The European Reformations Sourcebook

The European Reformations Sourcebook

Second Edition

Edited by

Carter Lindberg

WILEY Blackwell

To Emma, Caleb, and Nathan, and Teddy and Claudia

Contents

Preface to the Second Edition

I am grateful to all the readers whose use of this text contributed to the decision to revise it. I have endeavored in this revision to incorporate the many helpful critiques and suggestions from readers, especially for additional and lengthier selections from Luther and Calvin. Also, in response to reader critiques, I have deleted the "Legacies" chapter of the first edition by moving most of its material to the documentary narrative of earlier chapters. The "legacies" of the Reformations, however, continue to impact the present. I am thinking here in particular of gender issues and early modern theological and literal attacks on Jews and Judaism. I have included some documents by and about women, but the documents pertinent to the Reformations and the Jews would have extended the text far beyond the publisher's word limit. These two topics of course have pre- as well as post-Reformations history that continues to influence the present. However, the limitations of space ought not to dictate silence on these significant topics. Thus, I highly recommend the following for excellent access to pertinent documents and references for further study: For women and the Reformations start with Kirsi Stjerna, *Women and the Reformation* (Oxford: Blackwell, 2009) and Susan C. Karant-Nunn and Merry E. Wiesner-Hanks, eds., *Luther on Women: A Sourcebook* (Cambridge: Cambridge University Press, 2003); for primary sources see the some 180 titles in the series "The Other Voice in Early Modern Europe" (http://www.othervoiceineme.com). For the Reformations and the Jews start with Brooks Schramm and Kirsi Stjerna, eds., *Martin Luther, the Bible, and the Jewish People: A Reader* (Minneapolis: Fortress Press, 2012) with its extensive bibliography.

The revised *Sourcebook* is designed as a companion volume to the second, revised, edition of my textbook, *The European Reformations*, excepting chapters 1 ("Historiography") and 15 ("Legacies"). Thus, the chapters in the *Sourcebook* correlate with the chapters in the textbook as indicated by the chapter heading, e.g., "The Late Middle Ages," etc. The *Sourcebook* cover also relates to the textbook cover. Both covers are from the altarpiece in Wittenberg parish church by Lucas Cranach the Elder. The textbook cover is the central panel of the altarpiece depicting the Lord's Supper as communion that draws in the congregation. The present collection's cover is the predella (panel below the central panel) that illustrates Luther preaching to the congregation, one hand on the Bible, the other hand pointing to Christ on the cross.

Together these panels present the Reformations' focus on Word and sacrament. An excellent discussion of this altarpiece is by Bonnie Noble, *Lucas Cranach the Elder: Art and Devotion of the German Reformation* (Lanham: University Press of America, 2009).

The basic goal of this revision remains that of the original: *Ad fontes!* – "To the sources!" Yet a word of caution is in order. The sources alone may yield different stories for, as Mark U. Edwards (1994) has noted, an important question is: What did contemporaries know, and when did they know it? For an example of this issue of the selection and reception of sources with regard to the Reformations and the Jews see Wallmann (1987) and Wendebourg (2012). Without the sources, however, we remain clueless about how we got this way.

Again, I am grateful for the support and guidance given by the editors at Wiley Blackwell, especially Rebecca Harkin, whose good cheer and encouragement made this revision possible. I am delighted to add that, since the first edition, Teddy and Claudia have joined the original dedicatees Emma, Caleb, and Nathan.

Preface to the First Edition

Ad fontes! – "to the sources" – the watchword of the Renaissance Humanists remains a salutary exhortation. The contemporary classroom equivalent is "don't take your instructor's word for it – look it up yourself!" Such historical and contemporary slogans express awareness that interpretations of events and ideas – whether past or present – bear the imprint of the interpreter. Without at least a cursory acquaintance with the sources, we are at the mercy of our teachers; or, even worse, we are unduly influenced by the spirit of the times. Acquaintance with the primary texts has the potential to liberate us from being passive recipients of others' views of the past. The more conversant we are with the works of our distant mothers and fathers, the more able we are actively to engage in dialogue with them and to gain clues to "how we got this way." Such engagement and dialogue are not as easy and straightforward as they may seem, but without the texts themselves they cannot occur.

The following collection of texts is intended to facilitate the beginning of dialogue with the participants of the European Reformations. The collection, designed as a companion volume for my textbook *The European Reformations* (Blackwell, 1996), provides some of the sources of the narrative and interpretations of that text and also follows the chapter sequence of the textbook. I hope the following selections will provide a glimpse of the excitement and riches that await those who will take up the Renaissance challenge to go back to the sources.

In order to provide as much space as possible for the sources themselves, I have minimized introductions to bare-bones sketches at the start of each chapter. More information on the entries may be gained from their bibliographical references, the textbook, and *The Oxford Encyclopedia of the Reformation* (editor-in-chief Hans Hillerbrand, 4 vols., New York: Oxford University Press, 1996). The entries are numbered seriatim in each chapter. References to entries in other chapters are indicated by chapter and entry number (e.g., 1.2 = chapter 1, entry 2).

An editor of an anthology faces a doubly painful task: first, deciding what to include, and then deciding how to tailor that first decision. Wherever possible, I have selected texts available in English translation so that readers may more easily find what I omitted. The Bibliography is limited, with one or two exceptions, to the works from which I selected sources.

I am grateful to two of my graduate students – Rod Martin and Peter Vogt – for searching for texts and providing criticism and suggestions. The usual caveat applies: their work improved this project, but they are not to blame for remaining problems. I am also grateful to the editorial staff of Blackwell Publishers for encouraging and supporting this project with their usual good humor and expertise.

One of the pleasures of writing is the privilege of dedicating one's work. Our grand-children, Emma, Caleb, and Nathan, provided joy and inspiration by their visits during work on this project: Nathan by arriving during the midst of it all! Caleb (three) by making my study the base of his operations against dragons and pirates; and Emma (five) for providing needed perspective ("Grandpa, why don't you ever write a children's book?"). They remind me that *ad fontes* is more than old texts.

Abbreviations

BC   *The Book of Concord. The Confessions of the Evangelical Lutheran Church*, ed. Robert Kolb and Timothy J. Wengert. Minneapolis: Fortress Press, 2000

CStA   *Calvin-Studienausgabe*, ed. Eberhard Busch et al., 8 vols. Neukirchen-Vluyn: Neukirchener Verlagsgesellschaft, 1994–2011

LW   *Luther's Works*, ed. Jaroslav Pelikan and Helmut Lehmann, 55 vols. St. Louis: Concordia/Philadelphia: Fortress Press, 1955–86. Supplemental volumes 56–75, ed. Christopher Boyd Brown., St. Louis: Concordia, 2009– References are to volume and page, thus 31: 318 = vol. 31, p. 318

WA   *D. Martin Luthers Werke: Kritische Gesamtausgabe*, 58 vols. Weimar: Böhlau, 1883–

1

The Late Middle Ages

By the eve of the Reformation, European society had experienced the natural disaster of the plague (1.1) and social challenges to authority (1.2) that, along with widespread perceptions of ecclesiastical corruption, prompted a general sense of moral crisis (1.3). The social distress and crisis of values heightened apocalyptic fears and anxiety about eternal salvation. Popular religious agitation, often out of the control of the church, either turned in upon itself in penitential processions of flagellants or lashed out in pogroms against Jews believed to be behind contemporary sufferings (1.1). Social criticism depicted an upside-down world with the pope as Antichrist, and yearned for reform and rebirth. The invention of printing (1.4) enabled widespread distribution of these concerns; it also spread biblical texts in vernacular translations, and provided the laity with edifying literature. Moralists and Humanists exposed political and ecclesiastical corruption as well as human folly (1.5). Such preaching and literature, suffused with calls for reform, also contained a potent mix of nationalism, anticlericalism, and Humanist aspirations for renewal of the church and society that foreshadowed the great German Peasants' War of 1525. For example, the "Piper of Niklashausen" (1.6) attracted a mass peasant audience before his execution by the local bishop. Anticlerical satires echoed the proverb "the closer to Rome, the less Christian." One of the sharpest and most read of these polemics against Rome was *Vadiscum oder die Römische Dreifaltigkeit* ("Vadiscus ["wandering observer"] or the Roman Trinity") (1.7) by the poet laureate Ulrich von Hutten (1488–1523). The political form of anticlericalism appeared as "grievances" (*Gravamina*) against exploitation of the empire by the Roman Church that were first expressed at the Council of Constance (1417) and continued well into the Reformation at the Imperial Diets (1.8).

While the papacy reiterated its central role in the economy of both salvation and human society (1.9), its medieval doctrinal formulations came under increasing criticism from the conciliar movement (1.11–14). Following the death of Boniface VIII (1303), the papacy moved to Avignon, a city on the border of France under French

The European Reformations Sourcebook, Second Edition. Edited by Carter Lindberg.
© 2014 John Wiley & Sons, Ltd. Published 2014 by John Wiley & Sons, Ltd.

control. The Avignon papacy, sometimes called the "Babylonian Captivity of the Church," required massive funding both to make up for its loss of Roman revenue and to carry out its institutional programs. One of the instruments developed to meet papal financial needs was the indulgence (1.9–10). Clement VI's *Unigenitus Dei Filius* affirmed a treasury of merits derived from Christ and the saints. The pope, a kind of spiritual bookkeeper, could draw on this treasury and issue "checks" to balance the accounts of Christians with a merit-deficit – even if they were in Purgatory. After the papacy returned to Rome, there was a conflicted papal election that resulted in rival popes. The efforts to resolve the resultant schism in the Western church led to a brief period of three rival popes, and then efforts to resolve the schism by means of a council (1.11–15). Papal reaction throughout this period strove for independence from councils and reaffirmation of authority (1.16–17). Luther's call for a general council fell under the condemnation issued by Pius II (1.16). Such papal reactions were unable to stifle criticisms unleashed by Wyclif and Hus (1.18–19) among others.

In the face of these crises late medieval piety strove to ascend to salvation through ethical and spiritual renewal by penance, among other spiritual exercises. The sacrament of penance facilitated progress from vice to virtue in the midst of worldly temptations and attacks by demons. Scholastic theology (1.20) expressed this motif of ascent through the phrase *facere quod in se est* ("to do what is in one"), and mysticism expressed it by imitating Christ and by ascending to union with God (1.21–24). The evangelical strain in the various forms of mysticism is glimpsed in the prayer of Thomas à Kempis (1.25) and the preaching of Staupitz, Luther's monastic superior and pastor (1.26). Nevertheless, late medieval piety was marked by a nagging uncertainty concerning the effectiveness of penance, and indeed salvation itself, both dreadfully conditioned by the refrain that "no one knows whether he is worthy of the love or hate of God" (Ecclesiastes 9:1). Pastoral instructions on "how to live" (catechisms) and "how to die" (*ars moriendi*) tended to exacerbate rather than to relieve such uncertainty. The most popular late medieval catechism, Dietrich Kolde's *Christenspiegel* ("Mirror of a Christian") (1. 27), exemplifies this uncertainty with its 46 chapters listing sins (several hundred!), exhortations to penance, and pleas for Marian intercession. Kolde's "Mirror" went through 19 printings before 1500 and 28 afterward.

The intellectual foundations and methods developed by the Renaissance Humanists (1.28–29) provided tools for both criticism and reform of the medieval church. The Humanist motto "back to the sources" referred to the classics of both pagan and Christian literature, which were at this time increasingly available through the recovery and improvement of scholarship in languages and historical studies. The basic source of theology, of course, was the Bible. Medieval exegetes found confirmation of the teachings of the church in even the most obscure biblical verse by ingenious interpretative means. The literal sense of the Bible was like a husk to be broken in order to get to the kernel of the matter, to reach the secrets of revelation. The Franciscan Nicholas of Lyra's (d. 1349) turn from speculative interpretations to a more literal interpretation was of great significance (1.30) for the Reformations. By the fifteenth century his biblical commentaries had won approval and no exegete could ignore him. The verse *Si Lyra non lyrasset, Litherus non saltasset* ("Had Lyra not played his lyre, Luther would not have danced!") suggests the importance of the recovery of the historical and grammatical sense of Scripture.

The Humanists' desire for a "rebirth" of classical culture was not antiquarianism but a search for sources for the renewal of their contemporary cultural and religious life. In this process the traditional dogmatic warrants for the authority of the church and the interpretation of the gospel came under scrutiny. In the face of authoritarian reactions, the Humanists used satire with devastating effect against not only clerical dogmatism and scholastic theology, but also the ignorance, superstition, and fear they perceived in much medieval piety (1.31–33).

1.1 Jean de Venette: *Chronicle*
Birdsall & Newhall 1953: 48–52

In A.D. 1348, the people of France and of almost the whole world were struck by a blow other than war. . . .

All this year and the next, the mortality of men and women, of the young even more than the old, in Paris and in the kingdom of France, and also, it is said, in other parts of the world, was so great that it was almost impossible to bury the dead. People lay ill little more than two or three days and died suddenly, as it were in full health. He who was well one day was dead the next and being carried to his grave. Swellings appeared suddenly in the armpit or in the groin – in many cases both – and they were infallible signs of death. . . . Wherefore in many towns timid priests withdrew, leaving the exercise of their ministry to such of the religious as were more daring. In many places not two out of twenty remained alive. . . .

In the year 1349, while the plague was still active and spreading from town to town, men in Germany, Flanders, Hainaut, and Lorraine uprose and began a new sect on their own authority. Stripped to the waist, they gathered in large groups and bands and marched in procession through the crossroads and squares of cities and good towns. There they formed circles and beat upon their backs. . . . They flogged their shoulders and arms with scourges tipped with iron points so zealously as to draw blood. . . .

Some said that this pestilence was caused by infection of the air and waters, since there was at this time no famine nor lack of food supplies, but on the contrary great abundance. As a result of this theory of infected water and air as the source of the plague the Jews were suddenly and violently charged with infecting wells and water and corrupting the air. The whole world rose up against them cruelly on this account. In Germany and other parts of the world where Jews lived, they were massacred and slaughtered by Christians, and many thousands were burned everywhere, . . .

1.2 Social Tensions: *The Reformation of the Emperor Sigismund* (c.1438)
Strauss 1971: 6, 14–16, 21, 25, 28, 31

It is plain that the Holy Father, the pope, and all our princes have abandoned the task set them by God. It may be that God has appointed a man to set things right. . . .

One of the causes of ill will that has come between bishops and priests is the bishops' practice of taxing priests illegally and intimidating them with lawsuits if they fail to pay. They make it a special habit to threaten priests who live with concubines, because these men are afraid of being placed under the ban and usually pay up willingly to escape the bishop's wrath. Thus the bishop gets his money while he permits illicit practices to continue. . . . Secular priests ought to be allowed to marry. In marriage they will live more piously and honorably, and the friction between them and the laity will disappear. . . .

You may ask: How can this new order be introduced? . . . The new order must come, for it is the will of God. The time is near as you shall learn. . . .

Nowadays a man going to a city to buy or sell will come away saying "They have cheated me." Everything in the city is sold at too high a price; this is why knights and country people show so much ill will towards burghers. If all things were shared in the city, if people associated to own and do things in common, all these evils would disappear. . . .

There have now arisen great merchant companies whose members collaborate in far-flung trading ventures. It matters little whether their merchant luck goes well or ill; they arrange things in such a way that they come out ahead. They can lose nothing. They work all sort of deceit, and cities and countryside are ruined because of them. There should be laws made against the incorporation of such companies. . . .

Now I maintain that neither forest nor field should ever be closed to peasants . . .

It will come to pass that the lowly are raised up and the mighty humbled, as Jesus Christ says in the Gospel. . . .

Be it known that it is God's will to have a new state and order come into being appropriate to the Christian faith. . . .

However, the spiritual princes are opposed to divine order. And yet this may be a good sign, for we may come all the sooner into a reformation, seeing how their name and honor grow daily more despised. . . .

But nothing can be completed until he arises whom God has chosen for the task. . . .

1.3 The Crisis of Values: "Reynard the Fox" (1498)
Strauss 1971: 91–3, 95–6

[Reynard:] "We live in a perilous time. Lords and prelates set examples for us to follow – everyone can see that. Lesser folk notice what the mighty do. Who does not know that the king himself is a robber and a conniver? . . . No one tells him the truth; neither his chaplain nor his father confessor says to him, 'You have done wrong.' Why don't they? Because they like to enjoy their share of the loot. . . .

"Thus our king the lion has sitting in council with him a select band of robbers, whom he holds in great honor and makes the greatest among his nobles. But let the poor wretch Reynard take a chicken, and you'll see them pounce upon him and scream, 'To the gallows with him!' Little crooks are hanged; big crooks govern our lands and cities. I grew wise to this long ago, nephew, which is why I seek my own profit in life. Sometimes I think that, since everybody does it, this is the way it ought to be. . . .

"There is hardly a parish where the priest does not have a concubine, living in sin and shame, producing children like husbands in normal wedlock. Such priests are solicitous for their offspring and advance them as best they can, . . . Nowadays money calls the tune, and a priest's bastard is dubbed lord or lady. Show me a country where the priests do not levy the toll or run the village mills. Spreading wickedness by their own examples, they pervert the whole world! . . . "

[Reynard's skill at lying and flattery not only gets him off the charges against him at court but also gains him honors. The tale concludes:]

He who has not learned Reynard's craft is not made for this world and his advice is not heeded. But with the aid of the art of which Reynard is past master, success and power are within everyone's reach. For this reason our world is full of Reynards, and we find them at the pope's court no less than at the emperor's. Simon is now on the throne. Money counts, and nothing else. He who has money to give gets the benefice; he who has not does not get it. Whoever knows Reynard's cunning best is on his way to the top.

1.4 Jakob Wimpfeling: The Origins of Printing, from *Epitome Rerum Germanicarum* (1505)
Plöse & Vogler 1989: 33–4

In the year 1440 . . . Johannes Gutenberg rendered a great and well-nigh divine blessing to the whole world by the invention of a new kind of writing. For this man was the first to invent the art of printing in the city of Strasbourg. From there he went to Mainz where he successfully perfected it. . . .

Our countrymen distinguished themselves in this art not only in Strasbourg, but also where they set up this enterprise in other places. . . . Thus Sixtus Rusinger went to Naples from Strasbourg in 1471, and was the first [there] to show how books can be printed. For this he was highly honored by King Ferdinand [of Aragon and Naples] and the local nobles . . .

Many prominent and famous men have praised the art of printing. . . . "O Germany, you are the inventor of an art more useful than anything from the ancients for you teach how to copy by printing books."

1.5 Sebastian Brant: *The Ship of Fools*
Zeydel 1962: 57, 84–5, 208–9, 333–4

For profit and salutary instruction, admonition and pursuit of wisdom, reason and good manners: also for contempt and punishment of folly, blindness, error, and stupidity of all stations and kinds of men: with special zeal, earnestness, and labor compiled at Basel by Sebastian Brant, doctor in both laws.

11. Contempt of Holy Writ

A fool is he who has forsook
His faith in Writ and Holy Book
And thinks that he can live as well
Without a God, without a hell,
Despising preachment with a sneer
As though he could not see or hear . . .
There is so much of Holy Writ,
Of Testament both Old and New,
That everything's been proved to you.
We'll not require assurance queer
From Niklashausen's shepherd-seer.
The Lord doth verily proclaim:
Who sins on earth, in hell finds shame,
And who on earth in prudence lives,
To him eternal praise God gives . . .

63. Of Beggars

Bold begging charms full many a fool,
For begging has become the rule
And ranks among our best professions:
Church orders teem with rich possessions
And yet lament their pauper state.
Poor cadgers, ah, the pity's great!
Rank pauperdom, that's your class,
Though heaps of wealth you should amass,
And Prior shouts: "Bring more, bring plus!"
His is a sack that's bottomless!
Quite similar are the relic-vendors,
The pious dealers and pretenders . . .
"In this bag you will the hay
That once in bygone ages lay
Beneath the crib at Bethlehem."
"An ass bone here of Balaam."
"Of Michael's wing I have a feather."
"St. George's steed once wore this tether!"
"See here St. Clara's laced-up shoes."
To beg some men will always choose,
Though they could work if but they would,
They're young and strong, their health is good,
Save that their back they'll not incline,
These sluggards have a corpse's spine . . .

103. Of the Antichrist

St. Peter's ship is swaying madly,
It may be wrecked or damaged badly,
The waves are striking 'gainst the side
And storm and trouble may betide.
But little truth is now asserted
And Holy Writ is quite perverted,
It's now defined some other way
From what the tongue of truth would say.
Forgive me, you whom I may hit.
In th' large ship Antichrist does sit,
He's sent a message out to man,
False things he spreads wher'er he can,
Creeds, dogmas false in every way
Now seem to grow from day to day.
The printers make the case more dire,
If some books went into the fire
Much wrong and error would be gone . . .
The Antichrist is very near. . . .

1.6 "The Piper of Niklashausen," A Report of His Preaching (1476)
Benrath 1967: 236–9

He claimed that the Virgin Mary, the Mother of God, had appeared to him and revealed the wrath of God against the human race and especially against the priesthood . . .

There shall be more perfect grace in the Tauber valley than in Rome or anywhere else.

Whoever comes to the Tauber valley shall receive all perfect grace, and if he dies he shall go straight to heaven . . .

The Emperor is a villain, and along with the pope is nothing.

The Emperor gives to the princes, dukes, knights, and servants what he gains through taxes from the common people. Woe to those poor fools.

The clergy have many benefices; that should not be. They should have no more than is sufficient to maintain themselves.

They shall be struck dead, and in short it will come about that the priest might try to cover his tonsured head with his hand so that he will not be recognized.

The fish in the water and the animals in the field shall belong to all.

The princes of the world and the church have so much. What should it take for the common people to have enough?

It must come to pass that the princes and lords have to work for a day's wage. . . .

1.7 Ulrich von Hutten: *Vadiscum oder die Römishe Dreifaltigkeit* (1519)
Bentzinger 1983: 72–5

Three things Rome holds dear: the authority of the pope, relics of the saints, and the indulgence trade.

Three things costly in Rome: women, horses, and documents.

Three things cheap in Rome: fever, pestilence, and the poor.

Three things usually brought from Rome: depraved conscience, corrupted stomach, empty purse.

Three things necessary for the petitioner in Rome: much money, many instructions, many lies.

Three things found in all Rome's streets: holy places, broken columns, and whores. . . .

Three things customary in Rome: fleshly pleasures, costly clothing, respect for no one.

Three things banned in Rome: fasting, worship, telling the truth. . . .

Three are the citizens of Rome: Simon, Judas, and the people of Gomorrah.

Three things everyone wants in Rome: short masses, good money, good times.

Three things Rome has more than anywhere else in the world: old buildings, the Pope, and greed.

Three things expensive in Rome: official positions, law, and love.

Three things one kisses in Rome: hands, rears, and altars. . . .

Three things demanded in Rome: presents, favors, and power. . . .

Three things Rome is terrified to hear: General Councils, reformation, and that the Germans might see.

Three things calamitous to Rome: unity of the Princes, the peoples' true understanding, and that Roman villainy become known.

Three things are great sins in Rome: poverty, fear of God, and piety.

Three things help people advance in Rome: money, audacity, and arrogance. . . .

Three things valued in Rome: getting money, crusading against the Turks, indulgences for building churches. . . .

Three things held true in Rome: Roman sanctity, wisdom of the papists, German dullness.

Three wares sold in Rome: Christ, clerical income, women.

1.8 Jacob Wimpfeling: *Grievances of the German Nation* (1515)
Strauss 1971: 42–3, 45–7

It is not that we deny our debt to Rome. But we ask: Is Rome not also indebted to us? Have not two of our compatriots, clever and skillful men hailing from Strassburg and Mainz, invented the noble art of printing, which makes it possible to propagate the correct doctrines of faith and morals throughout the world and in all languages? . . . [O]ur compatriots crowd the road to Rome. They pay for papal reservations and dispensations. They appear before papal courts – and not always because they have appealed a case to Rome, but rather because their cases have been arbitrarily transferred there. Is there a nation more patient and willing to receive indulgences, though we well know that the income from them is divided between the Holy See and its officialdom? Have we not paid dearly for the confirmation of every bishop and abbot?

Let therefore the Holy Apostolic See and our gracious mother, the Church, reduce at least the most severe of the taxes she has placed on our country. . . . For the sums of money our prelates must send to Rome are taken from the pockets of poor burghers, rural clerics, and impoverished peasants, and many a husband and father cannot nourish his family for the taxes he must pay. Such a reduction of our tribute might well prevent the outbreak of violent insurrection of our people against the Church. . . . It would not take much for the Bohemian [Hussite] poison to penetrate our German lands . . .

I need say nothing of indulgences here, except to point out that the many conflicting interpretations of penance and indulgences given in sermons must confuse the faithful, while the prolific distribution of indulgences is likely to incline people to immoral lives. We all know how heavy a burden on our nation these indulgences have become, to say nothing of confessional letters which, by the way, are not available for small change . . . but will cost a man a week's household money or more.

1.9 Pope Boniface VIII: *Unam Sanctam* (1302)
Petry 1962: 505–6

The true faith compels us to believe that there is one holy catholic apostolic church, and this we firmly believe and plainly confess. And outside of her there is no salvation or remission of sins. . . . Therefore there is one body of the one and only church, and one head, not two heads, as if the church were a monster. And this head is Christ and his vicar, Peter and his successor; . . . By the words of the gospel we are taught that the two swords, namely, the spiritual authority and the temporal are in the power of the church. . . . The former is to be used by the church, the latter for the church; the one by the hand of the priest, the other by the hand of kings and knights, but at the command and permission of the priest. Moreover, it is necessary for one sword to be under the other, and the temporal authority to be subjected to the spiritual; . . . And we must necessarily admit that the spiritual power surpasses any earthly power in dignity and honor, because spiritual things surpass temporal things. . . . For the truth itself declares that the spiritual power must establish the temporal power and pass judgment on it if it is not good. . . . Therefore if the temporal power errs, it will be judged by the spiritual power, and if the lower spiritual power errs, it will be judged by its superior. But if the highest spiritual power errs, it can not be judged by men, but by God alone. For the apostle says: "But he that is spiritual judgeth all things, yet he himself is judged of no man" [I Cor. 2:15]. Now this authority, although it is given to man and exercised through man, is not human, but divine. . . . We therefore declare, say, and affirm that submission on the part of every man to the bishop of Rome is altogether necessary for his salvation.

1.10 Pope Clement VI: *Unigenitus Dei Filius* (1343)
Clarkson 1955: 319–20

The only-begotten Son of God [has] . . . redeemed us not with perishable things, with silver and gold, but with his own precious blood. . . . This merciful shedding of his blood . . . was to gain a great treasure for the Church militant. Thus our good Father has willed to enrich his children, so that there may be an infinite treasure for men; . . .

This treasure . . . (Christ) has committed to the care of St. Peter, who holds the keys of heaven, and to his successors, His own vicars on earth, who are to distribute it for the good of the faithful. And they are to apply it with compassion for a proper and reasonable cause, for the benefit of those who are truly sorry and who have confessed, at times for the complete remission of the temporal punishment due to sin, at times for the partial remission, sometimes in a general grant, sometimes to individuals, as they judge pleasing to God.

It is also known that the merits of the Mother of God and of all the elect, from the first just man until the last, add something to the store of this treasure. There is no reason to fear about exhausting or decreasing these merits, because, as has been said, the merits of Christ are infinite, and because, in proportion to the number of men who are drawn to justice by the application of these merits, the store of merits increases.

1.11 Pope Sixtus IV: *Salvator Noster* (1476)
Kidd 1941: 224

And, in order that the salvation of souls may be the more easily procured at a time when they are more in need of the prayers of others and the less capable of aiding themselves; anxious, as we are, by apostolic authority to succor from the Treasury of the Church the souls in purgatory . . . we . . . out of the plenitude of our authority, concede and grant that, if any relatives, friends or other Christians, moved by piety for the souls exposed to purgatorial fire for the expiation due to them by divine justice, during the said ten years, do, for the repairing of the church of Saints, give a fixed proportion of money, or value thereof, in accordance with the ordinance of the Dean. and Chapter of said church or of our Collector, and visit the said church, or send messengers of their own appointment during the said ten years, will that plenary remission by way of prayer shall, as aforesaid, avail and provide for plenary remission to those souls in purgatory for whom they have paid the said proportion of money or the value thereof. . . .

1.12 Marsilius of Padua: *Defensor Pacis* (1324)
Petry 1962: 511–12

2. The general council of Christians or its majority alone has the authority to define doubtful passages of the divine law, and to determine those that are to be regarded as articles of Christian faith, belief in which is essential to salvation; and no partial council or single person of any position has the authority to decide these questions.

3. The gospels teach that no temporal punishment or penalty should be used to compel observance of divine commandments. . . .
14. No bishop or priest has coercive authority or jurisdiction over any layman or clergyman, even if he is a heretic. . . .
17. All bishops derive their authority in equal measure immediately from Christ, and it cannot be proved from the divine law that one bishop should be over or under another, in temporal or spiritual matters.
18. The other bishops, singly or in a body, have the same right by divine authority to excommunicate or otherwise exercise authority over the bishop of Rome, . . .

1.13 Conciliarism: Opinion of the University of Paris (1393)
Thatcher & McNeal 1905: 328–9, 332

If the rival popes, after being urged in a brotherly and friendly manner, will not accept either of the above ways [resignation or arbitration], there is a third way which we propose as an excellent remedy for this sacrilegious schism. We mean that the matter shall be left to a general council. This general council might be composed, according to canon law, only of prelates, or, since many of them are very illiterate, and many of them are bitter partisans of one or the other pope, there might be joined with the prelates an equal number of masters and doctors of theology and law from the faculties of approved universities. Or if this does not seem sufficient to anyone, there might be added besides one or more representatives from cathedral chapters and the chief monastic orders, in order that all decisions might be rendered only after most careful examination and mature deliberation.

1.14 Pierre D'Ailly: Conciliar Principles (1409)
Petry 1962: 527

[T]he Church in certain cases can hold a general council without the authority of the Pope. . . . In the first place, if, in the event of a vacancy in the [Apostolic] See, heresy or some other persecution of the Church were to appear, which ought to be counteracted by a general council. Secondly, if, in a case where necessity or manifest utility dictated the summoning of a council, the Pope were mad or heretical, or otherwise useless or lacking in this matter, or, if required to act on this, refused or culpably (damnabiliter) neglected to call a council. Thirdly, if there were several contenders for the Papacy so that the whole Church obeyed no single one of them, nor appeared at the call, of any one or even two of them at the same time – just as is the case in the present schism. In these and in similar cases, therefore, it is clear from what has been said that the Church can and should assemble a general council without the authority of the Pope . . .

1.15 The Council of Constance: *Haec Sancta* (1415) and *Frequens* (1417)
Petry 1962: 533, 536

Haec sancta (6 May 1415): This holy synod of Constance . . . declares that this synod, legally assembled, is a general council, and represents the catholic church militant and has its authority directly from Christ; and everybody, of whatever rank or dignity, including also the pope, is bound to obey this council in those things which pertain to the faith, to the ending of this schism, and to a general reformation of the church in its head and members. Likewise it declares that if anyone, of whatever rank, condition, or dignity, including also the pope, shall refuse to obey the commands, statutes, ordinances, or orders of this holy council, or of any other holy council properly assembled, in regard to the ending of the schism and to the reformation of the church, he shall be subject to the proper punishment; . . .

Frequens (9 October 1417): A good way to till the field of the Lord is to hold general councils frequently, because by them the briers, thorns, and thistles of heresies, errors, and schisms are rooted out, abuses reformed, and the way of the Lord made more fruitful. . . . We therefore decree by this perpetual edict that general councils shall be held as follows: The first one shall be held five years after the close of this council, the second one seven years after the close of the first, and forever thereafter one shall be held every ten years. One month before the close of each council the pope, with the approval and consent of the council, shall fix the place for holding the next council. If the pope fails to name the place the council must do so.

1.16 Pope Pius II: *Execrabilis* (1460)
Kidd 1941: 222–3

An abuse, at once execrable and unheard of hitherto, has appeared in our day to the effect that certain persons, imbued with the spirit of rebellion, zealous not for wiser judgment but to escape from sin already committed, have presumed to appeal to a future Council from the Roman Pontiff; . . . How contrary this is to the sacred canons and how injurious to the Christian republic, anyone may understand who is acquainted with law. . . .

Anxious therefore to expel this pestilential poison far from the Church of Christ, we condemn such appeals and reprobate them as erroneous and damnable; voiding and annulling the same, if such appeals have hitherto been found to have been interposed; and we decree and declare that they are vain, pestiferous, and of no effect.

If, however, anyone shall do anything to the contrary, of whatever estate, rank, order or condition he be, even though he be distinguished as of Imperial, royal or pontifical dignity, let him *ipso facto* incur the sentence of execration and be incapable of absolution, save by the Roman Pontiff and at the point of death.

1.17 Pope Leo X: *Pastor Aeternus* (1516)
Thulin 1966: 27

The pope alone has the power, right, and full authority, extending beyond that of all councils, to call, adjourn, and dissolve the councils. This is attested not only by the Holy Scriptures as well as the statements of the Holy Fathers and our predecessors on the throne at Rome, but even the councils themselves . . .

It is necessary for the salvation of souls that all Christian believers be subject to the pope at Rome. The Holy Scriptures and the Holy Fathers testify to this, as does the bull of Pope Boniface VIII of blessed memory, which begins with the words "Unam Sanctam." Therefore, with the approval of the holy council now in session, we renew and consider this very same bull to be valid. All this is done for the salvation of believing souls, for the strengthening of the supreme authority of the pope at Rome and of the Holy See, and for the unity and power of the church which has been entrusted to him.

1.18 John Wyclif: "On Indulgences"
Vaughan 1845: 192–8

I confess that the indulgences of the pope, if they are what they are said to be, are a manifest blasphemy, inasmuch as he claims a power to save men almost without limit, and not only to mitigate the penalties of those who have sinned, by granting them the aid of absolution and indulgences, that they may never come to purgatory, but to give command to the holy angels, that when the soul is separated from the body, they may carry it without delay to its everlasting rest . . .

They suppose, in the first place, that there is an infinite number of supererogatory merits, belonging to the saints, laid up in heaven, and above all, the merit of our Lord Jesus Christ, which would be sufficient to save an infinite number of other worlds, and that, over all this treasure, Christ hath set the pope. Secondly, that it is his pleasure to distribute it, and, accordingly, he may distribute therefrom to an infinite extent, since the remainder will still be infinite. Against this rude blasphemy I have elsewhere inveighed. . . .

This doctrine is a manifold blasphemy against Christ, inasmuch as the pope is extolled above his humanity and deity, and so above all that is called God – pretensions which, according to the declarations of the apostle, agree with the character of the Antichrist; for he possesses Caesarean power above Christ, who had not where to lay his head. . . .

1.19 John Hus: *The Treatise on the Church*
Schaff 1917: 87, 143, 208, 211

If he who is to be called Peter's vicar follows in the paths of virtue, we believe that he is his true vicar and the chief pontiff of the church over which he rules. But, if he walks in the opposite paths, then he is the legate of antichrist at variance with Peter and Jesus Christ. . . .

No pope is the manifest and true successor of Peter, the prince of the apostles, if in morals he lives at variance with the principles of Peter; and if he is avaricious, then is he the vicar of Judas, who loved the reward of iniquity and sold Jesus Christ. And by the same kind of proof the cardinals are not the manifest and true successors of the college of Christ's other apostles unless the cardinals live after the manner of the apostles and keep the commands and counsels of our Lord Jesus Christ. . . .

It is clear that the pope may err, and the more grievously because, in a given case, he may sin more abundantly, intensely and irresistibly than others. . . .

In view of these things it is to be held that to rebel against an erring pope is to obey Christ the Lord.

1.20 Gabriel Biel: "Doing What is in One"
Ozment 1974: 148–9

You ask what it means for a man to do what is in him. Alexander of Hales answers as follows. "If we want to know what it means for one to do what is in him, let us first note that every man by nature possesses right reason. This uprightness of reason consists of a natural understanding of what is good. It is given to every man by the Creator, and by it every soul can know its origin, God, . . . It knows further that it should seek the good from its Creator, that all men should beg what they still lack from their Origin. If a man acts in accordance with this innate knowledge and directs his will to him whom he knows to be his praiseworthy Creator, then he does what is in him. This is generally what it means for any man to do what is in him. The infidel in mortal sin, however, needs more light, for his faith is unformed, lacking in charity. But this unformed faith can still make two things clear to him: divine justice which damns those who are false and divine mercy which saves the righteous. Knowledge of the former creates fear, and knowledge of the latter hope. To fear God's justice and hope in his mercy is to do what is in one." So Alexander. From this we can now say that he does what is in him who, illumined by the light of natural reason or of faith, or of both, knows the baseness of sin, and having resolved to depart from it, desires the divine aid [i.e. grace] by which he can cleanse himself and cling to God his maker. To the one who does this God necessarily grants grace – but by a necessity based on the immutability of his decisions, not on external coercion, as Alexander also declares.

1.21 Johannes Tauler, OP: Sermon Extract
Shrady 1985: 80

What, then, does true detachment . . . really mean? It means that we must turn away and withdraw from all that is not God pure and simple; that we reflect in the light of reason on our words and thoughts and deeds in an understanding spirit to see if there is perhaps anything that is not oriented toward God as its sole and supreme Good. Let us rid ourselves of anything that is not directed toward Him. This applies not only to those who wish to lead a spiritual life, but to all good men. . . . This degree of detachment is imperative if one wishes to receive the Holy Spirit and His gifts. It is essential to turn totally to God and away from all that is not God.

1.22 *Theologia Deutsch*
Hoffman 1980: 61, 70, 93, 113, 125

The Scriptures, the Truth, and the Faith proclaim that sin is nothing but a turning away on the part of the creature from the unchangeable Good toward the changeable.

This is to say that the creature turns from the Perfect to the imperfect, to separateness, to the partial, and pre-eminently to itself. . . .

It should also be pointed out that eternal bliss is rooted in God alone and nothing else. . . .

In other words, bliss or blessedness does not depend on any one created thing or on a creature's work but only on God and His works. . . .

In this spiritual poverty and humility one finds and understands that all humans are bent upon and turned toward the self, evil practices, and wickedness. One also sees that because of this inclination, it becomes necessary and useful to have order, rules, law, and commands. Law and command make our blindness evident to us and constrain wickedness into order. . . .

[T]he illumined ones [are] guided by the true Light. They do not practice the ordered life in expectation of reward. . . .

They are not so concerned about the outcome, how a particular behavior will turn out, how soon, and so on. Their concern is rather that things will work out well, in peace and inner ease. . . .

There is a kind of love that must be called utterly false, namely when one loves with an eye to reward. For instance, one holds righteousness dear, not for righteousness's sake but in order to acquire something thereby. And if someone loves another person because of that person's possessions, or if we love God for an ulterior purpose, for the sake of a certain thing we want to possess, that is all love gone astray . . .

But true Love is informed and guided by the true Light and knowledge. The true eternal divine Light inspires love to embrace nothing but the truly simple, perfect Good, for no other reason but goodness itself, and not in order to receive it as a reward or any one thing from God, but just out of love of goodness, because it is good and should therefore properly be loved.

1.23 Ludolf of Saxony: *Vita Jesu Christi*
Benrath 1967: 112–14

The sinner who desires to cast off the burden of his sin and to gain rest for his soul hears first of all how God invites the sinner to grace, and says: Come to me all who suffer and are burdened by the load of sins, I will refresh you and you shall find rest for your souls here and in the future. The sick also hear of the faithful, solicitous physician and go to him in thorough contrition, conscientious confession, and with the earnest resolve always to shun evil and to do the good. Secondly, the sinner, who already believing in Christ and reconciled to him through penance, shall strive with greater care to adhere to his physician and come to him in trustful relationship. . . . Thereby he takes very good care that he does not read superficially of his life, but rather he shall follow it step by step through the day. . . . Also, he shall so read the life of Christ that it is consulted for the power of imitating him, for it is of little use if he reads it without imitating it. . . .

As much as he endeavors to become conformed to him through imitation of his virtues, so much will he be near and transfigured to him in the fatherland in the clarity of his majesty. Thus go to every individual phase of Christ's life and all of his individual virtues, and endeavor to imitate him as a true disciple. . . .

1.24 Gerard Zerbolt: *The Spiritual Ascents*
Engen 1988: 263, 271, 292

Then think and shape in yourself such an affection as if your soul had suddenly to depart: How freely you would leave all delight behind, how gratefully you would take up every labor and penance, if you were able still to have your life. . . .

On another occasion, place before your eyes the image of some dying man, and carefully note the form, means, and order by which he comes to die. . . . Then think how the body leaves the soul and suddenly stands before the Judge's tribunal to receive the sentence which will never again be changed from that moment down through all the ages. Then follow the bier to the burial and see how that poor body, for which so many delights were sought, is given over to the earth, food for the worms consigned to eternal oblivion. From these and similar meditations, see that the joy and delight of this world are like a point that passes, a mere shadow, and a man is like a traveling guest who stays but one night. . . .

See how great is the ascent . . . from fear to hope; so great also is the distance within this ascent and the work of climbing. But he who has advanced well thus far is drawing nearer to purity and charity, though he still has some steps to ascend. . . .

The way that leads to life is narrow, surrounded by enemies on the right and on the left who shoot flaming arrows against the climbers and gravely wound them. Lying in wait, those enemies bend their bows and take aim at those advancing toward pure and spotless hearts. They throw out chains, that is, affection for the lower things, to catch the feet and thus drag them down . . . thus you may see a thousand falling to the left of this way, and ten thousand to its right . . .

1.25 Thomas à Kempis: *The Imitation of Christ*
Klug 1966: 30

Lord, I know that you sometimes permit
trouble and temptation to come to me.
I cannot escape them,
but, driven by my need,
I must come to you for help

that you may work this out for my good.
O God, I feel uneasy and depressed
because of this present trouble.
I feel trapped on every side,
yet I know I have come to this hour,
so that I may learn that you alone
can free me from this predicament.
Lord, deliver me,
for what can I do without you,
helpless as I am?
Lord, give me patience in all my troubles.
Help me, and I will not be afraid,
no matter how discouraged I may be.
Let me bear this trouble patiently
until the storm has passed
and my heart is calm again.
Your power, Lord, can take this trouble from me,
as you have done many times before.
No matter how hard it is for me, it is easy for you, O Lord.

1.26 Johannes von Staupitz: Sermon Extracts
Benrath 1967: 135–7

It is not right when some make the simple folk believe that diligent confession and a worldly gift grants a papal indulgence and they thereby attain the forgiveness of sins. For the clink of the coin that falls into the money box will not free the sinner of his sins. Forgiveness requires first and above all else a truly contrite heart. Also it is beyond doubt that the person may attain forgiveness of his sins by a true, honest contrition even without all the indulgences that he can avail himself of. But it is incredible and without any basis to attain pardon of sins even with the highest papal grace if there is not first a true, heartfelt contrition over sins. . . .

It is the greatest foolishness to think sins may be greater than God's mercy. The mercy of God is without measure and infinitely great. No one who seeks it will be denied it. Even he who is not aware of particular sins, shall recognize his need and turn to Christ, that Christ may help him. Christ has opened to us the well of God's righteousness.

1.27 Dietrich Kolde: *A Fruitful Mirror or Small Handbook for Christians* (1508)
Janz 1982: 111, 116–17, 120, 126–7

Who knows whether God does not hear the prayer of his chosen friends? Indeed, who cannot fairly hope that God will not reject the prayer of his faithful? But it is nevertheless not certain whether he will do it, or for whom, or when, unless it is revealed. . . .

Since we want Mary the mother of God to protect us in the hour of death under the cloak of her maternal kindness, there are many devout people who conceive and carry out the idea of making Mary a beautiful cloak of good works under which Mary may cover and protect them when they die. First, there are many people who vow to Mary that they will convert from their great sins. . . . These people offer a beautiful acceptable gift to Mary's cloak. The second group of good hearts fasts on Saturday as an offering to Mary's cloak. The third group hears a mass every day in honor of Mary. The fourth group reads her a rosary every day, which gives Mary great pleasure. The fifth reads fourteen Hail Marys to the cloak of our dear lady, the first seven in honor of Mary's seven joys and the second seven in honor of Mary's seven sorrows. The sixth gives one or three or more meals a week to the poor for the cloak. The seventh gives alms. Some of them give a hundred Te Deums. Some give thirty vigils or more. Some read five or six psalters. Thus the cloak, with which Mary will cover and protect us, is made large and complete. And one hopes that Mary will use the cloak to cover and protect all those who help with it and are in the state of grace in the hour of death. . . .

It is very blessed and meritorious for a person to say the rosary to our dear lady every day or three times a week, i.e., fifty Hail Mary's interspersed with five Our Fathers. And if someone were to read our dear lady's psalter with fervor he would earn even more. . . . Also, Mary obtains forgiveness of all sins for those who thus devoutly honor her with repentant heart. God generally gives them the grace to die well too. . . .

[Five signs of a good Christian]: The first is that a good Christian grieves whenever he thinks of his sins. . . . The second is that a good Christian condemns himself to have God send suffering to him. . . . The third is, a good Christian is truthful. . . . The fourth is, a good Christian always puts more care and effort into pleasing and serving God than into anything else. . . . The fifth is, that a good Christian has great love for Jesus Christ. . . . Further, a good Christian has great love and devotion for the holiest sacrament, and for Mary the most worthy mother of our dear Lord Jesus Christ, and for the holy woman Saint Ann, from whom came the virgin flesh of Mary the mother of God, blessed in eternity. Amen. . . .

There are three things I know to be true that frequently make my heart heavy. The first troubles my spirit, because I will have to die. The second troubles my heart more, because I do not know when. The third troubles me above all. I do not know where I will go.

1.28 François Rabelais: On Education
Englander 1997: 92

Therefore, my son [Pantagruel], I beg you to devote your youth to the firm pursuit of your studies and to the attainment of virtue. . . . It is my earnest wish that you shall become a perfect master of languages. First of Greek, as Quintilian advises; secondly, of Latin; and then of Hebrew, on account of the Holy Scriptures; also of Chaldean and Arabic, for the same reason; and I would have you model your Greek style on Plato's and your Latin on that of Cicero. Keep your memory well stocked with every tale from history, . . . Of the liberal arts, geometry, arithmetic, and music, I gave you some smattering while you were still small, at the age of five or six. Go on and learn the rest, also the rules of astronomy. But leave divinatory astrology and Lully's art [magic] alone, I beg you, for they are frauds and vanities. . . . [Law and natural science are also encouraged]

At some hour of the day also, begin to examine the Holy Scriptures. First the New Testament and the Epistles of the Apostles in Greek; and then the Old Testament, in Hebrew. . . .

But because, according to the wise Solomon, Wisdom enters not into the malicious heart, and knowledge without conscience is but the ruin of the soul, it befits you to serve, love, and fear God, to put all your thoughts and hopes in Him, and by faith grounded in charity to be so conjoined with Him that you may never be severed from Him by sin. . . .

1.29 Lorenzo Valla: *The Falsely Believed and Forged Donation of Constantine*
Benrath 1967: 478–9. Cf. LW 60: 158–84

I know that men have long waited for me to make this reproach to the Roman Popes. . . . For already for some centuries the popes have either not recognized the Donation of Constantine [an early medieval fictional narrative legitimating papal authority over the emperor] as fabricated or false, or they themselves have made it up, or they have later walked in the deceitful steps of their predecessors. And although their duplicity is obvious, they have defended it as true and thereby dishonored the majesty of the papacy, the memory of the ancient popes, and the Christian religion, and compounded everything with murder, destruction, and infamy. They maintain that the city of Rome, the kingdom of Sicily and Naples, all of Italy, Gaul, Spain, Germany, Britain, indeed the entire West belongs to them. All of this is contained in the document of the Donation. . . .

I maintain that Constantine not only made no such Donation, and not only that the Roman pope can make no regulations on it, but what is more that if both be true this double papal rule is terminated due to the crime of the possessor, for we see that the decline and the devastation of the Italians and many of other countries have flowed from this source alone. If the water source is bitter, so also is the stream; if the root is impure, so also are the branches; if the leaven is spoiled, so also is the whole dough. But if the stream is bitter, then one should plug the source; if the branches are impure the cause comes from the roots. If the dough is spoiled, then one must also avoid the leaven. Or are we able to pass off as legitimate the beginning of papal power in which we recognize the origin of all sorts of criminality and all kinds of vices?

1.30 Nicholas of Lyra: Interpretation of the Bible
Benrath 1967: 52–5

God . . . has the power not only to use a word in order to denote something . . . but also through the word . . . to signify other matters. Therefore all other books have in common the fact that they denote something with their words. But the particularity of this book is that the matters denoted here through words signify still something else. On the first level, one receives the literal historical sense mediated through the meaning of the words; on the second level through the meaning mediated by the matter itself, one receives the mystical or spiritual sense which in general is threefold: (1) If the matters denoted by the words are related to what is to be believed in the New Testament, then one retains the allegorical sense. (2) If they are related to what we should do, it is the moral or tropological sense. (3) If, however, they are related to what we may hope for in the future blessedness, then it is the anagogical sense . . . thus the verse: *Litter gesta docet, quid credas allegoria; Moralis quid agas, quo tendas anagogia* ["The letter teaches what happened; allegory teaches what you should believe; the moral sense teaches what you should do; the anagogical sense teaches to what you are to strive."].

The word "Jerusalem" provides an example of these four interpretations:

(1) [literally] . . . it means the one-time capital in the kingdom of Judah . . .

(2) [morally] . . . "Jerusalem" means the believing soul. . . .

(3) [allegorically] . . . "Jerusalem" signifies the militant church in her battles on earth. . . .

(4) [anagogically] . . . "Jerusalem" signifies the triumphant church. . . .

Those who desire to advance in the study of Holy Scripture must begin with the understanding of the literal sense. . . .

With God's help I will remain with the literal sense. . . .

1.31 Desiderius Erasmus: *Praise of Folly* (1509)
Radice 1971: 152–4, 156, 164–5, 178, 180–1

Then there are the theologians, a remarkably supercilious and touchy lot. . . .

[T]hey interpret hidden mysteries to suit themselves: how the world was created and designed; through what channels the stain of sin filtered down to posterity; by what means, in what measure and how long Christ was formed in the Virgin's womb; how in the Eucharist, accidents can subsist without substance. . . . What was the exact moment of divine generation? Are there several filiations in Christ? Is it a possible proposition that God the father could hate his son? Could God have taken the form of a woman, a devil, a donkey, a gourd or a flintstone? If so, how could a gourd have preached sermons, performed miracles, and been nailed to the cross? . . .

These subtle refinements of subtleties are made still more subtle by all the different lines of scholastic argument, so that you'd extricate yourself faster from a labyrinth than from the tortuous obscurities of realists, nominalists, Thomists, Albertists, Ockhamists and Scotists – and I've not mentioned all the sects, only the main ones. Such is the erudition and complexity they all display that I fancy the apostles them-selves would need the help of another holy spirit if they were obliged to join issue on these topics with our new breed of theologian. . . .

The whole tribe [of clergy] is so universally loathed that even a chance meeting is thought to be ill-omened – and yet they are gloriously self-satisfied. In the first place, they believe it's the highest form of piety to be so uneducated that they can't even read. Then when they bray like donkeys in church, repeating by rote the psalms they haven't understood, they imagine they are charming the ears of their heavenly audience with infinite delight. Many of them too make a good living out of their squalor and beggary, bellowing for bread from door to door, and indeed making a nuisance of themselves in every inn, carriage or boat, to the great loss of all other beggars. This is the way in which these smooth individuals, in all their filth and ignorance, their boorish and shameless behaviour, claim to bring back the apostles into our midst! . . .

Then the Supreme Pontiffs, who are the vicars of Christ: if they made an attempt to imitate his life of poverty and toil, his teaching, cross, and contempt for life, and thought about their name of Pope, which means Father, or their title of Supreme Holiness, what creature on earth would be so cast down? . . .

As if indeed the deadliest enemies of the Church were not these impious pontiffs who allow Christ to be forgotten through their silence, fetter him with their mercenary laws, misrepresent him with their forced interpretations of his teaching, and slay him with their noxious way of life!

1.32 Erasmus, "Letter to Martin Dorp" (1515)
Olin 1975: 66, 72

But you, good Dorp, write almost as if the book *Folly* has alienated from me the whole theological profession. "What was the need," you ask, "for lashing out so fiercely at the theological profession?" . . . I want to ask you if you really think the whole theological profession has been attacked, if something was said against stupid and incompetent theologians who were in fact unworthy of such a title? . . .

Not even through the guise of my creature Folly did I dare to mention a complaint that I often hear people repeating, yes, people who are themselves theologians, and I mean real theologians, men of integrity, gravity, and learning and who drink deeply of the doctrine of Christ from its very fonts [i.e., the Bible]. These men, whenever they are among those to whom they can speak their minds freely, deplore this more recent brand of theology which has crept into the world, and long for the ancient one. What is holier, what more venerable, what can get right to the flavor and spirit of Christ's heavenly doctrine than the ancient theology? But this other type of theology, not to mention the base and monstrous nature of its crude, artificial style, its ignorance of good scholarship, and its ineptitude of expression, has been so adulterated by Aristotle, by trifling human inventions, and even by secular laws that I can hardly say it savors of the genuine and pure Christ. For it happens that when we fix too steadily on human traditions, we lose sight of the archetype. . . . What connection is there, I ask, between Christ and Aristotle? Between the petty fallacies of logic and mysteries of eternal wisdom? What is the purpose of this maze of disputations? How much of it is deadening and destructive by the very fact that it breeds contention and disagreement!

1.33 Ulrich von Hutten: *Letters from Obscure Men* (1515)
Manschreck 1965: 12–13

[Y]ou charged me to write you oft, and propose from time to time knotty points in Theology, which you would straightway resolve better than the Courticians at Rome: therefore, I now write to ask your reverence what opinion you hold concerning one

who on a Friday, that is on the sixth day of the week – or on any other fast day –
should eat an egg with a chicken in it?

For you must know that we were lately sitting in an inn in the *Campo dei Fiori*,
having our supper, and were eating eggs, when on opening one I saw that there was
a young chicken within.

This I showed to a comrade; whereupon quoth he to me, "Eat it up speedily, before
the taverner sees it, for if he mark it, you will have to pay . . . for a fowl. For it is the
rule of the house that once the landlord has put anything on the table you must pay
for it – he won't take it back. And if he sees that there is a young fowl in that egg, he
will say 'Pay me for that fowl! Little or big, 'tis all one'."

In a trice I gulped down the egg, chicken and all.

And then I remembered that it was Friday!

Whereupon I said to my crony, "You have made me commit a mortal sin, in eating
flesh on the sixth day of the week!"

But he averred that it was not a mortal sin – nor even a venial one, seeing that such
a chickling is accounted merely as an egg, until it is born.

He told me, too, that it is just the same in the case of cheese, in which there are
sometimes grubs, as there are in cherries, peas, and new beans: yet all these may be
eaten on Fridays, and even on Apostolic Vigils. But taverners are such rascals that they
call them flesh, to get the more money.

Then I departed and thought the matter over. . . .

I am in a mighty quandary, and know not what to do. . . .

It seemeth to me that these young fowls in eggs are flesh, because their substance
is formed and fashioned into the limbs and body of an animal, and possesseth a vital.
principle.

It is different in the case of grubs in cheese, and such-like because grubs are
accounted fish, as I learnt from a physician who is also skilled in Natural Philosophy.

Most earnestly do I entreat you to resolve the question that I have propounded.
For if you hold that the sin is mortal, then, I would fain get shrift here, ere I return to
Germany.

2

The Dawn of a New Era

Later in life, Luther recollected that although he became a monk to save his soul (2.1), he had remained uncertain about salvation. In response to this anxiety, Luther's prior, Staupitz (cf. 1.26), sent him to Wittenberg to study and teach. In the course of lecturing on the Bible, Luther had his "conversion" experience (2.2), and began to develop the characteristic themes of his theology (2.3) and to critique scholastic theology (2.4). Luther's dismay over his parishioners' thinking indulgences freed them of all sin (2.5–9) motivated his "Ninety-five Theses" to discuss the meaning of the sacrament of penance (2.10). Luther's order, the Augustinian Eremites, meeting in Heidelberg (April 1518) provided him the opportunity to further explicate his theology. There, Luther gained a number of young adherents who went on to become Reformers, above all Martin Bucer (2.11) and Johannes Brenz. The official response to the "Theses" came from Prierias, the pope's theologian (2.12). Prince Frederick, pressed to surrender Luther to Rome as a heretic, requested that Luther receive a hearing in Germany from Cardinal Cajetan (2.13; see 2.14). At the Leipzig debate in midsummer 1519 Luther publicly affirmed that the Roman Church is neither historically nor doctrinally superior to the Greek Church, and that biblical authority stands above that of pope and council. The Leipzig Humanist Petrus Mosellanus, whose oration on theological disputation opened the debate, described the major participants (2.15). The Leipzig debate forced major personal and public intellectual and spiritual issues concerning reform of the church, faith and works, the sacraments, church authority, the relation of church and society, as well as questions concerning the secular order such as usury, poor relief, and social structures in general. Humanist support for Luther at this time is evident in the letter by Wolfgang Capito, later a reformer in Strasbourg (2.16) In early June 1520, Luther responded to charges that justification by grace alone through faith alone would lead to the neglect of good works with his *Treatise on Good Works* (2.17). Written in German, the *Treatise* focuses on Christian ethics rooted in the First Commandment, and foreshadows his formulations in the Large and Small Catechisms of 1529. The Ten Commandments are not

The European Reformations Sourcebook, Second Edition. Edited by Carter Lindberg.
© 2014 John Wiley & Sons, Ltd. Published 2014 by John Wiley & Sons, Ltd.

merely prohibitions but positive exhortations to serve others. All self-chosen works intended for salvatory merit (e.g., prayers, fasts, pilgrimages) are rejected; the only good works are those commanded by God (e.g., serving one's neighbor through everyday activities). Eight reprints within the year, and six further reprints and a Latin translation in 1521, indicate its popular reception.

Luther's three so-called Reformation treatises (2.18–20) followed in rapid succession that same year, 1520. *To the Christian Nobility of the German Nation Concerning the Improvement of the Christian Estate* appeared in mid-August and the entire run of 4,000 copies quickly sold out. Luther argued that since clerical authorities are incapable of improving the church, reform becomes the responsibility of secular authority. Luther's view of the priesthood of all believers removed the class distinction between clergy and laity, undercut an ecclesial ideology of papal supremacy and canon law, and facilitated secular national-political, social, and economic viewpoints.

Luther's *The Babylonian Captivity of the Church* (October 1520) aimed at the heart of Roman clericalism and monasticism: the doctrine of the sacraments. The title pointedly compares the captivity of the Jews under the Babylonian Empire to the captivity of Christians under papal tyranny. Papal tyranny denies the cup to the laity; and by the doctrine of transubstantiation and the sacrifice of the mass displaces the promise of God by ecclesial action. The tract was written in Latin because it is a theological confrontation of scholastic sacramental theology and canon law.

The Freedom of a Christian (November 1520) proclaimed that a Christian is liberated from the anxiety or pride associated with the religiosity of self-achievement because Christ has fulfilled the law for those who trust his promise. Thus as the good tree bears good fruit, so the Christian who trusts God's promise in Christ is freed from religious self-absorption and freed for serving others. The tract appeared in Latin and German. The Latin edition was accompanied by an open letter to Pope Leo that addresses him as an equal and offers the pope advice for reform of the church. Whether or not Leo ever read this letter, he had already signed, on 15 June, the bull "Exsurge Domini" that threatened Luther's excommunication.

Papal condemnation of Luther appeared in June 1520 (2.21), and soon Luther was summoned to appear before the Diet of Worms. The papal nuncio's report (2.22) indicates the attitudes present in Worms and other areas of the empire. Luther had his "hearing" (2.23–24) before the Diet in late April and was then placed under imperial ban (2.25). Widespread uncertainty about Luther's fate is reflected in Albrecht Dürer's diary entry (2.26).

2.1 Martin Luther: Recollections of Becoming a Monk
LW 54: 338

I was made a monk by my own power against the will of my father and mother, of God and the devil, for in my monastic life I honored the pope with such reverence that I would defy all papists who have lived or still live [to outdo me]. I took the vow not for the sake of my belly but for the sake of my salvation, and I observed all the statutes very strictly.

2.2 Luther's Conversion
LW 34: 336–7

Though I lived as a monk without reproach, I felt that I was a sinner before God with an extremely disturbed conscience. . . . I did not love, yes, I hated the righteous God who punishes sinners, and secretly . . . I was angry with God. . . . Thus I raged with a fierce and troubled conscience. Nevertheless, I beat importunately upon Paul at that place [Rom. 1:17], most ardently desiring to know what St. Paul wanted.

At last, by the mercy of God, meditating day and night, I gave heed to the context of the words, namely, "In it the righteousness of God is revealed, as it is written, 'He who through faith is righteous shall live.'" There I began to understand that the righteousness of God is that by which the righteous lives by a gift of God, namely by faith. And this is the meaning: the righteousness of God is revealed by the gospel, namely, the passive righteousness with which the merciful God justifies us by faith, as it is written, "He who through faith is righteous shall live." Here I felt that I was altogether born again and had entered paradise itself through open gates. There a totally other face of the entire Scripture showed itself to me. Thereupon I ran through the Scriptures from memory. I also found in other terms an analogy, as, the work of God, that is, what God does in us, the power of God, with which he makes us strong, the wisdom of God, with which he makes us wise, the strength of God, the salvation of God, the glory of God.

2.3 Luther's Theological Emphases
LW 12: 311; LW 35: 366, 368–72, 374–5

The proper subject of theology is man guilty of sin and condemned, and God the Justifier and Savior of man the sinner. Whatever is asked or discussed in theology outside this subject is error and poison. . . .

The little word "law" you must here not take in human fashion as a teaching about what works are to be done or not done. That is the way with human laws; a law is fulfilled by works, even though there is no heart in the doing of them. But God judges according to what is in the depths of the heart. For this reason, his law too makes its demands on the inmost heart; it cannot be satisfied with works, . . .

Faith, moreover, comes only through God's Word or gospel which preaches Christ, saying that he is God's Son and a man, and has died and risen again for our sakes, . . .

So it happens that faith alone makes a person righteous and fulfils the law. . . . Thus good works emerge from faith itself. . . .

Sin, in the Scripture, means not only the outward works of the body but also all the activities that move men to do these works, namely, the inmost heart, with all its powers. . . . And the Scriptures look especially into the heart and single out the root and source of all sin, which is unbelief in the inmost heart. As, therefore, faith alone makes a person righteous, and brings the Spirit and pleasure in good outward works, so unbelief alone commits sin, and brings forth the flesh and pleasure in bad outward works, . . .

Unbelief is the root, the sap, and the chief power of all sin. . . .

Grace actually means God's favor, or the good will which in himself he bears toward us, by which he is disposed to give us Christ and to pour into us the Holy Spirit. . . .

Faith is a living, daring confidence in God's grace, so sure and certain that the believer would stake his life on it a thousand times. This knowledge of and confidence in God's grace makes men glad and bold and happy in dealing with God and with all creatures. . . .

Righteousness, then, is such a faith. It is called "the righteousness of God" because God gives it, and counts it as righteousness for the sake of Christ our Mediator, and makes a man to fulfil his obligation to everybody. . . .

Flesh and spirit you must not understand as though flesh is only that which has to do with unchastity and spirit is only that which has to do with what is inwardly in the heart. Rather, . . . Paul calls everything "flesh" that is born of the flesh – the whole man, with body and soul, mind and senses – because everything about him longs for the flesh. Thus you should learn to call him "fleshly" too who thinks, teaches, and talks a great deal about lofty spiritual matters, yet does so without grace. . . .

On the contrary, you should call him "spiritual" who is occupied with the most external kinds of works, as Christ was when he washed the disciples' feet [John 13:1–14] and Peter when he steered his boat and fished. Thus "the flesh" is a man who lives and works, inwardly and outwardly, in the service of the flesh's gain and of this temporal life. "The spirit" is the man who lives and works, inwardly and outwardly, in the service of the Spirit and of the future life. . . .

Thus we have it that faith justifies without any works; and yet it does not follow that men are therefore to do no good works, but rather that the genuine works will not be lacking. Of these the work-righteous saints know nothing. They dream up works of their own in which there is no peace, joy, confidence, love, hope, boldness, or any of the qualities of true Christian work and faith.

2.4 Luther: "Disputation Against Scholastic Theology" (1517)
LW 31: 10–12

17. Man is by nature unable to want God to be God. Indeed, he himself wants to be God, and does not want God to be God.
29. The best and infallible preparation for grace and the sole means of obtaining grace is the eternal election and predestination from God.
30. On the part of man, however, nothing precedes grace except ill will and even rebellion against grace.
33. And this is false, that doing all that one is able to do can remove obstacles to grace. This in opposition to several authorities.
34. In brief, man by nature has neither correct precept nor good will.
40. We do not become righteous by doing righteous deeds but, having been made righteous, we do righteous deeds. This in opposition to the philosophers.
50. Briefly, the whole of Aristotle is to theology as darkness is to light. This in opposition to the scholastics. [cf. 1.32–33]

2.5 "Official Catalogue" of Relics in the Wittenberg Castle Church
Hillerbrand 1964: 47–9

Five particles of the milk of the Virgin Mary. One piece of the tree where Mary nursed the Lord near the Garden of Balsam. Four pieces of the hair of Mary. Three pieces of the shirt of Mary. . . . Two pieces of the veil of Mary which was sprinkled with the blood of Christ under the Cross. . . . One piece of the diaper in which he [Jesus] was wrapped. Thirteen pieces of the manger of Jesus. One piece of the cradle. Two pieces of the hay. One piece of the straw on which the Lord lay when he was born. . . . One piece of the bread of which Christ ate with his disciples during the Last Supper. . . . One piece of the burning bush which Moses saw. . . . One piece of the robe of Christ. . . . One piece of the beard of the Lord Jesus. . . . One large piece of one nail which was driven through the hands or feet of the Lord Jesus. . . .

All in all: five thousand and five pieces. An indulgence of one hundred days for each piece. There are eight halls and each hall has an indulgence of one hundred and one days in addition. Blessed are those who participate therein.

2.6 Archbishop Albert of Mainz: The Commission of Indulgences
Hillerbrand 1964: 37–41

We do herewith proclaim that our most holy Lord Leo X, by divine providence present Pontiff, has given and bestowed to all Christian believers of either sex who lend their helpful hand for the reconstruction of the cathedral church of St. Peter, the Prince of the Apostles, in Rome, complete indulgence as well as other graces and freedoms, which the Christian believer may obtain according to the apostolic letter dealing with this Matter. . . .

Here follow the four principal graces granted in the apostolic bull. . . .

The first grace is the complete remission of all sins. . . . Moreover, through such forgiveness of sins the punishment which one is obliged to undergo in purgatory on account of the offence of the Divine Majesty is all remitted and the pain of purgatory is altogether done away with. . . .

Because the conditions of men are many and diverse, it is not possible to establish a general fee. We have therefore fixed the following rates [for an indulgence]:

Kings, queens, and their sons, archbishops and bishops, and other great rulers should pay . . . twenty-five Rhenish guilders.

Abbots, prelates of cathedral churches, counts, barons, and others of the higher nobility and their wives shall pay for each letter of indulgence ten such gold guilders. Other lesser prelates and nobles, as also the rectors of famous places, and all others who take in, either from steady income or goods or other means, 500 gold guilders should pay six guilders.

Other citizens and merchants, who ordinarily take in 200 such gold florins, should pay three florins.

Other citizens, merchants, and artisans, who have their families and income of their own, shall pay one such guilder; those of lesser means, pay only one half. . . .

But those who do not have any money should supply their contribution with prayer. For the kingdom of heaven should be open to the poor no less than to the rich . . .

The second principal grace is a letter of indulgence, entailing the greatest, exceedingly quickening and hitherto unheard of powers, which will continue beyond the eight years designated in the present bull. . . .

The third principal grace is the participation in all the possessions of the Church universal; . . . contributors . . . together with their deceased relatives, who have departed this world in a state of grace, shall from now on, and for eternity, be partakers in all petitions, intercessions, alms, fastings, prayers, in each and every pilgrimage, even those to the Holy Land; . . . and all other spiritual goods which have been, or shall be, brought forth by the universal, most holy Church militant or by any of its members. . . .

We also declare that in order to obtain these two most important graces, it is not necessary to make confession, or to visit the churches and altars, but merely to procure the confessional letter. . . .

The fourth distinctive grace is for those souls which are in purgatory, and is the complete remission of all sins . . . in this wise: that the same contribution shall be placed in the chest by a living person as one would make for himself. . . .

Moreover, preachers shall exert themselves to give this grace the widest publicity, since through the same, help will surely come to departed souls, and the construction of St. Peter will be abundantly promoted at the same time. . . .

2.7 Tetzel: A Sample Sermon
Hillerbrand 1964: 41–3

Behold, you are on the raging sea of this world in storm and danger, not knowing if you will safely reach the harbour of salvation. . . .

You should know that all who confess and in penance put alms into the coffer . . . will obtain complete remission of all their sins. . . . Why are you then standing there? Run for the salvation of your souls! . . .

Don't you hear the voices of your wailing dead parents and others who say, "Have mercy upon me, have mercy upon me, because we are in severe punishment and pain. From this you could redeem us with a small alms and yet you do not want to do so." Open your ears as the father says to the son and the mother to the daughter . . . "We have created you, fed you, cared for you, and left you our temporal goods. Why then are you so cruel and harsh that you do not want to save us, though it only takes so little? You let us lie in flames so that we only slowly come to the promised glory." You may have letters which let you have, once in life and in the hour of death . . . full remission of the punishment which belongs to sin. . . .

2.8 A Contemporary Description of Indulgence Selling
Kidd 1911: 19–20

He gained by his preaching in Germany an immense sum of money, all of which he sent to Rome; and especially at the new mining works at St. Annaberg, where I, Frederick Mecum, heard him for two years, a large sum was collected. It is incredible what this ignorant and impudent friar gave out. He said that if a Christian had slept with his mother, and placed the sum of money in the Pope's indulgence chest, the Pope had power in heaven and earth to forgive the sin, and, if he forgave it, God must do so also. Item, if they contributed readily and bought grace and indulgence, all the hills of St. Annaberg would become pure massive silver. Item, so soon as the coin rang in the chest, the soul for whom the money was paid, would go straightway to heaven. The indulgence was so highly prized, that when the commissary entered a city, the [Papal] Bull was borne on a satin or gold-embroidered cushion, and all the priests and monks, the town council, schoolmaster, scholars, men, women, maidens, and children, went out to meet him with banners and tapers, with songs and procession. Then all the bells were rung, all the organs played; he was conducted into the church, and the Pope's banner displayed; in short, God himself could not have been welcomed and entertained with greater honor.

2.9 "The Robbing of Tetzel"
Joestel 1992: 15–16

In 1517 there lived an impoverished and indebted knight, Christoph Haake von Stülpe, whose estate was completely rundown. Negotiations in nearby Jüterbog with his principal creditor, the Cistercian cloister, did not provide a solution. However, while he was in the city he witnessed all the fuss over Tetzel's selling of indulgences. The sight of so much money flowing into Tetzel's oaken indulgence chest gave him an inspiration.

When Tetzel finally left Jüterbog and traveled toward the cloister of Zinna, he was overtaken and robbed in a swampy area by the knight and his men. Tetzel, enraged, shouted to the robbers: "You shall be cursed and damned for eternity!" The knight raised his viser, and Tetzel saw the laughing face of Haake whom Tetzel had sold an indulgence for fifty gulden that remitted the future sin of robbery.

2.10 Luther: "The Ninety-five Theses" (1517)
LW 31: 25–33

1. When our Lord and Master Jesus Christ said, "Repent" [Matt. 4:17], he willed the entire life of believers to be one of repentance.
2. This word cannot be understood as referring to the sacrament of penance, that is, confession and satisfaction, as administered by the clergy.
5. The pope neither desires nor is able to remit any penalties except those imposed by his own authority or that of the canons.

6. The pope cannot remit any guilt, except by declaring and showing that it has been remitted by God; or, to be sure, by remitting guilt reserved to his judgment. . . .

13. The dying are freed from all penalties, are already dead as far as the canon laws are concerned, and have a right to be released from them.

20. Therefore the pope, when he uses the words "plenary remission of all penalties," does not actually mean "all penalties," but only those imposed by himself.

21. Thus those indulgence preachers are in error who say that a man is absolved from every penalty and saved by papal indulgences.

27. They preach only human doctrines who say that as soon as the money clinks into the money chest, the soul flies out of purgatory.

37. Any true Christian, whether living or dead, participates in all the blessings of Christ and the church; and this is granted him by God, even without indulgence letters.

43. Christians are to be taught that he who gives to the poor or lends to the needy does a better deed than he who buys indulgences.

45. Christians are to be taught that he who sees a needy man and passes him by, yet gives his money for indulgences, does not buy papal indulgences but God's wrath.

52. It is vain to trust in salvation by indulgence letters, even though the indulgence commissary, or even the pope, were to offer his soul as security.

75 To consider papal indulgences so great that they could absolve a man even if he had done the impossible and had violated the mother of God is madness.

81. This unbridled preaching of indulgences makes it difficult even for learned men to rescue the reverence which is due the pope from slander or from the shrewd questions of the laity.

82. Such as: "Why does not the pope empty purgatory for the sake of holy love and the dire needs of souls that are there if he redeems an infinite number of souls for the sake of miserable money with which to build a church? The former reasons would be most just; the latter is most trivial."

86. Again: "Why does not the pope, whose wealth is today greater than the wealth of Crassus, build this one basilica of St. Peter with his own money rather than with the money of poor believers?"

94. Christians should be exhorted to be diligent in following Christ, their head, through penalties, death, and hell;

95. And thus be confident of entering into heaven through many tribulations rather than though the false security of peace [Acts 14:22].

2.11 Bucer's Description of Luther at the Heidelberg Disputation (1518)
Junghans 1967: 214–15

As certainly as our most distinguished [debaters] tried with all their power to unseat him, they could not with all their hairsplitting expositions pull him even a finger's breadth from his standpoint. His gracefulness was marvelous when he answered; his patience was incomparable when he listened. When he refuted objections you could have perceived the astuteness of Paul, not that of Duns Scotus [d. 1308; medieval scholastic]. It was amazing how he so easily pulled answers from his repertoire of Holy Scripture to give very brief and well-informed answers.

The following day [April 26, 1518] I had a confidential and for me good private conversation with him. . . . Whatever I wanted to learn he explained with complete clarity. He agrees with Erasmus in everything, indeed in this regard he even appears to surpass him, teaching openly and freely what he [Erasmus] only insinuates. . . . He has succeeded that in Wittenberg all those usual writers [the scholastics] have been dismissed, and the Greek language, Jerome, Augustine, and Paul are openly taught.

2.12 Prierias: *Dialogue Against the Arrogant Theses of Martin Luther on the Power of the Pope* (1518)
Löscher 1723: 11–40

1. The universal church is, in its essence, the assembly of all who believe in Christ. The true universal church in its power is the Roman Church, the head of all churches, and the Sovereign Pontiff. The Roman Church is represented by the College of Cardinals, however in its power it is the Pope who is the head of the Church, though in another manner than Christ.
2. As the universal church cannot err when it decides on faith or morals, so also a true council cannot err if it does its best to know the truth. . . . Accordingly, the Roman Church and the pope cannot err when he in his capacity as pope comes to a decision, that is, when he comes to a decision in consequence of his office and thereby does his best to know the truth.
3. Whoever does not hold to the teaching of the Roman Church and the pope as an infallible rule of faith, from which even Holy Scripture draws its power and authority, is a heretic.
4. The Roman Church can establish something with regard to faith and morals not only by words but also by acts. And there is no difference therein, except that the word is more suitable for this than the act. In this same sense custom acquires the power of law, for the will of a prince expresses itself in acts. . . . It follows that as he is a heretic who wrongly interprets Scripture, so also is he a heretic who wrongly interprets the teaching and acts of the Church in so far as they relate to faith and morals.

    Corollary: Whoever says in regard to indulgences that the Roman Church cannot do what she has actually done is a heretic.

2.13 Luther's Hearing before Cardinal Cajetan at Augsburg (1518)
Thulin 1966: 36–8

The cardinal addressed me in a friendly manner and said, "You have stirred up all Germany with your disputation on the indulgences. If you want to be a member of the church and have a pope who is gracious, then recant everything. In that case nothing shall happen to you . . ." He simply wanted me to recant what I had written. Thereupon I replied that I could not do this, but offered henceforth to remain silent. He refused to agree to this. I said that I also could not do the other thing, and then left him. . . .

When thereafter I returned to him, he wanted me simply to recant. Then I became very angry . . . and said, "I cannot recant unless someone teaches me something that is better. I cannot abandon the Scriptures." When he got nowhere with me with his "Revoca," he shouted in Italian, "Friar, friar, yesterday you were very reasonable, but today you are completely mad!" He then confronted me with the papal bull [Extravagante] of Clement VI. However, I said that the pope had misinterpreted the Scriptures, and I argued against the pope. Cajetan became very angry and said, "Recant or don't ever return [Revoca aut non revertere]!" I took the words, "don't ever return!" to heart. I spent a few more days in Augsburg and wrote two letters to the cardinal in which I made known to him my views. Since he did not answer me, Doctor Staupitz supplied me with a horse and the senate provided me with an old outrider who knew the roads. At night Langenmantel helped me get out of the city through a little gate. Thus I traveled on horseback without riding breeches, boots, spurs, and sword, until I got to Wittenberg. The first day I rode eight miles, and when I reached the inn that evening and dismounted in the stable I was so tired that I couldn't stand but slumped down into the straw.

2.14 Georg Spalatin: Recollections of
Frederick the Wise on Luther
Spalatin 1851: 161, 164–5

In this year 1519 in the month of February, Bishop Lorenz of Würzburg died, one of the lineage of Bibra. He was an honorable, pious, wise man who just before his death wrote to the Elector Prince Frederick of Saxony in his own hand concerning Dr. Martin Luther: "Your Beloved will indeed not allow the pious man, Dr. Martin, to draw back for that would be an injustice to him." The Elector of Saxony was so pleased with the Bishop's words that he paraphrased them in his own hand and sent them to me, Spalatin. . . .

[In 1520, Frederick met Erasmus in Cologne and asked whether] he too thought Dr. Martin Luther had erred in his writing and preaching. [Erasmus] gave his answer in Latin: "Yes, namely in two ways, first he attacked the Pope's crown; and second, the monks' bellies." The Elector smiled with amusement at this answer. Thereafter there was hardly a year up to his end that he didn't recall it. Subsequently, [some] Cardinals disputed with the Elector at Cologne about Dr. Martin Luther in order to suppress him and Christian teaching. Also at that time there, an ecclesiastical Elector said to [Frederick]: "O, my dear lord, if Dr. Martin Luther had only written in Latin and not in German."

2.15 Peter Mosellanus: Description of Luther, Karlstadt,
and Eck at the Leipzig Debate
Junghans 1967: 81–3

Martin is of medium form. He has a thinner body, exhausted equally by concerns and studies so that whoever looks closely can count nearly all his bones. He is still of a youthful and fresh period of life, and has a sharp and clear voice. His erudition and knowledge of Scripture are astonishing; he has nearly everything at his fingertips. He understands Greek and Hebrew so well that he can form a judgment on their interpretation. Also, he is not lacking for material to discuss for he has at his disposal an enormous wealth of things and words. . . . In addition, in terms of his life and conduct he is sociable and friendly. He displays nothing stoical or surly, and is always in good form. In social settings he is a humorous and witty entertainer, always lively and carefree with a cheerful countenance, even when enemies fiercely threaten him, so that one cannot easily believe that this man pursues such difficult work without godly power. But there is one fault: When he refutes anyone he does so a little too sharply than is proper for a theologian, and for one who desires to renew the godly. I don't know whether he has this failing in common with all who learn later in life.

One sees the same with Karlstadt only to a lesser degree, except that he is of a smaller stature and has a dark and sunburned face. His voice is unclear and boring. His memory is weak and his temper is obvious.

On the other hand, Eck's figure is tall, his body is strong and burly. He has a full and entirely German voice that resonates from his chest so that he could be a match not only for a dramatic actor but even for the town crier. His voice however is more brusque than expressive. . . . His mouth, his ears, generally his whole visage are such that one certainly might take him for any butcher or violence-loving soldier rather than a theologian. In what concerns him he has command of an excellent memory; when it falls into a corresponding understanding his mind is a masterpiece of nature. But if he fails to understand something, he lacks astuteness of judgment, and all the remaining gifts are nothing. This is the reason why, when he is disputing, he gathers so many texts and citations without any selection, and does not note that since many of these are inane they have nothing to do with the matter at hand and are rather unbelievable and sophist. He spreads about a lot of mixed fodder to the audience, who for the most part are dull and mindless, so that he produces such an effect that he is awarded the victory. Thereby he possesses an unbelievable brashness that he covers with remarkable craftiness. When he realizes he has walked into his opponent's trap, he gradually steers the disputation to another point. But many times he also adopts the meaning of his opponent with other words, and then attributes his own nonsensical reasoning to his opponent with astonishing skill.

2.16 Capito: Letter of Support to Luther (February 1519)
Junghans 1967: 215–16

The Swiss lands and the lands on the Rhine up to the North Sea are supporting the true friends of Luther, and these are very powerful. All told they are no strangers to learned studies. The Cardinal Matthias Schinner, Count Diebold III von Geroldseck, a learned and an extraordinarily honorable bishop [Christoph von Utenheim, Bishop of Basel] and not a few others of us belong among them. As these recently heard that you are in danger, they offer you not only subsistence but also protection where you could live openly or in concealment. . . .

Together we have printed your works, as you know, from the Froben publishing house. Immediately after the Frankfurt book fair, we distributed them with much luck in Italy, France [3,000 copies sold in two weeks!], Spain, and England, whereby we believe to provide for the common good by openly proclaiming the truth as far as possible.

2.17 Luther: *Treatise on Good Works* (June 1520)
LW 44: 23, 26–7, 70–1

The first thing to know is that there are no good works except those works God has commanded, just as there is no sin except that which God has forbidden. Therefore, whoever wants to know what good works are as well as doing them needs to know nothing more than God's [Ten] commandments. . . .

The first, highest, and most precious of all good works is faith in Christ. . . . For in this work all good works exist, and from faith these works receive a borrowed goodness. . . .

It further follows from this that a Christian man living in this faith has no need of a teacher of good works, but he does whatever the occasion calls for, and all is well done. . . .

We may see this in an everyday example. When a husband and wife really love one another, have pleasure in each other, and thoroughly believe in their love, who teaches them how they are to behave one to another, what they are to do or not to do, say or not to say, what they are to think? Confidence alone teaches them all this, and even more than is necessary. For such a man there is no distinction in works. He does the great and the important as gladly as the small and unimportant, and vice versa. . . .

[W]hat help would it be for you if you were to perform all the miracles of the saints . . . and yet were found guilty of having disregarded your neighbor's need and of having therefore sinned against love? For Christ at the last day will not ask how much you have prayed, fasted, pilgrimaged, done this or that for yourself, but how much good you have done to others, even to the very least [Matt. 25:40, 45]. . . .

2.18 Luther: *To the Christian Nobility of the German Nation Concerning the Reform of the Christian Estate* (1520)
LW 44: 126–7, 129–31, 133–4, 136, 158, 175, 177, 179, 189–90, 205–6, 212–16

The Romanists have very cleverly built three walls around themselves. Hitherto they have protected themselves by these walls in such a way that no one has been able to reform them. As a result, the whole of Christendom has fallen abominably.

In the first place . . . they have made decrees and declared that the temporal power had no jurisdiction over them, but that on the contrary, the spiritual power is above the temporal. In the second place, when the attempt is made to reprove them with the Scriptures, they raise the objection that only the pope may interpret the Scriptures. In the third place, if threatened with a council, their story is that no one may summon a council but the pope. . . .

Let us begin by attacking the first wall. It is pure invention that pope, bishops, priests, and monks are called the spiritual estate while princes, lords, artisans, and farmers are called the temporal estate. This is indeed a piece of deceit and hypocrisy. Yet no one need be intimidated by it, and for this reason: all Christians are truly of the spiritual estate, and there is no difference among them except that of office. . . . This is because we all have one baptism, one gospel, one faith, and are all Christians alike; for baptism, gospel, and faith alone make us spiritual and a Christian people. . . . [W]e are all consecrated priests through baptism. . . .

It follows from this argument that there is no true, basic difference between laymen and priests, princes and bishops, between religious and secular, except for the sake of office and work, but not for the sake of status. . . .

Therefore, just as those who are now called "spiritual," that is, priests, bishops, or popes, are neither different from other Christians nor superior to them, except that they are charged with the administration of the word of God and the sacraments, which is their work and office, so it is with the temporal authorities. They bear the sword and rod in their hand to punish the wicked and protect the good. . . .

I say therefore that since the temporal power is ordained of God to punish the wicked and protect the good, it should be left free to perform its office in the whole body of Christendom without restriction and without respect to persons, whether it affects pope, bishops, priest, monks, nuns, or anyone else. . . .

For these reasons the temporal Christian authority ought to exercise its office without hindrance, regardless of whether it is pope, bishop, or priest whom it affects. Whoever is guilty, let him suffer. . . .

The second wall is still more loosely built and less substantial. The Romanists want to be the only masters of Holy Scripture, although they never learn a thing from the Bible all their life long. They [try] . . . to persuade us that the pope cannot err in matters of faith. . . .

[T]heir claim that only the pope may interpret Scripture is an outrageous fancied fable. They cannot produce a single letter [of Scripture] to maintain that the interpretation of Scripture or the confirmation of its interpretation belongs to the pope alone. . . . They themselves have usurped this power. . . .

The third wall falls of itself when the first two are down. When the pope acts contrary to the Scriptures, it is our duty to stand by the Scriptures, to reprove him and to constrain him, according to the word of Christ, Matthew 18 [:15–17]. . . .

The Romanists have no basis in Scripture for their claim that the pope alone has the right to call or confirm a council. . . . Even the Council of Nicea, the most famous of all councils was neither called nor confirmed by the bishop of Rome, but by the emperor Constantine. . . .

They have no authority to prevent a council, or even worse yet at their mere whim to pledge it, impose conditions on it, or deprive it of its freedom. When they do that they are truly in the fellowship of Antichrist and the devil. . . .

[T]he Christian nobility should set itself against the pope as against a common enemy and destroyer of Christendom. . . . The German Christian nobility should ordain, order, and decree that henceforth no further benefice shall be drawn into the hands of Rome, . . . If this happened they would sit up and take notice in Rome. They would not think that the Germans are always dull and drunk, but have really become Christian again. . . .

We also see how the priesthood has fallen, and how many a poor priest is overburdened with wife and child, his conscience troubled. Yet no one does anything to help him, though he could easily be helped. . . . And this is what I say: according to the institution of Christ and the apostles, every city should have a priest or bishop, as St. Paul clearly says in Titus 1 [:5]. And this priest should not be compelled to live without a wedded wife, but should be permitted to have one, as St. Paul writes in I Timothy 3 [:2, 4] and Titus 1 [:67]. . . .

I will not conceal my real opinion or withhold comfort from that pitiful band who with wives and children have fallen into disgrace and whose consciences are burdened because people call them priests' whores and their children priests' children. . . .

Before God and the Holy Scriptures marriage of the clergy is no offense. . . . For Christ has set us free from all man-made laws, especially when they are opposed to God and the salvation of souls, as St. Paul teaches in Galatians 5[:1] and I Corinthians 10[:23]. . . .

One of the greatest necessities is the abolition of all begging throughout Christendom. Nobody ought to go begging among Christians. It would even be a very simple matter to make a law to the effect that every city should look after its own poor, if only we had the courage and the intention to do so. No beggar from outside should be allowed into the city whether he might call himself pilgrim or mendicant monk. Every city should support its own poor, and if it was too small, the people in the surrounding villages should also be urged to contribute, since in any case they have to feed many vagabonds and evil rogues who call themselves mendicants. In this way, too, it could be known who was really poor, and who was not. . . .

Above all, the foremost reading for everybody, both in the universities and in the schools, should be Holy Scripture – and for the younger boys, the Gospels. And would to God that every town had a girls' school as well, where the girls would be taught the Gospel for an hour every day either in German or in Latin. . . . [T]oday even the great, learned prelates and the very bishops do not know the gospel.

Enough has now been said about the failings of the clergy, . . . We will now devote a section to the failings of the temporal estate.

In the first place, there is a great need for a general law and decree in the German nation against extravagant and costly dress. . . .

It is also necessary to restrict the spice traffic, which is another of the great ships in which money is carried out of German lands. . . .

But the greatest misfortune of the German nation is certainly the *zynskauf* [usurious sale of loans and capital interest]. . . . This traffic has not existed much longer than a hundred years, and it has already brought almost all princes, endowed institutions, cities, nobles, and their heirs to poverty, misery, and ruin. . . . The devil invented the practice, and by confirming it [legalized by Lateran V in 1512] the pope has brought woe upon the whole world. . . .

In this connection, we must put a bit in the mouth of the Fuggers and similar [banking] companies. How is it possible in the lifetime of one man to accumulate such great possessions, worthy of a king, . . .

Finally, is it not lamentable that we Christians tolerate open and common brothels in our midst, . . .?

In this matter of brothels, and in other matters previously mentioned, I have tried to point out how many good works the temporal government could do, and what the duty of every government should be, so that everyone may learn what an awful responsibility it is to rule and sit in high places. . . . It is the duty of authorities to seek the best for those they govern. . . .

[T]he care of young people ought to be the chief concern of the pope, bishops, the ruling classes, and of the councils. They want to exercise authority far and wide, and yet they help nobody. For just this reason a lord and ruler will be a rare sight in heaven, even though he build a hundred churches for God and raise up all the dead! . . .

2.19 Luther: *The Babylonian Captivity of the Church* (1520)
LW 36: 18, 27–31, 35–8, 47–8, 51–2, 58–9, 66, 74, 78, 92, 106–7, 116, 124

To begin with, I must deny that there are seven sacraments, and for the present maintain that there are but three: baptism, penance [later dropped as a sacrament], and the bread. All three have been subjected to a miserable captivity by the Roman curia, and the church has been robbed of all her liberty. . . .

The first captivity of this sacrament, therefore, concerns its substance or completeness, which the tyranny of Rome has wrested from us. . . . The sacrament does not belong to the priests, but to all men. The priests are not lords, but servants in duty bound to administer both kinds to those who desire them, as often as they desire them. If they wrest this right from the laity and deny it to them by force, they are tyrants. . . .

The second captivity of this sacrament is less grievous as far as the conscience is concerned, yet the gravest of dangers threatens the man who would attack it. . . .

[W]hen the Evangelists plainly write that Christ took bread . . . and blessed it, and when the Book of Acts and the Apostle Paul in turn call it bread . . . we have to think of real bread and real wine, . . . Since it is not necessary, therefore, to assume a transubstantiation effected by divine power, it must be regarded as a figment of the human mind, for it rests neither on the Scriptures nor on reason, as we shall see. . . .

Moreover, the church kept the true faith for more than twelve hundred years, during which time the holy fathers never, at any time or place, mentioned this transubstantiation (a monstrous word and a monstrous idea), until the pseudo philosophy of Aristotle began to make its inroads into the church in these last three hundred years . . .

The third captivity of this sacrament is by far the most wicked abuse of all, in consequence of which there is no opinion more generally held or more firmly believed in the church today than this, that the mass is a good work and a sacrifice. And this abuse has brought an endless host of other abuses in its train, so that the faith of this sacrament has become utterly extinct and the holy sacrament has been turned into mere merchandise, a market, and a profit-making business. . . . On these the priests and monks depend for their entire livelihood. . . .

Let this stand, therefore, as our first and infallible proposition – the mass or Sacrament of the Altar is Christ's testament, which he left behind him at his death to be distributed among his believers. . . .

A testament as everyone knows, is a promise made by one about to die, in which he designates his bequest and appoints his heirs. A testament, therefore, involves first, the death of the testator, and second, the promise of an inheritance and the naming of the heir. . . .

You see, therefore, that what we call the mass is a promise of the forgiveness of sins made to us by God, and such a promise as has been confirmed by the death of the Son of God. For the only difference between a promise and a testament is that the testament involves the death of the one who makes it. . . .

If the mass is a promise, as has been said, then access to it is to be gained, not with any works, or powers, or merits of one's own, but by faith alone. For where there is the Word of the promising God, there must necessarily be the faith of the accepting man. It is plain therefore, that the beginning of our salvation is a faith which clings to the Word of the promising God, who, without any effort on our part, in free and unmerited mercy takes the initiative and offers us the word of his promise. . . . First of all there is God's Word. After it follows faith, after faith, love; then love does every good work, for it does no wrong, indeed, it is the fulfilling of the law [Rom. 13:10]. In no other way can man come to God or deal with him than through faith. That is to say, that the author of salvation is not man, by any works of his own, but God through his promise; . . .

However, faith is not a work, but the lord and life of all works. Who in the world is so foolish as to regard a promise received by him, or a testament given to him, as a good work, which he renders to the testator by his acceptance of it? . . .

[I]t is a manifest and wicked error to offer or apply the mass for sins, for satisfactions, for the dead, or any needs whatsoever of one's own or of others. You will readily see the obvious truth of this if you firmly hold that the mass is a divine promise which can benefit no one, except only him who believes with a faith of his own. Who can receive or apply, in behalf of another, the promise of God, which demands the personal faith of each one individually? . . .

Now there is yet a second stumbling block that must be removed, and this much greater and the most dangerous of all. It is the common belief that the mass is a sacrifice, which is offered to God. . . .

Over against [this] . . . we must resolutely set the words and example of Christ. For unless we firmly hold that the mass is the promise or testament of Christ, as the words clearly say, we shall lose the whole gospel and all its comfort. . . . Moreover, we have the example of Christ on our side. When he instituted this sacrament and established this testament at the Last Supper, Christ did not offer himself to God the Father, nor did he perform a good work on behalf of others, but sitting at the table he set this same testament before each one and proffered to him the sign. . . .

[Re baptism] Now, the first thing to be considered about baptism is the divine promise, which says: "He who believes and is baptized will be saved" [Mark 16:16]. This promise must be set above all glitter of works, vows, religious orders, and whatever else man has introduced, for on it all our salvation depends. But we must so consider it as to exercise our faith in it, and have no doubt whatever that, once we have been baptized, we are saved. . . .

For the truth of the promise once made remains steadfast, always ready to receive us back with open arms when we return. . . .

Thus it is not baptism that justifies or benefits anyone, but it is faith in that word of promise to which baptism is added. This faith justifies, and fulfills that which baptism signifies. . . .

[Re vows] [A]ll vows should be completely abolished and avoided, whether of religious orders, or about pilgrimages or about any works whatsoever, that we may remain in that which is supremely religious and most rich in works – the freedom of baptism. . . .

Therefore I advise no one to enter any religious order or the priesthood, indeed, I advise everyone against it – unless he is forearmed with this knowledge and understands that the works of monks and priests, however holy and arduous they may be, do not differ one whit in the sight of God from the works of the rustic laborer in the field or the woman going about her household tasks, but all works are measured before God by faith alone, . . .

[Re marriage] We have said that in every sacrament there is a word of divine promise, to be believed by whoever receives the sign and that the sign alone cannot be a sacrament. Nowhere do we read that the man who marries a wife receives any grace of God. There is not even a divinely instituted sign in marriage, nor do we read anywhere that marriage was instituted by God to be a sign of anything. . . .

Furthermore, since marriage has existed from the beginning of the world and is still found among unbelievers, there is no reason why it should be called a sacrament of the New Law and of the church alone. The marriages of the ancients were no less sacred than ours, nor are those of unbelievers less true marriages than those of believers, and yet they are not regarded as sacraments. . . .

[Re ordination] Of this sacrament the church of Christ knows nothing; it is an invention of the church of the pope. Not only is there nowhere any promise of grace attached to it, but there is not a single word said about it in the whole New Testament. . . .

Let everyone, therefore, who knows himself to be a Christian, be assured of this, that we are all equally priests, that is to say, we have the same power in respect to the Word and the sacraments. However, no one may make use of this power except by the consent of the community or by the call of a superior. (For what is the common property of all, no individual may arrogate to himself, unless he is called.) And therefore this "sacrament" of ordination, if it is anything at all, is nothing else than a certain rite whereby one is called to the ministry of the church. Furthermore, the priesthood is properly nothing but the ministry of the Word – the Word, I say; not the law, but the gospel. . . .

[I]t has seemed proper to restrict the name of sacrament to those promises which have signs attached to them. The remainder, not being bound to signs, are bare promises. Hence there are, strictly speaking, but two sacraments in the church of God – baptism and the bread. For only in these two do we find both the divinely instituted sign and the promise of forgiveness of sins. The sacrament of penance, which I added to these two, lacks the divinely instituted visible sign, and is, as I have said, nothing but a way and a return to baptism. . . .

2.20 Luther: *The Freedom of a Christian* (1520)
LW 31: 344–6, 348–9, 358–61, 363, 372–3

To make the way smoother for the unlearned – for only them do I serve – I shall set down the following two propositions concerning the freedom and the bondage of the spirit:

A Christian is a perfectly free lord of all, subject to none.

A Christian is a perfectly dutiful servant of all, subject to all.

These two theses seem to contradict each other. If, however, they should be found to fit together they would serve our purpose beautifully. . . .

One thing, and only one thing, is necessary for Christian life, righteousness, and freedom. That one thing is the most holy Word of God, the gospel of Christ, . . .

[R]emember . . . that faith alone, without works, justifies, frees, and saves; . . . Here we must point out that the entire Scripture of God is divided into two parts: commandments and promises. . . . [T]he commandments show us what we ought to do but do not give us the power to do it. They are intended to teach man to know himself, that through them he may recognize his inability to do good and may despair of his own ability. . . .

[T]hen, being truly humbled and reduced to nothing in his own eyes, he finds in himself nothing whereby he may be justified and saved. Here the second part of Scripture comes to our aid, namely, the promises of God. . . . Thus the promises of God give what the commandments of God demand and fulfil what the law prescribes so that all things may be God's alone, both the commandments and the fulfilling of the commandments. He alone commands, he alone fulfills. . . .

Let us now turn to the second part, the outer man. Here we shall answer all those who offended by the word "faith" and by all that has been said, now ask, "If faith does all things and is alone sufficient unto righteousness, why then are good works commanded? We will take our ease and do no works and be content with faith." I answer: not so, you wicked men. . . . This is the place to assert that which was said above, namely, that a Christian is the servant of all and made subject to all. Insofar as he is free he does no works, but insofar as he is a servant he does all kinds of works. . . .

In doing these works, however, we must not think that a man is justified before God by them, for faith, which alone is righteousness before God, cannot endure that erroneous opinion. . . . [T]he works themselves do not justify him before God, but he does the works out of spontaneous love in obedience to God and considers nothing except the approval of God, whom he would most scrupulously obey in all things. . . .

The following statements are therefore true: "Good works do not make a man good, but a good man does good works; evil works do not make a man wicked, but a wicked man does evil works." . . .

From this it is easy to know how far good works are to be rejected or not, and by what standard all the teachings of men concerning works are to be interpreted. If works are sought after as a means to righteousness, . . . and are done under the false impression that through them one is justified, they are made necessary and freedom and faith are destroyed; and this addition to them makes them no longer good but truly damnable works. They are not free, and they blaspheme the grace of God since to justify and to save by faith belongs to the grace of God alone. . . . We do not, therefore, reject good works; on the contrary, we cherish and teach them as much as possible. We do not condemn for their own sake but on account of this godless addition to them and the perverse idea that righteousness is to be sought through them; . . .

Our faith in Christ does not free us from works but from false opinions concerning works, that is, from the foolish presumption that justification is acquired by works. Faith redeems, corrects, and preserves our consciences so that we know that righteousness does not consist in works, although works neither can nor ought to be wanting; just as we cannot be without food and drink and all the works of this mortal body, yet our righteousness is not in them, but in faith; and yet those works of the body are not to be despised or neglected on that account. . . .

2.21 Pope Leo X: "Exsurge domine" (June 15, 1520)
Thulin 1966: 48–9

Bishop Leo, a servant of the servants of God.

Arise, O Lord [Ps. 7:6], judge thy cause; . . . Now a wild boar from the forest threatens to ravage the vineyard, indeed, a wild animal threatens to pluck its fruit [Ps. 80:12–13].

Arise, Peter, and in accord with your position as protector and guardian, with which you have been charged by God, attend with zeal the cause of the holy Roman church. . . .

[W]e herewith condemn . . . by virtue of this decree . . . the same Martin, his assenters, patrons, followers, and supporters, and demand and command that they be considered to be such by all Christian believers, both male and female. . . . In addition, we forbid all Christian believers under no circumstances to read, express, preach, praise, or print the writings of the same Martin . . . so that his memory may be completely obliterated from the fellowship of Christian believers. . . . Yes, they are to burn them. . . . And in order to increase the disgrace of the same Martin and those in accord with him . . . they, under every penalty to the law, are personally to seize Luther, his assenters, patrons, followers, and supporters, and at our request to hold them captive and send them to us, in payment of which good deed they are to receive a suitable reward and remuneration from us and the papal throne. . . .

2.22 The Papal Nuncio's Reports from the Diet of Worms
Thulin 1966: 53–5, 59

Against us are a host of poor German nobles, who have conspired together under Hutten's leadership, and, thirsting for the blood of priests, would like to fall upon us at once.

They refuse to let me have the dwelling that was rented for me . . . even though I am willing to pay more dearly than others; they erase my name on the door, and a thousand other crude and impudent pranks are played that are most strange and incredible. . . .

A while ago at Augsburg they were selling a picture of Luther with a halo; it was offered for sale here without the halo, and all the copies were disposed of in a trice before I could get one. Yesterday I saw Luther with a book and Hutten with a sword on one and the same page of a pamphlet. Above them was printed in handsome letters, "To the champions of Christian freedom, M. Luther and Ulrich von Hutten (in Latin)." . . .

In Antwerp Luther's writings are being printed in Spanish, presumably upon the urging of the Marranos [Spanish Jews who had converted to Christianity], whom one ought to ship from Flanders back to Spain; the emperor has promised us his assistance. In Ghent the [Augustinian] Eremites proclaim Luther's gospel in all the streets as being the teaching of St. Paul, yes, even of Christ. It has been reported to the emperor that the dioceses of Utrecht and Münster, as well as the other bishoprics of Lower Germany have been corrupted by the rot of this heresy. In Holland Luther's doctrine is openly propagated; the only reason why this is possible lies in the fact that Erasmus is a Hollander; even the emperor's councilors know about this and talk about it freely. . . .

The emperor has answered the University of Vienna to the effect that it is to burn the books of Luther at once.

Furthermore, his father confessor informed me as an eyewitness that today in a privy council he has resolved and given orders that one of his secretaries depart with utmost despatch for Antwerp and other cities in Flanders for the purpose of completely stamping out Luther's books, arresting his followers, and taking the most drastic preventive measures. . . .

No one knows a way of confronting the heresy; even those who fear Luther speak in his favor. . . .

[O]nly the emperor sides with us. That too, after all, is of great significance, if he does not desert us because of fear of a popular movement or in response to the wicked advice of his entourage. Outside of this the whole world is our enemy, and the mad dogs, the Germans, are equipped with weapons of the spirit and of the body, and know quite well how to boast that they no longer are stupid beasts like their ancestors, but have now diverted the Tiber into their Rhine, and that Italy has now surrendered the treasures of knowledge to them. . . .

2.23 Luther before Emperor and Empire
at the Diet of Worms (1521)
Thulin 1966: 64–5

[T]he secretary spoke up in these words:

"Come then: answer the question of his majesty, whose kindness you have experienced in seeking a time for thought. Do you wish to defend all your acknowledged books, or to retract some?" This the secretary said in Latin and in German. . . .

Dr. Martin himself replied in Latin and German, . . .

"Most serene emperor, most illustrious princes, concerning those questions proposed to me yesterday on behalf of your serene majesty, whether I acknowledged as mine the books enumerated and published in my name and whether I wished to persevere in their defense or to retract them, I have given to the first question my full and complete answer, in which I still persist and shall persist forever. These books are mine and they have been published in my name by me. . . .

"In replying to the second question, I ask that your most serene majesty and your lordships may deign to note that my books are not all of the same kind.

"For there are some in which I have discussed religious faith and morals simply and evangelically. . . . Thus if I should begin to disavow them, I ask you, what would I be doing? Would not I, alone of all men, be condemning the very truth upon which friends and enemies equally agree, striving alone against the harmonious confession of all?

"Another group of my books attacks the papacy and the affairs of the papists as those who both by their doctrines and very wicked examples have laid waste the Christian world with evil that affects the spirit and the body. . . . If, therefore, I should have retracted these writings, I should have done nothing other than to have added strength to this [papal] tyranny and I should have opened not only windows but doors to such great godlessness. It would rage farther and more freely than ever it has dared up to this time. . . .

"I have written a third sort of book against some private and (as they say) distinguished individuals – those, namely, who strive to preserve the Roman tyranny and to destroy the godliness taught by me. Against these I confess I have been more violent than my religion or profession demands. But then, I do not set myself up as a saint; neither am I disputing about my life, but about the teaching of Christ. It is not proper for me to retract these works. . . .

"Therefore, I ask by the mercy of God, that your most serene majesty, most illustrious lordships, or anyone at all who is able, either high or low, may bear witness, expose my errors, overthrowing them by the writings of the prophets and the evangelists. Once I have been taught I shall be quite ready to renounce every error, and I shall be the first to cast my books into the fire. . . .

"Since then your serene majesty and your lordships seek a simple answer, I will give it in this manner, neither horned nor toothed: Unless I am convinced by the testimony of the Scriptures or by clear reason (for I do not trust either in the pope or in councils alone, since it is well known that they have often erred and contradicted themselves), I am bound by the Scriptures I have quoted and my conscience is captive to the Word of God. I cannot and I will not retract anything, since it is neither safe nor right to go against conscience.

"I cannot do otherwise, here I stand, may God help me, Amen."

2.24 Charles V: Message to his Council (April 19, 1521)
Thulin 1966: 67

You know that I am descended from the most Christian emperors of the noble German nation, from the Catholic kings of Spain, the archdukes of Austria and the dukes of Burgundy. . . . I am determined to support everything that these predecessors and I myself have kept. . . . For it is certain that a single friar errs in his opinion which is against all of Christendom and according to which all of

Christianity will be and will always have been in error both in the past thousand years and even more in the present. For that reason I am absolutely determined to stake on this cause my kingdoms and seigniories, my friends, my body and blood, my life and soul. . . . And after having heard the obstinate answer which Luther gave yesterday, April 18, in the presence of us all, I declare to you that I regret having so long delayed to proceed against this Luther and his false doctrine and I am no longer willing to hear him speak more, but I am making it clear that immediately, according to the mandate, he be taken back keeping the tenor of his safe-conduct without preaching or admonishing the people with his bad doctrine and making sure that no disorder results.

2.25 The Edict of Worms (May 26, 1521)
Jensen 1973: 79–81, 85–7, 101–3, 109–11

To the honor and praise of God, . . . it is our duty to help subdue the enemies of our faith and bring them to the obedience of the divine majesty . . . , and to keep the Christian religion pure from all heresy or suspicion of heresy, according to and following the ordinance and custom observed by the Holy Roman Church. . . . For this reason – after having learned of the mistakes and heresies of a certain Martin Luther . . . who teaches iniquity, preaches false doctrines, and writes, in both Latin and German, evil things against our Catholic faith and the Holy Roman and Universal Church . . . imperiling and endangering Christian souls, and bringing future confusion to all the public affairs of our Holy Mother Church – if we do not put an end to this contagious confusion, it could lead to the corrupting of all faithful nations and to their falling into abominable schisms. . . .

Item. He changes and dishonestly infects the inviolable laws of the sacred sacrament of marriage. . . .

Item. As for the holy order of the priesthood (through which the precious body and blood of our Lord is consecrated) and the power and authority of the keys of our Holy Mother Church: not only does Luther despise them by saying that they are common to all men, children, and women, but in addition, he provokes the seculars to wash their hands in the blood of the priests.

Item. The Vicar of God here upon the earth, our Holy Father the pope, the true successor of Saint Peter, is called several infamous names by Luther. The pope is also blasphemed and persecuted. . . .

Item. He despises and condemns the doctrines and authorities which the holy doctors preceding us have left for our instructions, and he degrades with all his might the devotion that we have for our saints.

Item. He says that there are no such things as superiority and obedience. He destroys all civil police and hierarchical and ecclesiastical order, so that people are led to rebel against their superiors, spiritual and temporal, and to start killing, stealing, and burning, to the great loss and ruin of public and Christian good. . . .

For this reason we forbid anyone from this time forward to dare, either by words or by deeds, to receive, defend, sustain, or favor the said Martin Luther. On the contrary, we want him to be apprehended and punished as a notorious heretic, as he deserves. . . . Those who will help in his capture will be rewarded generously for their good work. . . .

And so as to prevent poisonous false doctrine and bad examples from being spread all over Christendom, and so that the art of printing books might be used only toward good ends, we, after mature and long deliberation, order and command you by this edict that henceforth, under penalty of confiscation of goods and property, no book dealer, printer, or anybody else mention the Holy Scriptures or their interpretation without having first received the consent of the clerk of the city and the advice and consent of the faculty of theology of the university, which will approve those books and writings with their seal. . . .

Item. Furthermore, we declare in this ordinance that if anyone, whatever his social status may be, dares directly or indirectly to oppose this decree – whether concerning Luther's matter, his defamatory books or their printings, or whatever has been ordered by us – these transgressors in so doing will be guilty of the crime of *lèse majesté* and will incur our grave indignation as well as each of the punishments mentioned above. . . .

2.26 Albrecht Dürer's Diary: Rumors of Luther's Capture (1521)
Thulin 1966: 71–2

On Friday before Pentecost in the year 1521 the news reached Antwerp that Martin Luther had treacherously been taken captive. . . . Whether he still lives, or whether they have murdered him – which I do not know – he has suffered this for the sake of the Christian truth and because he has rebuked the unchristian papacy which, with its encumbrance of human laws, has striven against freedom in Christ; and also because we have been robbed and plundered of [the labors of] our blood and sweat, shamefully and blasphemously ravaged by indolent folk, while thirsty and sick people had to die of hunger. My most serious concern is that God may possibly still want to let us remain under the influence of the false and blind doctrine which those men, whom they call father, have fabricated and set up, so that consequently in many places the divine word is falsely expounded or possibly not even presented. . . .

Therefore, let everyone who reads the books of Doctor Martin Luther observe how transparently clear his doctrine is when he teaches the holy Gospel. Therefore they are to be held in high honor, and not to be burned; . . .

God, if Luther is dead, who will from now on present the Gospel to us so clearly! O God, to think of what he might have been able to write for us in another ten or twenty years! O all you good Christian people, help me diligently to bewail this God-inspired man and to request God to send us another spiritually enlightened man.

3

Implementation of Reforms

The implementation of reforms flowed from the Reformers' reading of the Bible. It seemed clear to Humanists and Reformers alike that the clerical and ecclesiastical positions they opposed stemmed from biblical illiteracy (3.1). While the overwhelming majority of people could not read, the importance of a vernacular Bible should not be underestimated. Most people would have been within range of someone who could read and therefore could hear the Bible read in their own language. Erasmus (3.2) emphasized that the Bible should be available to everyone, and Luther and his colleagues worked to provide a textually and theologically reliable German translation of the Bible (3.3). Once the Bible was accessible, the question became how to read it (3.4–5; see 1.31). Biblical translation and literacy required linguistic competence, and thus not only an educated ministry but an educated laity (3.6). The implementation of biblical theology led not only to critiques of scholastic theology (3.7–9; cf. 1.32–33, 2.4), but to public challenge of canon law and episcopal authority with the rejection of clerical celibacy (3.11–13; cf. 2.19). The Reformers' affirmation of clerical marriage not only attacked church doctrine and authority, but in affirming women as companions and friends countered the centuries of misogyny illustrated by the influential manual "Hammer of Witches" written by two Dominican inquisitors (3.10). The defamation of women and the dismissal of women's intellectual capabilities by excluding them from education (cf. Kenney 1998, 10) was at least partially addressed by Luther's exhortation for public education that would include women (4.12–13) and his view that "all Christians, . . . even women, are priests. So when women baptize, they exercise the function of priesthood legitimately . . . as part of the public ministry of the church . . ." (LW 40:23; cf. Appold 2012). The effort to close cloisters was empowering to some women. Ursala of Münsterberg explained her decision to leave her convent to her Catholic cousins (3.14). Argula von Grumbach – the "Bavarian Judith" to Protestants, and "Lutheran Medea" to Catholics – engaged in theological controversies including her defense of the young Ingolstadt student Seehofer, accused of adhering to the Reformation (3.15). Katharina Schütz Zell married a pastor in

The European Reformations Sourcebook, Second Edition. Edited by Carter Lindberg.
© 2014 John Wiley & Sons, Ltd. Published 2014 by John Wiley & Sons, Ltd.

Strasbourg, became his partner in ministry, and was widely published (3.16). At the same time, there were women religious whose life in the cloister enabled education and leadership they were loath to surrender. Katherine Rem strongly rejected her brother's efforts to persuade her to leave her convent (3.17). And Caritas Pirckheimer, the highly respected humanist abbess of the Nuremberg cloister of St. Clare's, strove to protect the cloister's sisters from forced removal and successfully fought the city council's mandate to close the cloister (3.18).

While the Reformers agreed on clerical marriage, they read the biblical text differently on other issues such as religious images (3.19). During Luther's protective custody at Wartburg Castle (May 1521–March 1522), Karlstadt filled the leadership vacuum in Wittenberg. In consultation with the Wittenberg theologians, the town council endorsed changes in the mass, elimination of images, and reform of poor relief (3.20). The town council reported ensuing reforms (3.21). The situation in Wittenberg intensified with the arrival of the Zwickau Prophets (3.22–23), and became so serious that Luther returned (3.24–25), and by means of his Invocavit Sermons proceeded to slow the tempo of reform. By this point it was increasingly clear that Luther and Karlstadt had differing theologies (3.26–27).

3.1 Thomas More to Martin Dorp (1515)
Naphy 1996: 9–10

Once I was at a dinner and there was an Italian merchant there. His education was as vast as his wealth – and he had a lot of money. There was also a monk at the dinner who was trained in theology and a great debater. . . . No matter what anyone said, no matter how carefully and cautiously qualified or thought out, it was no sooner said than [the monk] would tear it to pieces with a syllogism. It did not matter at all that the topic had nothing to do with theology or philosophy and was totally unconnected to his entire profession. When dinner started he had assured everyone that nothing was beyond him when he said that he could argue both sides of any issue. In time the merchant turned the conversation to topics more related to theology. . . . Finally, to get a laugh, the merchant said that it was better, that is, less sinful, to keep a mistress than to chase around town after lots of women. This brought forth a strong rebuttal from the theologian. . . . [The monk] said that it was the famous opinion of the excellent author of that marvellous book, *A Direction for Men Who Keep Mistresses* that keeping a mistress at home was worse than bedding ten prostitutes somewhere else. This was because, firstly, the kept woman was a bad example and secondly, she was more convenient and therefore the chance for sinning greater. . . . When [the merchant] realised that the theologian did not know his Bible as well as he knew trivial things, he started to argue with him and based his statements on authority. As they were needed, he made up brief "biblical" quotations to back up his opinions. After he had made up the quotations (which were totally unknown) he proceeded to give chapter and verse for them: one from Paul, one from Peter and a third from a Gospel. He was very careful to give even the chapter numbers but, if a book had only sixteen chapters, he deliberately placed his quotation in the twentieth. What was the theologian left to do! Before he had been unbeatable, like a curled-up porcupine defended by its quills. These made-up quotations were more difficult for him. It took some fancy footwork but he did manage to get around them. He knew nothing about the Bible and not once did he doubt that the quotations were real. He thought it was a serious sin to refuse to accept the Bible but a greater disgrace to be defeated. This in spite of being surrounded on all sides! Do you know how this clever Proteus finally got out of the trap! Whenever some fake view was put to him, supposedly drawn from the Bible, he said: "An excellent quotation indeed, sir, but I understand that passage this way." Then he would give a view based on alternative interpretations. He admitted that in one sense the passage supported his opponent but that the other meaning was his escape route.

3.2 Erasmus: *Paraclesis* (1516)
Benrath 1967: 527–9

In all the other disciplines produced by human diligence, nothing is so hidden and covert that the keen perception of the mind has not investigated it, nothing so difficult that has not been conquered by hard work. But why do we not study this philosophy [of Christ] with the eagerness we ought even though we confess by our name Christian to belong to Christ? Platonists, Pythagoreans, Academics, Stoics, Cynics, Peripatetics, and Epicureans know in detail the teachings of their sects or at least know them by heart; they fight for them and would rather die than desert the banners of their masters. Why do not we even more have such a mind for our master and head, Christ? . . .

I am totally against those who do not want the Holy Scripture to be read by the laity in their vernacular, as if Christ had taught so obscurely that he can be hardly understood even by a few theologians or as if the defense of the Christian religion depended on its not being known! Perhaps it is better if the secrets of kings are concealed, but Christ desires that his mysteries be known as widely as possible. I desire that everyone including women read the gospels and the Pauline letters. These ought to be translated into all languages so that not only the Scots and the Irish but also the Turks and the Saracens could read and understand them. The first step is certainly to learn them in whatever manner. . . . Thus I would like the farmer to sing Scripture as he plows, the weaver to hum it as he weaves, the traveler to pass the boredom of his journey with such stories. Let the conversation of all Christians therefore relate to the Scripture.

3.3 Luther: "On Translating: An Open Letter" (1530)
LW 35: 182, 187–9, 195

[Y]ou ask why in translating the words of Paul in Romans 3[:28] . . . I rendered them thus: "We hold that a man is justified without the works of the law, by faith alone." You tell me, besides, that the papists are making a tremendous fuss, because the word *sola* (alone) is not in Paul's text, and this addition of mine to the words of God is not to be tolerated. . . .

I shall show why I chose to use the word *sola* . . . I have constantly tried, in translating, to produce a pure and clear German, . . .

Here, in Romans 3[:28], I knew very well that the word *solum* is not in the Greek or Latin text; the papists did not have to teach me that. It is a fact that these four letters *s o l a* are not there. And these blockheads stare at them like cows at a new gate. At the same time they do not see that it conveys the sense of the text; it belongs there if the translation is to be clear and vigorous. I wanted to speak German, not Latin or Greek, since it was German I had undertaken to speak in the translation. But it is the nature of our German language that in speaking of two things, one of which is affirmed and the other denied, we use the word *solum* (*allein*) along with the word *nicht* [not] or *kein* [no]. For example, we say, "The farmer brings *allein* grain and *kein* money". . . .

We do not have to inquire of the literal Latin, how we are to speak German, as these asses do. Rather we must inquire about this of the mother in the home, the children on the street, the common man in the marketplace. We must be guided by their language, the way they speak, and do our translating accordingly. That way they will understand it and recognize that we are speaking German to them. . . .

Now I was not relying on and following the nature of the languages alone, however, when, in Romans 3[:28] I inserted the word *solum* (alone). Actually the text itself and the meaning of St. Paul urgently require and demand it. For in that very passage he is dealing with the main point of Christian doctrine, namely, that we are justified by faith in Christ without any works of the law. . . . But when all works are so completely cut away – and that must mean that faith alone justifies – whoever would speak plainly and clearly about this cutting away of works will have to say, "Faith alone justifies us, and not works." The matter itself, as well as the nature of the language, demands it.

3.4 Luther: *A Brief Instruction on What to Look For and Expect in the Gospels* (1521)
LW 35: 119–20

Be sure, moreover, that you do not make Christ into a Moses, as if Christ did nothing more than teach and provide examples as the other saints do, as if the gospel were simply a textbook of teachings or laws. Therefore you should grasp Christ, his words, works, and sufferings, in a twofold manner. First as an example that is presented to you, which you should follow and imitate. . . . However this is the smallest part of the gospel, on the basis of which it cannot yet even be called gospel. For on this level Christ is of no more help to you than some other saint. His life remains his own and does not as yet contribute anything to you. In short this mode [of understanding Christ as simply an example] does not make Christians but only hypocrites. You must grasp Christ at a much higher level. Even though this higher level has for a long time been the very best, the preaching of it has been something rare. The chief article and foundation of the gospel is that before you take Christ as an example, you accept and recognize him as a gift, as a present that God has given you and that is your own. This means that when you see or hear of Christ doing or suffering something, you do not doubt that Christ himself, with his deeds and suffering, belongs to you. On this you may depend as surely as if you had done it yourself, indeed as if you were Christ himself. See, this is what it means to have a proper grasp of the gospel, that is, of the overwhelming goodness of God,

. . . This is what preaching the Christian faith means. . . .

Therefore make note of this, that Christ as gift nourishes your faith and makes you a Christian. But Christ as an example exercises your works. These do not make you a Christian. Actually they come forth from you because you have already been made a Christian. As widely as a gift differs from an example, so widely does faith differ from works, for faith possesses nothing of its own, only the deeds and life of Christ. Works have something of your own in there, yet they should not belong to you but to your neighbor.

So you see that the gospel is really not a book of laws and commandments which requires deeds of us, but a book of divine promises in which God promises, offers, and gives us all his possessions and benefits in Christ.

3.5 Jörg Vögeli: Letter to Konrad Zwick (1523)
Oberman 1981: 103–4

As far back as I can remember and, I think, even way before that, God's gospel was proclaimed to the people. But it was of little help. . . . Those who desired to be esteemed, moralized it so much that not one little word of the gospel was left that had not been given a moralistic meaning. Thus the delusion arose that moral virtues and the display of external works could raise us to heaven, and that everyone is able to do the good by his own power and innate reason; but that is a delusion . . .

Some (and they were the most learned) proposed the Spirit of the gospel and faith in Christ, but distorted it in so many ways that I and other simple folk could not understand what the gospel would be. . . . Due to all this I always questioned whether I did not understand the preacher or the preacher did not understand the gospel in its true, essential meaning. It had always seemed to me (for I had read none of the biblical books) that the royal road to heaven had many confusing labyrinthine paths. I thought faith could not be so complicated and incomprehensible because people in the past who were no sharper than us had comprehended it, and God's grace had been poured out no more then than now. But now I have read the books of Martin Luther in which he speaks of the Christian faith, and there I have happily noted that he speaks thoroughly of things, and explains Scripture from Scripture itself so reasonably that no doubt exists. He shows the path by which one can come to the understanding of God, that is, to faith in Him.

3.6 Philipp Melanchthon: "On Improving the Studies of Youth" (1518)
Spitz 1974: 169–70

Greek letters should be added to Latin, so that reading the philosophers, theologians, historians, orators, poets, wherever you turn, you may gain the very substance, not the shadow of things. . . . Here, above all, the erudition of the Greeks, which comprises the universal knowledge of nature, is necessary, so that you can discuss behavior fitly and fully . . .

For this purpose history is altogether indispensable, and to it alone, if I should be so bold, I would, by Hercules, not have been unwilling to yield whatever praises the whole world of the arts deserves. . . . No part of life, neither public nor private, can remain unaffected by it. Both public as well as personal concerns are indebted to it. And I do not know if our world would suffer less harm without the sun, its soul as it were, than without history, the principle of all civil activities. Our forebears have often insisted unanimously that the Muses were born from memory. Hence, lest I am mistaken, it is shown that every kind of art flows from history . . .

For this very reason I said that the church, deprived of the use of letters, had somewhere corrupted true and genuine piety with human traditions. . . .

There remains then, young men, for you to hear, that although it is this way and the things that are excellent are hard, nevertheless diligence overcomes difficulty, . . . Therefore take hold of sound studies and turn over in your mind what the poet says: He has half done who has begun. Dare to know, cultivate the ancient Latins, embrace Greek, without which Latin cannot be rightly pursued. These will nourish the talent for the use of all letters more gently and will render it more elegant whatever its origin. . . .

3.7 Melanchthon: "Theses Against Scholastic Theology" (1520)
Oberman 1981: 57–8

1. The beginning and foundation of justification is faith.
2. Love is a work of faith.
3. The distinction between faith formed in love [formata] and faith in the pure facts without love to God and the neighbor [informis] is a fiction.
4. For the so-called "faith without love" is no faith, but a false opinion.
5. Namely, love necessarily follows faith.
6. Faith and love are works of God not of nature.
7. If the essence of Christianity exists in the inner Sabbath rest and perfect freedom,
8. it follows that satisfaction is not a part of penance;
9. likewise it follows that there is no external sacrifice in Christianity.
10. Thus the Mass is not a sacrifice.
11. The Mass is also not a work whose fruit one can give to another.
12. Just as baptism benefits only him who has actually been baptized, so the Mass helps only those who themselves have partaken.
13. For like baptism, the Mass is also a sacramental sign through which the Lord testifies that the forgiveness of sins has been given.
14. Because the essence [Summa] of our justification is faith, one cannot call works meritorious;
15. rather, what is more, all human works are in reality sin.
16. Because the keys are given to all Christians in the same manner, the primacy of Peter cannot be based on divine law. . . .

3.8 Andreas Bodenstein von Karlstadt:
"The 151 Theses" (1517)
Kähler 1952: 8–37

7. The teaching of Augustine in the area of morals yields to no one (contrary to the canonists).
24. No good merits precede grace (contrary to common opinion).
34. Man before grace cannot fulfill the law.
36. God extends his justice to men not because they are upright of heart but that they may become so.
38. Grace makes it possible for us to invoke God (contrary to common opinion).
39. Any good work we do is not by our initiation (contrary to common opinion).
40. It is heresy to hold that God's gifts depend upon our works.
83. Justification does not follow but precedes the doers of the law.
84. The law without grace is the letter that kills, with grace the Spirit gives life.
85. Grace makes us lovers and doers of the law.
105. The law of faith written on the fleshly tablets of our hearts is love itself, diffused in our hearts through the Holy Spirit (cf. Rom. 5:5).
136. There is no righteous person on earth who does not sin through those just acts by which he does well (cf. Ecc. 7:20).
137. However, God does not wish the righteous to be worthy of condemnation by this sin, only humbled.
138. The righteous man, therefore is simultaneously good and evil [bonus et malus], son of God and son of the world.

3.9 Karlstadt: *The Meaning of the Term "Gelassen" and Where in Holy Scripture It is Found* (1523)
Furcha 1995: 135, 136, 139, 145, 162

Gelassen means about the same as *verlassen* – abandoned, forsaken. When I want to write or say, "We ought to abandon foreign money," I might substitute the term Gelass for abandon and say "We ought to detach ourselves from foreign money." . . .

However, we may also circumscribe the term "detached" or "abandoned" by numerous Latin words such as *deserere, renunciare, dimittere*, and the like. Note at once how the love of a wife surpasses and cuts out the love of father and mother. Likewise, the love of God ought to supersede all love and delight (which we have toward creatures). Nowhere other than in God ought a person be content. Yes, we must leave all creatures if we want to have God as our protector and indweller or Lord. . . .

All pleasure is sin. Soon a person violates this and burns himself with eating and drinking. It would be better for us were we to sprinkle food and drink with ashes than to have our food praised in song; for the nature of our pleasure prevents us from knowing God and his divine works. . . .

It is dangerous to use even the smallest thing with pleasure. For, as Christ says, everything one hankers after becomes one's heart and treasure. It turns us into servants and takes possession as a lord possesses his cattle. Therefore, we ought to ask for, seek, take, and enjoy every necessity with fear for the simple reason that we are unworthy of anything good. . . .

Someone might ask at this point what am I to abandon if I wish to become a disciple of Christ? And what are the goods called which one must renounce when one becomes a disciple of Christ? To this the prophets answer as follows, "You must renounce all things in heaven and on earth and sincerely and permanently divest yourself of them, never again to possess them with longing or in hope." . . . Note there that I must love God alone. . . . Were I to love something besides God, I should not love God with my whole heart. For that place in my heart which loves something else is taken away from God; hence, I cannot love God with all my heart. This love is the spiritual circumcision, i.e., a cutting away from the heart of all creatures, Deut. 30:6, Jer. 3:22. . . .

Your honor and your desiring of honor must die and must drop off like a pus-filled boil which has been cauterized, . . . When God's glory, honor, praise, will, and love rule in us with might, then ego, I-ness and everyone's self or self-absorption must wither and become nothing. This is the very characteristic and nature of faith – to see God's glory and our shame, God's virtue and strength and our wickedness and weakness . . . God's something and being. . . . And, on the other side, to know our nothingness.

3.10 "The Hammer of Witches" (1486)
Summers 1928: 41–4

[R]easons why there are more superstitious women found than men . . . [T]hey are more credulous; and since the chief aim of the devil is to corrupt faith, therefore he rather attacks them. . . . The second reason is, that women are naturally more impressionable, and more ready to receive the influence of a disembodied spirit; . . .

The third reason is that they have slippery tongues, and are unable to conceal from their fellow-women those things which by evil arts they know, and, since they are weak, they find an easy and secret manner of vindicating themselves by witchcraft. . . . All wickedness is but little to the wickedness of a woman. . . .

There are also others who bring forward yet other reasons, of which preachers should be very careful how they make use. For it is true that in the Old Testament the Scriptures have much that is evil to say about women, and this is because of the first temptress, Eve, and her imitators; yet afterwards in the New Testament we find a change of name, as from Eva to Ave (as S. Jerome says), and the whole sin of Eve taken away by the benediction of Mary. Therefore preachers should always say as much praise of them as possible.

But because in these times this perfidy is more often found in women than in men, as we learn by actual experience, if anyone is curious as to the reason, we may add to what has already been said the following: that since they are feebler both in mind and body, it is not surprising that they should come more under the spell of witchcraft.

3.11 Karlstadt: *Exposition of Numbers 30 Which Speaks of Vows* (1522)
Furcha 1995: 52, 80, 99

This booklet concludes on the basis of . . . Holy Scripture that priests, monks, and nuns may and ought to marry and enter upon the marital state with a good conscience and [in keeping with] God's will without having to obtain a Roman dispensation or release which is totally unnecessary. It advises above-named persons to cast off their deceitful living habits along with gowns and scowls and to enter upon a true Christian life. . . .

Since it is much better, and more pleasing to God, that nuns and monks take husbands and wives, and raise children in God's teaching and love, and that they are pleasant rather than that they mumble in churches and pray without any understanding, neither teaching children nor anyone else the word of God, and being envious of each other and not graciously inclined toward anyone, they ought, above all else, choose, seek, and do what is best.

To wit, because nuns and monks commit such beastly sins which are best left untold because they are worse even than common unchastity and adultery, and happen because of their strong nature and their tendency to uncleanness, it would be a thousand times better for them to change than to be driven to such beastly sins. Marriages are to be instituted in order to avoid unchastity, as Paul teaches [I Cor. 7]. . . .

Anyone who is inclined to chastity ought to remain chaste, but without making any vows until after the sixtieth year; for under that age he does what is wrong and the pastor must declare his vow inadmissible. Refuse those who are younger than sixty, 1 Tim. 5:9 ff. . . .

What the holy fathers fled, our monks seek out; what holy women bemoaned pleases our nuns. They hear and read of how much such women as Sarah, Rebekkah, Rachel, Lea, and Hanna would have liked to give birth to children and what pain and suffering they endured to prevent the label of unfruitfulness. Our nuns, however, forget the assistance for which they were created. They despise the commandment to multiply. They laugh at the raising of children and reject that which is divine and, what is more, they do what is of the devil, popish, and inferior. I would very much like to see the pope showing me a spiritual order of believers who have avoided the marriage bed. Priests and all the spirituals before him had wives according to the law. Aaron, the Levites, the prophets, and the apostles of Christ were married. The antichrist's rule alone is extramarital and of satanic standing. . . .

Read the Bible and take your children out of cloisters, you lay folks – the sooner, the better – and give them in marriage. You will thus serve God, be good parents, and assist your children in gaining their salvation. Amen.

3.12 Luther: *The Judgment of Martin Luther on Monastic Vows* (1521)
LW 44: 310–11

Is the taking of vows not a human institution, pure and simple? Is it not based on tonsure, garb, food, drink, days, places, postures, and other ceremonies? Where did God command any of them? Where did he command this poverty, this obedience, this chastity? Well then, so what? Are you still in doubt that it is wrong to make such vows, or that it always was? By divine decree these things are optional, but by human decree you make them obligatory. . . . By the same argument he never wanted celibacy to be made obligatory, but left it a matter of free choice. God did not want it to take on the nature of sin if someone chose to marry. Yet by your vow you make celibacy lifelong, as well as obligatory under the law. Since it can no longer be denied that they are simply doctrines of men, what else is there to do then, but to demonstrate here that the vows of the religious as well as the whole idea of monasticism are against the freedom of the gospel, and are forbidden by divine commands?

3.13 Luther: *The Estate of Marriage* (1522)
LW 45: 38–40. Cf. LW 59: 220–30

The world says of marriage, "Brief is the joy, lasting the bitterness." Let them say what they please; what God wills and creates is bound to be a laughingstock to them. . . .

Now the ones who recognize the estate of marriage are those who firmly believe that God himself instituted it, brought husband and wife together, and ordained that they should beget children and care for them. For this they have God's word, Genesis 1[:28], and they can be certain that God does not lie. They can therefore also be certain that the estate of marriage and everything that goes with it in the way of conduct, works, and suffering is pleasing to God. Now tell me, how can the heart have greater good, joy, and delight than in God, when one is certain that his estate, conduct, and work is pleasing to God? . . .

Now observe that when that clever harlot, our natural reason . . . takes a look at married life, she turns up her nose and says, "Alas, must I rock the baby, wash its diapers, make its bed, smell its stench, stay up nights with it, take care of it when it cries, heal its rashes and sores, and on top of that care for my wife, provide for her, labor at my trade, take care of this and take care of that, do this and do that, endure this and endure that, and whatever else of bitterness and drudgery married life involves? What, should I make such a prisoner of myself? O you poor wretched fellow, have you taken a wife? Fie, fie upon such wretchedness and bitterness! It is better to remain free and lead a peaceful, carefree life; I will become a priest or a nun and compel my children to do likewise."

What then does Christian faith say to this? It opens its eyes, looks upon all these insignificant, distasteful, and despised duties in the Spirit, and is aware that they are all adorned with divine approval as with the costliest gold and jewels. It says, "God, because I am certain that thou hast created me as a man and hast from my body begotten this child, I also know for a certainty that it meets with thy perfect pleasure. I confess to thee that I am not worthy to rock the little babe or wash its diapers, or to be entrusted with the care of the child and its mother. How is it that I, without any merit, have come to this distinction of being certain that I am serving thy creature and thy most precious will? O how gladly will I do so, . . . for I am certain that it is thus pleasing in thy sight."

A wife too should regard her duties in the same light, as she suckles the child, rocks and bathes it, and cares for it in other ways; . . . These are truly golden and noble works.

3.14 Ursala of Münsterberg: A Nun Explains Her Leaving the Convent (1528)
Wiesner-Hanks 1996: 41, 45, 49, 51, 53

I have learned that both your graces have been very uncivil because I left the convent in Freiberg along with two other women and have left my order. Your graces assume that this happened because of thoughtless impertinence. . . .

Through this [work], your graces will discover that this has not happened out of thoughtlessness, but because I am accountable to the judgment of God for my soul, . . .

[S]ince faith alone is now our salvation and unbelief our damnation, we find this place and situation [i.e., the convent] wholly the antithesis of it, both in words and works. And even the vows (in which salvation should rest, as they say) throw us who journey to God into uncertainty and eternal damnation; therefore we had to leave. . . .

No one can deny that chastity is a quality that God alone can create in human hearts and bodies; how, then, are we so arrogant as to pledge and sacrifice what is God's [to give] and not ours? . . . And therefore everything else that follows from these vows, that is rules, statutes, constitutions, and new traditions that come to them, are for the most part opposed to God's Word and faith. These are indeed a road which bypasses God, which is strongly forbidden in the First Commandment, which presses on the conscience with the hard threat of the law. . . .

The second reason that we must leave convent life is this: . . . we now recognize from holy Scripture that faith is the only work [necessary for] our salvation; similarly, unbelief is the only reason for our damnation. . . .

3.15 Argula von Grumbach
Matheson 1995: 144–5, 76–7, 85–6, 107

I am called a follower of Luther, but I am not. I was baptised in the name of Christ; it is him I confess and not Luther. But I confess that Martin, too, as a faithful Christian, confesses him. God help us never to deny this, whether faced by disgrace, abuse, imprisonment, breaking on the wheel and even death – God helping and enabling all Christians in this. Amen. . . .

How in God's name can you and your university [Ingolstadt] expect to prevail, when you deploy such foolish violence against the word of God; when you force someone to hold the holy Gospel in their hands for the very purpose of denying it, as you did in the case of Arsacius Seehofer? When you confront him . . . and use imprisonment and even the threat of the stake to force him to deny Christ and his word?

Yes, when I reflect on this my heart and all my limbs tremble. What do Luther and Melanchthon teach you but the word of God? You condemn them without having refuted them. Did Christ teach you so, or his apostles, prophets, or evangelists? . . .

For my part, I have to confess, in the name of God and by my soul's salvation, that if I were to deny Luther and Melanchthon's writing I would be denying God and his word, which may God forfend for ever. Amen. . . .

Are you not ashamed that [Seehofer] had to deny all the writings of Martin, who put the New Testament into German, simply following the text? That means that the holy Gospel and the Epistles and the story of the Apostles and so on are all dismissed by you as heresy. It seems there is no hope of a proper discussion with you. . . .

I beseech you for the sake of God, and exhort you by God's judgment and righteousness, to tell me in writing which of the articles written by Martin or Melanchthon you consider heretical. In German not a single one seems heretical to me. And the fact is that a great deal has been published in German, and I've read it all. Spalatin sent me a list of all the titles. I have always wanted to find out the truth. . . .

Your Princely Grace cannot afford such cashiers as these Franciscans who take nothing and yet rake in everything. It is not I who judge, but Christ in Matthew 23: "Woe to you, Pharisees, you brood of vipers, you who eat up and devour the houses of widows, all under the semblance of a lengthy prayer. The eternal fire is prepared for you." As far as I can see the endowment of so many canons and priests and that whole swarm of others does nothing but provide for lovers and their concubines. That is painfully obvious. The pope has followed the advice of the devil; he has forbidden women, and for the sake of money permitted concubines. . . .

3.16 Katharina Schütz Zell: Writings on Reformation and Marriage
McKee 2006: 69, 73–7

Indeed an evil teaching is more dangerous than a wicked life. Teaching affects many others, but with a wicked life the greatest harm is to the self. I must also say a little about the teaching, not only for my husband, but for the whole multitude of those who preach the Gospel, such as Luther, with all those who serve the Gospel with him, whose names are too many to count. I say then to the poison brewers, yes, to those who pour out all the worst kinds of poison, who are still in Strasbourg and in all the lands, whether they still wear gray hoods [Franciscans . . .] or black hoods [Augustinians . . .], or used to wear them, "If the teaching of Luther and his followers is false, why have you not shown its falsity and overcome it with clear godly scripture?" . . .

What else do all these three together [Roman Catholic opponents: Johannes Cochlaeus, Conrad Treger, and Thomas Murner] do than fence with vain arguments of straw and devise many lies? With these they make big books and thus only deafen the people with their prattle, by which means they intend to keep their godless existence. They fight against the faith, by doing what they intend – not rightly but falsely – to maintain their own and not God's good work and holy service. From that [their own service] they have up to now gained wealth and sensual pleasure so they want to keep their stock in trade, which the Gospel cut off from them – and that they cannot bear!

They also fight against clerical marriage, which has indeed clear and bright – not faint – grounds in godly scripture, in the Old and New Testaments, so that children and fools can read and understand, as I have shown and proved to the bishop of Strasbourg with a long writing. There I have compared marriage and harlotry with each other according to the teaching of godly scripture. Would to God that the bishop would finally become so angry with me that he would allow everyone to read this writing! However, . . . they [Roman clergy] intend to defy God and to put these scriptural teachings behind them again by force. For this, I must say, they have two reasons.

The first reason is that the pope and bishop and their servants, vicars and their fellows, do not raise so much tax money for harlotry from married people as from harlots and knaves. If a priest has a (legally married) wife, he behaves like any other honorable citizen and gives the bishop no tax for it [his married life] because God has given it to him freely. If priests (who are supposed to be celibate) have harlots, they must have their lords' permission and fairly pay them a tax for this permission since they are in feudal relationship to their lords the pope and bishops. . . .

Another reason they resist clerical marriage is that, should priests have (legal) wives, they would have to choose one and give up the others. They would not be able to behave as they do with the prostitutes: throwing out one, taking in another. . . .

I have helped to raise up clerical marriage. With God's help I was also the first woman in Strasbourg who opened the way for clerical marriage, . . . I myself married a priest with the intention of encouraging and making a way for all Christians – as I hope has also happened.

3.17 Katherine Rem: A Nun Rejects the Reformation (1523)
Wiesner-Hanks 1996: 29

You have wished us the correct understanding of Jesus Christ. We thank you for that. . . . We regard you as one of the false prophets that Jesus warned us against. . . . Therefore you have also come with many good words and wanted to lead us astray and make us despondent. You should not think that we are so foolish that we place our hope in the convent and in our own works. Rather we place our hope in God. He is the true lord and rewarder of all things. . . . You have shocked us because you actually wanted to come to us. If you don't come in kinship, stay out. If you want to straighten us out, then we don't want your [message] at all. . . .

3.18 Caritas Pirckheimer: *A Journal of the Reformation Years 1524–1528*
MacKenzie 2006: 88–90, 92–3

And so at 11 o'clock in the morning the ferocious wolves, both males and females [parents of younger nuns], came to my precious lambs, entered the church, drove out all the people and locked the church door. . . . Then they wanted me to use force and order the children [the three "children" were 23, 20, and 19] to go out into the church alone. I did not want to do this either and left it up to the children. None of them would cross the threshold in any way. The mothers [of the nuns] then asked the men to finish things up, for the crowd was getting closer. They were afraid there would be a riot. I then spoke to the men and told them to go in and speak with the children so that they would cooperate. I could not and would not force them to do what was repugnant to them. . . . The children embraced me, wept loudly and begged that I not let them go. But unfortunately I could not help them. . . .

The mothers told their children they should obey them according to God's commandment. They wanted them to leave the convent. For they were there to redeem their souls from hell. Here their children were in the jaws of the devil and in good conscience they could no longer allow that. The children cried out that they did not want to leave the pious, holy convent. They were not in hell at all. If they were dragged out, however, they would plunge into the abyss of hell. On Judgment Day, before the stern judge, they would demand their souls of them. Although they were their mothers, their daughters owed them no obedience in those matters that could damage their souls. . . .

There stood my poor little orphans among the vicious wolves and defied them with all their strength. . . .

Katharina Ebner [one of the sisters] said, "Here I stand and will not yield. No one shall be able to force me out. If I am removed by force, however, it shall never be by my will in eternity. I will appeal to God in heaven and to all the world on earth." When she was speaking Held [one of the men] took her under his arms and began to pull and drag her away. . . . Some sisters stopped at the chapel door. They heard the quarreling, shouting and dragging away amid the great screaming and weeping of the children. Four people grabbed each one with two pulling in front and two pushing from behind. And so the dear sisters Ebner and Teztel fell over each other at the threshold. Poor sister Teztel almost had her foot severed. . . .

Frau Ebner threatened her daughter that if she did not walk before her she would push her down the stairs to the pulpit. She threatened to throw her on the floor so hard that she would bounce. When they broke into the church amid much cursing and swearing, an incredible screaming, shouting and weeping began before they tore off the holy garments of our order and dressed them with worldly clothes. . . .

What happened afterwards to the poor children among the vicious wolves we cannot know.

3.19 Karlstadt: *On the Abolition of Images and That There Should Be No Beggars Among Christians* (1522)
Lietzmann 1911

See how God forbids all kinds of images, . . . God says you shall not worship them, you shall not even honor them. Therefore, God forbids all veneration [of images] and breaks down the papist refuge which by their agility always does violence to the Scriptures and makes black white and evil good. Notwithstanding, one of them may say: Indeed, I do not worship images. I do not honor them for their sake, but rather for the sake of the saints whom they represent. God answers briefly and with few words, Thou shalt not worship them. Thou shalt not honor them. Gloss as you can, you shall in fact not worship them. You shall not bend your knee before them; you shall not light candles before them . . .

Now I will and shall say to pious Christians that all of you who stand in fear of an image have idols in your hearts. . . .

Thus shall you deal with them, says God (Deut. 7:5): You shall overturn and overthrow their altars. You shall break their images to pieces. You shall hew down their pillars and burn up their carved images. We have no godly altars but rather heathen or human ones, as noted in Ex. 20:4. Therefore Christians shall abolish them. . . . The highest authorities should also abolish images. . . .

[O]ur magistrates should not wait until the priests of Baal purge out their wooden vessels and required hindrances. For they will never begin to do it. The highest civil authorities should command and do this. . . .

I have written too much and too little concerning idols, therefore I must write the following more briefly. In short, I can say that I have a sure sign when I come into a city that there are no Christians, or if there are, they are discouraged and few, if I see men begging for a living.

There shall be no beggar among you because the Lord your God blessed you in the earth which he gave you to possess (Deut. 15:4). . . .

If one of your brothers who dwells in the gate of your city comes to poverty, you shall not harden and shut your heart; you shall also not close your hand but rather open it to the poor and lend him what he needs. . . . Thus where one falls into poverty, everyone, and in particular the highest civil authority, should have compassion upon the poor and no one should stop the heart, but rather open his hands and lend the poor brother what he needs. Therefore Christian magistrates should be particularly diligent to help our own. . . . Not that we should suffer burdens and need ourselves, and the others live in pleasure. But rather in this way, we have food and drink and our wives, children, servants, relatives are also provided for, we shall have enough and be satisfied and help our fellow citizens and neighbors. The citizens in every city, and the farmers in every village, shall provide for their poor brethren, lending them what they need. Also princes, officials, mayors, judges, village-mayors, and other magistrates shall examine the way and comfortable means whereby the poor brothers and sisters, each according to his station, will be maintained, and that no one be allowed to run after bread. For this reason it is fitting that students who beg for their living be sent to their parents, for they learn much more roguery and indecency in beggary than virtue and learning. It is much better that they learn the craft of their parents than that they run after bread. Otherwise they serve nothing other than the papistic, unlearned, and deceitful priests.

It is also proper that the highest civil authorities direct their attention to the strong beggars who are able to work, and force them to work in order to support themselves. But also that they give them aid and help to begin their craft or work. Whether one desires to be a printer, goldsmith, baker, tailor, shoemaker, or learn a similar craft, or to begin to employ and promote, they shall help everyone according to his requirements. For they shall lend their brethren what they need.

If it happens that one may return the help he received without burden, they shall take the same and help others. But if the former would be so burdened by returning what was lent him, the benefactor should not demand it or expect it for he has done good. . . .

Also the income from the parish endowments, when they are available through the renunciation or death of the priests, shall come into the above-mentioned [common] chest to be lent by the council to everyone in the city. . . .

Also I would like to see that the income of the stoney churches be devoted to the above-mentioned chest and brotherly help. . . .

3.20 The Wittenberg Movement: The University Report to Elector Frederick (1521)
Oberman 1981: 77–80

Most Gracious Lord, we have conveyed both orally and in writing Your Electoral Grace's desires to the Augustinians. We find that as a whole they have given three reasons for their present way of celebrating Mass. . . .

First because a great number of unchristian abuses – clerical as well as secular – have everywhere penetrated the celebration of the Mass, . . . namely that the Mass is thought of as a good work by which we reconcile God, offering and giving him something for our sins. . . . Therefore the Augustinians will no longer celebrate Mass because celebration of the Mass according to the present praxis bestows reason and power on this abuse. . . .

Second, Masses as they are now celebrated, are against the custom and use instituted by Christ and the Apostles for Christ communed with the Twelve and the Apostles in community, and never for one person alone, as indeed Paul forbade private Masses to the Corinthians [see I Cor. 11:21, 33].

Third, Christ instituted and commanded distribution under both species [bread and wine]. But because Masses as now held are so ordered that participants are given only one form, they do no know how such a Mass shall be confirmed with a good conscience. . . .

It is certain that the abuse of the Mass is among the greatest sins on earth. . . .

Therefore . . . we request that Your Electoral Grace take this matter seriously and as quickly as possible abolish such abuses of the Mass in Your Electoral Grace's lands. . . .

3.21 The Wittenberg Movement by the End of 1522
Junghans 1967: 212–13

In addition, the Propst in Wittenberg [Justus Jonas, provost of the Castle Church, later dean of the Theology Faculty] took a woman named Felckin in marriage. A Franciscan monk has become a shoemaker and married a citizen's daughter. Another Franciscan has become a baker and taken a wife. And an Augustinian has become a cabinet-maker and taken a wife. Doctor Feldkirch [Johann Dölsch] has married his cook.

The Town Council has informed the Franciscans and Augustinians they shall vacate the cloister before mid-Lent [March 30th]. And they have taken note of all the treasures in the cloister. All prostitutes are expelled. If anyone is living illegitimately with a woman, he must marry her or give up the relationship. The Council has appointed and ordered fourteen men who shall inform all the poor people of this; the Council gives to those of the clergy each according to his need, an old priest six gulden, a young one shall learn a trade. . . .

The town church is closed every day. Only on Sunday is there a German mass and preaching in it. And the people go to the holy sacrament and receive it themselves at the altar and take the chalice themselves in their hands and drink the blood of Christ.

At Lochau our bishop [Franz Günther] conducts the German mass in the parish church, and the people also receive the Lord's Supper in both kinds. They also take both the bread and wine at the altar. . . .

Monks and priests let their tonsures grow out and take wives.

3.22 Nicholas Hausmann: A Report Concerning the Zwickau Prophets (1521)
Zuck 1975: 30

[Quotation from Nicholas Storch, one of the prophets:] Those in authority live only in lust, consume the sweat and blood of their subjects, eat and drink night and day, hunt, run, and kill. . . . Everyone therefore should arm himself and attack the priests in their fat nests, beating, killing, and strangling them, because once the bellwethers are removed, the sheep are easier to handle. Afterward the land-grabbers and noblemen should be attacked, their property confiscated, and their castles destroyed. . . .

The external, audible divine word which is preached by the priests in the daily mass for the living and the dead is sheer tomfoolery because they [the priests] celebrate it after overloading their bellies with good food and their heads with fine wine, not to mention their frolicking at night with "Frau Venus." . . . Like magicians they dress up in silk and velvet of all colors, make gestures like monkeys when they take the bread and wine in the sacrament of the altar, and, to top it off, speak in Latin so that the poor layman does not know at all whether he is betrayed, sold, or what, and doesn't know what it is all about. If he [the layman] does not give them [the priests] his purse, heaven is closed to him. . . .

You can receive the forgiveness of sins without all this nonsense, in your own quiet home or wherever you are, if you believe in the revelation of the Spirit. . . .

Don't you believe that God has another word which he will reveal to you through the Spirit? Why should God be chained to the creature? . . . He is absolutely free. He does what he wills. Thus the external, audible word of the priests is not the word of God but their own. . . .

No child should be baptized with water in the church because all you see in such baptisms is wet water; it is the same as if one would sprinkle or immerse a dog in it . . . because children have no faith. But without faith it is impossible to please God. Accordingly, one should not baptize infants with water, because the water remains what it is, water.

3.23 Melanchthon: Report to Frederick on the Situation in Wittenberg (1521)
Oberman 1981: 81–2

I must report these things without reservation. Your Majesty is not unaware how many dangerous dissensions of all kinds regarding the Word of God have arisen in Your Majesty's city, Zwickau. Indeed, there were people detained there who have striven for all possible kinds of changes. Now three men from among the master-minds of this unrest have shown up here [in Wittenberg], two uneducated weavers and one educated [literatus]. I have heard them. What they say has the ring of the miraculous to it: They have been sent to teach by the clear voice of God; between them and God there is intimate conversation; they can foretell the future; in short, they are prophets and apostles. I can hardly express how strongly they have impressed me. . . . For they give numerous indications that they are grasped by the Spirit; but only Martin [Luther] can judge. Therefore because now the Gospel and at the same time the honor and peace of the church are at stake, one must endeavor by all means to get the people to meet with Martin; they themselves call upon him.

I would not trouble Your. Highness with this letter if the matter were not so impor-tant that it requires a prompt decision. On the one hand we must be careful not to suppress the Spirit of God [I Thess. 5:19]; on the other hand however, we must not be captivated by Satan.

3.24 Luther: Letter to Elector Frederick (1522)
LW 48: 391–2

I have written this so Your Electoral Grace might know that I am going to Wittenberg under a far higher protection than the Elector's. I have no intention of asking Your Electoral Grace for protection. Indeed I think I shall protect Your Electoral Grace more than you are able to protect me. And if I thought that Your Electoral Grace could and would protect me, I should not go. The sword ought not and cannot help in a matter of this kind. God alone must do it – and without the solicitude and co-operation of men. . . .

Since Your Electoral Grace wishes to know what to do in this matter and thinks that you have done too little, I humbly answer that Your Electoral Grace has already done far too much and should do nothing at all. God will not and cannot tolerate your worrying and bustling, or mine. He wishes the matter to be left [in his hands] and no one else's. . . .

Inasmuch as I do not intend to obey Your Electoral Grace, Your Electoral Grace is excused before God if I am captured or put to death. Before men Your Electoral Grace should act as an elector, obedient to the authorities and allowing His Imperial Majesty to rule in your cities and lands over both life and property, as is his right according to the Imperial constitution; . . . For no one should overthrow or resist authority save him who ordained it; otherwise it is rebellion and an action against God. But I hope they will have the good sense to recognize that Your Electoral Grace occupies too lofty a position [to be expected] to become my executioner. . . . For Christ has not taught me to be a Christian at another's expense. If they are so unrea-sonable as to command Your Electoral Grace to lay hands on me, I shall at once tell Your Electoral Grace what to do. [In any case] I shall see to it that Your Electoral Grace suffers no harm and danger in body, estate, or soul on my account, whether Your Electoral Grace believes this or not.

3.25 Luther: *The Invocavit Sermons* (1522)
LW 51: 70–4, 77–8, 83, 85

The summons of death comes to us all, and no one can die for another. Every one must fight his own battle with death by himself, alone. We can shout into another's ears, but every one must himself be prepared for the time of death, for I will not be with you then, nor you with me. Therefore every one must himself know and be armed with the chief things which concern a Christian. And these are what you, my beloved, have heard from me many days ago.

In the first place, we must know that we are the children of wrath, and all our works, intentions, and thoughts are nothing at all. . . .

Secondly, that God has sent his only-begotten Son that we may believe in him and that whoever trusts in him shall be free from sin and a child of God, . . .

Thirdly, we must also have love and through love we must do to one another as God has done to us through faith. For without love faith is nothing, . . . And here, dear friends, have you not grievously failed? . . .

Fourthly, we also need patience. . . .

And here dear friends, one must not insist upon his rights, but must see what may be useful and helpful to his brothers, as Paul says, . . . "All things are lawful for me, but not all things are helpful" [I Cor. 6:12]. For we are not all equally strong in the faith, . . . Therefore we must not look upon ourselves, or our strength, or our prestige, but upon our neighbor, for God has said through Moses: I have borne and reared you, as a mother does her child [Deut. 1:31]. What does a mother do to her child? First she gives it milk, then gruel, then eggs and soft food, whereas if she turned about and gave it solid food, the child would never thrive [see I Cor. 3:2; Heb. 5:12–13]. So we should also deal with our brother, have patience for him for a time, have patience with his weakness and help him bear it; we should also give him milk-food, too [I Pet. 2:2; see Rom. 14:1–3], as was done with us, until he, too, grows strong, and thus we do not travel heavenward alone, but bring our brethren, who are not now our friends, with us. . . . I would not have gone so far as you have done, if I had been here. The cause is good, but there has been too much haste. For there are still brothers and sisters on the other side who belong to us and must still be won. . . .

Take note of these two things, "must" and "free." The "must" is that which necessity requires, and which must ever be unyielding; as, for instance, the faith, which I shall never permit anyone to take away from me, but must always keep in my heart and freely confess before every one. But "free" is that in which I have choice, and may use or not, yet in such a way that it profit my brother and not me. Now do not make a must out of what is "free," as you have done, so that you may not be called to account for those who were led astray by your loveless exercise of liberty. For if you entice any one to eat meat on Friday, and he is troubled about it on his deathbed, and thinks, Woe is me, for I have eaten meat and I am lost! God will call you to account for that soul. . . .

Love, therefore, demands that you have compassion on the weak, as all the apostles had. . . .

In short, I will preach it, teach it, write it, but I will constrain no man by force, for faith must come freely without compulsion. Take myself as an example. I opposed indulgences and all the papists, but never with force. I simply taught, preached, and wrote God's Word; otherwise I did nothing. And while I slept [see Mark 4:26–9], or drank Wittenberg beer with my friends Philip and Amsdorf, the Word so greatly weakened the papacy that no prince or emperor ever inflicted such losses upon it. I did nothing; the Word did everything. Had I desired to foment trouble, I could have brought great bloodshed upon Germany; indeed, I could have started such a game that even the emperor would not have been safe. But what would it have been? Mere fool's play. I did nothing; I let the Word do its work. . . .

Therefore it should have been preached that images were nothing and that no service is done to God by erecting them; then they would have fallen of themselves. That is what I did. . . .

Now, although it is true and no one can deny that the images are evil because they are abused, nevertheless we must not on that account reject them, nor condemn anything because it is abused. This would result in utter confusion. God has commanded us in Deut. 4[:19] not to lift up our eyes to the sun [and the moon and the stars], etc., that we may not worship them, for they are created to serve all nations. But there are many people who worship the sun and the stars. Therefore we propose to rush in and pull the sun and stars from the skies. No, we had better let it be. Again, wine and women bring many a man to misery and make a fool of him [Ecclus. 19:2, 31:30]; so we kill all the women and pour out all the wine. Again, gold and silver cause much evil, so we condemn them. Indeed, if we want to drive away our worst enemy, the one who does us the most harm, we shall have to kill ourselves, for we have no greater enemy than our own heart. . . .

3.26 Luther: *Against the Heavenly Prophets* (1525)
LW 40: 83, 103–4, 146–8, 207, 222–3

However, we must see to it that we retain Christian freedom and do not force such laws and works on the Christian conscience, as if one through them were upright or a sinner. Here questions are in order concerning the place which images, foods, clothing, places, persons, and all such external things, etc., ought to have. Whoever does not teach according to this order certainly does not teach correctly. From which you now see that Dr. Karlstadt and his spirits replace the highest with the lowest, the best with the least, the first with the last. Yet he would be considered the greatest spirit of all, he who has devoured the Holy Spirit feathers and all. . . .

We have noted above how Dr. Karlstadt and image-breakers of his kind do not interpret Moses' commandment as referring to the constituted authority, as is proper, but to the disorderly populace. That is certainly not the right spirit and attitude. For, as I have said, where the populace has the right and power to carry out a divine commandment, then one must thereafter give in and permit them to carry out all the commandments. Consequently, whoever arrives on the scene first must put to death murderers, adulterers, thieves, and punish rogues. And thereby justice, jurisdiction, dominion, and all authority would fall apart. Matters would take their course in accordance with the proverb: Give a rogue an inch and he takes a mile. . . .

After that, such disorder will gain in momentum, and the masses will have to kill all of the wicked. For Moses, when he commands the people to destroy images (Deut. 7[:16]), also commands them to destroy without mercy those who had such images in the land of Canaan. For this killing is just as strictly commanded as the destruction of images, which commandment these factious spirits so obstinately introduce and emphasize. . . .

Since our murderous spirits apply Moses' commandment to the masses, and do not have God's judgment over the wicked, but themselves judge that those who have images are wicked and worthy of death, they will be compelled by such a commandment to engage in rebellion, in murdering and killing, as works which God has commanded them to do. Let the Allstedtian [Thomas Müntzer] spirit be an example, who already had progressed from images to people, and who publicly called for rebellion and murder contrary to all authority. . . .

Now when God sends forth his holy gospel he deals with us in a twofold manner, first outwardly, then inwardly. Outwardly he deals with us through the oral word of the gospel and through material signs, that is, baptism and the sacrament of the altar. Inwardly he deals with us through the Holy Spirit, faith, and other gifts. But whatever their measure or order the outward factors should and must precede. The inward experience follows and is effected by the outward. God has determined to give the inward to no one except through the outward. For he wants to give no one the Spirit or faith outside of the outward Word and sign instituted by him, as he says in Luke 16[:29], "Let them hear Moses and the prophets." . . .

Again, in external matters which they believe God has not directly ordered, they act like incendiaries as if they were out of their minds. . . . They advocate the murder of godless rulers, will endure no injustice, and assume, in many cases, a pretense of humility and piety of much importance to themselves but of no meaning before God. . . .

From this you can grasp that Dr. Karlstadt's theology has not gotten beyond teaching how we are to imitate Christ, making of Christ only an example and lawgiver. From this only works can be learned. He does not know and teach Christ as our treasure and the gift of God, from which faith follows, and which is the highest of doctrines. . . .

In closing, I want to warn everyone truly and fraternally to beware of Dr. Karlstadt and his prophets. . . .

3.27 Karlstadt: *Several Main Points of Christian Teaching Regarding Which Dr. Luther Brings Andreas Carlstadt Under Suspicion Through False Accusation and Slander* (1525)
Furcha 1995: 342, 347, 373

My dear brothers, although Dr. Luther knew and praised me before our falling out as one who knew something of the articles of Christian teaching, the poor man now allows his anger to get the better of him. He defames me. . . . Dr. Luther brazenly accuses me against his own better judgment of not knowing or caring about the main articles of Christian teaching. . . .

What knavery Dr. Luther uses in his booklet *Against the Heavenly Prophets* I will briefly note. He leans on the backs of critters or washers, and uses clever tricks which prove me right in calling him a subtle Sophist. The trick of the critter he uses as follows: Attorneys whom the peasants call "critters" have the habit of washer-women – fast tongues and sharp words. And when such "critters" bring evil and unjust matters to court and fear that their antagonist will support his good cause with firm arguments, they reach down into their bag of defamations. . . . These taunts and lies they throw about as a hedgehog throws about his bristles. They do not do this in the hope of saving their cause, for they themselves know that it is a lost cause, but rather to force their adversary to direct much energy and work to their defamations so that his cause is left undefended. Or else, he is so moved by anger that he no longer knows where he stands.

This is what Dr. Luther does. . . .

It is not good enough to serve for nothing and do good unto the neighbor as Christ did and Dr. Luther says. . . . We must, above all else, be like Christ in our inner being and have the likeness of Christ. These are higher and more essential articles than to love the neighbor for nothing in word and deed. This stock-blind Dr. Luther simply does not know that the example and wisdom of Christ went before us, commanding us to walk in such wisdom. I know that Dr. Luther does not understand how Moses wrote of Christ in this case and what God demands of his people above all else; that is why he pulls his load as a blind old horse pulls his cart. . . .

4

Social Welfare and Education

Religious and theological perspectives influenced medieval attitudes to poverty, begging, and the developing profit economy. The religious significance of almsgiving as a good work, the efforts to distinguish the worthy from the unworthy poor, the difference between voluntary and involuntary poverty, the social unrest related to increasing poverty, and the biblical and canon law prohibitions of usury were all factors in the efforts of society to cope with growing numbers of poor people (4.1–4) and the development of early modern capitalism. Reformation theology accelerated the development of social legislation designed to restrict begging and to maximize alleviation of social conditions by the rationalization and secularization of poor relief. Luther's first extended treatment of the Lord's Supper (4.5), addressed specifically to the laity, viewed communion with God as the source for helping one's neighbor. By the early sixteenth century the excesses of the developing profit economy, or usury in medieval terminology, weighed heavily upon farmers and wage earners and all too often drove them to poverty when they could not pay their debts (4.6). Luther, among others, called for government controls on business practices and interest rates (4.7–8). Karlstadt and Luther also proposed social welfare legislation that became a model for evangelical cities and territories (4.9–11). Along with the elimination of begging and the provision of social welfare, the Reformers were keen to establish public education for the well-being of the community. Until the advent of humanism, education was almost entirely under the aegis of the church and its theology. In the popular mind, education was a waste of time unless one aspired to the professions of theology, law, or medicine. Hence, there was the widespread attitude that on the one hand the "learned are daft" ("Gelehrte sind verkehrte"), and on the other hand that youth ought to be out earning a living, not sitting in school. Hence Luther's appeals to city magistrates and parents to establish and support schools (4.12–13). For Luther, ignorance is not a virtue; thus his efforts to inculcate the Christian ABCs of the Ten Commandments, the Creed, and the Lord's Prayer were the foundations of his Small and Large Catechisms (4.14–15). The Small Catechism was intended for

The European Reformations Sourcebook, Second Edition. Edited by Carter Lindberg.
© 2014 John Wiley & Sons, Ltd. Published 2014 by John Wiley & Sons, Ltd.

use in the home where parents are to teach the basics of the gospel to their children. In contrast to the length and complexity of Kolde's catechism (1.27), Luther addresses children, and hence their parents, with basically one simple question, "What is this?" or "What does this mean?" Already in his 1526 "German Mass and Order of Service," Luther was advocating addressing people at the level of their questions and issues. The Large Catechism (roughly four times the length of the Small Catechism) was intended for the education of pastors, a pressing need that became evident during the visitations of evangelical parishes to provide both assessment and instruction to those pastors and parishes that embraced the Reformation (see "Instructions for the Visitors of Parish Pastors in Electoral Saxony," 1528; LW 40: 263–320). The 1529 Latin translation of the "Large Catechism" influenced Calvin's *Institutes of the Christian Religion*.

4.1 Canon Law
Lindberg 1993: 173–4

We should not show our liberality indifferently to all who come to us. But we should know . . . the quality of the beggar, the capacity of the donor, . . . the reason for the demand, . . . the quantity being requested. . . .

The order of charity is indeed such that you first provide for your relatives and that you help them with kindness, but not that you make them rich. . . . Nothing should be given to simulators, harlots, and hunters of alms because when you give to them you give not to the person but to a most worthless species to which nothing should be given; unless they are in extreme necessity, in which case give to the person and not to the species. . . . The same can be said about heretics and the anathematized. . . .

[T]he righteous should be preferred to the unrighteous, the good to the bad, the member of the family to the stranger, the religious to the nonreligious, and it should be given to the best, the nearest member of the family or the most religious, rather than to the less good, or the one who is not from your near family or the less religious . . . unless this . . . person is in such a great indigence that he would die without our help. . . .

4.2 Johann Geiler of Kaysersberg: "Concerning Begging"
Sachsse & Tennstedt 1980: 36

A necessary matter, not only here [Strasbourg] but throughout Christendom, would be to take care that alms be rightly dispensed to the poor and not given to the unworthy who need it least of all. . . . We owe it out of our own humanity to provide for the poor and to be zealous in this matter. Therefore the Emperor and the assembly of princes should take over this, as it has been suggested but in vain. Therefore it is necessary that every community support their own poor. By God's grace there is a large amount of alms in this city through various contributions. The difficulty, however, lies in their distribution. It would be necessary for this purpose that a few be chosen to take on the business of administration [of alms]. And an ordinance would be necessary according to which the able-bodied beggars or children who could earn their bread would be urged to work, and only those unable to work be provided with alms. Also, they [the poor] must be divided into six or seven groups with each group under the direction of one whose abilities are trusted. It is too much to expect that one person would be able to keep things in order for six or seven groups. Other measures must be conceived whereby this inordinate mess can be straightened out.

4.3 The Nuremberg Begging Order of 1478
Sachsse & Tennstedt 1980: 64–6

The honorable city council has been informed often and emphatically, fully and credibly, that some beggars and beggaresses live a life without fear of God, even lives that are unseemly and unbecoming. Also that there are some who come here to Nuremberg for alms, demanding and taking them, even though they are not needy. And because alms, when they are given, are a particularly praiseworthy, meritorious, virtuous, and good work, and because those that take alms without need or falsely are thereby burdened by a heavy and manifest wrong, the above-named, our councilors, to the praise of God but also from necessity, undertake to prevent such dishonesty and danger from swindling whereby poor, distressed persons are deprived from their support by alms. To this end they desire to establish and earnestly command that the following ordinance, avoidance of which shall incur the herein contained penalties, shall be enforced and kept, according to which everyone is to comply:

First, . . . neither citizens nor visitors – men or women – in this city of Nuremberg may beg either day or night unless permission to do so is granted by . . . the honorable council.

And whoever has received such permission shall not beg unless they openly wear the beggar's badge that is given them. Whoever begs without permission and the badge shall remain a year and a mile away from this city. . . .

Beggars will not be permitted to beg if they have children with them among whom one is eight years old and without disability because they could very well earn their own bread. However, if a man or woman beggar has four or five children, all under seven years, and also a child over eight to watch the rest, then the elected lords shall be entitled to make an allowance. . . .

The beggars who are permitted to beg here and who are not cripples, lame, or blind shall not sit idly at the begging place in front of the church on any work day, but rather do spinning or other work they are able to perform in their situation. . . .

Also, that beggar, be he citizen or visitor, who is permitted to beg, and who has a nasty looking injury on his body or his limbs, the sight of which could cause detriment [to the well-being] of pregnant women, shall cover such wounds and not allow them to be openly visible or displayed. . . .

If a student desires to seek alms here, he shall not be allowed unless he goes punctually to school and behaves as an obedient student. The schoolmaster shall appropriately punish students who behave otherwise. . . .

4.4 Luther: "Foreword" to Mathias Hütlin's *The Book of Vagabonds* (1510)
WA 26: 638–9, 643–4. See also LW 59: 236–9

This booklet about the trickery of beggars was first printed by someone who called himself *Expertum in truffis*, that is, a fellow experienced in roguery . . . It seemed to me a good thing that this booklet should not be neglected but rather should become known everywhere so that one can see and understand how the devil rules so powerfully in the world, and so that it could help enlighten people to be on the lookout for him [the devil]. . . .

Therefore every town and village should know and be acquainted with its own poor, listing them in a register so that they can help them. But foreign beggars ought not be tolerated without a letter or seal, for there is far too much roguery among them, as mentioned by this booklet. And if a town were aware of its poor, then such roguery would soon be discovered and forbidden. I myself in recent years have been fooled by these vagabonds and blabber-mouths more than I wish to confess. Therefore, he who will be warned, be warned and do good to his neighbor according to Christian love, manner, and command. May God help us. Amen. . . .

[Excerpt:] *Falling Sickness* [*Grantnern*]. The eighth chapter concerns the *Grantnern*. They are beggars who say in the farmhouses, "Oh, my dear friend, look, I am afflicted with the falling sickness of Saint Valentine, or Saint Kurin, or Saint Vitus, or Saint Anthony, and I vowed to give to these beloved saints an offering of six pounds of wax, an altar cloth, and a silver salver (etc.). Now I have to get this from the contributions and help of pious people. Therefore, I beg you to contribute a. penny, some flax or some yarn for the altar cloth. May God and the dear saints protect you well from plagues and days of illness." Note this false trick: some fall down even in front of churches, they take soap in their mouths in order to have foam come out as thick as a fist. And they pierce their nostrils with a straw to bleed as if they had the plague. And it's all knavery. These are vagabonds who infest all the countries. Likewise, many of them provide for themselves this way by saying: "Be aware, dear friend, that I am the son of a butcher, of an artisan. Once a beggar came to my father's house and begged for the sake of Saint Valentine. My father gave me a penny to give to him. I said, 'Father, this is a trick!' My father commanded me to give it to him, but I didn't. At that moment I got the falling sickness. I vowed to Saint Valentine to give three pounds of wax as well as a sung mass. And thus now I have to ask and beg this from pious people because I promised to do so. Otherwise I would have had enough by my own means. Therefore I beg you for your contribution and help. . . .

Everything he says is lies. He has asked for more than twenty years for these three pounds of wax and the mass, but with the fruits of his begging he gambles, drinks, and buys women. And there are many who use even more subtle words than these noted here. Some have letters and seals confirming their situation is true. . . .

But if the *Grantner* use many words and speak of great wonders and how they have taken vows; and if they use their tongues skillfully, that is a sign that they have been in this business a long time. They are no doubt false, for they talk up those who believe them and take a nut from their tree. Beware of them and don't give them anything. . . .

4.5 Luther: *The Blessed Sacrament of the Holy and True Body of Christ and the Brotherhoods* (1519)
LW 35: 50–2, 67–9

The significance or effect of this sacrament is fellowship of all the saints. . . .

This fellowship consists in this, that all the spiritual possessions of Christ and his saints are shared with and become the common property of him who receives this sacrament. . . . [I]t is like a city where every citizen shares with all the others the city's name, honor, freedom, trade, customs, usages, help, support, protection, and the like, while at the same time he shares all the dangers of fire and flood, enemies and death, losses, taxes, and the like. For he who would share in the profits must also share in the costs, and ever recompense love with love. Here we see that whoever injures one citizen injures an entire city and all its citizens; whoever benefits one [citizen] deserves favor and thanks from all the others. So also in our natural body, as St. Paul says in I Corinthians 12[:25–6], where he gives this sacrament a spiritual explanation, "The members have [the same] care for one another; if one member suffers, all suffer together; if one member is honored, all rejoice together." This is obvious: if anyone's foot hurts him, yes, even the little toe, the eye at once looks at it, the fingers grasp it, the face puckers, the whole body bends over to it, and all are concerned with this small member; again, once it is cared for all the other members are benefited. This comparison must be noted well if one wishes to understand this sacrament, for Scripture uses it for the sake of the unlearned. . . .

In conclusion, the blessing of this sacrament is fellowship and love, by which we are strengthened against death and all evil. This fellowship is twofold: on the one hand we partake of Christ and all saints; on the other hand we permit all Christians to be partakers of us, in whatever way they and we are able. Thus by means of this sacrament, all self-seeking love is rooted out and gives place to that which seeks the common good of all; and through the change wrought by love there is one bread, one drink, one body, one community. This is the true unity of Christian brethren. Let us see, therefore, how the neat-looking brotherhoods, of which there are now so many, compare and square with this.

The Brotherhoods

First let us consider the evil practices of the brotherhoods. One of these is their gluttony and drunkenness. After one or more masses are held, the rest of the day and night, and other days besides, are given over to the devil; they do only what displeases God. Such mad reveling has been introduced by the evil spirit. . . . Temporal lords and cities should unite with the clergy in abolishing it. . . . And the brotherhood is also supposed to be a special convocation of good works; instead it has become a collecting of money for beer. What have the names of Our Lady, St. Anne, St. Sebastian, or other saints to do with your brotherhoods, in, which you have nothing but gluttony, drunkenness, useless squandering of money, howling, yelling, chattering, dancing, and wasting of time? If a sow were made the patron saint of such a brotherhood she would not consent. . . .

If men desire to maintain a brotherhood, they should gather provisions and feed and serve a tableful or two of poor people, for the sake of God. The day before they should fast and on the feast day remain sober, passing the time in prayer and other good works. Then God and his saints would be truly honored; . . . Or they should gather the money which they intend to squander for drink, and collect it into a common treasury, each craft for itself. Then in cases of hardship, needy fellow work-men might be helped to get started, and be lent money, or a young couple of the same craft might be fitted out respectably from this common treasury. These would be works of true brotherhood; they would make God and his saints look with favor upon the brotherhoods, of which they would then gladly be the patrons. . . .

4.6 Anonymous: "What is Loan-Interest Other than Usury?" (1522)
Plöse & Vogler 1989: 85–7

Peasant: Greetings! God be with you, dear sir.
Businessman: Greetings to you, peasant! What brings you here?
P: I've come because I'd like to see what you're doing.
B: . . . I sit here and count my money.
P: Dear sir, shall I sit here with you for awhile? I'd really like to chat with you.
B: My dear little peasant, chat away! What do you want to discuss?
P: Dear sir, who has given you so much money that you have to sit here and count it?
B: What are you asking, who gives me the money? I'll tell you. A peasant comes and asks me to lend him 10 or 20 gulden. So I ask him whether he has a good meadow or a good field. He says, "Yes, sir, I have a good meadow and a good field which together are worth a 100 gulden." So I say to him: "Well then if you will pledge the property as security, and give me a gulden every year, I will lend you 20 gulden." At this the peasant is happy and says: "I will happily do it." [I say:] "But I tell you, if you do not deliver on your annual payment, I will take your property for my own." The farmer agrees and assigns it to me. I lend him the money; he pays me the interest for one, two, or three years. Thereafter he cannot manage the interest payments so I receive the property and turn out the peasant. Thus I receive the property and the money. The same thing happens with tradesmen. One has a good house for which I lend him money until it becomes mine. In this way I get a great amount of property and money. That's what passes my time.
P: I thought only Jews practiced usury. Now I learn you do it too.
B: Usury! There's no one here associating with usury. What the peasant brings me is interest.
P: If you're not engaged in usury, then why is there interest on your loans? What is interest on loans other than usury? For you loaned the money on security and receive annual interest on it, as when a Jew loans for a pledge. But you would give it such a subtle name, calling it interest.
B: You're talking as if of usury. Has not our Lord God said we should assist one another in need and extend our hands to one another?

P: Yes, but has not our Lord God said, "You shall not take interest from money lent to another if the interest is usury?"

B: You're a good fellow. If I should take nothing from the money I lend out, who will increase my pile of money?

P: I see and hear that your only concern is to increase your pile of money, and to have much money and property. And thus you go about with your fat cheeks and great belly saying, "Out of the way, here I come!" But truly I say to you that it [usury] is a great and serious sin.

B: May God give you peasants the fever! What do you mean, my fat belly? Has the devil clean carried you away, that you abuse me in my own house? Would it also be wrong if the parsons take no interest from lent money? Scram in the name of a thousand devils! What do I have to do with you?

P: . . . when someone tells you the truth you strike out left and right. [You're] like an ass with a sack on its head that wants to get it off but the sack is too heavy; it remains on his neck. Thus the name usurer sticks to you.

B: May you get the plague and boils! Had I expected this I would not have said as much about how I get my property and money. I think the devil has shit on me with you. . . .

4.7 Luther: *Trade and Usury* (1524)
LW 45: 245, 247, 258, 270–2

I suppose that my writing will be quite in vain, because the mischief has gone so far and has completely gotten the upper hand in all lands; . . . Nevertheless, I have been asked and urged to touch upon these financial evils and expose some of them so that, even though the majority may not wish to do right, at least some people – however few they are – may be delivered from the gaping jaws of avarice. . . .

First. Among themselves the merchants have a common rule which is their chief maxim and the basis of all their sharp practices, where they say: "I may sell my goods as dear as I can." They think this is their right. Thus occasion is given for avarice, and every window and door to hell is opened. What else does it mean but this: I care nothing about my neighbor; so long as I have my profit and satisfy my greed. . . . There you see how shamelessly this maxim flies squarely in the face not only of Christian love but also of natural law. How can there be anything good then in trade? How can it be without sin. . . .

I have already said that Christians are rare people on earth. This is why the world needs a strict, harsh temporal government which will compel and constrain the wicked to refrain from theft and robbery, and to return what they borrow (although a Christian ought neither to demand nor expect it). This is necessary in order that the world may not become a desert, peace vanish, and men's trade and society be utterly destroyed; . . .

On the trading companies I ought to say a good deal, but the whole subject is such a bottomless pit of avarice and wrongdoing that there is nothing in it that can be discussed with a good conscience. Who is so stupid that he cannot see that the trading companies are nothing but pure monopolies? . . . They control all commodities, deal in them as they please, and practice without concealment all the tricks that have been mentioned. They raise or lower prices at their pleasure. They oppress and ruin all the small businessmen, like the pike the little fish in the water, just as if they were lords over God's creatures and immune from all the laws of faith and love. . . .

Kings and princes ought to look into this matter and forbid them by strict laws. But I hear that they have a finger in it themselves, . . . They hang thieves who have stolen a gulden or half a gulden, but do business with those who rob the whole world and steal more than all the rest, so that the proverb remains true, "Big thieves hang little thieves."

4.8 Luther: "That Clergy Should Preach Against Usury" (1540)
WA 51: 331–2, 361–4, 367–9

I ask, for God's sake, that all preachers and pastors not keep silent or refrain from preaching against usury, and that they exhort and warn the people. We cannot prevent usury . . . nevertheless we might through our exhortation rescue some from such a Sodom and Gomorrah. . . . Therefore let each of us be led by our conscience and office to be responsible at times throughout the year to exhort our congregations and also instruct them to guard against usury and greed. Thereby we remove the mask from the rogue [the usurer] by which he adorns himself as if he were righteous and good. . . .

I have been told that in the Leipzig market the interest is thirty percent, and in the Naumberg market the interest is forty percent; whether it is even more, I don't know. Shame on you! Will this not finally lead to the Devil? . . . [Such interest ruins everyone, meanwhile the usurer] in the process suffers no danger in body or goods, does no work, sits by the stove and bakes apples. Thus a usurer might sit at home and devour the whole world in ten years. . . .

It is not proper for us preachers to approve it [usury]. In this regard let us be bishops, i.e., be on guard and watch, for it concerns our salvation. First, we shall scold and condemn usury from the pulpit, and diligently and straight out repeat the text (see Neh. 5 et al.), namely: Whoever loans something and gets more in return is a usurer and is condemned as a thief, robber, and murderer.

. . . [I]f you clearly know and are acquainted with a usurer, do not administer the sacrament to him or grant him absolution as long as he does not repent! . . . [L]et the usurer lie as a pagan in death, and do not bury him among other Christians! . . . For because he is a usurer and idolater, because he serves mammon, he is unbelieving and he cannot have or receive the forgiveness of sins nor the grace of Christ nor the communion of the saints. He has condemned himself, separated and banned himself, so long as he does not confess his sins and repent.

This talk will perhaps seem to be somewhat harsh. Perhaps it will also be frightening to some. Above all it will appear frightening to the small usurers; I mean those who take only five or six percent. However, to the great devourers of the world, those who can never take a high enough percentage, one can never be sufficiently harsh, for they have given themselves over to mammon and the devil. They let us cry out and not once inquire about it. It is in particular of these I have spoken; they should be given over in life and death to the devil, and there should be no Christian fellowship with them.

4.9 Social Welfare Legislation: The City of Wittenberg (1522)
Lietzmann 1935: 4–6

1. It is unanimously resolved that all income from the churches, all of the brother-hoods, and the guilds shall be collected together and brought into a common chest. Two from the city council, two from the community, and a secretary are to be delegated who shall receive and possess such income in order to provide for the poor people.
2. Moreover, henceforth the endowed income of priests, when it is freed through the death of a priest, will also be collected in the same common chest; . . .
3. Likewise, no beggars shall be tolerated in our city, rather one shall urge them to work or expel them from the city. But they who because of age or sickness or other misfortune have fallen into poverty shall be provided for from the common chest through the appropriate delegated manner.
4. Likewise, there shall be no Terminey [wandering mendicants] among us.
5. Likewise, no monks shall be allowed to beg in our city, but rather they are allowed the income they now have. In addition they shall [henceforth] support and maintain themselves by the work of their hands.
6. Likewise, everything which the cloisters among us now have is to be inventoried, . . . [including] the incomes they possess and collect yearly.
7. Likewise, no foreign students will be allowed in our city. If one or more desire to study with us, then they must provide themselves with food and drink, for we will allow no one to beg nor to ask for alms.
8. Likewise, neither wandering begging monks with relics nor any kind of monks begging alms . . . shall be tolerated. . . .
9. Likewise, loans shall be made from the common chest to poor artisans who without this are unable to support themselves daily by their trade, in order that they may be able to provide for themselves. When they are established, however, they can repay the loan without any interest; but if they are unable to repay the loan, it shall be pardoned for God's sake.
10. Likewise, the common chest shall provide for poor orphans, the children of poor people, and maidens who shall be given an appropriate dowry for marriage.
11. Moreover, where such income is not sufficient for such good works or does not extend itself far enough, then shall others, be they priests or citizens, according to what they have, yearly contribute a sum of money for the maintenance of the multitude of the poor. . . .
16. In case our fellow citizens and residents are burdened by interest rates that are too high, for example, five to six percent, or do not have the means for a deposit, we will loan them the main sum from the common chest, and they will repay the capital at four percent annually until it is repaid. . . .

17. Likewise, particular regard shall be given to the children of poor people. Boys sent to school and studies who because of poverty are unable to remain there, shall be given the means [to remain in school] so that at all times there will not be lacking learned people to preach the Holy Gospel and the Scriptures, and also in worldly government. Those not sent to school shall be supported [in studying] trades and crafts, for in such things particular care is needed.

4.10 Social Welfare Legislation: Leisnig (1523)
LW 45: 178, 182–3, 189, 192

In order that our Christian faith – in which all the temporal and eternal blessings won by our Lord and Savior Christ out of pure grace and mercy are granted unto us by the eternal God – may bear fruit in brotherly love, and this love truly express itself in deeds of tender kindness, we, the aforesaid general parish assembly, acting unanimously, for ourselves and our posterity have ordained, established, and set up a common chest, . . .

The administration of the common chest shall be set up in the following manner: annually . . . a general assembly of the parish shall convene here in the town hall. There, by the grace of God united in true Christian faith, they shall elect from the entire assembly ten trustees or directors for the common chest who shall be without exception the best-qualified individuals; namely, two from the nobility, two from the incumbent city council; three from among the common citizens of the town; and three from the rural peasantry. The ten thus duly elected shall immediately assume the burden and responsibility of administration and trusteeship of the common chest. They shall do so voluntarily and with a good Christian conscience, for the sake of God and the general welfare. . . .

This common chest or receptacle shall be kept in that part of our church where it is safest, and shall be provided with four separate and distinct locks, each having its own key, so that the nobility shall have one of the keys, the council another, the town citizenry the third, and the rural peasantry the fourth. . . .

Every Sunday in the year, from eleven o'clock until two hours before vespers, the ten directors shall meet in the parsonage or in the town hall, there to care for and exercise diligently their trusteeship, making their decisions and acting in concert in order that deeds of honor to God and love to the fellow-Christian may be continued in an unbroken stream and be used for purposes of improvement. . . .

Those individuals in our parish and assembly who are impoverished by force of circumstances and left without assistance by their relatives, if they have any capable of helping, and those who are unable to work because of illness or old age and are so poor as to suffer real need, shall receive each week on Sunday, and at other times as occasion demands, maintenance and support from our common chest through the ten directors. This is to be done out of Christian love, to the honor and praise of God, so that their lives and health may be preserved from further deterioration, enfeeblement, and foreshortening through lack of shelter, clothing, nourishment, and care, and so that no impoverished person in our assembly need ever publicly cry out, lament, or beg for such items of daily necessity. For this reason the ten directors shall constantly make diligent inquiry and investigation in order to have complete and reliable knowledge of all these poor. . . . The names of the poor whom they have discovered and decided to help, together with the action taken, shall be legibly entered in the minutes so that the resources of our common chest are distributed in orderly fashion. . . .

Wherever . . . the resources and stores of our common chest, as itemized above, should prove insufficient . . . we the nobility, council, craft supervisors, gentry, and commoners dwelling in the city and villages of our whole parish, for ourselves and our posterity, and by virtue of this our fraternal agreement, have unitedly resolved and consented that every noble, townsman, and peasant living in the parish shall, according to his ability and means, remit in taxes for himself, his wife, and his children a certain sum of money to the chest each year, in order that the total amount can be arrived at and procured which the deliberations and decisions of the general parish assembly, on the basis of investigation in and experience with the annual statements, have determined to be necessary and sufficient. . . .

4.11 *A Conversation Concerning the Common Chest of Schwabach, Namely by Brother Heinrich, Knecht Ruprecht, Spitler, and Their Master of the Wool Trade* (1524)
Schade 1966: 3.196–206

Brother: Thanks be to God. O Master, I have heard something good.
Master: What is it?
Brother: A common chest has been established.
Master: Praise and thanks be to God that even the poor are being considered! Who are the directors?
Brother: Hans Heller and Hans Volkmer. They have pledged and sworn to collect [resources] into the common chest, and the alms will be distributed to the poor on Walpurgis [May Day eve].
Kemerin: I'll bet! They will collect and distribute, all right; Heller to his belly and Volkmer to his beer needs.
Master: Oh, these two will not do that because they are good Lutherans. . . .
Kemerin: How will the church be maintained?
Master: That [i.e., the church] means community when this little word stands by the other, as by chest or need. All the needs of the church and city can be met from this; otherwise [under the old system of begging] there would be no money left in existence. . . .
Kemerin: But the common chest will still make poor people because many will give to it what might be necessary for his own needs. Also, many will give up his own inheritance.
Knecht Ruprecht: That is something to be concerned about.
Master: Yes, if our lords desire to act as our parsons, monks, and nuns who have done a good job attracting the people and given nothing in return no matter how poor and wretched the people become. But my lords will act more wisely and with understanding.

Brother: Therefore we shall beseech God for understanding and wisdom. . . .

Master: It's high time we ask God so that the devil with his false spirit does not harm us in the love to God and the neighbor.

Knecht: Yes, it is also of necessity a good thing that one decree more than two overseers [for the common chest].

Brother: Also, so that my lords not be suspect in this [venture], the overseers should solemnly vow and make no accounts without the will and knowledge of the whole community, or be permitted to do their accounting before twelve or sixteen citizens, elected from the community. Also, the overseers shall be relieved each year, except for the eldest, and others be appointed in their place.

Knecht: Thus the community shall willingly help with body and goods.

Master: Without any doubt my lords will consider all these needs in an orderly manner.

Brother: I ask you, dear Master, read the booklet by Luther on the order of the common chest.

Master: I will read it. . . .

4.12 Luther: *To the Councilmen of All Cities in Germany that They Establish and Maintain Christian Schools* (1524)
LW 45: 348, 350, 356–7, 367–71, 373

First of all, we are today experiencing in all the German lands how schools are everywhere being left to go to wrack and ruin. . . . The carnal-minded masses are beginning to realize that they no longer have either the obligation or the opportunity to thrust their sons, daughters, and relatives into cloisters and foundations, and turn them out of their own homes and property and establish them in others' property. For this reason no one is any longer willing to have his children get an education. "Why," they say, "should we bother to have them go to school if they are not to become priests, monks, or nuns? 'Twere better they should learn a livelihood to earn." . . .

Therefore, I beg all of you, my dear sirs and friends, for the sake of God and our poor young people, not to treat this matter [the establishment of public schools] as lightly as many do, . . . For it is a grave and important matter, and one which is of vital concern, both to Christ and the world at large, that we take steps to help the youth. By so doing we will be taking steps to help ourselves and everybody else. . . . My dear sirs, if we have to spend such large sums every year on guns, roads, bridges, dams, and countless similar items to insure the temporal peace and prosperity of a city, why should not much more be devoted to the poor neglected youth – at least enough to engage one or two competent men to teach school? . . .

Since a city should and must have [educated] people, and since there is a universal dearth of them and complaint that they are nowhere to be found, we dare not wait until they grow up of themselves; neither can we carve them out of stone nor hew them out of wood. Nor will God perform miracles as long as men can solve their problems by means of the other gifts he has already granted them. Therefore, we must do our part and spare no labor or expense to produce and train such people ourselves. . . .

After all, temporal government has to continue. Are we then to permit none but louts and boors to rule, when we can do better than that? That would certainly be a crude and senseless policy. . . .

Let us suppose that there were no soul, no heaven or hell, and that we were to consider solely the temporal government from the standpoint of its worldly functions. Does it not need good schools and educated persons more than the spiritual realm? . . .

Only one thing is lacking, the earnest desire to train the young and to benefit and serve the world with able men and women. The devil very much prefers coarse blockheads and ne'er-do-wells, lest men get along too well on earth. . . .

Finally, one thing more merits serious consideration by all those who earnestly desire to have such schools and languages established and maintained in Germany. It is this: no effort or expense should be spared to provide good libraries or book repositories, especially in the larger cities which can well afford it. For if the gospel and all the arts are to be preserved, they must be set down and held fast in books and writings. . . . This is essential, not only that those who are to be our spiritual and temporal leaders may have books to read and study, but also that the good books may be preserved and not lost, together with the arts and languages which we now have by the grace of God. . . .

4.13 Luther: *A Sermon on Keeping Children in School* (1530)
LW 46: 238–9, 242, 252, 256

[T]emporal authority is a creation and ordinance of God, and that for us men in this life it is a necessary office and estate which we can no more dispense with than we can dispense with life itself, since without such an office this life cannot continue. That being true, it is easy to understand that God has not commanded and instituted it only to have it destroyed. On the contrary, he wills to have it maintained, . . . to protect those who do good and to punish those who do wrong. Now who will maintain this office except us men to whom God has committed it, and who truly need it? . . . And what men are capable of doing it? Certainly not those who would rule only with the fist, as many now think to do. For if men were to rule solely by the fist, the end result would surely be a bestial kind of existence: whoever could get the better of another would simply toss him into the discard pile. We have enough examples before our eyes to see what the fist can accomplish apart from wisdom or reason. . . .

Indeed, there is need in this office [of civil service] for abler people than are needed in the office of preaching, so it is necessary to get the best boys for this work; for in the preaching office Christ does the whole thing, by his Spirit, but in the worldly kingdom men must act on the basis of reason – wherein the laws also have their origin – for God has subjected temporal rule and all of physical life to reason (Genesis 2[:15]). . . .

At this point I should also mention how many educated men are needed in the fields of medicine and the other liberal arts. Of these two needs one could write a huge book and preach for half a year. Where are the preachers, jurists, and physicians to come from, if grammar and other rhetorical arts are not taught? For such teaching is the spring from which they all must flow. . . .

But I hold that it is the duty of the temporal authority to compel its subjects to keep their children in school, especially the promising ones we mentioned above. For it is truly the duty of government to maintain the offices and estates that have been mentioned, so that there will always be preachers, jurists, pastors, writers, physicians, schoolmasters, and the like, for we cannot do without them. . . .

4.14 Luther: *The Small Catechism* (1529)
BC 347–9, 352–3, 357

Preface: The deplorable, wretched deprivation that I recently encountered while I was a visitor has constrained and compelled me to prepare this catechism, or Christian instruction, in such a brief, plain, and simple version. Dear God, what misery I beheld! The ordinary person, especially in the villages, knows absolutely nothing about the Christian faith, and unfortunately many pastors are completely unskilled and incompetent teachers. Yet supposedly they all bear the name Christian, are baptized, and receive the holy sacrament, even though they do not know the Lord's Prayer, the Creed, or the Ten Commandments! As a result they live like simple cattle or irrational pigs and despite the fact that the gospel has returned, have mastered the fine art of misusing all their freedom. . . .

Therefore, my dear sirs and brothers, who are either pastors or preachers, I beg all of you for God's sake to take up your office boldly, to have pity on your people who are entrusted to you, and to help bring the catechism to the people, especially to the young. . . .

Although no one can or should force another person to believe, nevertheless one should insist upon and hold the masses to this: that they know what is right and wrong among those with whom they wish to reside, eat, and earn a living. For example, if people want to live in a particular city, they ought to know and abide by the laws of the city whose protection they enjoy, no matter whether they believe or are at heart scoundrels and villains. . . .

[O]nce the people have learned the text well, then teach them to understand it, too, so they know what it means. . . .

The Ten Commandments

The Fourth Commandment
You are to honor your father and mother.
What is this? Answer:
We are to fear and love God, so that we neither despise nor anger our parents and others in authority, but instead honor, serve, obey, love, and respect them.

The Fifth Commandment
You are not to kill.
What is this? Answer:
We are to fear and love God, so that we neither endanger nor harm the lives of our neighbors, but instead help and support them in all of life's needs.

The Seventh Commandment
You are not to steal.
What is this? Answer:
We are to fear and love God, so that we neither take our neighbors' money or property nor acquire them by using shoddy merchandise or crooked deals, but instead help them to improve and protect their property and income.

The Lord's Prayer

The Fourth Petition
Give us today our daily bread.
What is this? Answer:
In fact, God gives daily bread without our prayer, even to all evil people, but we ask in this prayer that God cause us to recognize what our daily bread is and to receive it with thanksgiving.
What then does "daily bread" mean? Answer:
Everything included in the necessities and nourishment for our bodies, such as food, drink, clothing, shoes, house, farm, fields, livestock, money, property, an upright spouse, upright children, upright members of the household, upright and faithful rulers, good government, good weather, peace, health, decency, honor, good friends, faithful neighbors, and the like.

4.15 Luther: *The Large Catechism* (1529)
BC 440–1, 443, 449–51

The Lord's Prayer

We have now heard what we are to do and believe. . . . Now follows the third part, how we are to pray. We are in such a situation that no one can keep the Ten Commandments perfectly, even though he or she has begun to believe. . . . Consequently, nothing is so necessary as to call upon God incessantly and to drum into his ears our prayer that he may give, preserve, and increase in us faith and the fulfillment of the Ten Commandments and remove all that stands in our way and hinders us in this regard. That we may know what and how to pray, however, our Lord Christ himself has taught us both the way and the words, as we shall see.

But before we explain the Lord's Prayer part by part, the most necessary thing is to exhort and encourage people to pray, as Christ and the apostles also did. The first thing to know is this: It is our duty to pray because of God's command. For we heard in the Second Commandment, "You are not to take God's name in vain." Thereby we are required to praise the holy name and to pray or call upon it in every need. For calling upon it is nothing else than praying. . . .

This God requires of us; it is not a matter of our choice. It is our duty and obligation to pray. . . .

This is the first and most important point, that all our prayers must be based on obedience to God, regardless of our person, whether we are sinners or righteous people, worthy or unworthy. We must understand that God is not joking, but that he will be angry and punish us if we do not pray, just as he punishes all other kinds of disobedience. Nor will he allow our prayers to be futile or lost, for if he did not intend to answer you, he would not have ordered you to pray and backed it up with such a strict commandment.

In the second place, what ought to impel and arouse us to pray all the more is the fact that God has made and affirmed a promise: that what we pray is a certain and sure thing. As he says in Psalm 50[:15], "Call on me in the day of trouble; I will deliver you," and Christ says in the Gospel in Matthew 7[:7–8], "Ask, and it will be given you," etc. . . . "For everyone who asks receives." Such promises certainly ought to awaken and kindle in our hearts a longing and love for prayer. For by his Word, God testifies that our prayer is heartily pleasing to him and will assuredly be heard and granted, so that we may not despise it, cast it to the winds, or pray uncertainly.

You can hold such promises up to him and say, "Here I come, dear Father, and pray not of my own accord nor because of my worthiness, but at your commandment and promise, which cannot fail or deceive me." . . .

Furthermore, we should be encouraged and drawn to pray because in addition to this commandment and promise, God takes the initiative and puts into our mouths the very words and approach we are to use. In this way we see how deeply concerned he is about our needs, and we should never doubt that such prayer pleases him and will assuredly be heard. So this prayer is far superior to all others that we might devise ourselves. . . . Thus there is no nobler prayer to be found on earth, for it has the powerful testimony that God loves to hear it.

The Fourth Petition

"Give us today our daily bread."

Here we consider the poor breadbasket – the needs of our body and our life on earth. . . .

To put it briefly, this petition includes everything that belongs to our entire life in this world, because it is only for its sake that we need daily bread. Now, our life requires not only food and clothing and other necessities for our body, but also peace and concord in our daily activities, associations, and situations of every sort with the people among whom we live and with whom we interact – in short, in everything that pertains to the regulation of both our domestic and our civil or political affairs. For where these two spheres are interfered with and prevented from functioning as they should, there the necessities of life are also interfered with, and life itself cannot be maintained for any length of time. Indeed, the greatest need of all is to pray for the civil authorities and the government, for it is chiefly through them that God provides us daily bread and all the comforts of life. Although we have received from God all good things in abundance, we cannot retain any of them or enjoy them in security and happiness were he not to give us a stable, peaceful government. For where dissension, strife, and war prevail, there daily bread is already taken away or at least reduced.

It would therefore be fitting if the coat of arms of every upright prince were emblazoned with a loaf of bread instead of a lion or a wreath of rue [an herb], or if a loaf of bread were stamped on coins, in order to remind both princes and subjects that is through the princes' office that we enjoy protection and peace and that without them we could neither eat nor preserve the precious gift of bread. . . .

Thus, you see, God wishes to show us how he cares for us in all our needs and faithfully provides for our daily sustenance. Although he gives and provides these blessings bountifully, even to the godless and rogues, yet he wishes us to ask for them so that we may realize that we have received them from his hand and may recognize in them his fatherly goodness toward us.

5

The Reformation of the Common Man

The question "What makes a Christian?" (5.1, 5.5) gained increasing urgency as streams of radical reform welling up from those convinced they had a divinely inspired mandate for immediate implementation of reform merged with those who perceived a direct connection between Christian freedom (2.20) and political and economic freedom (5.10). The growing tension and then open conflict were rooted on the one hand in the ever more burdensome obligations placed upon the peasants by both territorial and local rulers through the imposition of Roman law, and on the other hand in the peasant appropriation of John Wyclif's (1320–84) argument that the law must correspond to evangelical justice. The concept of "godly law" in opposition to Roman law spread through Europe with the Bohemian Hussite movement. In short, the peasant movements were willing to acknowledge only those laws based in the Bible. Karlstadt and Thomas Müntzer hoped to lead this "Reformation of the Common Man" with their claims of direct communication with the Holy Spirit colored by apocalyptic expectation (5.2, 5.3). The biblical "great reversal" of the first and the last was seen to apply to the princes and the peasants. Karlstadt's reply (5.4) to Luther's Invocavit Sermons (3.25) demanded that every local congregation implement changes immediately without regard to the weak in faith and those who might be offended. As Luther reaffirmed his opposition to forced reform (5.6), Müntzer's denunciations of the authorities and calls for the elimination of the godless became ever bolder until, on the eve of the battle at Frankenhausen, he proclaimed that "God instructs all the birds of the heavens to consume the flesh of the princes; whilst the brute beasts are to drink the blood of the big wigs" (5.7). But it was the peasants who were consumed: 6,000 dead, 600 captured, including Müntzer, who soon afterward was executed. Both Luther. and Müntzer understood themselves to be theologians rather than politicians, and so their social-political conflicts were rooted in opposing views of divine revelation (3.24–25; 5.8–10, 5.12). For Luther, issues of justice remained in the realm of law and reason; for Müntzer, they were matters of gospel

---

The European Reformations Sourcebook, Second Edition. Edited by Carter Lindberg.
© 2014 John Wiley & Sons, Ltd. Published 2014 by John Wiley & Sons, Ltd.

and revelation. The remaining entries (5.13–22) provide some perspectives on these issues in light of the Peasants' War.

5.1 Müntzer to Luther (1520)
Matheson 1988: 18–19, 21–2

The council has appointed one, most benign father to seek your advice in my case against those who incriminate me. . . . You are my advocate in the Lord Jesus. I beg you not to lend your ears to those who are defaming me. . . .

It is not my work I am doing, but that of the Lord. . . . If you advise me to write against these assertions . . . I will do so, so that the adversaries of the cross may learn to revere the name of God and to silence the blasphemous mouth, so that the light which comforts us may shine forth on all who are in the house of the Lord. Please indicate what in all this you regard as Christian. I firmly believe I have been snatched from my original danger for other struggles with this world. He who plucked me from the loathsome swamp will snatch me from the paw of the beast and the lion and the dragon, so that I will not fear even if I walk in the midst of the shadow of death, for the Lord is with me as a strong warrior. He himself will provide the voice and the wisdom which none of our adversaries will be able to resist. What more can I desire! Fare thee well in Christ, model and beacon to the friends of God! . . .

Thomas Müntzer, whom you brought to birth by the gospel.

5.2 Müntzer: *Prague Manifesto* (1521)
Matheson 1988: 357–61

I, Thomas Müntzer of Stolberg, do declare before the whole church and the whole world – wherever this letter may be shown – that I can testify with Christ and all the elect who have known me from my youth up, to having shown all possible diligence, more than any other man known to me, in pursuing better instruction about the holy and invincible Christian faith. For at no time in my life (God knows I am not lying) did I learn anything about the true exercise of the faith from any monk or priest, or about the edifying time of trial which clarifies faith in the spirit of the fear of God, showing the need for an elect man to have the seven-fold gift of the holy spirit. I have not heard from a single scholar about the order of God implanted in all creatures, not the tiniest word about it; while as to understanding the whole as a unity of all the parts those who claim to be Christians have not caught the least whiff of it – least of all the accursed priests. I have heard from them about mere Scripture, which they have stolen from the Bible like murderers and thieves; . . . for they themselves have never heard it from God, from his very mouth. . . . For anyone who does not feel the spirit of Christ within him, or is not quite sure of having it, is not a member of Christ, but of the devil. . . .

Take note of this text, if you happen to have any brains in your head: Heaven and earth will pass away, my word will never pass away. If it is only written in books, nowhere else, and God spoke only once and then vanished into thin air, then it surely cannot be the word of the eternal God. Then it is just a creaturely thing, entering the memory in an external way, all of which is contrary to the true order and contrary to the rule of the holy faith, as Jeremiah says. That is why all the prophets speak in this way: "Thus says the Lord"; they do not say "Thus said the Lord", as if it were past history; they speak in the present tense. . . .

In order to bring such teaching to the light I am willing to sacrifice my life for God's sake, God will do wonderful things with his elect, especially in this land. For the new church will begin here, this people will be a mirror for the whole world. Therefore I summon every single person to help in the defense of God's word. . . . If you refuse God will let you be struck down by the Turks in the coming year.

5.3 Müntzer to Melanchthon (1522)
Matheson 1988: 43–4, 46

Greetings, instrument of Christ. Your theology I embrace with all my heart for it has snatched many souls from the snares of the hunters. That your priests are taking wives I commend, lest the Roman pretence continue to oppress you. What I disapprove of is this: that it is a dumb God whom you adore, for because of your ignorance about propagation you cannot distinguish between the elect and the reprobate; as a result you totally reject the coming church in which the knowledge of the Lord will dawn in all its fullness. But this error . . . arises wholly from all ignorance of the living word. Look to the Scriptures, on which we rely to trample down the world; they say quite unambiguously: Man does not live by bread alone but by every word which proceeds from the mouth of God; note that it proceeds from the mouth of God and not from books. . . . O most beloved, see to it that you prophesy, otherwise your theology will not be worth a cent. Think of your God as at hand and not distant; believe that God is more willing to speak than you are prepared to listen. We are brim full of desires. This hinders the finger of the living God from piercing his tablets. By your arguments you drag men to matrimony although the bond is not yet an immaculate one, but a Satanic brothel, which is as harmful to the church as the most accursed perfumes of the priests. Do not [let?] these passionate desires impede your sanctification! . . .

Our most beloved Martin acts ignorantly because he does not want to offend the little ones; . . . But the tribulation of Christians is already at the door; why you should consider that it is still to come, I do not know. Dear brothers, leave your dallying, the time has come! Do not delay, summer is at the door. Do not make peace with the reprobate, for they impede the mighty working of the Word. Do not flatter your princes; otherwise you will live to see your undoing, . . . Should you wish I will back up all I have said from the Scriptures, from the order of creation, from experience, and from the clear word of God. You delicate biblical scholars, do not hang back. I can do no other.

5.4 Karlstadt: *Whether One Should Proceed Slowly* (1524)
Sider 1978: 50, 52, 61–2, 64–5, 70

Upon my report, dear brother [Bartel Bach, town clerk in Joachimstal] . . . you wrote to me that for yourself you would like to move slowly hereafter, . . . in order to avoid offending the weak. You do nothing other than what the whole world now does which shouts: "Weak, weak, sick, sick, not too fast, slowly, slowly." . . .

[W]e should do all God's commands according to our ability and should not wait until the foolish or weak follow. . . .

See here! . . . I ask whether one should not stop coveting other people's goods until the others follow? May one steal until the thieves stop stealing? . . .

It is also the same with the removal of the God-blaspheming and Christ-blaspheming images or masses. Where we, who confess God, rule and find idols, we should remove them and behave toward them as God commanded. . . .

Some [i.e., Luther], however, resist God's prohibition and Word. . . . Because of the weak, they say, one should delay and not proceed at all. . . .

We should take such horrible things [i.e., idols] from the weak, and snatch them from their hands and not consider whether they cry, scream, or curse because of it. The time will come when they who now curse and damn us will thank us. By a comparison, I will show you that he who would forcibly break the will of fools would manifest toward them the brotherly love which is genuine and best. . . . Therefore, I ask whether, if I should see that a little innocent child holds a sharp pointed knife in his hand and wants to keep it, would I show him brotherly love if I would allow him to keep the dreadful knife as he desires with the result that he would wound or kill himself, or when I would break his will and take the knife? You must always say that if you take from the child what brings injury to him, you do a fatherly or brotherly Christian deed. For Christ has depicted for us genuinely Christian and brotherly love in the passages where he says: "If your hand offends you, cut it off and throw it from you" (Matt. 18:1–8). Christ said that in order to point to genuine brotherly love. . . .

The conclusion therefore is this: Where Christians rule, there they should consider no government, but rather freely on their own hew down and throw down what is contrary to God, even without preaching. Such offenses are numerous – for example, the mass, images, the idolatrous flesh which the priests now devour, etc. . . .

5.5 Luther: *Letter to the Christians at Strassburg in Opposition to the Fanatic Spirit* (1524)
LW 40: 66–70

I have learned how the new prophets are appearing in various regions, and, as some of you have written to me, . . . Dr. Karlstadt has started disturbance among you with his fanaticism in the matter of the sacrament, images, and baptism. This he has also done elsewhere, and he blames me for his banishment.

Now my very dear friends, I am not your pastor. No one has to believe me. Each one is responsible for himself. I can warn every one, I can thwart no one. . . .

My sincere counsel and warning is that you be circumspect and hold to the single question, what makes a person a Christian? Do not on any account allow any other question or other art to enjoy equal importance. . . .

I might well endure his [Karlstadt's] uproar against images. . . . But I will not endure any one inciting and driving Christians to works of this kind, as if one cannot be a Christian without their performance. . . . For we know that no work can make a Christian, and that such external matters as the use of images and the keeping of the

Sabbath are, in the New Testament, as optional as all other ceremonies enjoined by the Law. Paul says, "We know that 'an idol has no real existence'" [I Cor. 8:4]. If so, why then should the Christian conscience be ensnared and tortured on account of something that has no reality? If it has no existence, let it be of no account, whether it falls or stands, . . .

Ask your evangelists, my dear sirs and brothers, to turn you away from Luther and Karlstadt and direct you always to Christ, but not, as Karlstadt does, only to the work of Christ, wherein Christ is held up as an example, which is the least important aspect of Christ, and which makes him comparable to other saints. But turn to Christ as to a gift of God or, as Paul says, the power of God, and God's wisdom, righteousness, redemption, and sanctification, given to us. For such matters these prophets have little sympathy, taste, or understanding. Instead they juggle with their "living voice from heaven," . . . They make for confused, disturbed, anxious consciences, and want people to be amazed at their great skill, but meanwhile Christ is forgotten. . . .

5.6 Luther: *Letter to the Princes of Saxony Concerning the Rebellious Spirit* (1524)
LW 40: 50–2, 57–9

Satan . . . made himself a nest at Allstedt, thinking he can fight us while enjoying our peace, protection, and security. . . .

I am especially glad that none of ours start a disturbance of this kind. They themselves boast that they do not belong to us, and have learned and received nothing from us. They come from heaven, and hear God himself speaking to them as to angels. What is taught at Wittenberg concerning faith and love and the cross of Christ is an unimportant thing. "You yourself must hear the voice of God," they say, "and experience the work of God in you. . . . The Bible means nothing. It is Bible – Booble – Babel," etc. . . . I have never read or heard of a more arrogant, imperious holy spirit (if such there be) he [Müntzer] wants to enforce faith in an immediate and dictatorial manner. . . .

I have already heard earlier from the spirit himself here in Wittenberg, that he thinks it necessary to use the sword to carry out his undertaking. . . .

Though I realize full well that Your Princely Graces will know how to deal in this matter better than I can advise, yet I am in duty bound to do my part and respectfully to pray and exhort you to look into this matter carefully. Your obligation to maintain order requires you to guard against such mischief and to prevent rebellion. . . .

As far as doctrine is concerned, time will tell. For the present, your Graces ought not to stand in the way of the ministry of the Word. Let them preach as confidently and boldly as they are able and against whomever they wish. . . .

But when they want to do more than fight with the Word, and begin to destroy and use force, then your Graces must intervene . . . and banish them from the country. . . . For we who are engaged in the ministry of the Word are not allowed to use force. Ours is a spiritual conflict in which we wrest hearts and souls from the devil. It is written in Dan. [8:25] that the Antichrist shall be vanquished without human hand. . . .

If we Christians justified our damaging of churches and our violence by Jewish examples, then it would follow that we are to put all non-Christians to death. For the Jews were as strictly bidden to put to death Canaanites and Amorites [Exod. 23:23] as they were to destroy images. But all the Allstedtian spirit would gain by this would be the shedding of blood. All who did not hear his heavenly voice would be put to the sword by him, . . .

5.7 Müntzer to the People of Erfurt (1525)
Matheson 1988: 158–9

To our heartily loved brothers, the whole congregation of Erfurt. . . .

[W]e urgently beg you to give no more credence to platelickers like these [Lutherans], and to let nothing prevent you any longer from helping ordinary Christian people to fight with us against the godless, wicked tyrants.

Help us in any way you can, with men and cannons, so that we can carry out the commands of God himself in Ezekiel, chapter 34, where he says: "I will rescue you from those who lord it over you in a tyrannous way. I will drive the wild beasts away from your land." In chapter 39 of the same prophet God goes on to say: "Come, you birds of the heaven and devour the flesh of the princes; and you wild beasts drink up the blood of all the big wigs." Daniel says the same thing in chapter 7: that power should be given to the common man, Revelations 18 and 19. Almost all of the pronouncements of scripture testify that the creatures must be set free if the pure word of God is to dawn. . . .

Thomas Müntzer on behalf of the ordinary Christian people.

5.8 Müntzer to Frederick the Wise (1524)
Matheson 1988: 110–13

The critical situation has made it imperative to prepare for, and take action against, every manifestation of unbelief. . . . In view of all this it has been ordained by God that I should be put forward, as Ezekiel says, as a wall in front of our poor, disintegrating Christianity; not just to punish part of it as some imagine, but to seize it in its entirety by the roots, which God has already done in several places where it was opportune. But Satan is driving the godless scholars to their downfall, like the monks and priests before them, for they let their rascally nature peep out when they treated the holy spirit of Christ as the butt of their scorn and derision, denouncing him as a devil when he appeared in many of the elect. This is what that mendacious man, Luther, does in the scandalous letter about me which he sent to the dukes of Saxony (cf. 5.6). There is not a hint of a brotherly exhortation in it; he just barges his way in like some pompous tyrant, full of ferocity and hate. I beseech you, therefore, for the sake of God, to consider earnestly what sort of farce may ensue if I pay him back for his loud mouth. . . .

Finally, here is my earnest judgement: The Christian faith which I preach may not be in accord with that of Luther but it is identical with that in the hearts of the elect throughout the earth, Psalm 67. For even if someone were born a Turk he still has the beginning of the same faith, that is, the movement of the holy spirit, as it is written of Cornelius, Acts 10. So if I am to be brought to trial before the Christian people then an invitation, announcement, and communication must be sent to every nation, to those who have, in faith, endured trials quite beyond their strength, have plumbed the despair of the heart, and are continually meditating on this. People like that I would gladly thole [have] as my Judges. . . . So why should I then, throw pearls to the swine who publicly mock and, deride the holy spirit, since Christ has said that they are born of the devil? What should induce me to let my patience be exploited to cover up their shame? It would be just the same as their present advice: Christians should suffer and let themselves be martyred and should not defend themselves. That, however, would be of great benefit to the tyrants, a fine cover-up to let them practise their shameful deeds.

5.9 Müntzer: *Vindication and Refutation* (1524)
Matheson 1988: 327–8, 333–5, 348

A highly provoked Vindication and a Refutation of the unspiritual soft-living Flesh in Wittenberg, whose robbery and distortion of Scripture has so grievously polluted our wretched Christian Church. . . .

[T]here is nothing so very surprising about Doctor Liar [Luther], that most ambitious of all the biblical scholars, becoming a more arrogant fool every day, covering himself up with your [God's] Holy Scripture and most deceitfully arming himself with it, but in no way renouncing fame and easy living. . . . Without true or just cause he has made me a laughing-stock among his scornful, jeering, ruthless companions and has jeeringly traduced my name in the eyes of the simple, making me out to be a satan or a devil, although I am a ransomed member of your body. . . .

[T]hat indulgent fellow, Father Pussyfoot, comes along and says I want to stir up an insurrection. . . .

The poor flatterer tries to use Christ to cover himself, adducing a counterfeit type of clemency which is contrary to Paul's text in I Timothy 1. In his book about trade [4.7] however, he says that the princes should not hesitate to join the thieves and robbers in their raids. He suppresses here, however, the basic reason for all theft. He is a herald, who hopes to earn gratitude by approving the spilling of people's blood for the sake of their earthly goods; something which God has never commanded or approved. Open your eyes! What is the evil brew from which all usury, theft and robbery springs but the assumption of our lords and princes that all creatures are their property? The fish in the water, the birds in the air, the plants on the face of the earth – it all has to belong to them! Isaiah 5. To add insult to injury, they have God's commandment proclaimed to the poor: God has commanded that you should not steal. But it avails them nothing. For while they do violence to everyone, flay and fleece the poor farm worker, tradesman and everything that breathes, Micah 3, yet should any of the latter commit the pettiest crime, he must hang. And Doctor Liar responds, Amen. It is the lords themselves who make the poor man their enemy. If they refuse to do away with the causes of insurrection how can trouble be avoided in the long run? If saying that makes me an inciter to insurrection, so be it! . . .

Sleep softly, dear flesh! I would prefer to smell you roasting in your own arrogance in a pot or in a cauldron by the fire, Jeremiah 1, smitten by God's wrath, and then stewing in your own juice. May the devil devour you! Ezekiel 23. Your flesh is like that of an ass; it would be a long time cooking and would turn out to be a tough dish indeed for your mealy-mouthed friends. . . .

5.10 Müntzer: *Sermon to the Princes* (1524)
Matheson 1988: 234, 245–51

And so, my dear brothers, if we are to rise up out of this mire and become true pupils of God, taught by God himself, John 6, Mt. 23, we will need the vast resources of his strength, sent down to us from above, in order to punish such unspeakable wickedness and nullify it. . . .

Therefore, my dearest, most revered rulers, learn true judgment from the mouth of God himself. Do not let yourself be seduced by your hypocritical priests into a restraint based on counterfeit clemency and kindness. . . .

Now if you are to be true rulers, you must seize the very roots of government, following the command of Christ. Drive his enemies away from the elect; you are the instruments to do this. My friend, don't let us have any of these hackneyed posturings about the power of God achieving everything without any resort to your sword; otherwise it may rust in its scabbard. . . . Do not, therefore, allow the evil-doers, who turn us away from God, to continue living, Deut. 13, for a godless man has no right to live if he is hindering the pious. . . .

Hence the sword, too, is necessary to eliminate the godless, Rom. 13. To ensure, however, that this now proceeds in a fair and orderly manner, our revered fathers, the princes, who with us confess Christ, should carry it out. But if they do not carry it out, the sword will be taken from them. . . .

For the godless have no right to live, unless by the sufferance of the elect, as is written in the book of Exodus, chapter 23. . . .

5.11 The Twelve Articles of the Upper Swabian Peasants (1525)
Baylor 1991: 231–45

First, . . . we want to have the full power for a whole congregation to select and elect its own pastor, and also the power to remove him, if he acts improperly . . .

Second, since a just tithe has been established in the Old Testament, and fulfilled in the New (as the whole Epistle to the Hebrews says), we will gladly pay the just grain tithe to the full – but in the proper way. It should be given to God and distributed to his people, paid to a pastor who clearly proclaims the word of God. . . . We are willing that henceforth our churchwardens, chosen by the congregation, collect and receive this tithe. From it they shall give the parson, who has been elected by the whole congregation, enough to maintain himself and his family modestly, according to the determination of the whole congregation. And whatever is left over should be distributed to the destitute people. . . .

We will not pay the "small tithe" [on animals] at all. Since the lord God created cattle freely for mankind (Genesis 1), we regard it as an improper tithe which has been contrived by people. . . .

Third, until now it has been the custom for us to be regarded as a lord's personal property, which is deplorable since Christ redeemed us all with the shedding of his precious blood. . . . Thus, Scripture establishes that we are and will be free. . . . Without a doubt, as true and just Christians, you will also gladly release us from serfdom, or show us from the gospel that we should be serfs.

Fourth, until now it has been the custom that no poor man has been allowed the right to hunt game or fowl or to catch fish in flowing water. We think that this is completely improper and unbrotherly; rather, it is selfish and not compatible with the word of God. . . .

Fifth, we also have grievances concerning the use of woodlands. For our lordships alone have appropriated all the woods, and when the poor man needs wood, he must buy it at double the price. It is our conviction that, regardless of the kind of woods involved . . . it should revert to the whole community. . . .

Sixth, we have a serious grievance concerning labor services, which increase from day to day. We want . . . some understanding, and accordingly not to be so severely burdened. . . .

Seventh, henceforth we no longer want to be burdened by a lordship; . . . Lords should not force or compel their peasants, seeking to get more services or other dues from them without payment. The peasant should be able to use and enjoy his property in peace, without being burdened. . . . But if the lord is truly in need of services, the peasant should be at his disposal willingly and obediently, but at an hour and season that are not to the peasant's detriment, and the peasant should be properly paid for his services.

Eighth, we are aggrieved, especially those that have their own land, because these lands cannot sustain the payments [taxes and fees] on them, and because these peasants must then forfeit the land and are ruined. [We demand] that lords let honorable people inspect these pieces of property and establish a payment that is equitable, so that the peasant does not work for nothing. For every laborer is worth his wage. . . .

Ninth, we are burdened by the great outrage that new laws are constantly being made, so that we are punished not according to the facts of a case, but sometimes out of envy and sometimes out of favoritism. . . .

Tenth, we are aggrieved that some have appropriated meadowland as well as fields which belong to the community. . . . We will take these properties into our hands again, unless they have in fact been legally bought. . . .

Eleventh, we want the custom termed heriot [this feudal obligation required a dead peasant's family to make a payment to a lord for the death of "his" serf] to be completely abolished. For we will never accept that the property of widows and orphans should be taken from them so shamelessly. . . .

Twelfth, it is our conclusion and final conviction that if one or more of the articles we have composed here is not in accordance with the word of God, we will retract these articles, if they can be shown to be improper according to the word of God. . . .

5.12 Luther: *Admonition to Peace. A Reply to the Twelve Articles of the Peasants in Swabia* (1525)
LW 46: 17–19, 21–4, 31–2, 40, 42

The peasants who have now banded together in Swabia have formulated their intolerable grievances against the rulers in twelve articles, and have undertaken to support them with certain passages of Scripture. Now they have published them in printed form. The thing about them that pleases me most is that, in the twelfth article, they offer to accept instruction gladly and willingly, . . . to the extent that it can he done by clear, plain, undeniable passages of Scripture. And it is indeed right and proper that no one's conscience should be instructed or corrected except by Holy Scripture. . . .

This, then, is a great and dangerous matter. It concerns both the kingdom of God and the kingdom of the world. If this rebellion were to continue and get the upper hand, both kingdoms would be destroyed and there would be neither worldly government nor word of God, which would ultimately result in the permanent destruction of all Germany. Therefore it is necessary for us to speak boldly and to give advice without regard to anyone. It is also necessary that we be willing to listen and allow things to be said to us, so that we do not now – as we have done before – harden our hearts and stop our ears, and so that God's wrath not run its full course. . . .

To the Princes and Lords

We have no one on earth to thank for this disastrous rebellion, except you princes and lords, and especially you blind bishops and mad priests and monks, whose hearts are hardened, even to the present day. . . . [Y]ou do nothing but cheat and rob the people so that you may lead a life of luxury and extravagance. The poor common people cannot bear it any longer. The sword is already at your throats, but you think that you sit so firm in the saddle that no one can unhorse you. This false security and stubborn perversity will break your necks, as you will discover. . . .

If it is still possible to give you advice, my lords, give way a little to the will and wrath of God. A cartload of hay must give way to a drunken man – how much more ought you to stop your raging and obstinate tyranny and not deal unreasonably with the peasants. . . . Try kindness first, for you do not know what God will do to prevent the spark that will kindle all Germany and start a fire that no one can extinguish. . . .

The peasants have just published twelve articles, some of which are so fair and just as to take away your reputation in the eyes of God and the world. . . .

To the Peasants

So far, dear friends, you have learned only that I agree that it is unfortunately all too true that the princes and lords who forbid the preaching of the gospel and oppress the people unbearably deserve to have God put them down from their thrones [Luke 1:52] because they have sinned so greatly against both God and man. And they have no excuse. Nevertheless, you, too, must be careful that you take up your cause justly and with a good conscience. . . . And you must most seriously consider not merely how strong you are and how wrong the princes are, but whether you act justly and with a good conscience.

Therefore, dear brethren, I beg you in a kindly and brotherly way to look carefully at what you are doing and not to believe all kinds of spirits and preachers. . . . Just listen attentively, as you offer many times to do. I will not spare you the earnest warning that I owe you, even though some of you have been so poisoned by the murderous spirits that you will hate me for it and call me a hypocrite. . . .

In the first place, dear brethren, you bear the name of God and call yourselves a "Christian association" or union, and you allege that you want to live and act according to divine law. Now you know that the name, word, and titles of God are not to be assumed idly or in vain, . . .

I say all this, dear friends, as a faithful warning. In this case you should stop calling yourselves Christians and stop claiming that you have the Christian law on your side. . . . So again I say, however good and just your cause may be, nevertheless, because you would defend yourselves and are unwilling to suffer either violence or injustice, you may do anything that God does not prevent. However, leave the name Christian out of it. . . .

In saying this it is not my intention to justify or defend the rulers in the intolerable injustices which you suffer from them. They are unjust, and commit heinous wrongs against you; that I admit. . . .

Your name and title ought therefore to indicate that you are people who fight because they will not, and ought not, endure injustice or evil, according to the teaching of nature. You should use that name, and let the name of Christ alone, for that is the kind of works that you are doing. If, however, you will not take that name, but keep the name of Christian, then I must accept the fact that I am also involved in this struggle and consider you as enemies who, under the name of the gospel, act contrary to it, and want to do more to suppress my gospel than anything the pope and emperor have done to suppress it. . . .

Admonition to Both Rulers and Peasants

Now, dear sirs, there is nothing Christian on either side and nothing Christian is at issue between you; both lords and peasants are discussing questions of justice and injustice in heathen, or worldly, terms. . . . For God's sake, then, take my advice! Take a hold of these matters properly, with justice and not with force or violence and do not start endless bloodshed in Germany. . . .

I, therefore, sincerely advise you to choose certain counts and lords from among the nobility and certain councilmen from the cities and ask them to arbitrate and settle this dispute amicably. . . .

5.13 Aspects of Müntzer's Military Campaign
Scott & Scribner 1994: 147

On Sunday morning [April 29] Pfeiffer, Müntzer, and their followers, together with the Eichsfeld contingent which had joined them on the boggy ground at Görmar sporting a yellow-and-green flag, marched to Ebeleben, where they sacked the castle, tearing down and smashing whatever they could, drank up the wine, seized the corn in sheaves in the fields, fished out the ponds, then attacked and plundered the nunnery at Marksussra, likewise the castle of Almenhausen and others, and sent back many wagons piled high with booty to the lower parish [St. Blasius] in Mühlhausen. . . .

5.14 The Massacre of Weinsberg (April 16, 1525): Report of the Parson Johann Herolt
Scott & Scribner 1994: 158

On the holy Easter Day, 16 April, as the peasants were encamped at Neckarsulm, a carter called Semelhans arrived who had brought salt into the castle of Weinsberg. He reported that the nobles and cavalry had gone down into the town, leaving almost no one in the castle. . . . So the peasants scaled the walls, captured the countess and her children, plundered the castle, and then appeared before the town. But the townsfolk were peasant supporters and opened the gates and towers to the peasants and let them in.

Then Lucifer and all his angels were let loose; for they raged and stormed no differently than if they were mad and possessed by every devil. First they seized the count, then the nobility and the cavalry, and some were stabbed as they resisted. Dietrich von Weiler fled into the church tower, and as he called down to the peasants for mercy, offering them money, someone fired a shot up at him and hit him, then climbed up and threw him out of the window. They then led lord Ludwig, Count of Helfenstein . . . to a field in the direction of Heilbronn and with him thirteen nobles, among whom were two ensigns, Rudolf von Eltershofen and Pleickhart von Ruchzingen. There they made a circle and made the well-born and the noble run the gauntlet with their servants, twenty-four persons in all. The count offered to give them a barrel of money if they would let him live, but there was no way out but to die. When the count saw that, he stood stock still until they stabbed him. Rudolf von Eltershofen went into the ring with his arms crossed and gave himself up willingly to death. Thus, all these were driven through by lances contrary to all the rules of war and afterwards dragged out naked and let lie there. May Almighty God have mercy on them and us! After all this, they set alight to the castle and burnt it, and then marched off to Würzburg.

5.15 Müntzer to the People of Allstedt (1525)
Matheson 1988: 140–2

Even if there are only three of you whose trust in God is unperturbable and who seek his name and honor alone, you need have no fear of a hundred thousand. So go to it, go to it, go to it! The time has come, the evil-doers are running like scared dogs! Alert the brothers, so that they may be at peace, and testify to their conversion. It is absolutely crucial – absolutely necessary! Go to it, go to it, go to it! Show no pity, . . . Pay no attention to the cries of the godless. They will entreat you ever so warmly, they will whimper and wheedle like children. Show no pity, as God has commanded in the words of Moses, Deuteronomy 7; and he has revealed the same thing to us too. Alert the villages and towns and especially the mineworkers and other good fellows who will be of use. We cannot slumber any longer. . . .

Go to it, go to it, while the fire is hot! Don't let your sword grow cold, don't let it hang down limply! Hammer away ding-dong on the anvils of Nimrod, cast down their tower to the ground! As long as they live it is impossible for you to rid yourselves of the fear of men. One cannot say anything to you about God as long as they rule over you. Go to it, go to it, while it is day! God goes before you; follow, follow! . . .

Thomas Müntzer, a servant of God against the godless.

5.16 Müntzer's Revolutionary "Ring of Justice" in the Camp of the Frankenhausen Army
Scott & Scribner 1994: 239

At that time [during the camp at Frankenhausen] Matern von Gehofen, Georg Buchner, and the Rev. Steffan Hartenstein appeared at Artern as emissaries of count Ernst von Mansfeld. They ordered the town gates, which were shut, to be opened. Thereupon the citizens of Artern opened the gates and admitted the emissaries in [apparent] good faith. Immediately, however, they shut the gates once more and cruelly captured and bound the emissaries, and led them with the booty out of Artern. In the field they held common counsel whether to execute the prisoners there and then, seeing that they had the hangman with them, but put off a decision and brought them instead to Frankenhausen, where they were held captive. When Thomas Müntzer arrived here in Frankenhausen and called a common assembly in the square by the gate, the said prisoners were brought into the ring and presented. In the presence of the entire troop – several thousand men – Müntzer publicly enquired whether anyone had charges to lay against them. At that a person from the said district [Artern] . . . stepped forward to interrogate Matern von Gehofen by torture, while . . . [another person] from Artern did likewise to the Rev. Steffan Hartenstein. We citizens of Frankenhausen approached Müntzer to beg him not to execute the prisoners. . . . But the interrogation of the prisoners by torture was so cruel, so swift and intense that as a result they were beheaded with the sword.

5.17 Luther: *Against the Robbing and Murdering Hordes of Peasants* (1525)
LW 46: 49–50, 52

In my earlier book on this matter [*Admonition to Peace*], I did not venture to judge the peasants, since they had offered to be corrected and to be instructed; . . . But before I could even inspect the situation, they forgot their promise and violently took matters into their own hands and are robbing and raging like mad dogs. . . .

[T]hey are starting a rebellion, and are violently robbing and plundering monasteries and castles which are not theirs; by this they have doubly deserved death in body and soul as highwaymen and murderers. . . . [I]f a man is in open rebellion, everyone is both his judge and his executioner; just as when a fire starts, the first man who can put it out is the best man to do the job. For rebellion is not just simple murder; it is like a great fire, which attacks and devastates a whole land. Thus rebellion brings with it a land filled with murder and bloodshed; it makes widows and orphans, and turns everything upside down, like the worst disaster. Therefore let everyone who can, smite, slay, and stab, secretly or openly, remembering that nothing can be more poisonous, hurtful, or devilish than a rebel. It is just as when one must kill a mad dog; if you do not strike him, he will strike you, and a whole land with you. . . .

I will not oppose a ruler who, even though he does not tolerate the gospel, will smite and punish these peasants without first offering to submit the case to judgment. He is within his rights, since the peasants are not contending any longer for the gospel, but have become faithless, perjured, disobedient, rebellious murderers, robbers, and blasphemers, whom even a heathen ruler has the right and authority to punish.

5.18 Luther: *An Open Letter on the Harsh Book Against the Peasants* (1525)
LW 46: 63, 65, 67, 73, 80, 81

I have been obliged to answer your letter in a printed book because the little book that I published against the peasants has given rise to so many complaints and questions, as though it were un-Christian and too hard. . . .

If they think this answer is too harsh, and that this is talking violence and only shutting men's mouths, I reply, "That is right." A rebel is not worth rational arguments, for he does not accept them. You have to answer people like that with a fist, . . .

My good friends, you praise mercy so highly because the peasants are beaten; why did you not praise it when the peasants were raging, smiting, robbing, burning, and plundering in ways that are terrible to see or even to hear about? Why were they not merciful to the princes and lords, whom they wanted to exterminate completely? . . .

All my words were directed against the obdurate, hardened, blinded peasants, who would neither see nor hear, as anyone may see who reads them; and yet you say that I advocate the merciless slaughter of the poor captured peasants. If you are going to read books this way and interpret them as you please, what book will have any chance with you? . . .

My little book was not written against ordinary evildoers, but against rebels. You must make a very, very great distinction between a rebel and a thief, or a murderer, or any other kind of evildoer. A murderer or evildoer lets the head of the government alone and attacks only the members or their property; indeed, he fears the ruler. So long as the head remains, no one ought to attack such a murderer, because the head can punish. Everyone ought to await the judgment and command of the head, to whom God has committed the sword and the office of punishment. But a rebel attacks the head himself and interferes with the exercise of his sword and his office, and therefore his crime is not to be compared with that of a murderer. We cannot wait until the head gives commands and passes judgment, for the head himself is captured and beaten and cannot give them. Rather, everyone who can must run, uncalled and unbidden, and, as a true member, help to rescue his head by stabbing, hewing, and killing, and risk his life and goods for the sake of the head. . . .

Rebellion is no joke, and there is no evil deed on earth that compares with it. Other wicked deeds are single acts; rebellion is a flood of all wickedness . . . .

5.19 The Account of Hans Hut (1527)
Scott & Scribner 1994: 290

On 26 November 1527, Hans Hut confessed without torture. . . .

On the Sunday [May 14] before the day on which the peasants were defeated, Müntzer preached publicly in Frankenhausen: the lord God Almighty would now purify the world; he had taken power from the rulers and given it to their subjects, whereupon the rulers would tremble. In their infirmity the rulers would beg them [for mercy], but they should not be trusted for they would not keep faith with [their subjects]. God was on the subjects' side, for the peasants had painted a rainbow on every banner which they displayed, to which Müntzer explained: that (meaning the rainbow) is the [sign of the] League of God. After three days preaching to that effect, a rainbow appeared in the sky around the sun. Müntzer pointed to the rainbow, declaring to the peasants: you see now the rainbow, the league, the sign that God is on your side. You must fight valiantly and be bold! He, Hut, also saw the rainbow at that moment.

5.20 Johann Rühl, Mansfeld Councillor, to Martin Luther (1525)
Scott & Scribner 1994: 292

As the first shots were fired, which fell short, he [Müntzer] cried: "I told you, no shots will harm you." But the other shots reached their target. Then those who could ran towards the town. Müntzer hid himself, got into a house near the gate, took off his robe, and laid himself on a bed. A Saxon nobleman, Otto von Noppe, came into the house to take lodgings and one of his servants went upstairs, saw the person in bed, called out for his Junker, and asked, "Who's lying there? Who are you?" He said: "Ah! I'm a poor sick man." Then his bag was found in the course of the usual search, and in it the letter that count Albrecht had written to the camp. And he [von Noppe] said: "Whence do you have this letter? I suppose you are the priest?" He denied it at first, and then he admitted it, and was taken away and brought to duke George. . . .

Be it as it will with him, yet it is held by many who are favorable to you that you allowed them [the peasants] to be slain without pity by the tyrants, and that they can thereby become martyrs. It is said publicly in Leipzig that because the elector [Frederick the Wise] has died, you are afraid for your skin and play the hypocrite to duke George by approving of his deeds. I pass no verdict on that, however, but commend myself to your spirit, for I know the saying [in Latin]: Whoever takes up the sword will perish by the sword, and consequently that the authorities bear the sword as avengers [see Rom. 13:4]. It will be necessary in the course of time to underline this and you will be excused, for the innocent should always remained undamned.

5.21 Aftermath of the Peasants' War: Report of the Bernese Chronicler, Valerius Anshelm
Scott & Scribner 1994: 302–3

After this rebellious war was repressed and the hated peasants were once again in harness, with considerable bloodshed and more than 130,000 peasants slain in Upper Germany alone (among whom there were a number of citizens and nobles who had been forced to join the peasants), there was also such devastation that there was a great and lasting rise in the prices in all things, especially meat. This was followed by pestilence, so that the yoked peasants, having sweated [from their labors], now had to endure the cold sweat of death or prolonged sickness [i.e., the "sweating sickness"]. For a rough and tyrannical action they had to pay a rough and tyrannical price, for the lords, having gained their victory, became more ungracious and unjust than before. Those [nobles] who, out of fear and helplessness, had left their subjects without protection, and those – although few – who previously had shown grace and virtue, were now moved to more harshness, thinking that the ass would be kept in check and tamed with a tighter girdle and sharper bit. . . .

Over and above all this, all the articles which the peasants had initially demanded were not only rejected, but they were enforced with strict prohibitions and relentless punishments. In sum, what the peasants and their supporters undertook, namely, to free the Gospel and themselves through rebellion, was itself overthrown by rebellion, so that evangelical teaching and preaching were accused under the names of Luther, Zwingli, and the Anabaptists of being "evan-hellical" and rebellious. [The Gospel] was hated and shunned and in many places rooted out with severe destruction of life and property, or its introduction was prohibited under pain of such punishment. And so it was that the burdened peasantry had slipped their cart traces, but were now bound to the wagon with chains. This rebellious history should give an eternal example and an adequate warning to avoid rebellion and act with reason.

5.22 The Consequences of Luther's Stance during the Peasants' War: Hermann Mühlpfort, Mayor of Zwickau, to Stephan Roth at Wittenberg (1525)
Scott & Scribner 1994: 322–4

God be praised, there is peace in and around the city of Zwickau. God help us with his grace. Doctor Martin has fallen into great disfavor with the common people, also with both learned and unlearned; his writing is regarded as having been too fickle.

I am greatly moved to write to you about this, for the pastor [Nikolaus Hausmann] and the preachers here have been greatly disconcerted and amazed by the tracts recently issued, since one is clearly contrary to the other. . . .

It is true, as Martin writes, that rebellion should be put down, and it is entirely fitting that secular authority should punish, though they do it without being asked; but, contrary to his first tract, he conceded too much to one side – indeed, far too much, for the poor were to be strangled. I find that incomprehensible. I know what is happening in towns and villages, such that one should complain to God in heaven. . . .

What has moved me to write to you, besides Martin's rash tract, is that poverty has been so much forgotten. I also believe that my pious, Christian territorial princes, young and old, who were certainly innocent of this rebellion and of the bloodshed, could have averted rebellion in their lands if they had exercised control over the nobility, for they have always avoided shedding blood and have not ceased to protect the pious from the wicked. But I fear there will be more disobedience . . . I fear truly that more violence will erupt and the nobility will increase their arrogance further. There is such boasting and thumping. . . .

Oh God, if only the princes had followed Martin's advice and allowed some commissioners from the nobles and the towns to negotiate in God's name. . . .

6

The Swiss Connection: Zwingli and the Reformation in Zurich

Oswald Myconius initiated the Zurich invitation to Zwingli to become people's priest that prompted the enquiry about Zwingli's conduct (6.1). Led by Zwingli's preaching and backed by the town council (6.2), Zurich began emancipating itself from the power of its bishop, the Bishop of Constance, Hugo von Hohenlandenberg. At this point, the papacy was still more interested in procuring Swiss mercenaries (6.3) than in potential heresy in Zurich. Emboldened by Zwingli's preaching, some citizens, including the publisher Christopher Froschauer, broke the Lenten fast on Ash Wednesday in 1522 and had to appear before the town council (6.4–5). Zwingli supported the fast-breakers on the basis that practices lacking biblical support were not obligatory (6.6). His sermon influenced city magistrates to refrain from punishing Froschauer and to repeal the ordinance on Lenten fasting the following year. The next items on the reform agenda included repeal of mandatory clerical celibacy (6.7) and reform of the Great Minster (6.8), including a reform of the Latin school that introduced "prophesy" (cf. I Cor. 14:26–33), multi-lingual biblical study (6.9). The practice of "prophesy" was taken up in numerous Reformed areas throughout Europe. The town council decided Zwingli should write a summary of Christian doctrine (6.10) to instruct the pastors and the people in the faith and the reform of church practice. This first official statement of the Zurich Reformation was sent to the University of Basel, and the bishops of Constance, Chur, and Basel. Since there was no response by the deadline of May 1524, the council approved a systematic removal of images (6.11) and regulation of worship (6.12). Zwingli also clarified his relationship to Luther and to Scripture (6.13–14) as he prepared the Sixty-Seven Articles (6.15) for a public debate on reform called by the Zurich City Council. The debate (6.16) was attended by 600 people, including the Vicar of the Bishop of Constance, Fabri. The enthusiastic approval of Zwingli's teachings, and a magisterial order that they be enjoined upon all the priests of the canton, marks the official beginning of the Reformation in German Switzerland. The Lord's Supper, however,

The European Reformations Sourcebook, Second Edition. Edited by Carter Lindberg.
© 2014 John Wiley & Sons, Ltd. Published 2014 by John Wiley & Sons, Ltd.

remained a neuralgic point among the Reformers. All the Reformers rejected the medieval doctrine of transubstantiation (6.17–18), but their disagreement over eucharistic theology became the church-dividing issue between Luther on the one hand and Karlstadt, Hoen, and Zwingli on the other (6.19–23). Karlstadt's *Dialogue* continued the spiritualist attack on the externalization of worship that he began with his attack on images (3.19). Zwingli knew Karlstadt's idiosyncratic interpretation of Luke 22:19 ("This is my body"), but was more influenced by John 6:63 ("It is the spirit that gives life, the flesh is of no avail") and Hoen's symbolism. The Lord's Supper, the sacrament of communion and unity, became a major cause of disunity (cf. also 9.13–14). One consequence of this theological conflict was the loss of support for reform, especially among Humanists such as Erasmus and Willibald Pirckheimer, brother of Caritas, who placed reform of conduct and morality above reform of doctrine (6.24–25)

6.1 Zwingli's Invitation to Zurich (1518)
Potter 1978: 10–12

Myconius to Zwingli, 3 December 1518: You have friends here, and you have carping critics as well, not many of the latter while the former are numerous and good – there is no one that does not praise your scholarship to the heavens. . . . After I had extolled your uprightness, honesty and chastity . . . he [Canon Conrad Hofmann] left me thoroughly content, you can be sure. Three days later he came back to me and burst out as follows: "You recently specially commended Zwingli to me for his chastity, which pleased me well, but just now there has been some one with me who alleges that an official has recently brought an action against him for seducing his daughter. Please tell me if this is true."

Zwingli: [Myconius] has written to me that a rumor has been spread in Zurich about me, alleging that I have seduced the daughter of a high official, and that this has given offence to a number of my friends. I must answer this calumny so that you, dear friend, and others, can clear my life from these false rumors. . . . First, you know that three years ago I made a firm resolution not to interfere with any female: St Paul said it was good not to touch a woman. That did not turn out very well. . . .

As to the charge of seduction I needn't take long in dealing with that. They make it out to concern the daughter of an important citizen. . . . No one doubts that the lady concerned is the barber's daughter except possibly the barber himself who has often accused his wife, the girl's mother, a supposedly true and faithful wife, of adultery, blatant but not true. At any rate he has turned the girl, about whom all this fuss is being made, out from his house and for two years has given her neither board nor lodging. So what is the daughter of such a man to me? . . .

Further, feelings of shame have so far restrained me that when I was still in Glarus and let myself fall into temptation in this regard a little, I did so so quietly that even my friends hardly knew about it.

And now we will come to the matter before us and I will cast off what they call the last anchor taking no account of public opinion which takes a poor view of open resort to loose women. In this instance it was a case of maiden by day, matron by night, and not so much of the maiden by day but everybody in Einsiedeln knew about her . . . no one in Einsiedeln thought I had corrupted a maiden.

6.2 Mandate of the Zurich Mayor and Council for Scriptural Preaching (1520)
Kidd 1911: 385

That they all and generally preach in freedom (as is also granted by the papal laws) the holy Gospels and Epistles of the Apostles conformably with the word of God, and the true divine Scriptures of the Old and New Testament, and that they teach that which they receive and hold from the said Scriptures, and say nothing of other accidental innovations and rules.

6.3 Heinrich Bullinger: Account of Zwingli's Preaching Against Mercenary Service in 1521
Kidd 1911: 385

Zwingli preached at this time very earnestly against taking money [i.e., against mercenary service], saying that it would break up and disturb the pious Confederation. He spoke also against unions [treaties] with princes and lords. . . . Therefore, no one should enter into any unions; and if God helps a people out of unions, they should avoid entering into them again; for they cost much blood. "And I wish," said he, Zwingli, "that they had made a hole in [i.e., repudiated] the union with the Pope, and had given his messenger something to carry home on his back." He said also that one would be aroused about a voracious wolf, but they do not offer protection from the wolves which destroy men. They may well [aptly] wear red hats and mantles; for if one should shake them, ducats and crowns would fall out; if one should wring them, there would run from them his son's, brother's, father's, and good friends' blood.

6.4 The Affair of the Sausages
Kidd 1911: 390–1

Inquiry as to who had been eating flesh and eggs in Lent.

1 (a). Elsi Flammer, maidservant of the printer in the Niederdorf, said she had by her master's orders cooked some sausages on Ash Wednesday, and that the people's priest [Leo Jud] of Einsiedeln, Bartholomew Pur, and Michael Hirt, had eaten of them. Afterwards several vinedressers of her master's had eaten of this flesh. . . .

(c). Bartholomew Pur, the baker, said : On Ash Wednesday he and Master Ulrich [Zwingli], people's priest at the Great Minster, Master Leo Jud, people's priest at Einsiedeln, Master Laurence [Keller], parson of Egg, Henry Aberli, Michael Hirt the baker, Conrad Luchsinger, and Conrad Escher, were in the kitchen of the printer's [Froschauer's] house, and the printer produced two dried sausages. They cut them up and each had a little bit. All ate of them, except Master Ulrich Zwingli. . . .

6.5 Christopher Froschauer's Defense (1522)
Kidd 1911: 391–2

In the first place, prudent, gracious, pious and dear Lords, as it has come to your knowledge that I have eaten flesh in my house, I plead guilty, and in the following wise: I have so much work on hand, and it is costing me so much in body, goods, and work, that I have to get on and work at it day and night, holy day and work-a-day, so that I may get it ready by Frankfurt Fair. The work is the epistles of St. Paul. . . . Next, on further reflection, I find that the Almighty and gracious God has visited us and illuminated us with the light of the truth, i.e. with God's Word, which we must truly believe if we are to become really blessed; . . . and further, we must direct our lives and actions by the rule of the Gospel, else we are not Christians. . . . I have such confidence in you, my Lords, as to say that, if the Spiritualty [i.e., Bishop] put us under penalties, and it is neither against God nor holy Scripture, you will protect and defend us in our godly rights. But if you, my Lords, charge yourselves with the affair and put me under penalties, then I have nothing against it, though I have not offended either against you or against God with my eating of flesh.

6.6 Zwingli: *Concerning Choice and Liberty Respecting Food – Concerning Offense and Vexation – Whether Anyone Has Power to Forbid Foods at Certain Times – Opinion of Huldreich Zwingli* (1522)
Jackson 1987: 73, 110–12

First, Christ says, Matthew 15:17, "What goes in the mouth defiles not the man," etc. . . . These words of Christ, Mark speaks still more clearly, 7:15: "There is nothing outside a man, which by going into him can defile him; but the things which come out of a man are what defile him." So the meaning of Christ is, all foods are alike as far as defilement goes: they cannot defile at all. . . .

[Zwingli concludes his argument for Christian freedom in a series of statements.]

1. The general gathering of Christians may accept for themselves fasts and abstinence from foods, but not set these up as a common and everlasting law.
11. If he is to be cursed who preaches beyond what Paul preached, and if Paul nowhere preached the choice of a food, then he who dares command this must be worthy of a curse.
12. If we are not bound by any law but the law of love, and if freedom as to food injures not the love of one's neighbor, in case this freedom is rightly taught and understood, then we are not subject to this commandment or law.
13. If Paul command us to remain in the liberty of Christ, why do you command me to depart from it? Indeed, you would force me from it.
16. Finally, God spake to Peter, Acts 10:15: "What God has cleansed, you must not call common." And the Sabbath is subject to us, not we to the Sabbath, . . .

These points have forced me to think that the church officers have not only no power to command such things, but if they command them, they sin greatly; . . .

6.7 Petition of Certain Preachers of Switzerland to the Most Reverend Lord Hugo, Bishop of Constance, That He Will Not Suffer Himself to be Persuaded to Make Any Proclamation to the Injury of the Gospel, Nor Endure Longer the Scandal of Harlotry, But Allow the Priests to Marry Wives or at Least Would Wink at Their Marriages (1522)
Jackson 1987: 150, 156–9, 162, 164

We think that your most Reverend Fatherhood is not unaware how unsuccessfully and scantily the prescriptions in regard to chastity that have come down to our times from our predecessors have been kept by the general run of priests. . . .

We, then, having tried with little enough success alas! to obey the law . . . have discovered that the gift [of celibacy] has been denied unto us, and we have meditated long within ourselves how we might remedy our ill-starred attempts at chastity. And turning the matter over on all sides, we found nothing encouraging or propitious until we began to chew the cuds, as it were, like the cattle, over those words of Christ just quoted [Matt. 19:10–12]. . . . [Then] we found that the whole question was far easier than we had thought. For when he says, "All men cannot receive this saying," and again, "He that is able to receive it, let him receive it," he prescribes no punishment for them that cannot receive it. . . . Therefore our souls which had been nigh unto despair were mightily refreshed when we learned those who were unable to receive the saying were threatened with no punishment by him who can send both body and soul into hell. . . .

Hence we beseech your mercy, wisdom, and learning, illustrious Leader, to show yourself the first to lay hold upon the glory of taking the lead over all the bishops of Germany in right thinking upon Christianity, . . . and while others continue to thrust ill-feigned chastity upon the unfortunate general body of our fellow bishops, do you suffer those who are consumed with passion to marry wives, since this, as has been shown, will be lawful according to Christ and according to the laws of men. . . .

Influenced then by these passages we are at length persuaded that it is far more desirable if we marry wives, that Christ's little ones may not be offended, than if with bold brow we continue rioting in fornication. . . . [W]e think you are brave enough to do right. . . . And in fact you will have to refrain at least from interfering. For there is a report that most of the ecclesiastics have already chosen wives, not only among our Swiss, but among all peoples everywhere, and to put this down will certainly be not only beyond your strength but beyond that of one far more mighty, if you will pardon our saying so. Accordingly, scorn us not. . . .

6.8 Ordinance for Reform of the Great Minster (1523)
Kidd 1911: 425–7

1. First, inasmuch as divers troubles have arisen by reason of the clergy making overcharge, in the matter of tithes, fees, and burdens, whereof the ordinary man complains, the Provost and Chapter hereby agree to surrender all their church-dues at the

Great Minster, . . . Further, they agree that, at the Great Minster, no one shall be required to pay for baptism, for the administration of the sacraments, for spiritual advice, or for a grave-space, without a gravestone; though, if any one wishes to have a gravestone, he must pay for it. No one is to be required to set up candles at a funeral; though if any one wishes to stick them up, he must be at charges for them. And if any one wishes to have the bells tolled for the departed in the Minster only, then he need not pay; but, if in the Minster and in other churches as well, then he must pay the fee as hitherto. . . .

4. Further, it is thought good that the number of priests and clergy be reduced, so far as can be done with a good conscience, until no more persons remain than suffice for the preaching of God's Word and other Christian purposes. . . .

5. Further . . . it is resolved that well-learned, able, and honest men be appointed to give public lectures day by day in Holy Scripture, for an hour in the Hebrew, an hour in the Greek, and an hour in the Latin tongue, as is necessary for the right understanding of divine Scripture. . . .

7. Further, a schoolmaster shall be more liberally paid than hitherto, to diligently teach young boys . . . so that they shall not go to foreign places for school and learning . . . and a suitable dwelling-house shall be built for him.

12. And so soon as the prebends, offices, and arrangements aforementioned shall be honestly provided, any surplus of tithes, rents, and revenues shall be devoted to the relief of the needy in the hospital and of poor people at home. . . .

6.9 Institution of the Prophesy in Zurich
Junghans 1967: 271–2

As before under the papacy the hours of prime, terce, sext, and none were read and sung in the choir, we have resolved to read in their place at 8 AM in the choir . . . the holy biblical Scriptures in their original languages in order to gain true, good Christian understanding. This has been arranged by Zwingli in an orderly manner. All the pastors, preachers, canons, chaplains, and advanced students are to assemble and sit in the choir of the Great Minster. [The first meeting was on July 19, 1525.] Master Ulrich Zwingli opened with prayer . . . Then a student read the text . . . It was read in Latin, as the Bible was then translated into Latin. Then the Bible began to be read from the beginning, proceeding every day through the whole year except for Sunday and Friday [Market Day]. And when all the books of the Old Testament were completed, the Bible reading began again from the beginning. In these readings nothing but the Old Testament was read. After the student read the Latin text, Jacobus Ceporinus stood up and read the same text in Hebrew, the original language in which the Old Testament was written, and then explained the Hebrew text in Latin. After that, Zwingli read the same text in Greek from the Septuagint, and also explained it in Latin. He thus expounded the right understanding and use of the text. Finally, a preacher presented in German what had been taught, with a related prayer.

6.10 Zwingli: "Short Christian Instruction" (1523)
Pipkin 1984: 64–6, 68, 70–5

Now we have two salvations from the law: one is from the ceremonies, that is, external things or empty church performances. The other is from the punishment of our misdeeds. . . .

[W]e Christians are also free from all those laws imposed on us for the purpose of making us pious or good. Herein belong all the papal laws not grounded on the word of God: prohibition of foods, commands to chastity, vows, auricular confession, sacrifices, financial payments, indulgences and the whole worthless business. We are also free from humanly devised teachings devised by men, such as intercessions to the saints, purgatory, images, church decorations, ordering masses, the purchase of vigils and other things, etc.; for they are not based on the word of God. The foundation of everything is the sole word of Christ. . . . Finally, on the pretext that they are Christians, some want to exempt themselves from obedience to true government which we call the temporal. They are the worst enemies of the teachings of God. . . . However, a government shall command nothing that is against the honor of God and his word. . . .

Concerning images: it is reasonable for everyone to teach, as has been found, that images are forbidden by God – so that, after they have been instructed and strengthened, the unlearned and weak ones may soon accept what should be done with the images. . . .

[T]he images and the paintings which we have in the churches, . . . have created the danger of idolatry. Therefore, one should not leave them there any longer. . . .

If one wants to speak of the mass, one should first point out, so as not to offend anyone, that none of us wants to abolish or belittle the body and blood of Christ, or to teach that it is nothing – but that mass has a different purpose from that of eating and drinking the body and blood of Christ. . . .

However the claim of the priesthood to sacrifice Christ for other people has been invented in themselves without foundation in the word of God. As a result there arise two serious blasphemies of God – and two big sins.

The first blasphemy of God is that through it the great value and treasure of the sufferings of Christ is obscured. . . . For if we believe that he, once sacrificed, has redeemed and paid for eternity for us, that is, the believers, then it must be a blasphemy to undertake it again, just as if it has not previously been accomplished.

The other blasphemy and abomination consists in that no one can sacrifice anything higher than himself, . . . And, therefore, whoever calls himself a sacrificer takes Christ's honor away from him and gives it to himself. . . .

The two sins are these:

The first is that the wrong understanding of sacrifice has planted and encouraged all vices. For all robbers, usurers, traitors, murderers, and adulterers have believed that their matter becomes right if they let a mass be said for their misdeeds. . . .

The other sin is that one has collected so much temporal good with the mass and has taken it for the fabricated sacrifice. Even if it were a sacrifice it would still be an abomination to take money and rewards of temporal goods for it. . . .

If we now see that the mass is no special establishment of Christ, but considered by human beings as a sacrifice (where, nevertheless, this sacrament is nothing but the eating and drinking of the body and blood of Christ) then it should be a concern for all persons that such misuse will be abolished where one pretends to perform a sacrifice for others – nevertheless, with such discretion and prudence that a riot does not occur because of it. . . . For, in short, when Almighty God reveals his word, then people must see that they comply with it, or they will invite the wrath of God on themselves.

6.11 Removal of Relics and Organs (1524)
Kidd 1911: 442–3

At the Great Minster in Zurich were shrines . . . of the blessed martyrs Felix and Regula. And as the common people were for it, the bodies of the blessed martyrs were kept and buried therein. But the honorable Council and the Citizens also ordered at this time, in June, that they should be put thence and out of the church; and, should there be any corpses therein, they should be honorably interred, or secretly dispersed in the bone house. . . .

At this time, also the magistrates at Zurich ordered. that there should be no more playing of organs [the organ in the Great Minster was broken to pieces on December 9, 1527] in the city and in the churches, no ringing for the dead, and for and against the weather; no more blessing of palms, salt, water, and candles; and no more bringing to any one of the last baptism or extreme unction; but that all such superstitions should cease and be clean put away, inasmuch as they are all at variance with the clear word of God.

6.12 The Council's Mandate for Church-Going (1531)
Kidd 1911: 450

Whereas the mandate for Church-going put out last year [March 26], 1530, has been badly observed; and people, young and old, men and women, idly wander about hither and thither during sermon-time, on the bridges, down the alleys, by the gates and alongside the moats; therefore our Lords . . . earnestly command that every man shall strictly observe the mandate to go to Church on Sundays and Holy-days. And that no man may be able to fraudulently say that he went to another church, it is provided that henceforth the preachers in all the three churches shall begin to preach at one and the same time, convenient to all.

Our Lords further give notice hereby to the numbers of those who are free and well-off that on work-days they frequent the prayers and preaching more diligently and better. They have ordered, and it will henceforth be the rule, that the morning sermon shall take place every day, as hitherto, and that at 8 a.m. for half-an-hour there shall be a discourse and prayer.

6.13 Zwingli's View of Luther
Quellenbuch 1966: 99

What equipped me to preach the gospel and (in 1519 in Zurich) to preach on an entire Gospel (Matthew) one lesson after another? Has Luther done this? I however had begun to preach the gospel before I heard Luther anywhere be named, and for this purpose I began to learn Greek ten years ago so that I might learn the teachings of Christ from their own source. Others may judge the extent to which I accomplished this, however Luther, whose name was still unknown to me for two years, did not instruct me, since I was bound to the biblical writings alone. . . . But the papists say: But you must indeed be a follower of Luther because you preach just like Luther writes. I answered them: I preach just as Paul writes, why do you not then call me a follower of Paul? Indeed, I preach the Word of Christ; why do you not call me a Christian? Therefore this is nothing but a deceit. Luther, it strikes me, is an excellent fighter for God who searches through the Scriptures with greater keenness than anyone in the past thousand years. As long as the papacy has existed, no one has come close to his manly, undaunted courage with which he has assailed the pope and Rome. But whose is such a deed? God's or Luther's? Ask Luther himself: I know for sure, he says God's. Why then do you ascribe to others what Luther himself ascribes to God? Further, I will not bear Luther's name because I have read little of his teaching. But what I have read of his writings is in general so well-grounded in God's Word that it would be impossible for a creature to overcome it.

6.14 Zwingli: *Of the Clarity and Certainty of the Word of God* (1522)
Bromiley 1953: 83, 86–8, 92

The word Gospel is the equivalent of good news or tidings which God gives to men in matters of which they are either ignorant or doubtful. . . .

Those who defend the doctrines of men [i.e., the papists] say: [W]e understand the Gospel in a different way. And if there is a conflict between your understanding and ours, someone will have to decide between us and have authority to silence the one who is in error. And this they say in order to subject the interpretation of God's Word to men, thus making it possible to rebuke and suppress the evangelical preachers. . . . Not everything, they say, is told us in the Gospels. There are many good things which are never even thought of in the Gospel. Oh you rascals – you are not instructed or versed in the Gospel, and you pick out verses from it without regard to their context, and wrest them according to your own desire. . . . Here we come upon the canker at the heart of all human systems. And it is this: we want to find support in Scripture for our own view, and so we take that view to Scripture, and if we can find a text which, however artificially, we can relate to it, we do so, and in that way we wrest Scripture in order to make it say what we want it to say. . . .

The will of God is this, that he alone should be the teacher. And I intend to be taught by him and not by men, . . . For it is not for us to sit in judgment on Scripture and divine truth, but to let God do his work in and through it, for it is something which we can learn only of God. Of course, we have to give an account of our understanding of Scripture, but not in such a way that it is forced or wrested according to our own will, but rather so that we are taught by Scripture: and that is my own intention.

6.15 Zwingli: *The Sixty-Seven Articles* (1523)
Noll 1991: 39–46

1. All who say that the gospel is nothing without the confirmation of the church make a mistake and blaspheme God.
2. The sum of the gospel is that our Lord Jesus Christ, true Son of God, has made known to us the will of his heavenly Father, redeemed us from death by his innocence, and reconciled us to God.
3. Therefore, Christ is the only way to salvation for all who have been, who are, and who will be. . . .
8. From this follows, first, that all who live in this head are members and children of God. This is the church or the communion of saints, the bride of Christ, the *ecclesia catholica* [universal church].
16. In the gospel we learn that the teachings and traditions of men are of no use for salvation. . . .
18. Christ, who has once offered himself as a sacrifice, is for eternity a perpetually enduring and efficacious sacrifice for the sins of all believers. Therefore we conclude that the Mass is not a sacrifice but a memorial of the one sacrifice and a seal of redemption that Christ made good for us.
19. Christ is the only Mediator between God and us. . . .
24. Christians are not obligated to do works that God has not commanded. They may eat all foods at all times. From this we learn that decretals regulating cheese and bread are a Roman fraud. . . .
28. Everything that God permits or has not forbidden is proper. From this we learn that marriage is proper for all people.
34. The so-called spiritual estate has no justification in the teaching of Christ for its splendor.
35. But secular authority does have rightful power and is supported from the teaching and action of Christ. . . .
37. To these authorities all Christians are obliged to be obedient, with no exceptions;
38. So long as the authorities do not command anything in opposition to God.
39. Therefore all secular laws should be conformed to the divine will, which is to say, that they should protect the oppressed, even if the oppressed make no complaint. . . .
42. But if rulers act unfaithfully and not according to the guiding principles of Christ, they may be replaced by God.
49. I know of no greater offense than that priests are not allowed to have lawful wives, while they are allowed to pay concubines. What a disgrace!
54. Christ has borne all of our sorrow and labor. Whoever adds works of penance, which belongs to Christ alone, makes a mistake and blasphemes God.
56. Whoever forgives sin only for money is a comrade of Simon and Balaam, and is the true apostle of the devil.
57. The true holy Scripture knows nothing of a purgatory after this life.
62. Scripture recognizes no priests except those who proclaim God's Word. . . .

66. All spiritual leaders should humble themselves, and seek to exalt only the cross of Christ rather than their own purses. . . .
67. If anyone wishes to discuss with me taxes, tithes, unbaptized children, or confirmation, I am ready to provide an answer.

But let no one undertake to argue with sophistry or human wisdom, but let Scripture be the judge (Scripture breathes the Spirit of God), so that you can either find the truth or, if you have found it, hold on to it.

6.16 The First Zurich Disputation (January 23, 1523)
Jackson 1972: 50–8, 79–80

[Fabri:] I say that I shall not undertake to dispute anything here at Zurich. For, as I think, such matters are to be settled by a general Christian assembly of all nations, or by a council of bishops and other scholars as are found at universities. . . . According to my opinion whatever such things one would discuss should be brought before the universities, as at Paris, Cologne or Louvain. (Here all laughed, for Zwingli interrupted by asking: "How about Erfurt? Would not Wittenberg do?" Then the legate said: "No; Luther was too near." . . .).

Then Master Ulrich Zwingli spoke as follows: Pious brothers in Christ, the worthy Lord Vicar seeks so many evasions and subterfuges for the purpose of turning your simplicity from your understanding with artful, rhetorical, evasive words. . . . But we desire to speak of the truth (to find out), whether a man is bound by divine ordinance to keep that which on account of long usage has been set up as law by men. For we of course think (as also the pope's own decree says) that custom should yield to truth. As to claiming that such matters should be settled by a Christian assembly of all nations, or by a council of bishops, etc., I say that here in this room is without doubt a Christian assembly. . . .

Now finally, since reference is made to the judges which my Lord Vicar thinks cannot be found outside the universities, I say that we have here infallible and unprejudiced judges, that is the Holy Writ, which can neither lie nor deceive. These we have present in Hebrew, Greek and Latin tongues; these let us take on both sides as fair and just judges. . . .

Also we have here in our city, God be praised, many learned colleagues who are as sufficiently taught in these three languages as none at the universities just named and mentioned by the Lord Vicar. . . . Here in this room are sitting also doctors of the Holy Writ, doctors of canonical law, many scholars from the universities. They should hear the Scriptures which are referred to, have them read, to see if that is so which they try and pretend to support by divine Scriptures. And as if all that was not sufficient there are in this assembly many Christian hearts, taught doubtless by the Holy Spirit, and possessing such upright understanding, that in accordance with God's spirit they can judge and decide which party produces Scripture on its side, right or wrong, or otherwise does violence to Scripture contrary to proper understanding. . . .

[On the intercession of the saints] Zwingli: We know from the Old and New Testaments of God that our only comforter, redeemer, savior and mediator with God is Jesus Christ, in whom and through whom alone we can obtain grace, help and salvation, and besides from no other being in heaven or on earth.

The Vicar, laughing: I well know that Jesus Christ alone is the comfort, redemption and. salvation of all, and an intercessor and mediator between us and God, his heavenly Father, the highest round [rung] by which alone is an approach to the throne of divine grace and charity, according to Heb. 4:16. Nevertheless one may perhaps attain the highest round by means of the lower. It seems to me the dear saints and the Virgin Mary are not to be despised, since there are few who have not felt the intercession of the Virgin and the saints. I do not care what every one says or believes. I have placed a ladder against heaven; I believe firmly in the intercession of the much-praised queen of heaven, the mother of God, and another may believe or hold what he pleases. . . .

6.17 The Fourth Lateran Council (1215)
Clarkson 1955: 259

Indeed, there is but one universal Church of the faithful outside which no one at all is saved and in which the priest himself, Jesus Christ, is the victim; his body and blood are truly contained in the Sacrament of the Altar under the species of bread and wine, transubstantiated by the divine power – the bread into his body and the wine into his blood – that, for the enacting of the mystery of unity, we may take from his substance as he himself took from our substance. And no one can consecrate this sacrament except a priest who is rightly ordained according to the Church's powers that Jesus Christ gave to the apostles and to their successors. . . .

6.18 The Second Council of Lyons (1274)
Clarkson 1955: 260

Furthermore, the same holy Roman Church holds and teaches that there are seven sacraments of the Church. . . . The same Roman Church consecrates the sacrament of the Eucharist from unleavened bread, and she holds and teaches that in this sacrament the bread is truly transubstantiated into the body of our Lord Jesus Christ, and the wine into his blood.

6.19 Karlstadt: "Dialogue" on the Lord's Supper (1524)
Lindberg 1979: 41, 43–4, 47, 55–6. See also Burnett 2011: 163–204

Speakers: Gemser [a papist; at times a "new papist" of Wittenberg], Victus, and Peter, a layman [represents Karlstadt]. . . .
G. You are troubled about whether Christ is in the sacrament according to his humanity.
V. You guessed it. . . .
G. The priests make the bread nothing, leaving only the form of the bread there, and into this same form in place of the bread, they conform the body of Christ.

V. If I hear correctly it is not *sacramentum*, but rather *fermentum Pharisaeorum* [leaven of the Pharisees]. For the form of the bread remains ever so small and so great, so thick, and in every respect as before, until the priests breathe over it, or blow and cackle like geese. Therefore I ask whether Christ's body, arm, breast, bones, crown of thorns, nails, spear, are in the bread which is smaller than Christ's little finger was?

G. Yes.

V. Must he then shrink himself and crumple together, when the priests blow out such words? . . .

G. One should not question. . . .

P. Dear lords, with your permission, allow me to speak. Do not take it ill of me that I inquire for I understand that you are discussing the body and blood, bread and cup of the Lord Jesus Christ. . . . Dear sirs, speak understandably and in good German, for although I partly understand you, I don't understand you completely. . . .

G. *Touto* is a Greek pronoun which indicates a neuter noun. Now the word *artos*, in Latin *panis* (in German, "bread"), is masculine. Therefore the pronoun *touto* cannot be applied to it. Thus the opinion of those who say that the bread is the body, etc., does not pass examination, for the Greek language does not permit it. It would be equally unsuitable if I said in Latin, *Istud panis est hoc corpus meum*, or in German, "the bread is my body."

P. That's good.

G. It pleases you?

P. Yes indeed; for a long time I could not discover how it might be possible that the bread should become the body of Christ. I have always considered it this way: that Christ pointed to his body and thus said, "This is my body which will be given for you." For Christ did not point to the bread, nor did he say, "The bread is my body which will be given for you." But those who say that the bread is the body speak out of their peculiarities and lies, or at least promote their mischievousness. Listen, Jesus took the bread, and thanked God, and broke it, and gave it to his disciples, and said they should eat it in remembrance of him. And he placed in the middle of his word the origin and manner of his remembrance, namely, that his disciples should remember that he gave his body for them. Paul strongly conveys this meaning. Those speaking otherwise pervert God's Word and are perverted people.

G. Who has taught you this?

P. He whose voice I heard yet did not see; I also knew not how he came and went from me.

G. Who is he?

P. Our father in heaven.

G. Oh, if I also might have learned from him . . .

P. Thus to receive Christ means to accept Christ; that is, heartily and ardently to recognize Christ . . .

G. There you have struck the pope such a box on his ear that his entire countenance is blackened.

P. And all papists too.

G. And even the new papists [e.g., Luther]. But what must we do so that we accept or receive the body of Christ spiritually?

P. We must abandon [ourselves] and must not do anything.

G. That is too severe for me. Tell me, how should we, as you say, worthily receive the bread of the Lord?

He who has a passionate remembrance of the delivered up body of Jesus Christ and desires to prove that externally in the congregation in that he wants to eat the Lord's bread as Christ said, "Do this in memory of me," he is worthy to receive the Lord's bread. He who does not have the right remembrance of Christ is not fit as Christ wants him to be fit. . . .

6.20 Zwingli: "Letter to Matthew Alber Concerning the Lord's Supper" (1524)
Pipkin 1984: 131–2, 135–9, 141

I may not be silent concerning Carlstadt, who seasonably or unseasonably dragged the matter [the Eucharist] suddenly before the attention of the public. . . .

The gist of this matter can easily be gathered from the sixth chapter of John. Do not listen to those [i.e., Luther] who at once cry out, "Christ is not dealing there with this sacrament at all." . . .

What pray, could be said more plainly, clearly, transparently, or briefly than "It is the Spirit who gives life; the flesh profits nothing"? Does not this passage [John 6:63] sufficiently answer all those questions by which with greater curiosity than piety, they now declare that the substance of the bread is transformed into that of the flesh? . . . "The flesh profits nothing." . . . What does profit then? What follows: "The words I speak unto you are spirit and life." What words? "Whoever eats my flesh and drinks my blood has eternal life." [John 6:54] What flesh and what blood? Not that one which has fluids nor that one that has weight, but that which we know in our heart is a pledge of our salvation because it suffered death on the cross for us. These words, I say, believed by us and sunk into the depths of our souls win eternal life, for by faith alone are we justified. [Rom. 5:1] Therefore, the faith which is certain is that Christ crucified is our redemption and salvation. . . .

Carlstadt . . . wants the demonstrative pronoun to be changed so that when it said, "Jesus took bread, blessed and broke it and gave it to his disciples, saying, 'Take and eat; this is my body which is given for you,'" makes the pronoun "this" refer not to the bread, but to Christ himself, in the sense, "Take, eat; for I am going to give this, my body, for you." . . . If anyone approves this view of Carlstadt's, he will not offend me in the least, but I beg him also to consider mine. I think the hinge of the matter is to be found in the very short syllable, namely, in the word "is", the meaning of which is not always given by "is" but sometimes by "signifies." . . .

Put "signifies" for "is" here [words of consecration] and you have, "Take, eat, for this which I bid you do will signify to you or remind you of my body which presently is to be given for you." . . . The meaning of Christ's words becomes perfectly plain to this effect: "This feast signifies or is the symbol by which you will recall that my body, mine, the Son of God, your Lord and Master, was given for you." . . .

What, then, does this eating do? Nothing but make it plain to your brother that you are a member of Christ, and one of these who trust in Christ.

6.21 Zwingli: *Friendly Exegesis, That Is, Exposition of the Matter of the Eucharist, Addressed to Martin Luther by Huldrych Zwingli* (1527)
Pipkin 1984: 282–3, 354–7, 364–6

We make our inference thus: you affirm that the flesh is eaten; we deny it. Therefore, one or the other must be wrong. . . . [W]hat we are at swords' points over is not, as you say, whether he [Christ] said so and so or not, but whether what he said should be understood in one way or another. . . . For the contest is whether Christ meant by these words to set his carnal body before us to be eaten. . . . [T]he question under discussion is whether the words should be tortured into such an unnatural meaning or not. . . .

[Y]ou say a lot of things that I may properly pass by. They are so infantile and unworthy of a great theologian that I should grudge the labor of confuting things that fall as they do of themselves, if I were not afraid that whatever I bypass without answering, you would cry out, "Why did you not answer this point?" . . .

Now catachresis must be considered here. . . . Catachresis is a figure by which the literal and natural signification of anything is applied to a thing to which the literal signification does not belong. . . . This word "is", then, is transferred from its natural signification to one not literally belonging to it, when I point to a statue of Caesar and say, "This is Caesar." For that by which we say that a statue "is" what it is the statue of, is a different kind of "being" from the natural signification of "being" . . .

I followed Hoen of Holland . . . in explaining "is" is used for "signifies", . . . But that simple explanation which anyone could understand pleased me: "This bread signifies my body which is given for you." . . . [T]he point is simply this, that the force of the word "is" undergoes modification and has the value, "is a signification or representation of" . . .

So much for my exposition of my opinion in the matter of the Eucharist, most learned Luther. All your weapons I think either have been wrested from your hands or are on the point of falling from them of themselves . . . Our view is bound to prevail, beyond a doubt, but the victory will be a harder one with your opposition, for it will have to be wrought out with travail, when we should just come upon it with universal rejoicing . . . Remember how much the Lord has wrought for the world through you, all the glory which is dropping away from you because of your obstinate stubbornness in this one matter.

6.22 Luther: *Confession Concerning Christ's Supper* (1528)
LW 37: 171, 218–19

[Y]ou may be sure that it is pure imagination when anyone says that this word "is" means the same as "represents." No man can ever prove that from a single passage of Scripture. . . .

Our faith maintains that Christ is God and man, and the two natures are one person, so that this person may not be divided in two; therefore, he can surely show himself in a corporeal, circumscribed manner at whatever place he will. . . .

And if you could show me one place where God is and not the man, then the person is already divided and I could at once say truthfully, "Here is God who is not man and has never become man." But no God like that for me! For it would follow from this that space and place had separated the two natures from one another and thus had divided the person, even though death and all the devils had been unable to separate and tear them apart.

This would leave me a poor sort of Christ, if he were present only at one single place, as a divine and human person, and if at all other places he had to be nothing more than a mere isolated God and a divine person without the humanity. No, comrade, wherever you place God for me, you must also place the humanity for me. They simply will not let themselves be separated and divided from each other. He has become one person and does not separate the humanity from himself as Master Jack takes off his coat and lays it aside when he goes to bed.

6.23 The Marburg Colloquy and Articles (1529)
Ziegler 1969: 79–82, 85–6, 105

LUTHER.: Your argument comes down to this: Because we have a spiritual repast, a physical one is not needed. I reply that in no way do we deny the spiritual repast, which indeed we consistently teach and believe to be necessary. But from this it cannot be proved that the physical repast is useless or unnecessary. I do not inquire into whether it is necessary or not, for we are not here for this. It is written, "Take, eat, this is my body," and for this reason one must do it and believe it at all costs. One must do this! One must do this! Otherwise I could not be baptized., I could not believe in Christ! In many ways he gives himself to us: in preaching, in baptism, as often as a brother needs consolation, in the sacrament. Again and again the body of Christ is eaten, as he himself has commanded us to do. If he were to command me to eat dung, I would do so, assured that it were good for me. The servant doesn't brood over the wish of his lord. . . .

ZWINGLI: It is a prejudice, a preconception, which keeps Doctor Luther from yielding his point. He refuses to yield until a passage is quoted that proves that the body in the Lord's Supper is figurative. It is the prejudice of a heretic. . . . One cannot reason thus from Scripture! Comparison of scriptural passages is always necessary. Although we have no scriptural passage that says, "This is the sign of the body," we still have proof that Christ dismissed the idea of a physical repast. Since it is our task here to investigate scriptural passages, and since the passage in John 6 moves away from the physical repast, we must therefore take it into account. From this it follows that Christ did not give himself in the Lord's Supper in a physical sense. And finally, you yourself have acknowledged that it is the spiritual repast that offers solace. And since we are agreed on this major question, I beg you for the love of Christ not to burden anyone with the crime of heresy because of these differences. The fathers certainly did not condemn one another in this way when they disagreed. . . .

You spoke of taking the Scriptures literally. Much I agreed with, much I did not because it was perfectly childish, like saying, "If God commanded me to eat dung." The works that God commands are for our well-being. God is truth and light, and he leads us not into the darkness. Consequently he does not mean "This is my body" in a literal, actual, physical sense, which contradicts the Scriptures. It is the oracles of demons that are obscure, not the maxims of Christ. God does not work in this way. The soul is spiritual, the soul does not eat flesh. Spirit eats spirit.

Do not take offense at my words, for I desire your friendship, not the bitterness of your heart. I confront you willingly, Doctor Luther, and you, Master Philip.

LUTHER: I promise to control my feelings in deference to God and our gracious prince and lord. What is past is past. Let us look to the future! If we cannot agree on everything, we can still enter into fellowship – as we shall discuss in conclusion. . . .

If you think that God does not confront us with the incomprehensible, then I cannot agree with you. The virginity of Mary, the forgiveness of sins, and many others like this are incomprehensible – even the words "This is my body." . . .

I call upon you as before: . . . Give way, and give glory to God!

ZWINGLI: And we call upon you to give glory to God and to quit begging the question! The issue at stake is this: Where is the proof of your position? I am willing to consider your words carefully – no harm meant! You're trying to outwit me. I stand by this passage in the sixth chapter of John [verse 63] and shall not be shaken from it. You'll have to sing another tune!

LUTHER: You're being obnoxious! . . . You express yourself poorly and make about as much progress as a cane standing in a corner. You're going nowhere.

ZWINGLI: No, no, no! This is the passage that will break your neck!

LUTHER: Don't be so sure of yourself. Necks don't break this way. You're in Hesse, not Switzerland. . . .

ZWINGLI: You must excuse what I have just said. It is one of the expressions that we use.

LUTHER: Call upon God, that you may receive understanding.

OECOLAMPADIUS: Call upon him yourself, for you need it just as much as we!

6.24 Erasmus to Martin Bucer (1527)
Naphy 1996: 90–1

You have given a number of guesses as to why I have not joined your Church. First and foremost, I want you to know that my conscience has held me back. If I could have been convinced that this movement came from God I would have enlisted long ago. Also I see that there are a number of people in your camp who are completely unknown to Evangelical truth. . . . I knew some people who were excellent before they joined your side; what has become of them since, I do not know. As far as human judgement will allow, it seems to me that many of them have become worse and none have improved.

The third thing which has held me back is the constant in-fighting between the leaders. Leaving aside the Prophets and the Anabaptists, just look at the spiteful pamphlets written by Zwingli, Luther and Osiander against each other. I have always condemned the venom of the leaders but they are egged on by the actions of certain people. In actual fact, if you were what you brag of being, they would have set an example of godly and patient conduct which would have made the Gospel widely acceptable. . . . I am not overly upset with him [Luther] for treating me so badly. However, his betrayal of the Gospel, inciting the princes, bishops, false monks and theologians against good people have made everyone's burden (which is already bad enough) twice as heavy. . . . I foresee a violent and bloody century should those who are angry get their strength back, as they surely will. You can say that every crowd has its unruly elements. But surely it was the responsibility of the leaders to pay special attention to conduct and not even to speak to liars, false-witnesses, drunks, and fornicators. The Gospel would have looked good to everyone if the husband had found it made his wife nicer, if the teacher saw his student more obedient, if the magistrate had seen better-behaved citizens, if the employer found his employees more honest, if the buyer saw the merchant less deceitful. But, as things are now, the conduct of some people has thrown cold water on the enthusiasm of those who initially supported the movement: the sort of people who loved godliness and hated Pharisaism. The princes, some of whom were hopeful at the start, are now cursing as they contemplate the host which has appeared full of vagrants, fugitives, bankrupts, the naked, the destitute, and, primarily, evil people.

6.25 Willibald Pirckheimer: Humanist Disappointment with the Reformation (1530)
Plöse & Vogler 1989: 462–4

I confess that I initially also was a good Lutheran, as was also our blessed Albrecht [Dürer; cf. 2:26], for we hoped the Roman knavery as well as the roguishness of the monks and parsons would be improved. But as one watched and waited, matters got worse. . . .

For without works faith is dead as are also the works without faith. I also know, and it is the truth, that unbelievers do not put up with such roguishness and knavery as those calling themselves evangelicals bear. . . . [Consequences include] neither faith nor trust; there is no fear of God, no love to the neighbor; there is the loss of all honor and good morals, art, and learning; there is the seeking after nothing other than pleasure, honor, property, and money. . . . The giving of alms has disappeared for these knaves have also misused alms so that no one will give anymore. So also with confession and the sacrament, no one or few keep anything of the love of the Lord God. . . .

7

The Radical Reformations

Contemporary accounts of the rise of Anabaptism are polarized between Zwingli's description (7.1) of an irrational fanaticism set to undermine church and society, and an account of the first believers' baptism (7.2). The biblicism of the Radicals became apparent at the Second Zurich Disputation (7.3). Conrad Grebel, Felix Manz, and Balthasar Hubmaier insisted that all reforms required explicit biblical warrant. Since, in their view, infant baptism had no such warrant (7.5–6), it soon became the lightning rod of controversy (7.9). Indeed, believers' baptism in place of infant baptism became the distinguishing mark of Anabaptism, and in turn governed their views of the church, Christian life, and interpretation of the Scriptures. The disturbances which arose in Zurich over images, the mass, and the Christian life parallel those that earlier arose over the same issues in Wittenberg. Anabaptist leaders were not unaware of this as they referred to the works of Karlstadt and Müntzer (7.4). Efforts to counter the Anabaptist movement in Zurich escalated from dialogue to disputation to imprisonment, expulsion, and finally the death penalty (7.7–8, 7.11). One of the issues posed by the Radical Reformers was the relation between civil and church authority. The south German Anabaptist Michael Sattler led a conference at Schleitheim that set forth the pacifist position (7.10). Sattler himself was soon afterward captured, tried, and executed by Austrian Catholic authorities (7.12), increasingly concerned about rebellion (7.13).

From February 1534 to June 1535 Radicals such as Jan Matthys, Jan Bockelson (van Leiden), Bernhard Rothmann, and Bernd Knipperdolling sought to realize by force the New Jerusalem in the city of Münster (7.14). Before Catholic and Evangelical princes retook the city on June 25, 1535, John of Leiden established the rule of the second King David in Münster, and proclaimed that he, King John, would rule the world and slay other rulers. The Twelve Elders of the Tribes of Israel replaced the town council and provided detailed codes for all areas of life (7.15). After obtaining control of the city, they sent out an appeal to those of like mind to come and join them (7.16). Rothmann's booklet appealed to his besieged fellow citizens of the New Jerusalem in

The European Reformations Sourcebook, Second Edition. Edited by Carter Lindberg.
© 2014 John Wiley & Sons, Ltd. Published 2014 by John Wiley & Sons, Ltd.

Münster which had adopted community of goods (7.18) and polygamy (7.19). Rothmann argued (7.20–21), like Müntzer, that the elect must root out the godless, before the end came. Although Rothmann's fate is uncertain, John of Leiden, Knipperdolling, and Krechting were flayed alive and their bodies hung in iron cages on the church tower, where the cages remain (7.22).

7.1 Zwingli: *Refutation of the Tricks of the Baptists* (1527)
Jackson 1972: 131–7, 168, 170–1

This work is called a "Refutation of the Tricks, etc.," because this class of men [Anabaptists] so abounds and works in tricks that I have never seen anything equally oily or changeable. . . . [T]hey deceive not only the simple, but even the elect, . . . For you must know, most pious reader, that their sect arose thus. When their leaders, clearly fanatics, had already determined to drag into carnal liberty the liberty we have in the gospel, they addressed us who administer the word at Zurich first, kindly, indeed, but firmly, . . . They denounced infant baptism tremendously as the chief abomination, proceeding from an evil demon and the Roman pontiff. We met this attack at once, promised an amicable conference. It was appointed for Tuesday of each week. At the first meeting the battle was sharp but without abuse, as we especially took in good part their insults. Let God be the witness and those who were present, as well from their side as from ours. The second was sharper. . . . Within three, or at most four, days it was announced that the leaders of the sect had baptized fifteen brethren. Then we began to perceive why they had determined to collect a new church and had opposed infant baptism so seriously. We warned the church that it could not be maintained, . . . They had attempted a division and partition of the church, and this was just as hypocritical as the superstition of the monks. . . . Then . . . in great swarms they came into the city, unbelted and girded with rope or osiers, and prophesied, as they called it, in the market place and squares. They filled the air with their cries about the old dragon, as they called me, and his heads, as they called the other ministers of the word. They also commended their justice and innocence to all, for they were about to depart. They boasted that already they hold all things in common, and threatened with extremes others unless they do the same. They went through the streets with portentous uproar, crying Woe! Woe! Woe to Zurich. Some imitated Jonah, and gave a truce of forty days to the city. What need of more? I should be more foolish than they were I even to name all their audacity. . . . When the evil had somewhat subsided, so that the majority seemed likely to judge the matter impassively, joint meetings were appointed. . . . In the presence of the church the contest raged for three whole days more, with so great damage to them that there were few who did not see that the wretched people were struggling for the sake of fighting, and not to find the truth. . . . After that conference . . . the senate decreed that he should be drowned who rebaptized another. . . .

So much about their division and betrayal of the church. They have gone out from us, for they were not of us. . . .

In describing their deeds I shall be free and brief. They have their wives common in such a manner as to desert their own marriage partners and take others; so with the children, as to desert them and leave them for others to support. These fine fellows, when lust persuades, make common a brother's wife, even his virgin daughter. Though the very force of nature requires that they cherish their children by the sweat of the body, they make them common to others. . . .

At St. Gall public charges were made against two girls who had been of unblamed modesty until they had gone over to the Catabaptists, but whose modesty had suffered shipwreck when their bodies were immersed in catabaptism. They affirmed that they were betrothed in spiritual marriage, the rings being accepted, and in one night on one couch two Catabaptists had so loosed their virgin belts that the couch, groaning for a long time, at length, impatient of the burden, threw on the floor with one crash the two marriages. Those who heard the downfall swore solemnly that those spirits made such a sound that it appeared as if four bodies had fallen from on high. . . . But who can fittingly tell of the awful murder which a brother perpetrated upon his own brother [Thomas Schinker upon his brother Leonhard] in St. Gall? What ability in words can worthily set forth so great atrocity? Or who is so dull as not to see that God has set forth this example for the good of all, so as the more to deter from this pernicious sect? A brother calls in a brother who is thinking of no such thing into the presence of his father, mother, sisters and the whole family, and orders him to kneel in the midst. The fanatical fellow obeys, thinking his brother is going to show some wonder. Doubtless the parents had the same expectation, . . . But when this one had kneeled, the other seized a sword which he had brought for this purpose, drove it through his neck and cut off his head, which rolled to the feet of his parents, and left him lifeless. From his trunk poured a great quantity of blood. All there fell and became [as] lifeless in madness. The murderer himself shouted: The will of God is fulfilled. Like a madman he came into the city and cried out to the Burgomaster: I announce to you the Day of the Lord. For at that time they were appointing as the day of the Lord that Ascension Sunday that passed two years ago. I cannot jest here at that murderous sect, for the deed was too atrocious to admit any mirth. . . .

7.2 Anabaptism Begins (1525)
Kidd 1911: 454–5

From the Confession of fourteen imprisoned Anabaptists of Zollikon: . . . They admitted that they had been baptized, and had become "servants, bondmen, and subjects of God;" they would do whatever the Spirit of God prompted them, and not suffer themselves to be forced therefrom by any temporal magistrate. So far as they were not hindered by the Word of God, they would be my Lords' subjects. . . . Rudolph Thomunn, of Zollikon, deposed that he had eaten the Last Supper with the old assistant-curate [Brötli?] and the [parson] of Wytikon [William Röubli], and had invited them to his house. . . . There many had assembled, so that the room was full; there was much speaking and long readings. Then stood up Hans Bruggbach of Zumikon, weeping and crying out that he was a great sinner, and asking them to pray God for him. Whereupon Blaurock asked him if he desired the grace of God. "Yes," said he. Manz then stood up and said, "Who will hinder me from baptizing him?" Blaurock answered, "Nobody." So [Manz] took a bowl of water and baptized him in the name of God the Father, God the Son, and God the Holy Ghost. Whereupon James Hottinger stood up and desired baptism; and Felix Manz baptized him also. . . . Seeing the loaf on the table, Blaurock said, "Whosoever believes that God has redeemed him by His death and rosy-colored blood . . . comes and eats with me from this loaf and drinks with me of this wine." Then several ate and drank thereof.

7.3 The Second Zurich Disputation (1523)
Harder 1985: 240–1, 246

Then Dr. Balthasar Fridberger [Hubmaier] arose, saying: Lord Burgomaster and other dear brothers in Christ! Yesterday it became thoroughly clear from Scripture that there should be no images. . . . Thus we find also that God hates not only the adoration which takes place before the images but also the making of the image. Therefore he commands them to be burnt and those who make them, he curses, . . .

Huldrych Zwingli . . . expressed this opinion: Conrad Grebel has demanded of us that we discuss the abuses of the mass. I say therefore: All that is planted and added without being instituted by Christ is a true abuse. But since these things cannot be abolished all at once, it is necessary to preach God's Word against them firmly and courageously. . . .

Likewise concerning the vestments which the priest wears when he administers the mass: Although at first, when I wrote about the canon, I yielded on this point for the sake of the weak in faith, supposing it was a symbol of Christ's suffering, as is further explained in that booklet. I have now been informed differently by several that these vestments are derived from the vestments of the priest in the Old Law, from which there was good reason to consider the mass a sacrifice; therefore I have changed and withdrawn my former opinion.

Since, then, neither chanting nor vestments is of any use except to detract from right, true prayer, which is raising one's spirit to God, these things must be put away and abolished at the proper time so that no uproar or other disunity will arise among Christians. . . . For if anyone were to officiate at a mass at present without the vestments, there would be a disturbance.

Therefore, faithful, elect, dear brethren in Christ Jesus, I urge you for God's sake to take the Word of God in hand and present and preach it to your parishioners with the utmost clarity that they may learn from it what the mass is, and also that one may well have a mass without the vestments. If the people are thus built up, these things can be abolished without tumult. . . .

7.4 Conrad Grebel and Companions to Müntzer (1524)
Matheson 1988: 123, 125–8, 130–2

[Y]our writing against false faith and baptism was brought to us; . . .

[Y]ou – and Karlstadt too – are considered by us to be the purest proclaimers and preachers of the purest divine word. . . .

As far as baptism is concerned your writing pleases us greatly and we would like further information from you. Our information is that without Christ's rules about binding and unbinding not even an adult ought to be baptised. Scripture describes baptism as signifying that sins are washed away by faith and the blood of Christ (converting the heart of the baptised and that of the believer before and after); that it signifies that one is, and should be, dead to sin, walking in newness of life and spirit, and that one will certainly be saved if one lives out the faith as it is signified by the inward baptism; so it is not as if the water strengthens and increases faith, as the Wittenberg scholars say, or is a profound comfort, and one's last refuge on the deathbed. Likewise it is not a means of salvation, as Augustine, Tertullian, Theophylactus and Cyprian have taught, thereby slighting the faith and the suffering of Christ in regard to older adults and slighting the suffering of Christ in regard to the unbaptised little children. . . .

If you should fall into the hands of Luther and the dukes. . . . Be strong! You have the Bible (which Luther makes a bible, bauble, babel) as a defense against the idolatrous Lutheran laxity which he, and the learned pastors here, have planted throughout the world. . . . May God be gracious to you and to us, for our pastors are equally harsh and rage against us, denouncing us publicly from the pulpit as scoundrels and Satans disguised as angels of light. In time we will also see ourselves engulfed by persecution at their hands. . . . But you are far purer than our people here and those in Wittenberg, who slide each day from one distortion of Scripture into another and from one blindness into a still greater one. It is my belief, my firm conviction, that they want to become real papists and popes. Enough for now. May the Lord of hosts with his son Jesus Christ our saviour and his spirit and his word be with you and with us all.

Conrad Grebel, Andreas Castelberg, Felix Manz, Heinrich Aberli, Johann Panicellus, Hans Oggenfuss, Hans Hujuff, your fellow-countryman from Halle; your brothers and, for Luther, seven new little Müntzers. . . .

7.5 Mantz's Petition of Defense, Zurich (1524)
Harder 1985: 311–14

[I]nfant baptism is wrong and false, and has arisen from and been invented by that antichrist, the pope and his adherents, which is true as we know and believe from Holy Writ. . . .

I should have thought that all this would have been clear to you simply from the truth itself, for your shepherds [Zwingli et al.] have often asserted that the Scriptures, to which we are not to add or subtract anything, must be allowed to speak for themselves. Although this was the intention, it was never carried out and we have never been given opportunity to speak, nor has the Scripture been heard, for our speech is cut off in the throat as soon as they suppose that we are about to speak the truth. They interrupt and demand proof from the Scripture although they ought rather to furnish such proof and stand by the truth – God knows that they act thus! They know full well, much better than one could ever demonstrate, that Christ did not teach infant baptism and that the apostles did not practice it, but that, in accord with the true meaning of baptism, only those should be baptized who reform, take on a new life, lay aside sins, are buried with Christ, and rise with him from baptism in newness of life, etc. . . .

The entire New Testament Scripture is full of such passages and their like, from which I have now clearly learned and know for sure that baptism is nothing else than a dying of the old man and a putting on of a new, [that] Christ commanded to baptize those who had been taught, [that] the apostles baptized none except those who had been taught of Christ, and [that] nobody was baptized without external evidence and certain testimony or desire. . . .

7.6 Hubmaier to Oecolampadius on Baptism (1525)
Kidd 1911: 452–3

Baptism, say they [Zwingli and Leo Jud] is a mere sign. Why do we strive so much over a sign? The meaning of this sign and symbol, the pledge of faith until death in hope of the resurrection to the life to come, is more to be considered than the sign. This meaning has nothing to do with babes; therefore infant baptism is without reality. In Baptism a man pledges himself to God; in the Supper to his neighbor, to offer body and blood in his stead, as Christ for us. I believe, yea, I know, that it will not go well with Christendom until Baptism and the Supper are brought back to their own original purity. . . .

7.7 The Zurich Council Orders Infant Baptism, and Silence (1525)
Kidd 1911: 453–4

Whereas an error has arisen respecting baptism, as if young children should not be baptized until they come to years of discretion and know what the faith is; and whereas some have accordingly neglected to have their children baptized, our Lords the Burgomaster, Council, and Great Council, have had a disputation held about this matter to learn what Holy Scripture has to say about it. As they have learned from it that, notwithstanding this error, children should be baptized as soon as they are born, all those therefore who have hitherto allowed their children to remain unbaptized, must have them baptized within the next week: and whosoever will not do this, must with wife and child, goods and chattels, leave our city, jurisdiction, and dominions, or await what will be done with him. . . .

7.8 The Council Orders Anabaptists to Be Drowned (1526)
Kidd 1911: 455

Whereas our Lords the Burgomaster, Council, and Great Council, have for some time past earnestly endeavored to turn the misguided and erring Anabaptists from their errors; and yet several . . . to the injury of the public authority and the magistrates as well as to the ruin of the common welfare and of right Christian living, have proved disobedient; and several of them, men, women, and girls, have been by our Lords sharply punished and put into prison: Now therefore, by the earnest commandment, edict, and warning of our Lords aforesaid, it is ordered that no one in our town, country, or domains, whether man, woman, or girl, shall baptize another; and if any one hereafter shall baptize another, he will be seized by our Lords and, according to the decree now set forth, will be drowned without mercy. . . .

7.9 Zwingli: *Of Baptism* (1525)
Bromiley 1953: 139–41, 153–4, 156–8

[T]he Anabaptists claim that only those who know that they can live without sin ought to receive the sign of baptism. In so doing they make God a liar and bring back the hypocrisy of legal righteousness. . . . [I]s not that the height of presumption? As long as we are in the flesh, we are never without sin. . . .

But the Anabaptists do hold that they live without sin. This is proved by what they and some others write and teach concerning the . . . perseverance of saints. In this they are committed absolutely to the view that they can and do live without sin. How far that claim is borne out by their envy, lying, clamour, evil-speaking, and blasphemy I leave on one side. . . .

Clearly, then, baptism cannot bind us in such a way that we must not accept it unless we know that we can live without sin; for if that be the case, baptism was instituted in vain, for not one of us can claim to do that before God. Therefore we will turn to the Word of God and learn there both what baptism is and when it was instituted. As regards the first question, baptism is a covenant sign which indicates that all those who receive it are willing to amend their lives and to follow Christ. In short, it is an initiation to new life. Baptism is therefore an initiatory sign. . . .

[I]t is not the pouring of water which washes away sin. And that was what we once believed, although without any authority in the Word of God. We also believed that the water of baptism cleanses children from a sin which they never had, and that without it they would be damned. All these beliefs were erroneous, . . . Water-baptism cannot contribute in any way to the washing away of sin. . . . [A]lthough baptism may wash the body – and that is all that water-baptism can do – it cannot take away sin. Sin is taken away only when we have a good conscience before God. But no material thing can purge the conscience, . . . [T]he sacrament can never cleanse the soul, for it is only an external thing. The word which saves the soul is not the word outwardly spoken, but the word inwardly understood and believed. And it is to that water that Christ is here referring, . . . But that water can be none other than Christ himself. . . .

Hence water-baptism is nothing but an external ceremony, that is, an outward sign that we are incorporated and engrafted into the Lord Jesus Christ and pledged to live to him and to follow him. And as in Jesus Christ neither circumcision nor uncircumcision avails anything, but a new creature, the living of a new life (Gal. 6), so it is not baptism which saves us, but a new life. . . . The root of the trouble is that the Anabaptists will not recognize any Christians except themselves or any Church except their own. And that is always the way with sectarians who separate themselves on their own authority. . . . For if every blockhead who had a novel or strange opinion were allowed to gather a sect around him, divisions and sects would become so numerous that the Christian body which we now build up with such difficulty would be broken to pieces in every individual congregation. Therefore no innovations ought to be made except with the common consent of the churches, and not merely of a single church. For the judgment of Scripture is not mine or yours, but the churches. . . .

7.10 The Schleitheim Confession of Faith [Seven Articles] (1527)
Zuck 1975: 72–5

Dear brethren and sisters, we who have been assembled in the Lord at Schleitheim on the Border, make known in points and articles to all who love God that as concerns us we are of one mind to abide in the Lord as God's obedient children, [His] sons and daughters, we who have been and shall be separated from the world in everything, [and] completely at peace. . . .

The articles which we discussed and on which we were of one mind are these: (1) Baptism; (2) The Ban (Excommunication); (3) Breaking of Bread; (4) Separation from the Abomination; (5) Pastors in the Church; (6) The Sword; and (7) The Oath.

First: . . . Baptism shall be given to all those who have learned repentance and amendment of life, and who believe truly that their sins are taken away by Christ, and to all those who walk in the resurrection of Jesus Christ, and wish to be buried with him in death, so that they may be resurrected with him, and to all those who with this significance request it [baptism] of us and demand it for themselves. . . .

Second: . . . The ban shall be employed with all those who have given themselves to the Lord, to walk in his commandments, and with all those who are baptized into the one body of Christ and who are called brethren or sisters, and yet who slip sometimes and fall into error and sin, being inadvertently overtaken. . . .

Third: . . . All those who wish to break one bread in remembrance of the broken body of Christ, and all who wish to drink of one drink as a remembrance of the shed blood of Christ, shall be united beforehand by baptism in one body of Christ which is the Church of God and whose head is Christ. . . .

Fourth: . . . A separation shall be made from the evil and from the wickedness which the devil planted in the world; in this manner, simply that we shall not have fellowship with them [the wicked] and not run with them in the multitude of their abominations. . . .

Fifth: . . . The pastor in the Church of God shall . . . be one who out-and-out has a good report of those who are outside the faith. This office shall be to read, to admonish and teach, to warn, to discipline, to ban in the Church, to lead out in prayer for the advancement of all the brethren and sisters, to lift up the bread when it is to be broken, and in all things to see to the care of the body of Christ, in order that it may be built up and developed, and the mouth of the slanderer be stopped. . . .

Sixth: . . . The sword is ordained of God outside the perfection of Christ. It punishes and puts to death the wicked, and guards and protects the good. . . . In the perfection of Christ, however, only the ban is used for a warning and for the excommunication of the one who has sinned, without putting the flesh to death – simply the warning and the command to sin no more. . . .

Finally it will be observed that it is not appropriate for a Christian to serve as a magistrate. . . .

Seventh. We are agreed as follows concerning the oath: . . . Christ, who teaches the perfection of the Law, prohibits all swearing to his [followers], whether true or false – neither by heaven, nor by the earth, . . .

These are the articles of certain brethren who had heretofore been in error and who had failed to agree in the true understanding, so that many weaker consciences were perplexed, causing the name of God to be greatly slandered. Therefore there has been a great need for us to become of one mind in the Lord, which has come to pass. To God be praise and glory! . . .

7.11 The Banishment of Blaurock and Execution of Mantz
Harder 1985: 474–5

On Saturday, January 5, 1527, the Large and Small Councils of Zurich condemned to death Felix Mantz, the son of Hans Mantz, the canon. And so he was drowned in the afternoon of the same day, about three o'clock, and [they] beat his comrade, Jörg Blaurock, out of the city with rods on the very same day at about four. For Mantz had baptized persons in violation of the prohibition on penalty of death by drowning, and Blaurock had also returned to Milords' jurisdiction against their strict prohibition. And because with their preaching and rebaptism, many people agitated against the government, supposing that no Christian could be a ruler and no one should be put to death. . . . Against this Mantz, also Blaurock and Conrad Grebel, who had died previously, and their many adherents, many of whom lived in Zollikon, Huldrych Zwingli had to dispute often and suffer on account of rebaptism and because they thought that infants should not be baptized but allowed to grow up until they believed and could themselves request baptism. But although he amply defeated them with the Old and New Testaments before about 600 men and in the Grossmünster before men and women, they were still so hardheaded that no one could dissuade them, no matter how long they had to lie in the towers. And Milords had to endure great suffering, trouble, and work with them, for it was a very harmful sect and a rebellion against the government.

7.12 The Trial and Martyrdom of Michael Sattler (1527)
Williams 1957: 138–44

After many legal transactions on the day of his departure from this world, the articles against him being many, Michael Sattler . . . requested that they might once more be read to him and that he might again be heard upon them. . . .

Thereupon Michael Sattler requested permission to confer with his brethren and sisters, which was granted him. Having conferred with them for a little while, he began and undauntedly answered as follows: "In regard to the articles relating to me and my brethren and sisters, hear this brief answer:

"First, that we have acted contrary to the imperial mandate, we do not admit. . . .

"Secondly, that the real body of Christ the Lord is not present in the sacrament, we admit. For the Scripture says: Christ ascended into heaven and sitteth on the right hand of his Heavenly Father. . . . from which it follows that, if he is in heaven and not in the bread, he may not be eaten bodily.

"Thirdly, as to baptism we say infant baptism is of no avail to salvation. For it is written [Rom. 1:17] that we live by faith alone. . . .

"Fourthly, we have not rejected the oil [of extreme unction]. For it is a creature of God, and what God has made is good and not to be refused, but that the pope, bishops, monks, and priests can make it better we do not believe; for the pope never made anything good. . . .

"Fifthly, we have not insulted the mother of God and the saints. . . . But that she is a mediatrix and advocatess – of this the Scriptures know nothing, . . .As regards the saints, we say that we who live and believe are the saints. . . .

"Sixthly, we hold that we are not to swear before the authorities, for the Lord says [Matt. 5:34]: Swear not, but let your communication be, Yea, yea; nay, nay.

"Seventhly, when God called me to testify of his Word and I had read Paul and also considered the unchristian and perilous state in which I was, beholding the pomp, pride, usury, and great whoredom of the monks and priests, I went and took unto me a wife, according to the command of God; for Paul well prophesies concerning this to Timothy [I, 4:3]. . . .

"Eighthly, if the Turks should come, we ought not to resist them. For it is written [Matt. 5:21]: Thou shalt not kill. . . ."

The judge asked Michael Sattler whether he too committed it to the court. He replied: "Ministers of God, I am not sent to judge the Word of God. We are sent to testify and hence cannot consent to any adjudication, since we have no command from God concerning it. But we are not for that reason removed from being judged and we are ready to suffer and to await what God is planning to do with us. We will continue in our faith in Christ so long as we have breath in us, unless we be dissuaded from it by the Scriptures."

The town. clerk said: "The hangman will instruct you, he will dispute with you, archheretic."

Michael: "I appeal to the Scriptures."

Then the judges arose and went into another room where they remained for an hour and a half and determined on the sentence. In the meantime some [of the soldiers] in the room treated Michael Sattler most unmercifully, heaping reproach upon him. . . .

The judges having returned to the room, the sentence was read. It was as follows: "In the case of the attorney of His Imperial Majesty vs. Michael Sattler, judgment is passed that Michael Sattler shall be delivered to the executioner, who shall lead him to the place of execution and cut out his tongue, then forge him fast to a wagon and thereon with red-hot tongs twice tear pieces from his body; and after he has been brought outside the gate, he shall be plied five times more in the same manner. . . ."

After this had been done in the manner prescribed, he was burned to ashes as a heretic. His fellow brethren were executed with the sword, and the sisters drowned.

His wife, also after being subjected to many entreaties, admonitions, and threats, under which she remained steadfast, was drowned a few days afterward. Done on the 21st day of May, A.D. 1527.

7.13 Johann Eck: Letter to Duke George of Saxony on the Anabaptists (1527)
Junghans 1967: 380–2

I think it would be well for your princely grace to know how the Anabaptists have fared in Salzburg. Thus from humble obedience I will relate a few main items to your princely grace. . . . On October 25th, three were burnt in the city of Salzburg. They did not recant. Ten weeks ago, the goldsmith Georg Steiner, the purse-master in the brotherhood of Hans Hut and his companions, Andrae Schmidt, Christoph Teufel, a potter, and Wolfgang Winter, a tailor, have all four recanted. They were beheaded and burned. The widow Barbara Grünauer and the goldsmith's cook, Elsbeth, did not recant and were drowned on the same day. On November 4th, Wolf Baumann, a nobleman and judge from Dietmering, was beheaded. He recanted and wanted to give all his goods to save his life. Along with him a citizen, who had recanted, was beheaded. Two citizens, who did not recant, were burned on the same day. Also in an isolated farm house a half mile from Salzburg, eleven women and sixteen men were captured, of whom twenty-one recanted and were taken to Hall. The remaining six were taken back into the house, bound, and burned with the house on November 6th. On November 3rd, the Cardinal [Archbishop Matthaeus Lang] had proclaimed: Whoever has had himself rebaptized and denounces it within eight days will be granted grace; whoever is seized after that will be punished in body and possessions. Twenty-five women and sixteen men have renounced their baptism. The men in shirts and socks and with lit candles, the women without cloaks and with black crosses, stood before the church and were absolved and led into the church on the Sunday before St. Martin's [November 10]. Still, he [the Cardinal] had many imprisoned everywhere, including even a doctor of theology.

My gracious lord of Constance [Bishop von Hohenlandenberg] on Wednesday after St. Michael's [October 2] had a Lutheran monk burned. My gracious lord of Augsburg [Bishop Christof von Stadion], imprisoned a Lutheran pastor on November 20th. In Bavaria, Leonhard Spörle has led many astray. My gracious lord, Duke Wilhelm, had him beheaded on November 12th. He had recanted. His wife remains in prison; I do not know what will be done with her. In Burghausen, eighteen are imprisoned. My gracious lord commanded that those who recant shall be beheaded, and those who do not recant shall be burned. . . . As my gracious lord may see, a strict mandate has gone out against the Anabaptists. . . . For this sect is very alarming . . . more damage is to be feared from them than from the recent peasant rebellion. For this sect is deeply rooted in the cities. If now a rebellion starts it will spring up in the cities. There they would have cannons, powder and armor, and also men trained in war. And if the peasants, as before, rise up, all chaos would result, directed against the clergy, princes, and nobles. Therefore the princes and nobles have to be alert.

7.14 Bernard Rothmann: *A Confession of Faith and Life in the Church of Christ of Münster* (1534)
Zuck 1975: 90–3

[W]e do not like what the Catholics and Lutherans teach concerning Christ's works, the fruit of faith. The papists make little use of faith and also of the good works of Christ, for they are busy in works which are arranged by their idol, the Antichrist from Rome, and his tonsured monks, as all know well. But the Lutherans emphasize faith too much and think little about good works. The fruit of the true Gospel cannot be found among them, but rather the opposite, namely, sexual laxity, drunkenness, and gluttony, and whatever belongs to a fleshly life. . . .

[W]e must become modeled after Christ, so that we follow his footsteps in all obedience, that we do everything that God has commanded, and that we refrain from all unrighteousness. . . . Thus, with Scripture, we hold to the necessity of faith and of good works also. . . .

Concerning baptism, we hold to what the Scripture teaches, namely, that baptism is the covenant of a good conscience with God (I Pet. 3), . . . Up to now, they are all pushed into water, which you can do to cats and dogs. But there is no baptism, and there should be no baptism except belief. . . .

On Monday before Fastnacht [February 9, 1534], the papists, wearing weapons under their clothing, agreeing with the bishop and the canons, sought to take the city by force and deal with us as they wished. In order to prevent this, we then assembled our forces in the marketplace. The godless [probably Lutherans] set up fortifications in the Uberwasser [Church]. Since they were there, and we stood in the marketplace, praying to God who alone helps and protects us, they then opened two doors and let in the bishop's representatives and many people, in order to drive us out. They also marked themselves and all of the homes of the godless with wreaths of straw; all who were not so marked, were to be taken away and plundered. Wasn't that a treacherous deed? But the Almighty pitied us in our innocence, and with visible wonders, slew our enemies and drove them out. Since they couldn't reach their goal, because God wouldn't permit it, they left with their people.

Thus they have begun our present war. Only God knows what the end will be. We place ourselves under his protection, without fear for what man will do to us. . . .

7.15 The Twelve Elders of Münster: "Thirteen Statements of the Order of Life" and "A Code for Public Behavior" (mid-1534)
Zuck 1975: 95–7

The Scripture directs that those who are disobedient and unrepentant regarding several sins shall be punished with the sword:

1. Whoever curses God and his holy Name or his Word shall be killed (Lev. 24).
2. No one shall curse governmental authority (Ex. 22, Deut. 17), on pain of death.
3. Whoever does not honor or obey his parents (Ex. 20, 21) shall die.

4. Servants must obey their masters, and masters be fair to their servants (Eph. 6).
5. Both parties who commit adultery shall die (Ex. 20, Lev. 20, Matt. 5).
6. Those who commit rape, incest, and other unclean sexual sins should die (Ex. 22, Lev. 20).
13. Concerning slander, murmuring, and insurrection among God's people (Lev. 19): There shall be no slanderer or flatterer among the people.

. . . Whoever disobeys these commandments and does not truly repent, shall be rooted out of the people of God, with ban and sword, through the divinely ordained governmental authority.

"A Code for Public Behavior"

The elders of the congregation of Christ in the holy city of Münster, called and ordained by the grace of the most high and almighty God, desire that the following duties and articles be faithfully and firmly observed by every Israelite and member of the house of God.

1. What the Holy Scriptures command or prohibit is to be kept by every Israelite at the pain of punishment. . . .
7. What the elders in common deliberation in this new Israel have found to be good is to be proclaimed and announced by the prophet John of Leiden as faithful servant of the Most High and the holy government to the congregation of Christ and the entire congregation of Israel.
8. Lest among the sincere and unblemished Israelites open transgression against the Word of God be tolerated, and in order that the evildoer and transgressor, if apprehended at an obvious transgression, meet his just punishment, the swordbearer, Bernhard Knipperdoling, will punish him according to his deed. . . .
29. When a stranger who does not adhere to our religion, be it brother, countryman, or relative, comes to this our holy city, he is to be referred to the swordbearer, Knipperdoling, so that he can talk with him. This is not to be done by anyone else.
30. A baptized Christian is not to converse with any arriving person or pagan stranger and is not to eat with him, lest there arise the suspicion of treacherous consultation. . . .
33. If, according to God's will, someone is killed by the enemy or departs otherwise in the Lord, no one is to take his belongings, such as weapons, clothes, etc. They are to be brought to the swordbearer Knipperdoling, who in turn will pass them on to the elders, who will then give them to the lawful heirs.

7.16 Appeal to Outsiders to Join the "New Jerusalem" in Münster
Hillerbrand 1964: 253–4

Dear friends, you are to know and recognize the work God has done among us so that everyone might arise to the New Jerusalem, the city of the saints, for God wants to punish the world. Let everyone watch lest he through carelessness fall under the judgment. Jan Bokelson, the prophet of Münster, has written us with all his helpers in Christ that no one can remain free under the dragon of this world, but will suffer bodily or spiritual death. Therefore let no one neglect to come unless he wishes to tempt God. . . . Do not look after earthly goods, . . . Here are available sufficient goods for the saints. Therefore do not take anything along, except money and clothes and food for travel. Whoever has a knife, lance or rifle should take it along. Whoever does not have such should buy himself such, for the Lord will redeem us through his mighty hand and through his servants, Moses and Aaron. Therefore be careful and watch for the evil one. Gather half a mile from Hasselt near the mountain cloister on 24th March around noon. Be careful in all things. Be not there before the appointed day nor later, for we will not wait for any. Let no one neglect to come. If anyone stays behind, I will be innocent of his blood.

7.17 The Death of the "Prophet" Jan Matthijs
Hillerbrand 1964: 255–6

The following day Jan Matthijs took ten or twenty men and left the town with them. When they reached the enemy they became involved in fighting. Together with his fellows, Jan Matthijs was killed. He was pierced with a spear. Afterwards the soldiers cut off his head, tore his body into a hundred pieces, which they threw around. They put the head on a stick and held it high in the air. Then the soldiers shouted to the Anabaptists in the city that they should come out and get their mayor. They did not know that Jan had been the highest prophet in the city.

7.18 Communism in the City of Münster
Hillerbrand 1964: 257

The prophets, preachers, and the entire council deliberated and felt that everything should be held in common. It was first ordered that everyone who had copper money should bring it to the City Hall, where he would receive a different currency. This was done. After the prophets and the preachers had reached an agreement with the council in this matter, it was announced in the sermons that all things should be held in common. Thus they said in the sermon: "Dear brothers and sisters, inasmuch as we are one people, and are brothers and sisters one to another, it is God's will that we should bring our money, silver and gold together. Each one of us should have as much as any other. Therefore everyone is to bring his money to the chancellery near the City Hall. There the council will be present and receive the money." Likewise preacher Stutenbernt said: "A Christian should not have any money; everything which Christian brothers and sisters possess belongs to one as well as the other. You shall not lack anything, be it food, clothes, house, or goods. What you need, you shall receive, God will not suffer you to lack anything. One thing shall be held as much in common as the other. It belongs to all of us. It is mine as well as yours, and yours as well as mine." Thus they persuaded the people so that some of them brought their money, silver and gold, indeed everything they owned. But there was much inequality in Münster, where one supposedly had as much as any other.

Some people in the city turned in all their money, silver and gold and did not keep anything. Others turned in part and kept part. Still others did not turn in anything.

7.19 The Introduction of Polygamy in the City of Münster
Hillerbrand 1964: 259

Thus Jan van Leiden – together with the bishop, the preachers and the twelve elders – proclaimed concerning the married estate that it was God's will that they should inhabit the earth. Everyone should take three or four wives, or as many as were desired. However, they should live with their wives in a divine manner. This pleased some men and not others. . . .

Jan van Leiden was the first to take a second wife in addition to the one he had married in Münster. It was said that there was still another wife in Holland. Jan van Leiden continued to take more wives until he finally had fifteen. In similar fashion all the Dutchmen, Frisians and true Anabaptists had additional wives. Indeed, they compelled their first wives to go and obtain second wives for them. The devil laughed hard about this. Those who had old wives and wanted to take young ones had their way. . . . The Anabaptists in Münster, especially the leaders, such as Jan van Leiden and the twelve elders, were planning it well. They had done away with money, gold and silver, and had driven everyone from his property. They sat in the houses, held the property, and also wanted to have ten or twelve wives. I presume they called this the "right baptism."

7.20 Rothmann: *A Restitution of Christian Teaching, Faith, and Life* (1534)
Zuck 1975: 98–101

From the history of the people of God we learn that God brings about a restitution after each fall. . . .

God the Almighty rightly began the restitution, when he awakened Martin Luther. When Luther, however, would not further God's grace, but remained lying in his own pride and filth, then the Antichrist became evident, and the true Gospel began to appear. But the fullness of truth was magnificently introduced in Melchior Hofmann, John Matthys, and here in our brother, John of Leiden. Thus the Kingdom of Christ has begun in Münster. What has been restored by God in the New Zion will now be shown, point by point.

1. God has again restored the Scripture through us. He has abundantly made his will known to us. And as we earnestly put into practice what we understand, God teaches us further every day.

2. The Münsterites hold to the true understanding of Scripture . . . Everything is portrayed previously in the Old Testament, before it is dealt with in the New Testament. Much more, everything which we await in the New Testament, has been openly anticipated in the Old Testament. . . .

6. Baptism is here restored. The Antichrist began child-washing, and made an idol out of water, with his magic. True baptism belongs only to those who understand and believe in Christ.

7. Through God's grace, the true church has been restored to Münster. For 1,400 years, the truth has been falsified and repressed. . . . The true, holy church cannot be found either among Catholics or Evangelicals. The latter would have better remained papists, than to have taught half-truths, for a half-truth is no truth. . . .

10. The living communion of saints has been restored, which provides the basis for community of goods among us. . . . And accordingly everything which has served the purposes of self seeking and private property, such as buying and selling, working for money, taking interest and practising usury – even at the expense of unbelievers – or eating and drinking the sweat of the poor (that is, making one's own people and fellow-creatures work so that one can grow fat) and indeed everything which offends against love – all such things are abolished amongst us by the power of love and community. . . .

11. We have again been given a sound understanding of the Lord's Supper. . . . The Antichrist teaches that he can make a god out of bread . . . Rather, the Lord's Supper is a remembrance of the Lord. . . .

12. God has restored the true practice of holy matrimony amongst us. Marriage is the union of man and wife – "one" has now been removed – for the honor of God and to fulfill his will, so that children might be brought up in the fear of God. . . .

Freedom in marriage for the man consists in the possibility for him to have more than one wife. . . . This was true of the biblical fathers until the time of the Apostles, nor has polygamy been forbidden by God. . . .

But the husband should assume his lordship over the wife with manly feeling, and keep his marriage pure. Too often wives are the lords, leading their husbands like bears, and all the world is in adultery, impurity, and whoredom. Nowadays, too many women seem to wear the trousers. The husband is the head of the wife, and as the husband is obedient to Christ, so also should the wife be obedient to her husband, without murmuring and contradiction. . . .

13. Previously, there has been no true understanding of the glory of the Kingdom of Christ on earth. . . . We know, however, that this Kingdom must be fulfilled during our generation, and that the scriptural reference to the Kingdom of Christ must be awaited here on earth. . . .

With his well-armed servants, Christ will defeat the devil and all unrighteousness, and then He will enter into his Kingdom, in full justice and peace. . . . In sum, the people of Christ must inherit the earth. The prophets and the psalmist, together with Christ's parables and the Apocalypse, undeniably give proof of this. . . .

7.21 Rothmann: *Concerning Revenge* (1534)
Zuck 1975: 102–4

Now God has risen in his wrath against his enemies. Whoever wishes to be God's servant, must arm himself in the same way and manner. That time is now here. The day of wrath has begun meaningfully in our midst, and will spread over the entire world. . . .

Thus we, who are covenanted with the Lord, must be His instruments to root out the godless on the day which the Lord has prepared. . . .

Our duke and prince [John of Leiden] has appeared and has already been established upon the throne of David. . . . God has awakened the promised David, armed together with his people, for revenge and punishment on Babylon. You have now heard what will happen, what rich reward awaits us, and how gloriously we shall be crowned, if only we fight bravely. Whether we live or die, we know that we cannot be lost (II Tim. 2:5; II Cor. 6:9).

7.22 The Capture, Torture, Confession, and Execution of Jan van Leiden
Hillerbrand 1964: 264–6

Confession of Jan van Leiden, supposedly King of Münster, made on 25th July 1535, at Dülmen. . . .

The day after St Agnes was set as time of execution. The day before the king was asked if he wanted to confess his sins to a priest. He replied that he was not ashamed to converse and counsel with an understanding man and asked for Johann von Syburg, the Bishop's chaplain. . . . When Johann von Syburg afterwards returned to us he reported that this unfortunate man showed extraordinary remorse. He had confessed openly that even if he were executed ten times, he had deserved it. None the less, he could not be brought to see his error regarding baptism and the human nature of Christ. . . .

Knipperdoling, on the other hand, wanted no one to talk or counsel with him. Earlier, under torture, he had boasted that he was not aware of any shortcoming. He had only sought the glory of God and his salvation; all other matters had been secondary. . . .

When the king was led as the first to the place of execution, he knelt and said, with folded hands, "Father, into thy hands do I commend my spirit." Then he was tied to a stake and tortured with fiery and glowing tongs and eventually killed, presumably under the applause and pleasure of the priests, whom Münster has always had in abundance. Their joy would have been full if the Lutherans had been given the same punishment. I will not mention the king's steadfastness in enduring torture. He did not even say one word to acknowledge his pain. After all, in earlier times even pagans showed such virtue; it is also certain that Satan gives power and steadfastness to those whom he entangles in his snares. . . .

After the deserved punishment had been administered to these criminal men, they were put into three iron cages so that they could be seen and recognized from afar. These cages were placed high on the steeple of St Lamberti's Church as a perpetual memorial and to warn and terrify the restless spirits lest they attempt something similar in the future. Such was the evil ending of this tragedy.

8

Augsburg 1530 to Augsburg 1555: Reform and Politics

Imperial inability to enforce the Edict of Worms and prohibit the spread of reforms (8.1) and the Catholic conviction of evangelical inspiration of the Peasants' War hardened positions by the Diet of Speyer. Nevertheless, the Diet opened with one last appeal for a common program for reform (8.2). The imperial response, however, was to forbid innovations, demand the enforcement of the Edict of Worms, and promise the arrangement of a council. The cities declared such moves impossible (8.3). The Diet then closed with a binding resolution ("Recess," 8.4) for conduct governed by conscience until a National Assembly would meet. In the ensuing years imperial political preoccupation with the papacy, France, and the Turks, hindered imperial interference with Lutheran advances. Catholic reaction to evangelical development improved imperial–papal relations, and a Catholic majority among the Estates provided a receptive audience for the Proposition (8.5) of the second Diet of Speyer in 1529, where the majority reaffirmed the Edict of Worms (8.6). In response, the evangelical minority at the Diet lodged their famous protest (8.7). Within the year Charles V decided personally to settle the religious question at the next Diet to be held in Augsburg in 1530. Cardinal Legate Campeggio urged strict repression of the evangelicals (8.8) and the Bavarian dukes (8.9) and their Theology Faculty followed suit (8.10). Charles V, however, promised a fair hearing, and the Lutherans followed Brück's advice (8.11) and formulated a written confession of their faith (8.12). Cardinal Campeggio led the negative Roman Catholic response to the Augsburg Confession (8.13–14) that led to the Diet's resolution (8.15) to maintain the status quo until the imminent meeting of a council. Protestant concerns about the timing and outcome of the promised council prompted reflection on the legality of resisting the emperor (8.16–20). In 1547 the emperor defeated the Schmalkald League and imposed religious as well as political conditions upon the Protestants. The center of Lutheran resistance shifted to the city of Magdeburg, where a group of pastors set forth a confession (8.21) that included a doctrine of resistance. This first formal assertion of a theory of rightful resistance by Protestants influenced later

The European Reformations Sourcebook, Second Edition. Edited by Carter Lindberg.
© 2014 John Wiley & Sons, Ltd. Published 2014 by John Wiley & Sons, Ltd.

Calvinist developments. Bartholomai Sastrow, a lawyer in Greifswalt and then mayor of Stralsund, provides a glimpse of religious practice during the Interim (8.22). In 1555 Charles V finally achieved a working peace (8.23). The Peace of Augsburg provided legal recognition only to the Catholic and Lutheran churches, yet even this limited religious pluralism displaced the medieval sense of a sacral community, the *corpus Christianum*. A year later Charles abdicated the throne (8.24) in search of his own personal peace.

8.1 Reform Programme of the Bishop of Pomerania (1525)
Kidd 1911: 189–91

1. Hitherto you have held seven sacraments, but not rightly. Henceforward faith must be before all things the foundation of your salvation, and you must have no more sacraments than Christ ordained, namely, Holy Communion and Holy Baptism.
4. Henceforward there shall be no pilgrimages nor wanderings to holy places, since they aid no man's salvation.
6. Henceforward no ringing nor singing nor Masses nor Vigils for the dead are to be held: for they are of no use, and of no avail.
7. Henceforward no water, salt, ashes, palms, tapers, greenery, and the like are to be hallowed: for it is all nonsense and no good.
9. There are to be no more Orders, neither monks nor nuns; . . .
10. Bishops shall continue and remain; not anointing-bishops nor ordaining-bishops, but such as preach and teach and expound the pure Word of God and preside over the Church.
11. Henceforward there are to be no superstitious distinctions made of days and seasons, with all sorts of Feast Days, Fridays, Saturdays, Ember Days, Fast Days, and so on; but every day alike shall be the Lord's Day, for eating flesh or fish as every man likes or finds necessary, or according as the good God may bestow it.
13. Hymns and prayers in church are to be in German, so that every man may understand. *Salve regina* is not to be sung, for it conduces to God's dishonor. Holy Baptism is to be administered in German, without chrism and oil.
15. In no church shall the Consecrated Bread be reserved nor taken for God's Body except at the Communion, according to Christ's institution, nor carried about.
16. Pictures in houses and churches are not to be prayed to, nor to have any candles lit before them.
18. Brotherhoods and guilds are to direct and lay out their endowments, not on the Mass, but on the maintenance of the poor and other pious uses.
19. The daily Mass is an abomination to God: so henceforward it is not to be observed in any church or anywhere.
20. When a man desires to go to Holy Communion, he must cause the priest, his confessor, to inform him out of God's Word, and must also inform himself, how he should receive and take the bread and wine according to Christ's institution in both kinds.

21. If any one thinks that he can make satisfaction for his sins himself or can save himself apart from the merits of Christ . . . let him be damned!
22. All priests and monks and nuns are at liberty to leave their orders and marry.

8.2 The Speech from the Throne (1526)
Kidd 1911: 183

First, it is the gracious and express will, desire, and command of our most gracious Lord, His Imperial and Royal Spanish Majesty aforesaid, that the Electors, Princes, and Estates of the Holy Empire, together with the aforementioned commissioners and deputies of His Majesty, should at this present Diet deliberate, consider, and finally by common conference resolve upon measures, ways, and means whereby the Christian faith and the well established good Christian practice and order of the Church in general may be maintained until the meeting of a free Council, and here among the members of the Holy Empire unity of each with all may be secured; how, moreover, transgressors may be punished for their offences and, should one forcibly resist the punishment, how the authorities may assist each other; so that the Imperial Edict resolved upon by the above commissioners, together with the Estates of the Empire, may be observed by each and all, and obtain immediate execution.

8.3 The Declaration of the Cities (1526)
Kidd 1911: 183–4

We observe . . . that nothing in this Diet shall be undertaken or concluded to the injury of our holy Christian faith or to the laws or ancient customs of the Church, its doctrine, order, ceremonies, and usages; but that these shall, in accordance with His Majesty's Edict at Worms, be, throughout the Empire, maintained, executed, and ordained to be used, with the proviso that His Imperial Majesty will shortly repair to Rome to His Holiness the Pope, and with him will, as is fitting, announce and proclaim a General Council and common assembly of Christendom.

Now we, the representatives of the Free Cities of the Empire, willingly obedient in all subjection to His Majesty, as our right, only, and natural lord, in all that may forward the peace and unity of the Holy Empire, acknowledge ourselves also bound thereto. But your Electoral and Princely Graces know to what a great and grievous extent the errors, discords, and disagreements in the matter of the aforesaid articles, especially in respect of ceremonies and abuses, have of recent years increased and multiplied: and how impossible it has hitherto proved, and, as it may be presumed, will yet prove more impossible, to execute the Imperial Edict of Worms. . . .

We, therefore, the representatives of the Free Cities, doubt not but that . . . His Imperial Majesty will himself graciously consider that it would be extremely grievous, in the matter of ceremonies and abuses, to persist in imposing the Edict of Worms until a General Council.

Further, the date of His Majesty's Instructions is the twenty-third day of March last, at which time His Majesty was at one with His Holiness the Pope. But, as we are now informed, His Holiness has at this moment an army in the field against His Majesty. For this and other reasons we cannot suppose that a General Council or other common assembly of Christendom can, as His Imperial Majesty intended, be proclaimed and brought together. . . .

8.4 The Recess of the Diet (1526)
Kidd 1911: 185

Thereupon have we [the Commissioners], the Electors, Princes, Estates of the Empire, and ambassadors of the same, now here at this present Diet, unanimously agreed and resolved, while awaiting the sitting of the Council or a national Assembly . . . with our subjects, on the matters which the Edict published by His Imperial Majesty at the Diet held at Worms may concern, each one so to live, govern, and carry himself as he hopes and trusts to answer it to God and His Imperial Majesty.

8.5 The Speech from the Throne (1529)
Kidd 1911: 240–1

[Your] Imperial Majesty has no small grief and trouble that in the German nation . . . such evil, grave, perilous, and pernicious doctrines and errors have arisen in our holy faith, and are now daily increasing more and more. Thereby not only . . . are the Christian and laudable laws, customs, and usages of the Church held in contempt and disgrace, to the reproach and dishonor of God our Maker; but also to that of your Imperial Majesty and the Empire. In particular, the German nation, its estates, subjects, and allies are thereby roused and inflamed to grievous and pitiful revolts, tumults, war, misery, and bloodshed; while your Majesty's edicts and mandates, together with the recesses of the Empire, are so little regarded . . . that your Majesty is seriously displeased and in no mind (as indeed becomes the Head of Christendom) any further to tolerate or permit the same.

(2) Whereas then in the Recess lately made at Regensburg [May 28, 1527] . . . it was held that in the matter of differences and discords . . . there was no better way open to a fruitful result than by a General Council or, at least, a National Assembly. . . .

(3) And whereas now the relations between your Imperial Majesty and his Holiness the Pope are, by the grace of Almighty God, in such good Christian accord that, as your Majesty is assured, there is no refusal on the part of his Holiness to hold the General Council . . . it is your Majesty's gracious offer to urge His Holiness to allow the summoning of such a Council. . . .

(4) Meanwhile, it is your Majesty's will, intention, and strict command . . . that, until the assembly and holding of the aforesaid Council, no one, whether of spiritual or of temporal estate, shall, to the detriment of our true Christian faith, use violence or force against ancient usages and customs, or go over to any wrong or strange creed, or attach himself to any new sect, as may hitherto have happened in some places. . . .

(7) And whereas in the Recess of the Diet of Speier, made in the . . . year 1526, an article was comprised saying that "the Electors, Princes, and Estates of the Empire,

and the ambassadors of the same unanimously agreed and resolved, while waiting for the Council, with our subjects, in matters which the edict published by his Imperial Majesty at the Diet held at Worms may concern, each one so to live, govern, and carry himself as he hopes and trusts to answer it to God and his Imperial Majesty, etc." and whereas, from the same article, as hitherto understood, expounded, and explained at their pleasure by several of the Estates of the Holy Empire, marvelous great trouble and misunderstanding has arisen against our holy Christian faith, as also against the Magistrates through the disobedience of their subjects, and much other disadvantage, your Imperial Majesty conceives no small astonishment thereat: and to the end that, for the future, the said article may be no further taken and expounded at every man's pleasure, and that the consequences, which hitherto have proved so disastrous to our holy faith, may be averted, your Imperial Majesty hereby repeals, revokes, and annuls the above-mentioned article contained in the aforesaid Recess, now as then, and then as now, all out of your own Imperial absolute power. . . .

8.6 The Resolution of the Majority (1529)
Kidd 1911: 242

[T]he Electors, Princes, and other Estates have resolved that those who have hitherto held to the aforesaid Imperial Edict [of Worms] should continue to abide by the same till the coming Council, and hold their subjects thereto.

(6) That by the other Estates, with whom the other doctrine originated and with whom, to some degree, it cannot be abandoned without considerable tumult, trouble, and danger, all further innovation shall nevertheless be prevented till the coming Council, so far as is humanly possible.

(7) That, in particular, such doctrines and sects as deny the most worthy sacrament of our Lord Jesus Christ's Body and Blood shall in no wise be tolerated by the holy Empire of the German Nation, nor be henceforth suffered . . . to preach in public: nor shall the celebration of the holy Mass be done away: nor shall any one, in places where the new doctrine has got the upper hand, be forbidden to celebrate or to hear Mass, nor be hindered or forced therefrom. . . .

(9) Further, your. Imperial Majesty bids and commands every Estate, spiritual and temporal, . . . that, until the assembly and holding of the aforesaid Council, no one, whether of spiritual or temporal Estate, shall, by act or deed, in any wise use force against another to deprive and despoil him of authority, goods, rents, dues, and customs; . . .

8.7 The Resolution of the Minority (1529)
Kidd 1911: 243–5

You . . . know what objections we caused to be raised, both orally and in writing, on the last day of the late Diet, against certain points in the article for the preservation of peace and unity in view of the religious division imminent in the Empire, pending the Council. . . . You . . . should have sought means whereby we might have been able, with a good conscience and without objection, to come to an agreement with you for the interpretation of the late Recess of Speyer, where it might by difference of opinion be perverted; whereby, too, the late Recess (which hitherto was everywhere considered just, and that, so far, unanimously) should also remain in essence and substance as then. . . .

But whereas we have found that you . . . persist in the maintenance of your intention; and whereas (for stated and weighty reasons and objections which we have now and at all times wished, declared, and repeated) both for conscience' sake and because you, Beloved, and you Excellencies, in view of the imminent religious division abovementioned, have not reconciled yourselves to assist in the preservation of peace and unity pending the Council, we do not agree or consent herein; . . .

[O]ur great and urgent needs require us openly to protest against the said resolution . . . as being, in view of the said late Recess, null and void, and, so far as we ourselves and our people, one and all, are concerned, not binding. This we hereby presently do. We hereby protest to you . . . that we, for kindred reasons, know not how to, cannot, and may not, concur therein, but hold your resolution null and not binding and we desire in matters of religion (pending the said general and free Christian council or national assembly) by means of the godly help, power, and substance of the oft-mentioned late Recess of Speyer, so to live, govern, and carry ourselves, in our governments, as also with and among our subjects and kinsfolk, as we trust to answer it before God Almighty and his Roman Imperial Majesty, our most gracious Lord.

8.8 Cardinal Campeggio's Instructions to the Emperor (1530)
Kidd 1911: 256–7

In certain parts of Germany all the Christian rites which were given to us by the ancient holy fathers have been abrogated in accordance with the suggestions of these scoundrels; the sacraments are no longer administered, vows are not observed, marriages are contracted irregularly and within the degrees prohibited by the laws. . . .

And I, if there shall be need, will pursue them with ecclesiastical censures and penalties, omitting nothing that it may be needful to do. I will deprive the beneficed heretics of their benefices, and will separate them by excommunications from the Catholic flock. Your Highness also, with your just and awful Imperial Ban, will subject them to such and so horrible an extermination that either they shall be constrained to return to the holy Catholic faith, or shall be utterly ruined and despoiled both of goods and life. And if any there be, which God forbid, who shall obstinately persevere in that diabolical course . . . Your Majesty will then take fire and sword in hand, and will radically extirpate these noxious and venomous weeds. . . .

It will be well and to the purpose that when this magnificent and Catholic undertaking shall have been put firmly and directly on its way, there should be chosen, some few days after, efficient and holy inquisitors who, with the utmost diligence and assiduity, should go about seeking and inquiring if there be any (but far be it from them) who persist in these diabolical and heretical opinions, nor will by any means abandon them . . . in which case they shall be castigated and punished according to the rule and practice observed in Spain with regard to the Moors. . . .

8.9 Dukes William IV and Louis X of Bavaria to the Theological Faculty of Ingolstadt University (1530)
Reu 1930: 79

To the worthy, learned, dear, devout, and faithful dean and members of the theological faculty of our University at Ingolstadt.

By the grace of God, William and Louis, brothers, Dukes of Upper and Lower Bavaria, etc. – Greeting: Worthy, learned and devout, dear, faithful Ones! Since our most gracious lord and cousin, His Imperial Roman Majesty may upon his arrival in Germany be confidently expected to summon a general Diet at which the matters of our Christian religion and faith will be discussed first of all; and in order that this matter (as is proper) may be given the most thorough and careful treatment, and in order that the doctrines which Martin Luther and other new teachers during the past twelve years have set up in opposition to our Christian faith may be clearly shown to be erroneous and worthy of repudiation, therefore we order you at once to make a complete summary and catalogue of all such heresies, wrong doctrines, and slanderous statements, and to indicate how these views may be refuted so that we may obtain the list from you when we need it. This is our solemn order and command; and we will graciously acknowledge this service which you are bound to perform by virtue of your official position.

8.10 Johannes Eck: "404 Articles" on the Errors of the Reformers (1530)
Reu 1930: 97–9

All Catholics believe that, in the midst of these numerous tumults of wars and afflictions of Christianity, you most worshipful Emperor, are the divinely appointed, chosen, and consecrated instrument for stopping the decline of the Catholic faith, for helping the afflicted Church and the oppressed ecclesiastics, for saving the Christian empire from Soliman [*sic*] the Turk, . . . But Martin Luther, the Church's enemy within the Church, has refused to heed the high admonitions addressed to him by your Majesty and hurled himself into a veritable whirlpool of godlessness. . . . He . . . blasphemes God; he has no reverence for saints or sacraments and no respect for ecclesiastical or secular magistrates; he is contumelious and rebellious; . . . he kindles the fires of sedition throughout the empire; he is making ardent preparations for a deluge of Christian blood; he is arming the hands of the Germans in order that they may bathe in the blood of the Pope and Cardinals. Thus he has produced a vast offspring, much worse than himself, bringing forth broods of vipers. . . . [T]hey destroy the churches, demolish the altars, and trample upon the most holy Eucharist; they burn the images of Christ and the saints, extinguish the worship of God, cast the relics of the saints into the dirt; they steal the church's treasures. . . . Nevertheless most of them now have the audacity openly to glory in all their dreadfully execrable crimes and to fling out the boast that they can shield themselves behind the recess of the Diet of Speyer. . . .

For the purpose of stamping out their deceitful vaunts, I present myself before your most worshipful Majesty, ready to perform the same service that I performed at Leipzig against Luther and at Baden against Oecolampadius, namely to defend all the ordinances, usages, doctrines, and ceremonies of our Catholic religion and faith and to attack the arguments of the antagonists. Let them come on, these enemies of the church, these instruments of godlessness, these advocates of heresies, and vessels of iniquity. . . .

8.11 The Advice of Dr. Brück, Chancellor of Electoral Saxony (1530)
Kidd 1911: 258

Inasmuch as His Imperial Majesty's summons desires that every man's opinion and mind should have a hearing, it appears to us a good thing that the opinion wherein our side has hitherto stood and persisted, should be duly collected together in writing with well-grounded justification of the same from Holy Scripture, so that one may have it ready in writing to start with, since it is hardly likely that, in the handling of the affair, the preachers as well as the Estates will be allowed to take part. . . .

8.12 The Augsburg Confession (1530)
Tappert 1959: 23, 30–4

A Confession of Faith Presented in Augsburg by Certain Princes and
Cities to His Imperial Majesty Charles V in the Year 1530
Psalm 119:46
"I will also speak of thy testimonies before kings, and shall not be put to shame."

IV. Justification

It is also taught among us that we cannot obtain forgiveness of sin and righteousness before God by our own merits, works, or satisfactions, but that we receive forgiveness of sin and become righteous before God by grace, for Christ's sake, through faith, when we believe that Christ suffered for us and that for his sake our sin is forgiven and righteousness and eternal life are given to us. For God will regard and reckon this faith as righteousness, as Paul says in Romans 3:21–26 and 4:5.

VI. The New Obedience

It is also taught among us that such faith should produce good fruits and good works and that we must do all such good works as God has commanded, but that we should do them for God's sake and not place our trust in them as if thereby to merit favor before God. . . .

VII. The Church

It is also taught among us that one holy Christian church will be and remain forever. This is the assembly of all believers among whom the Gospel is preached in its purity and the holy sacraments are administered according to the Gospel. For it is sufficient for the true unity of the Christian church that the Gospel be preached in conformity with a pure understanding of it and that the sacraments be administered in accordance with the divine Word. It is not necessary for the true unity of the Christian church that ceremonies instituted by men, should be observed uniformly in all places. . . .

IX. Baptism

It is taught among us that Baptism is necessary and that grace is offered through it. Children, too, should be baptized, for in Baptism they are committed to God and become acceptable to him.

On this account the Anabaptists who teach that infant Baptism is not right are rejected.

X. The Holy Supper of our Lord

It is taught among us that the true body and blood of Christ are really present in the Supper of our Lord under the form of bread and wine and are there distributed and received. The contrary doctrine is therefore rejected.

8.13 Cardinal Legate Campeggio's Response to the Augsburg Confession (1530)
Kidd 1911: 289–93

Most Invincible, Imperial, and Catholic Majesty! . . .

In the first place, I say that in order to facilitate this business it will be very much to the point if your Catholic Majesty with your very great authority, and then with the help of such Catholic Princes as shall seem best to you, should with every care try and strive to bring into the right and Catholic road some of these Princes, even if you cannot bring all who have subscribed to these articles and propositions; and also some of the imperial Cities, which indeed, as your Serene Highness will see in the reply which will be given to you, being desirous of persevering in the assertion of the said articles proposed, have strayed far and entirely from the truth and the sincere faith of Christ. . . .

Your Highness must be aware that it was, and always will be, in the nature of heretics to be obstinate and hard, never willing to give way or consent to reason, nor to any authority, however clear and approved. This I am convinced will be the same with these, from the protestation they make and propound at the beginning. For though they try to cover it up and soften it down with fine words, yet it seems to me to say nothing else in the end than that, if the matter is not settled to their liking, they mean to persist in their opinion and in their appeal to a future Council – not because they are to be determined, either as regards belief or giving way, by any Council; but that they may be able to persist in their wrong opinions and evade the coming of Your Highness for their great good, and in this way (which God avert) reduce all Germany to their perverse opinions, fill it with tumults and seditions, as they have done up to now, and so be able also to contaminate the rest of Christendom. . . .

But let your Catholic Majesty with your illustrious Princes and good and true Christians, after having established a complete understanding and confederation, prepare to decide thoroughly to extirpate these heresies, proceeding against them with order and system by means of reason and justice, using you your temporal arms and I the spiritual, and thus zealously punish them as is right; which, with the help of God, will be easy for you. And in this glorious, holy, and very truly Catholic undertaking, your Serene Highness would show yourself to all the world to be as in name so in deeds, as I told you before, the true and undoubted successor of that Charles the Great. . . .

8.14 Confutation of the Augsburg Confession (1530)
Reu 1930: 350–2, 354, 382

To Article IV. In the fourth article the condemnation of the Pelagians, who thought that man can merit eternal life by his own powers without the grace of God, is accepted as Catholic. . . . [However] if any one would intend to disapprove of the merits that men acquire by the assistance of divine grace, he would agree with the Manichaeans rather than with the Catholic Church. For it is entirely contrary to Holy Scripture to deny that our works are meritorious. . . . Nevertheless, all Catholics confess that our works of themselves have no merit, but that God's grace makes them worthy of eternal life. . . .
To Article V. In the fifth article the statement that the Holy Ghost is given by Word and sacraments, as by instruments, is approved. . . . The mention, however, that they make of faith is approved so far as not faith alone, which some incorrectly teach, but faith which worketh by love, is understood . . . For in baptism there is an infusion, not of faith alone, but also, at the same time, of hope and love . . .
To Article VI. Their Confession in the sixth article, that faith should bring forth good fruits, is acceptable and valid. . . .

But in the same article their ascription of justification to faith alone is diametrically opposite the truth of the Gospel, by which works are not excluded; . . . On this account their frequent ascription of justification to faith is not admitted. . . .
To Article IX. The ninth article concerning Baptism . . . is approved and accepted, and they are right in condemning the Anabaptists, a most seditious class of men that ought to be banished from the boundaries of the Roman Empire. . . .
To Article X. The tenth article gives no offence . . . if only they believe that the entire Christ is present under each form, so that the Blood of Christ is no less present under the form of bread by concomitance than it is under the form of the wine, and the reverse. . . .
Conclusion. . . . [S]ince His Imperial Majesty perceives that the Elector, the princes and the cities agree on many points with the Catholic and Roman Church . . . His Holy Imperial Majesty is fully convinced, and hopes that the result will be, that when the Elector, princes and cities have heard and understood this Reply they will agree with

united minds in regard to those matters also in which they perhaps have not agreed hitherto with the Roman Catholic Church, and that in all other things above mentioned they will obediently conform to the Catholic and Roman Church and the Christian faith and religion. . . . [I]f this admonition, so Christian and indulgent, be unheeded, the Elector, princes and cities can judge that a necessary cause is afforded His Imperial Majesty that, as becometh a Roman Emperor and Christian Caesar and a defender and advocate of the Catholic and Christian Church, he must care for such matters as the nature of the charge committed to him and his integrity of conscience require.

8.15 The Recess of the Diet of Augsburg (1530)
Reu 1930: 391–2

His Imperial Majesty, for the benefit and prosperity of the Holy Empire, for the restoration of peace and unity, and for the purpose of manifesting His Majesty's leniency and special grace, has granted the Elector of Saxony, the five Princes, and the six Cities a time of grace from now until the 15th day of April next year in which to consider whether or not they will confess the other articles together with the Christian Church, His Holiness the Pope, His Imperial Majesty . . . until a general council shall be convoked. . . .

The Elector of Saxony, the five Princes, and the six Cities shall between now and said 15th day of April prohibit in their countries the printing, selling, and retailing of any new books dealing with religion, and it is His Majesty's earnest will and command that in the meantime all Electors, Princes, and Estates of the Holy Empire promote peace and unity in this respect; . . .

Neither the Elector of Saxony, the five Princes, the six Cities, nor their subjects shall make any attempt to induce or force the subjects of His Majesty and of the Holy Empire . . . to join their sects; nor shall they in any way molest those . . . who still wish to cling to the old Christian faith and usages. . . .

Inasmuch as no general council has been held in the Christian Church for many years, although . . . numerous abuses and errors may have taken root, His Imperial Majesty, for the purpose of a Christian reformation, has considered this matter with His Holiness the Pope, and resolved with all . . . here assembled at Augsburg, to use His influence in inducing His Holiness the Pope and all Christian kings and potentates to consent to the convocation of a general Christian council within six months of the conclusion of this Diet at a suitable place and to holding this council at the latest one year after convoking it, in the firm confidence and hope that thereby Christendom may be restored in spiritual and temporal matters to lasting peace and unity. Amen.

8.16 Luther: *Temporal Authority: To What Extent It Should Be Obeyed* (1523)
LW 45: 111–13, 125–6

[St. Peter in Acts 5:29] clearly sets a limit to the temporal authority, for if we had to do everything that the temporal authority wanted there would have been no point in saying, "We must obey God rather than men."

If your prince or temporal ruler commands you to side with the pope, to believe thus and so, or to get rid of certain books, you should say, ". . . Gracious sir, I owe you obedience in body and property; command me within the limits or your authority on earth, and I will obey. But if you command me to believe or to get rid of certain books, I will not obey; for then you are a tyrant and overreach yourself, . . ."

You must know that since the beginning of the world a wise prince is a mighty rare bird, and an upright prince even rarer. They are generally the biggest fools or the worst scoundrels on earth; therefore one must constantly expect the worst from them and look for little good, especially in divine matters which concern the salvation of souls. They are God's executioners and hangmen; his divine wrath uses them to punish the wicked and to maintain outward peace. . . .

What if a prince is in the wrong? Are his people bound to follow him then too? Answer: No, for it is no one's duty to do wrong; we must obey God (who desires the right) rather than men [Acts 5:29]. What if the subjects do not know whether their prince is in the right or not? Answer: So long as they do not know, and cannot with all diligence find out, they may obey him without peril to their souls. . . .

8.17 Judgment of the Saxon Jurists (1530)
LW 47: 8

We [Luther, Jonas, Melanchthon, Spalatin, and other theologians] are in receipt of a memorandum from which we learn that the doctors of law have come to an agreement on the question: In what situations may one resist the government? Since this possibility has now been established by these doctors and experts in the law, and since we certainly are in the kind of situation in which, as they show, resistance to the government is permissible, and since, further, we have always taught that one should acknowledge civil laws, submit to them, and respect their authority, inasmuch as the gospel does not militate against civil laws, we cannot invalidate from Scripture the right of men to defend themselves even against the emperor in person, or anyone acting in his name. And now that the situation everywhere has become so dangerous that events may daily make it necessary for men to take immediate measures to protect themselves, not only on the basis of civil law but on the grounds of duty and distress of conscience, it is fitting for them to arm themselves and to be prepared to defend themselves against the use of force; and such may easily occur, to judge by the present pattern and course of events. For in previously teaching that resistance to governmental authorities is altogether forbidden, we were unaware that this right has been granted by the government's own laws, which we have diligently taught are to be obeyed at all times.

8.18 Luther: Letter to Lazarus Spengler in Nuremberg (1531)
Zuck 1975: 134

We have placed this proposition before the jurists: If they find (as some think they do) that the imperial law teaches resistance as a matter of self-defense in such a case, we cannot check the course of temporal justice.

For as theologians we are obliged to teach that a Christian is not to offer resistance but to suffer everything. Nor is he to plead the shift: It is permissible to repel force by force.

If, therefore, the jurists are right in saying that a Christian may offer resistance, not as a Christian but as a citizen or member of the body politic, we let that pass.

We speak about the members of Christ and the body ecclesiastical; we know well enough that a Christian as a citizen or member of the body politic may bear the sword and a temporal office. We have often written of this matter.

But our office will not allow our advising a member of the body politic to offer such resistance; nor are we acquainted with their statute law. They will have to take this responsibility upon their conscience. . . .

8.19 Luther: *Dr. Martin Luther's Warning to his Dear German People* (1531)
LW 47: 3–14, 19, 30, 35–6, 52, 55

All right, if a war or a rebellion should break out as I fear . . . I wish to testify before God and all the world here in this writing that we, who are derisively called "Lutherans," neither counseled it or consented to it, nor, indeed, gave any cause for it; rather we constantly and ceaselessly pleaded and called for peace. The papists themselves know and have to admit that we have preached peace up till now and have also kept the peace, and that peace was also our ardent desire now at the diet. Consequently, if a war or a rebellion should break out, it can under no circumstances be said, "See, that is the fruit of Lutheran teaching." It will rather have to be said, "See, that is the papists' teaching and its fruit; they want peace neither for themselves nor for others.". . . .

Furthermore, if war breaks out – which God forbid – I will not reprove those who defend themselves against the murderous and bloodthirsty papists, nor let anyone else rebuke them as being seditious, but I will accept their action and let it pass as self-defense. I will direct them in this matter to the law and to the jurists. For in such an instance, when the murderers and bloodhounds wish to wage war and to murder, it is in truth no insurrection to rise against them and defend oneself. . . .

This is my sincere advice: If the emperor should issue a call to arms against us on behalf of the pope or because of our teaching, as the papists at present horribly gloat and boast – though I do not yet expect this of the emperor – no one should lend himself to it or obey the emperor in this event. All may rest assured that God has strictly forbidden compliance with such a command of the emperor. Whoever does obey him can be certain that he is disobedient to God and will lose both body and soul eternally in the war. For in this case the emperor would not only act in contravention of God and divine law but also in violation of his own imperial law, vow, duty, seal, and edicts. And lest you imagine that this is just my own idea or that such advice is dictated by my fancy, I shall submit clear and strong reasons and arguments to convince you that this is not my own counsel, but God's earnest, manifold, and stringent command. . . .

The first reason why you must not obey the emperor and make war in such an instance as this is that you, as well as the emperor, vowed in baptism to preserve the gospel of Christ and not to persecute it or oppose it. Now you are, of course, aware that in this case the emperor is being incited and duped by the pope to fight against the gospel of Christ, because our doctrine was publicly proved at Augsburg to be the true gospel and Holy Scripture. . . .

The second reason is this: Even if our doctrine were false – although everyone knows it is not – you should still be deterred from fighting solely by the knowledge that by such fighting you are taking upon yourself a part of the guilt before God of all the abominations which have been committed and will yet be committed by the whole papacy. This reason encompasses innumerable loathsome deeds and every vice, sin, and harm. In brief, the bottomless hell itself is found here, with every sin, all of which you share in if you obey the emperor in this instance. . . .

The third reason why you must refuse obedience to the emperor in such a call to arms is this: if you did otherwise you would not only burden yourself with all these abominations and help strengthen them, but you would also lend a hand in over-throwing and exterminating all the good which the dear gospel has again restored and established. . . .

And as I did above, I testify here again that I do not wish to incite or spur anyone to war or rebellion or even self-defense, but solely to peace. But if the papists – our devil – refuse to keep the peace and, impenitently raging against the Holy Spirit with their persistent abominations, insist on war, and thereby get their heads bloodied or even perish, I want to witness publicly here that this was not my doing, nor did I give any cause for it. . . .

8.20 Luther: Disputation Concerning the Right to Resist the Emperor (1539)
Zuck 1975: 134–5

If one may resist the pope, one may also resist all the emperors and dukes who contrive to defend the pope. . . . The pope . . . wishes . . . every soul . . . to go to hell for his sake. Hence it is necessary that one march against his soldiers that war under him and go out to meet them even though it mean a revolution. For we can not allow the dam-nation of souls. I am obliged to lay down my life for the emperor, but not my soul.

If the emperor defends the pope, who is a wolf, one is not to yield or stand for it, but one must attack him. . . . Self-defense is the natural course. The princes must resist the tyrants, a thing which the First Table [of the Decalogue] also requires. The emperor and Ferdinand are seeking first and foremost to get our goods, but still under the cover of the pope.

8.21 Nicholas Gallus et al.: A Confession of the Magdeburg Pastors Concerning Resistance to the Superior Magistrate (1550)
Zuck 1975: 137–8

We will undertake to show that a Christian government may and should defend its subjects against a higher authority which should try to compel the people to deny God's Word and to practice idolatry.

We scarcely expect to convince the Catholics that subjects may resist their Lord and a lower magistrate may resist a higher if he seeks to uproot the Christian religion, for the Catholics do not admit that we have the Christian religion and consequently think they have the right to make war upon us.

Our object is primarily to allay the scruples of those who do adhere to the true Word of God. . . .

But first we would address ourselves to the Emperor and beg him not to let the Pope persecute the Lord, Christ. But if your Majesty will not concede that Lutherans are Christians, bear in mind that Christ was considered a blasphemer, and He has shown us one mark of the true Church, namely that it should not constrain anyone with the sword as the Roman Church does. Obedience to God and to Caesar are not incompatible, provided each stays within his own proper sphere. Your Majesty has gone beyond your office and encroached upon the Kingdom of Christ. . . .

We will show from Holy Scripture that if a higher magistrate undertakes by force to restore popish idolatry and to suppress or exterminate the pure teaching of the Holy Gospel, as in the present instance, then the lower godfearing magistrate may defend himself and his subjects against such unjust force in order to preserve the true teaching, the worship of God together with body, life, goods, and honor.

The powers that be are ordained of God to protect the good and punish the bad (Romans 13), but if they start to persecute the good, they are no longer ordained of God.

There are to be sure degrees of tyranny and if a magistrate makes unjust war upon his subjects contrary to his plighted oath, they may resist, though they are not commanded to do so by God.

But if a ruler is so demented as to attack God, then he is the very devil who employs mighty potentates in Church and State. . . . [T]hen in the name of natural law and Scripture he may be resisted.

8.22 Sastrow's account of preaching during the Interim
Junghans 1967: 468–70

The Emperor remained in Speier a few days. They had there an evangelical preacher in the Franciscan cloister, in which he was prior, since all his brothers in the same cloister were good evangelicals. But they remained in their monastic habits. I had seen then the prior for four years standing in the pulpit in his monk's cowl and also going about the citizens on the streets. His preaching filled the church and people were even at the church door. He never referred to the pope or Luther in the least word. He was a learned man who was a highly gifted teacher of the evangelical religion. When the imperial majesty came there, he exchanged his monastic garb for secular clothes and fled. Similarly, the preacher at Worms as well as the evangelical preachers in the surrounding imperial cities fled, . . .

The same small town, Landau, had an evangelical preacher, a fine learned man. . . . But when the Emperor arrived there from the Diet of Augsburg, on the way to Speier, the evangelical preacher had to flee. In his place was assigned a papist preacher, a young, unlearned and nasty fellow, a godless, shameless, insolent papist knave. One time I was in Landau and stayed over Sunday. I went to church and saw the papal mass held, and heard the young rascal insolently preach. "The Lutherans," he said, "do not want one to pray to Mary the mother of God or to other saints. Listen my friends, I will tell you a true story: A man died. As he was passing away, his soul came before heaven. St. Peter closed the door and would not let him into heaven. Mary, the mother of God, was taking a stroll with her dear Son in front of heaven. The man addressed her and complained that St. Peter had refused him. He recounted how he had honored the holy virgin Mary while on earth, how many rosaries, Our Fathers, and Ave Marias he had prayed, how many candles he had lit in her memory. 'Yes, it is true, my dear Son,' Mary said to the Lord Christ. Then the Lord said: 'Have you not heard or read that I am the way and the truth, and the door to heaven?' Mary answered: 'If you are the door, I am the window.' She then took the man's soul by his head and tossed him through the window into heaven. What difference was it to him whether he entered heaven by the door or a window? What will the Lutheran rascals say now; that one should not pray to Mary?" What could be more godless and brazen in the light of the gospel and in the place where earlier the Word had been preached and taught purely?

8.23 The Peace of Augsburg (1555)
Kidd 1911: 363–4

In order to bring peace into the holy Empire of the Germanic Nation between the Roman Imperial Majesty and the Electors, Princes, and Estates: let neither his Imperial Majesty nor the Electors, Princes, etc., do any violence or harm to any state of the Empire on account of the Augsburg Confession, but let them enjoy their religious belief, liturgy and ceremonies as well as their estates and other rights and privileges in peace; . . .

Likewise the Estates espousing the Augsburg Confession shall let all the Estates and Princes who cling to the old religion live in absolute peace and in enjoyment of all their estates, rights and privileges.

However, all such as do not belong to the two above-named religions shall not be included in the present peace but be totally excluded from it. . . .

Where an archbishop, bishop or prelate or any other priest of our old religion shall abandon the same, his archbishopric, bishopric, prelacy, and other benefices, together with all their income and revenues which he has so far possessed, shall be abandoned by him without any further objection or delay. The chapters and such as are entitled to it by common law or the custom of the place shall elect a person espousing the old religion, who may enter on the possession and enjoyment of all the rights and incomes of the place without any further hindrance and without prejudging any ultimate amicable settlement of religion. . . .

[Adherents of the] Augsburg Confession shall be left to the free and untrammelled enjoyment of their religion, ceremonies, appointment of ministers . . . until the final settlement of religion shall take place. . . .

No Estate shall try to persuade the subjects of other Estates to abandon their religion nor protect them against their own magistrates. . . .

In case our subjects, whether belonging to the old religion or to the Augsburg Confession, should intend leaving their homes, with their wives and children in order to settle in another place, they shall neither be hindered in the sale of their estates . . . nor injured in their honor. . . .

8.24 Charles V: Abdication Speech, Brussels (1556)
Robinson 1906: 165–7

I had no inordinate ambition to rule a multitude of kingdoms, but merely sought to secure the welfare of Germany, to provide for the defence of Flanders, to consecrate my forces to the safety of Christianity against the Turk and to labor for the extension of the Christian religion. But although such zeal was mine, I was unable to show so much of it as I might have wished, on account of the troubles raised by the heresies of Luther and the other innovators of Germany and on account of serious war into which the hostility and envy of neighboring princes had driven me, and from which I have safely emerged, thanks to the favor of God.

This is the fourth time that I go to Spain, there to bury myself. I wish to say to you that nothing I have ever experienced has given me so much pain or rested so heavily upon my soul as that which I experience in parting from you today, without leaving behind me that peace and quiet which I so much desired. . . . I am no longer able to attend to my affairs without great bodily fatigue and consequent detriment to the affairs of the state. The cares which so great a responsibility involves; the extreme dejection it causes; my health already ruined; all these leave me no longer the strength sufficient for governing the states which God has confided to me. . . .

The last time that I went to Germany I had determined to do what you see me do today, but I could not bring myself to do it when I saw the wretched condition of the Christian state, a prey to such a multitude of disturbances, of innovations, of singular opinions as to faith, of worse than civil wars, and fallen finally into so many lamentable disorders. . . . In order that I might not be wanting in my duty I risked my strength, my goods, my repose and my life for the safety of Christianity and the defense of my subjects. . . .

I have carried out what God has permitted, since the outcome of our efforts depends upon the will of God. We human beings act according to our powers, our strength, our spirit, and God awards the victory and permits defeat. I have ever done as I was able, and God has aided me. I return to Him boundless thanks for having succored me in my greatest trials and in all my dangers.

I am determined then to retire to Spain, to yield to my son Philip the possession of all my states, and to my brother, the king of the Romans, the Empire. I particularly commend to you my son, and I ask of you in remembrance of me, that you extend to him the love which you have always borne towards me; moreover I ask you to preserve among yourselves the same affection and harmony. Be obedient towards justice, zealous in the observance of the laws, preserve respect for all that merits it, and do not refuse to grant to authority the support of which it stands in need.

Above all, beware of infection from the sects of neighboring lands. Extirpate at once the germs, if they appear in your midst, for fear lest they may spread abroad and utterly overthrow your state, and lest you may fall into the direst calamities.

9

The Genevan Reformation

Calvin's account of his conversion and development as a Reformer (9.1) does not mention the event that triggered his flight from France, the reaction to Nicholas Cop's All Saints' Day address as Rector to the University of Paris (9.2) with which Calvin was associated. Cop's mix of Luther's theology and French Humanism roused the ire of the Sorbonne scholastics. Calvin was thus convinced that reform of the church from within was impossible; the only options for a French evangelical were martyrdom or self-chosen exile. Not surprisingly, many French evangelicals did not share Calvin's conviction. They argued that external participation in Catholic worship did not compromise their inner faith. After all, if Jesus did not condemn Nicodemus for coming to him under the cover of night (John 3:1 ff.), why could they not also opt for discretion? Calvin's uncompromising condemnation of this so-called "Nicodemist" stance (9.3) led to the influx of some 5,000 French refugees into Geneva, causing social and political tensions with native Genevans. On a lighter note, one of Calvin's more satirical writings describes the "benefit" of relics (9.4). Two perspectives on the early reform movement in Geneva are provided by Michel Roset's *Chronicle* (9.5), composed while he was a civil servant in Geneva, and by Jeanne de Jussie of Geneva's Convent of the Poor Clares (9.6). Calvin supervised the preparation of the *Ecclesiastical Ordinances* (9.7), the basic statement of Geneva's church polity and the model for future Calvinist churches throughout Europe and North America. It informed Calvin's letter to Kaspar Olevianus for organizing the city churches in Heidelberg (9.8). François Bonivard, author of a number of tracts as well as the official history of Geneva, described the Consistory and Genevan poor relief (9.9). Calvin's *Institutes* (9.10) remains a theological masterwork. Throughout his life, Calvin emphasized the value of catechetical instruction. In Geneva, children's catechesis was held at noon every Sunday in the three city churches, with catechetical examinations four times a year on the Sunday before celebrating the Lord's Supper. In question-and-answer format the 1545 Geneva Catechism has 373 questions divided into four parts: Faith, Law, Prayer, The Sacraments (9.11). The "Ordinances Concerning Church Polity"

The European Reformations Sourcebook, Second Edition. Edited by Carter Lindberg.
© 2014 John Wiley & Sons, Ltd. Published 2014 by John Wiley & Sons, Ltd.

(9.12) completed the Ecclesiastical Ordinances of 1541 by adding certain rules for the rural churches.

Calvin's effort's to bring consensus between the Wittenbergers and the Swiss in relation to the Lord's Supper are exemplified by his "Short Treatise on the Lord's Supper" (9.13) and the letter to Zwingli's successor, Heinrich Bullinger (9.14). The "Agreement of Zurich" ("Consensus Tigurinus," 9.15) drawn up by Calvin and Bullinger unified the Reformation in Switzerland. Calvin was also notably involved in disputes over predestination and the doctrine of the Trinity. The former began with an attack by the Catholic theologian Albert Pighius, who argued that, if everything occurs by God's will and power, there was no need for humans to have any ethical concerns. Why punish sinners if God makes them sin? Does not the doctrine of double predestination vitiate all order and ethics, destroy all religion, and reduce humans to beasts? The controversy erupted within Geneva when Jerome Bolsec publicly challenged Calvin's teaching on predestination, claiming that Calvin made God the author of sin. Bolsec was imprisoned and then banished from Geneva in 1551. The vehement responses of the Geneva Company of Pastors (9.16) and Calvin (9.17) stimulated Bolsec's return to Catholicism and the publication of "biographies" of Calvin and Beza that described them as heretics, liars, hypocrites, and sexual deviants. The arrival in Geneva of Michael Servetus stimulated the dispute over the doctrine of the Trinity. His *On the Errors of the Trinity* (1531), that attacked the doctrine as ancient polytheism, was condemned by all sides. He was recognized during a visit to Geneva, arrested, tried for heresy, and burned at the stake in 1553 (9.18–22). Stirred by the Servetus case, Sebastian Castellio's argument for religious liberty (9.23) incensed Theodore Beza, Calvin's successor, who saw religious liberty as "a most diabolical dogma, because it means that everyone should be left to go to hell in his own way."

9.1 John Calvin: Conversion and Development
Calvin 1981: xl–xliv

God having taken me from my originally obscure and humble condition, has reckoned me worthy of being invested with the honourable office of a preacher and minister of the gospel. When I was as yet a very little boy, my father had destined me for the study of theology. But afterwards, when he considered that the legal profession commonly raised those who followed it to wealth, this prospect induced him suddenly to change his purpose. Thus it came to pass, that I was withdrawn from the study of philosophy, and was put to the study of law. To this pursuit I endeavoured faithfully to apply myself, in obedience to the will of my father; but God, by the secret guidance of his providence, at length gave a different direction to my course. And first, since I was too obstinately devoted to the superstitions of Popery to be easily extricated from so profound an abyss of mire, God by a sudden conversion subdued and brought my mind to a teachable frame, which was more hardened in such matters than might have been expected from one at my early period of life. Having thus received some taste and knowledge of true godliness, I was immediately inflamed with so intense a desire to make progress therein, that although I did not altogether leave off other studies, I yet pursued them with less ardour.

I was quite surprised to find that before a year had elapsed, all who had any desire after purer doctrine were continually coming to me to learn, . . . Being of a disposition somewhat unpolished and bashful, which led me always to love the shade and retirement, I then began to seek some secluded corner where I might be withdrawn from the public view; . . . Leaving my native country, France, I in fact retired into Germany, expressly for the purpose of being able there to enjoy in some obscure corner the repose which I had always desired, and which had been so long denied me. But lo! whilst I lay hidden at Basle, and known only to a few people, many faithful and holy persons were burnt alive in France; and the report of these burnings having reached foreign nations, they excited the strongest disapprobation among a great part of the Germans, whose indignation was kindled against the authors of such tyranny. . . . [I] t appeared to me, that unless I opposed them to the utmost of my ability, my silence could not be vindicated from the charge of cowardice and treachery. This was the consideration which induced me to publish my Institute of the Christian Religion. My objects were, first . . . to vindicate my brethren, whose death was precious in the sight of the Lord; and next, that as the same cruelties might very soon after be exercised against many unhappy individuals, foreign nations might be touched with at least some compassion towards them and solicitude about them. When it was then published, it was not that copious and laboured work which it now is, but only a small treatise containing a summary of the principal truths of the Christian religion; and it was published with no other design than that men might know what was the faith held by those whom I saw basely and wickedly defamed by those flagitious and perfidious flatterers. . . .

Wherever else I have gone, I have taken care to conceal that I was the author of that performance; and I had resolved to continue in the same privacy and obscurity, until at length William Farel detained me at Geneva. . . . Farel, who burned with an extraordinary zeal to advance the gospel, immediately strained every nerve to detain me. And after having learned that my heart was set upon devoting myself to private studies, for which I wished to keep myself free from other pursuits, and finding that he gained nothing by entreaties, he proceeded to utter an imprecation that God would curse my retirement, and the tranquillity of the studies which I sought, if I should withdraw and refuse to give assistance, when the necessity was so urgent. By this imprecation I was so stricken with terror, that I desisted from the journey which I had undertaken; . . .

9.2 Nicolas Cop: Rector's Address to the University of Paris (1533)
CStA 1.1: 11–25

Where shall our address begin and end in relation to the wealth of its themes? Now because the subject is greater than I can encompass with one address, I shall interpret the verses of the Gospel read today in church [Matt. 5:1–12] . . .

First we must examine the scope of this Gospel text and to what it refers. This will easily become evident from the description and comparison of the two major parts: gospel and law. The gospel is the good news and salvation-bringing proclamation of

Christ that he is sent by the Father in order to help us, to mediate eternal life to us. The law is grasped in the rules; it threatens and constrains, and promises no grace. The gospel, in contrast, works not with threats and imposes no commands, but rather teaches God's exceedingly great goodness. Thus whoever will purely and sincerely interpret the gospel, must orient everything to the description of the law and the gospel. If one does not follow this way of interpretation, one will never prevail in Christian philosophy. The evil sophists [the scholastic theologians sitting before Cop's pulpit!] are permanently addicted to this error, flailing empty straw, showing off with hair-splitting, but setting forth nothing about faith, nothing about the love of God, nothing about the forgiveness of sins, nothing about grace, nothing about justification and true good works. Rather, they spitefully gripe about everything, mess it up and stuff it with sophistical legalism. I ask you, you who are present here, not to put up with such heresies and blasphemies. . . .

The gospel promises the forgiveness of sins and justification free, gratis, for nothing. For we are not accepted by God because we fulfill the law but solely for the sake of the promise of Christ. . . .

9.3 Apology of John Calvin to the Gentlemen, the Nicodemites (1544)
CStA 3: 224–7, 242–5, 254–7

[A] faithful person living among the papists cannot under any circumstances participate in their idolatrous practices without offending God. This doctrine is surely clear. I have proved it by the testimony of Scripture and by such clear reasons that it is not possible to contradict it.

However, some find me too rigorous, and, what is more, complain that I have treated them inhumanely. . . . [I]t appears that they cannot bear it if someone reproaches them. But what pretence of being right do they give as an excuse, as if I have unjustly condemned them? They can only dish up this miserable thin gruel, a subterfuge, that if their inner affection is devoted to God, what does it matter how they appear before others. . . . I ask you, can God be content with such bifurcation? He who said that before him every knee should bend and every tongue confess his name [Phil. 2:10f.]; will he indeed tolerate that one bows before idols? . . .

The complaint heard from small and great, laity and clergy has little merit: What! Shall we abandon everything and flee without knowing where to go? Or else should we expose ourselves to death? . . . Can we not serve God and be obedient to his Word without suffering persecution? If they want to be good Christians only under this condition, then they must certainly paint an entirely new Jesus Christ. . . .

If the faithful in the early church had argued this way, what would have become of Christianity? . . .

Where is the similarity between the Nicodemites and Nicodemus? They point to his coming to Jesus in the night (John 3:2) and not publicly declaring to belong to his followers . . . [But] [a]fter his conversion, Nicodemus openly confessed him [Christ] in the daylight, indeed in the moment of great danger. . . . Nicodemus buried only Jesus' body. But today's Nicodemites bury body and soul, humanity and divinity, and do everything without honor. Nicodemus laid him in the grave because he was dead; but they want to bury him after his resurrection. Thus let them finally stop making Nicodemus a shield for their denying the Christian faith to the point of defiling themselves with idolatry. . . .

9.4 Calvin: *A Very Useful Account concerning the Great Benefit that Christianity will Receive if it takes an inventory of all the sacred bodies and relics which are in Italy, France, Germany, Spain, and other kingdoms and countries* (1543)
Calvin 1958: 287–341

I am not able to do what I'd like in this booklet because it would be necessary to have registers from everywhere to know which relics are said to be in which place in order to make comparisons. And then one would discover that each apostle has more than four bodies, and each saint at least two or three. . . .

Let us begin [the enumeration of relics] with Jesus Christ. Since his natural body could not be had . . . they have compensated by amassing in its place a thousand other pieces of rubbish. . . . Besides teeth and hair, the Abbey of Charroux in the diocese of Poitiers claims to have the prepuce, that is, the skin cut off at circumcision. I ask you, how did this skin come to them? St. Luke the Evangelist says that our Lord Jesus was circumcised, but in point of fact does not say that the skin was kept as a relic. . . . But to prove it is genuine, they [the monks of Charroux] say that some drops of blood fell from it. . . . However, even if we concede to them that the skin cut from Jesus Christ might be there or elsewhere, what shall we say of the foreskin shown at the Cathedral St. John Lateran in Rome? It is certain that there could not be more than one foreskin, it cannot be at both Rome and Charroux. Thus, there you are, an obvious falsehood. . . .

As for the Virgin Mary, because her body is no longer on earth they cannot have her bones. Otherwise, I think they would have made believe she had so many bones they could fill a large ossuary. Moreover, to have some part of her body they compensate with her hair and her milk. Her hair is displayed at St. Mary above Minerva in Rome, St. Salvador's in Spain, at Mascon, at Cluny, at Noyers, at St. Flour, at St James, and at many other places. Concerning her milk, there are so many places it is shown that they cannot be numbered. For there is no little village, nary a convent be it of monks or of nuns, however insignificant, where there is not her milk in more or less quantities. . . . There is so much [milk] that if the holy Virgin had been a cow, and had she continued to nurse her whole life, she would have had great difficulty to give so much. . . .

Because St. Sebastian has been given the office of healer of the plague, he is in high esteem and sought after. Thus his body has been multiplied into four entire bodies; one is at St. Laurence in Rome, another at Soissons, the third at Piligny near Nantes, the fourth near Narbonne, his birthplace. In addition, he has two heads: one at St. Peter's in Rome, and the other with the Dominican friars of Toulouse. It is true that they are empty according to the report of the Franciscans of Angiers who say they have the brain. One more thing: the Dominicans of Angiers have an arm; and there is another one at St. Sernin of Toulouse; and another at the shrine in Auverne; another at Montbrison, along with small pieces which are in numerous churches. All this considered, it's anyone's guess where the body of St. Sebastian really is. . . .

9.5 Michel Roset: *Chronicles of Geneva* (1562)
Kingdon 1974: 81–3, 85

Jacques Bernard, the guardian of the Franciscan convent in the Rive quarter and a citizen, who not long beforehand had been called to the knowledge of the Gospel, had presented to the Council five articles or propositions. These he, along with the other preachers, offered to maintain. On 20 May [1535] he obtained permission for publication of the propositions and Sunday, 30 May, was assigned as the day of open disputation. . . . The propositions maintained were, in summary: justification of men by Jesus Christ alone; the government of the Church depends on the Word of God alone; the adoration of a sole God who is sufficiently satisfied by way of atonement for our sins by the unique oblation made one time by Jesus Christ; Christ is the sole mediator between God and man, from which it follows that those who attribute to themselves some power, thinking to justify themselves through their works, are in error; the human and papal traditions which are called ecclesiastical are pernicious; it is idolatry and against God's wishes to adore with honor the Saints and statues; the mass does not contribute to our salvation, nor do prayers for the deceased; the Saints are not our intercessors. The disputations were continued for several days before a large audience. Among those in attendance were two persons who supported the party of the priests. One was named Caroli, a Doctor of the Sorbonne, the other Chappuisi, a citizen of the city and a monk of the convent in the Plainpalais quarter. Both were defeated and confessed to it, following which they have since themselves preached the Gospel.

After the disputations of July 1535, the Ministers and many of the citizens asked the Council for a declaration of judgment concerning these public debates. . . . The Council, which still hoped to avoid dangers and harmful consequences for humanitarian reasons, delayed, hoping to avoid trouble. On 23 July, it prohibited Farel from preaching at the church of the Madeleine, one of the largest parishes. . . . Nonetheless, on 8 August, he preached publicly at the church of Saint Pierre. As a result, he was reprimanded by the Council. On this same day, several citizens and small children entered the aforementioned church and broke the statues. From there, they went to the other churches. For this they too were summoned and reprimanded. However, they maintained that they had acted correctly. Their argument was so persuasive that the Council was unsure if it should chastise them. It did, however, suspend the destruction of that which remained until further and wiser deliberation. At the same time, it ordered a cessation of the mass and had the property of the convents inventoried because of the troubles. . . .

On 15 October, the Syndics and the Council, having once again asked the priests if they wished to say anything more concerning the disputations, prohibited them from administering the sacraments further and from wearing their habits.

In December 1535, when the city was continually besieged, the citizens sought out the idols and relics in the churches in order to leave nothing. Among others, four notable things were found. At the church of Saint Pierre, there was the arm of Saint Antoine upon which the most solemn oaths had been given. They found that it was the parched genital member of a stag. The brain of Saint Pierre, which had been held in great veneration, was found to be a pumice-stone. At the church of Saint Gervais, the priests said that under the main altar were buried Saints Nazarien, Celse and Panthaléon, called the holy bodies. They asked that they be canonized, but this was not done. If one pressed his ear to the monument, he heard beneath it a sound like the indistinct voices of men talking. There was also a hole through which the devout put their rosaries which were then so strongly held that they were not able to pull them out. The secret of all this was that under the altar there were great pots or earthen pipes situated so that they resounded at the least breeze. And, there were hooks cleverly placed below the hole so that the rosaries were held firmly.

9.6 Jeanne de Jussie: *The Short Chronicle. A Poor Clare's Account of the Reformation in Geneva*
Jussie 2006: 53, 60–1, 99, 112–13, 139, 170–2

Those Swiss Germans who had attacked the country did unspeakable harm to the land, and like disloyal, heretical dogs, they pillaged and burned all the churches, monasteries, and convents everywhere they went. . . .

They took the sacred host and trampled it under their feet, and some of them threw it into the fire or mud. They also took the blessed ointment for the sacrament of baptism and the blessed oil with which all good Christians are anointed in the last days of their illness, and they poured them on the ground in great horror and contempt – the Mohammedan Turks and infidel Jews could not have done worse – and they emptied the holy fonts. They spat on and shamefully wiped their bodies with the holy relics. . . .

The prince and grand heresiarch of that damnable sect was an Augustinian monk named Martin Luther. . . . [F]illed with wickedness and great self-pride, he set his mind to all sorts of malice and error, and he revived all the heresies and errors that had existed ever since the apostles' death, and he had them printed in Basel and carried straightaway through almost all of Christendom, and so his pestiferous venom poisoned all the kingdoms and lands of the Catholic Church. . . .

On that day [March 11, 1534] a young guard, a thief and bandit of the Lutheran sect, was executed. . . .

[A] woman who had been on the gibbet for about a year already, who had died in the religion of the holy mother church, miraculously turned to that Lutheran man who had been put on the gibbet the previous Thursday and was near her, opened her mouth wide, and bit him on the chin. Because it was an amazing thing, the news spread quickly through the town. Many people ran there to see it and to find out if it was true. The Lutherans tried to separate them with their pikes because the Christians were making fun of them, but she kept turning back. On that day, more than four thousand people from all estates saw the event and true thing. . . .

The next Friday a Lutheran apothecary died suddenly. His wife was a good Christian, and when she saw him near death, she did her duty to urge him back to God and make his confession. But he would not listen, and he asked and begged her to call for the accursed Farel. She said that she would not do it and that if he came she would leave the house because she would have nothing to do with such company, and so he died. Because he had died in his error, his father, who was a Christian, had him thrown out of his house and carried to the cemetery of the Madeleine . . . because he did not regard him as his son and his wife likewise regarded him as nothing more than a dog. The heretics took him and buried him in their fashion. Then they left. The little Christian children who had watched how they did it said to each other, "Those dogs did not put any holy water on their brother. Let's give him what he deserves to soothe his soul." All together they poured their urine on his grave. . . .

[Invasion of the St. Clare convent:] The poor lay brother opened the door with good intention, and that multitude came inside immediately. The poor lay brother stood frozen with fear. They ran immediately through the convent . . . destroying and smashing everything they found, images, books, and breviaries; they did worse things than they had done in any other church, . . . Like enraged wolves, they destroyed those fine images with great axes and hammers, especially going after the blessed crucifix which was wonderfully handsome, and the image of Our Lady; they left no image intact. . . .

[On August 30, 1535, the nuns left Geneva under guard because it was too dangerous to remain:] [T]hey had no one but God to comfort them, except a poor lay brother named Nicolas des Arnox, who was still so sick he could hardly stand. . . . In front of them and at their sides were at least three hundred archers, well armed to protect the syndics, which was a good thing. For when the wicked Genevans, who had already decided the night before to pillage and violate the sisters, gathered, there were soon at least five hundred of them, and they blocked the Serrière de Saint Antoine [a narrow street], on the sisters' path, thinking they would pull the young sisters aside and hold them back, and they stood in front of them. One of them came close to the poor simple nun – and mother vicaress was at her side to protect her . . . and he whispered in her ear, "Sister Jacquemine, come with me! I will treat you like my sister."

Mother vicaress replied, "Hah! Wicked guard, you are lying!" She shouted, "Monseigneur Syndic, look how poorly you are obeyed! Get these boys out of the road!"

At those words everyone froze, and when the syndic saw that band of wicked troublemakers, God made him very angry, and in a furious and horrible voice he swore on the blood of God, "If any man moves, he will have his head cut off mercilessly on the spot!" . . .

And God cause them to be terrified; they bared their teeth in malice and retreated and watched the sisters from a distance. The sisters continued on their way trembling with fear, there is no doubt. . . .

When they had crossed the bridge, although they did not yet find anyone to comfort them, it was a great relief to be out of the city limits and in monseigneur's lands [Savoy].

9.7 The Ecclesiastical Ordinances of 1541
Kingdon 1974: 97–103

In the name of the Almighty God, we the Syndics, the Small and Great Council . . . have ordained and established in our city and territory the observation and maintenance of the ecclesiastical polity which follows, since we see that it is taken from the Gospel of Jesus Christ.

First, there are four orders of offices which Our Lord has instituted for the government of His Church, namely: the pastors, secondly, the doctors, then the elders, otherwise called those delegated by the Seigneury, and, fourthly, the deacons. . . .

With regard to the pastors . . . their office is to announce the Word of God for the purpose of instructing, admonishing, exhorting and reproving, both in public and in private, to administer the sacraments, and to exercise fraternal correction with the elders or delegates. . . .

[I]n order that all the ministers maintain doctrinal purity and concord among themselves, it will be expedient that they meet together on one particular day of the week for a conference on the Scriptures. No one shall be exempt without a legitimate excuse. If anyone is negligent with respect to this, he is to be admonished. . . .

The proper office of the doctors is to instruct the faithful in sound doctrine so that the purity of the Gospel is not corrupted either by ignorance or by erroneous belief. . . .

However, since it is possible to profit from such [educational] lessons only if first instructed in languages and the humanities, and since also there is need to raise up the seed for the future so that the Church is not left a desert to our children, a *collège* must be established in order to instruct them and to prepare them for the ministry as well as for the civil government. . . .

[The Elders'] office is to watch over the life of each person, to admonish amicably those whom they see to be at fault and leading a disorderly life, and when necessary to report them to the Company, which will be authorized to administer fraternal correction and to do so in association with the others.

As this church is now organized, it will be desirable to elect two from the Small Council, four from the Council of Sixty, and six from the Council of Two Hundred. They should be men of virtuous lives, honest, without reproach and beyond all suspicion, above all God-fearing and of good spiritual prudence. And, they should be elected in such a manner that there will be some of them in each quarter of the city, so that their eyes will be everywhere. . . .

There were always two kinds of deacons in the early Church. Some were delegated to receive, dispense and preserve the property of the poor, daily alms as well as possessions, revenues, and pensions. Others were to care for and remember the sick and administer the food for the poor, a custom which we still retain at present. And, in order to avoid confusion, since we have both *procureurs* and *hospitalliers*, one of the four *procureurs* of the hospital shall be the receiver of all its property. And, he shall be sufficiently paid in order to better exercise his office. . . .

It will be necessary to watch diligently that the communal hospital is well maintained. It is as much for the sick as for the elderly who cannot work, and, in addition, for widows, orphaned children and other poor persons. . . .

It will also be necessary both for the poor of the hospital and for those of the city who do not have the means to help themselves, that there be a physician and a surgeon employed by the city. While practicing in the city, they shall be charged with the care of the hospital and the visitation of other poor persons. . . .

Moreover, in order to prevent begging which is contrary to proper polity, it will be necessary for the Seigneury to appoint several of its officers and to station them at the exits of the churches to remove from these places those who might resist. And, if there are offenders or recalcitrant individuals, they are to bring them to one of the Lord Syndics. Similarly, at other times, the *dizainiers* [officials in charge of the districts of the city] are to watch that the prohibition against begging is properly observed.

9.8 Calvin to Kaspar Olevianus regarding the churches in Heidelberg (1560)
CStA 8: 121–3

That there is some hope to be able to introduce a church order in the Pfalz pleases me very much. If perhaps for this purpose our local order can be of use, I will happily summarize the main points.

The pastors are selected by our Collegium [clerical assembly]. The candidates are given a text to interpret in order to test their skill. Then they are examined on the main points of doctrine. Finally, they have to preach before us as well as before the congregation. Two members of the Council are also present. If the candidates' training is found sufficient, we recommend them to the Council with testimonials, and it is in its power to reject the candidates if it finds anything unsuitable. If, after this process, they are accepted, then their names are published so that if anyone has any kind of unknown offence on their conscience, it can be indicated within eight days. Those whose election is approved through universal tacit agreement, we then entrust to God and the congregation.

Children are baptized only in a public preaching worship service because it appears nonsensical that the celebratory reception into the community occur only before a pair of witnesses. The father must be there, unless prevented by a pressing engagement, in order to answer the baptismal questions with the godparents. No one is permitted to be a godparent who does not recognize with us the same confession [of faith]. The banned are also excluded from this honor.

No one may come to the holy Supper of Christ who has not confessed his faith. For that reason four examinations are held annually in which the children are questioned and each one's progress is ascertained. Even if they begin each Sunday in the catechism lesson, in a certain sense passing exams, they still may not come to the Lord's Supper until according to the judgment of the pastor they have gained sufficient understanding of the main content of the faith. With respect to the adults, there is an annual inspection of each family. We allot the districts among ourselves so that the individual precincts can be visited by turns. The pastor is accompanied by one of the elders. Thereby newcomers may also then be examined. Those already received are exempted and only asked whether the home is orderly and peaceful, whether there is conflict with the neighbors, whether there happens to be any drunkenness, whether they are lazy and inactive in attending sermons.

The supervision of conduct is administered in the following manner. . . .

[N]o one is summoned [for discipline] except one who has received a personal admonition due to disobedience and gives a bad example to the community such as blasphemers, drunkards, whores, brawlers and quarrelers, dancers and leaders of balls, and suchlike people. He who has only slightly erred is reprimanded with friendly words and dismissed. The rebuke is stronger for more serious sins. Namely, the pastor then excommunicates the person, even if only for a brief period. . . . Anyone who stubbornly disdains church authority and does not repent of his defiance within a year's time will be expelled for a year by the Council. If anyone behaves in an especially impudent manner, the Council takes up the matter and punishes them. Whoever, in order to save his life, has renounced his evangelical faith to the papists and attended mass, is to face the community. The pastor then declares the matter from the chancel. Then the banned person kneels and humbly asks for forgiveness. . . . In order that the people cannot complain about excessive severity, the pastors not only place themselves under the same punishments, but each of the ban's rated offences carries with it at the same time the removal from office.

I think this summary is sufficient. From this you can already recognize the form [of the church order] which however I cannot provide [completely] to you. Simply set forth what you find useful for yourselves so that it is not difficult to exhort good wise men to advise what is best. . . .

9.9 François de Bonivard: *On the Ecclesiastical Polity of Geneva*
Kingdon 1974: 104–7

[The Consistory] was set up as follows: Of the four Syndics, one would always be Judge and Head of the Consistory with the assistance of certain laymen, some from the Small Council and others from the Council of Two Hundred, and the Preachers. They would be censors of morals before a case was referred to the temporal court for correction. Marital cases were handled in the same way. . . . If there were important cases, they were referred to the Small Council for judgment on the following Monday, as the Consistory met on Thursday. They had jurisdiction to excommunicate, barring from Communion those who were obstinate in their sin. . . .

Moreover, you must know that the magistrates of Geneva have not done as many others who have deprived the thief of his plunder, then have not rendered it to the robbed, but kept it for themselves. Knowing that the property of the Church appertains to such uses as we have heretofore mentioned, they have also applied it to the Ministers and Schools as we have stated above, which is for the service of truth. Next, it is applied to the service of charity, which is to nourish the poor, those unable to earn their living by the sweat of their brow as God commands; it also supports those who are strong and robust enough to nourish themselves but cannot feed their wives and children, because they have too great a number. Thus, aid is distributed to them in proportion to the burden which they have over and above that which they can support with their own hands. From the beginning of the abolition of papism, they took possession of the Convent of the Women of Saint Clare, chasing the sisters from it. Of it they made a hospital where are nourished not only the poor of the city, but those of all places from which their churches receive revenues. Transients have a free meal in the evening if they arrive here and breakfast the morning before they depart. The hospital has its own minister and its school-master and school-mistress for the boys and girls. . . . It is true that what remains of the property of the Church is employed for public uses, particularly for the fortification of the city and other defenses of war, which is only, after all, for the Church. Because, if the papal ecclesiastics wished to return to the thievery from which they were removed and they were not resisted, the poor would necessarily die of famine as previously. Thus the places where the affairs of piety govern have been delegated by good rules. There is the hospital where charity is exercised and close by the hospital, the *collège* where truth is taught.

Considering thus all the aforementioned things, do you know of any reason why Geneva ought not now call itself the true Church of God which has received and protected with all its power that which God first announced by His Prophets and later by His Son and the Apostles? . . .

9.10 Calvin: *Institutes of the Christian Religion*
Calvin 1960 (page numbers appear after citations)

Moreover, it has been my purpose in this labor to prepare and instruct candidates in sacred theology for the reading of the divine Word, in order that they may be able both to have easy access to it and to advance in it without stumbling. For I believe I have so embraced the sum of religion in all its parts, and have arranged it in such an order, that if anyone rightly grasps it, it will not be difficult for him to determine what he ought especially to seek in Scripture, and to what end he ought to relate its contents. . . . (4)

Nearly all wisdom we possess, that is to say, true and sound wisdom, consists of two parts: the knowledge of God and of ourselves. (35)

Consequently, we know the most perfect way of seeking God, and the most suitable order, is not for us to attempt with bold curiosity to penetrate to the investigation of his essence, which we ought more to adore than meticulously search out. . . . (62)

But a most pernicious error widely prevails that Scripture has only so much weight as is conceded to it by the consent of the church. As if the eternal and inviolable truth of God depended upon the decision of men! . . . Thus these sacrilegious men, wishing to impose an unbridled tyranny under the cover of the church, do not care with what absurdities they ensnare themselves and others, provided they can force this one idea upon the simple-minded: that the church has authority in all things. (75)

When we call faith "knowledge" we do not mean comprehension of the sort that is commonly concerned with those things which fall under human sense perception. For faith is so far above sense that man's mind has to go beyond and rise above itself in order to attain it. . . . From this we conclude that the knowledge of faith consists in assurance rather than in comprehension. . . .

For unbelief is so deeply rooted in our hearts, and we are so inclined to it, that not without hard struggle is each one able to persuade himself of what all confess with the mouth: namely, that God is faithful. . . .

Here, indeed, is the chief hinge on which faith turns: that we do not regard the promises of mercy that God offers as true only outside ourselves, but not at all in us; rather that we make them ours by inwardly embracing them. . . . Briefly, he alone is truly a believer who, convinced by a firm conviction that God is a kindly and well-disposed Father toward him, promises him all things on the basis of his generosity; who relying upon the promises of divine benevolence toward him, lays hold on an undoubted expectation of salvation. (559–62)

He is said to be justified in God's sight who is both reckoned righteous in God's judgment and has been accepted on account of his righteousness. Indeed, as iniquity is abominable to God, so no sinner can find favor in his eyes in so far as he is a sinner and so long as he is reckoned as such. Accordingly, wherever there is sin, there also the wrath and vengeance of God show themselves. Now he is justified who is reckoned in the condition not of a sinner, but of a righteous man; and for that reason, he stands firm before God's judgment seat while all sinners fall. If an innocent accused person be summoned before the judgment seat of a fair judge, where he will be judged according to his innocence, he is said to be "justified" before the judge. . . . [J]ustified by faith is he who, excluded from the righteousness of works, grasps the righteousness of Christ through faith, and is clothed in it, appears in God's sight not as a sinner but as a righteous man.

Therefore, we explain justification simply as the acceptance with which God receives us into his favor as righteous men. And we say that it consists in the remission of sins and the imputation of Christ's righteousness. (725–7)

Christian freedom, in my opinion, consists of three parts. The first: that the consciences of believers, in seeking assurance of their justification before God, should rise above and advance beyond the law, forgetting all law righteousness. . . .

The second part, dependent upon the first, is that consciences observe the law, not as if constrained by the necessity of the law, but that freed from the law's yoke they willingly obey God's will. . . .

The third part of Christian freedom lies in this: regarding outward things that are of themselves "indifferent" [adiaphora], we are not bound by God by any religious obligation preventing us from sometimes using them and other times not using them, indifferently. . . . (834, 836, 838)

No one who wishes to be thought religious dares simply deny predestination, by which God adopts some to hope of life, and sentences others to eternal death. . . . We call predestination God's eternal decree, by which he determined with himself what he willed to become of each man. For all are not created in equal condition; rather eternal life is fore-ordained for some, eternal damnation for others. (926)

[W]e should contemplate the evident cause of condemnation in the corrupt nature of humanity – which is closer to us – rather than seek a hidden and utterly incomprehensible cause in God's predestination. And let us not be ashamed to submit our understanding to God's boundless wisdom so far as to yield before its many secrets. For, of those things which it is neither given nor lawful to know, ignorance is learned; the craving to know, a kind of madness. (957)

Accordingly, those whom God has adopted as his sons are said to have been chosen not in themselves but in his Christ; . . . But if we have been chosen in him, we shall not find assurance of our election in ourselves; and not even in God the Father, if we conceive him as severed from his Son. Christ, then, is the mirror wherein we must, and without self-deception may, contemplate our own election. For since it is into his body the Father has destined those to be engrafted whom he has willed from eternity to be his own, that he may hold as sons all whom he acknowledges to be among his members, we have been inscribed in the book of life if we are in communion with Christ. (970)

But however these deeds of men are judged in themselves, still the Lord accomplished his work through them alike when he broke the bloody scepters of arrogant kings and when he overturned intolerable governments. Let the princes hear and be afraid.

But we must, in the meantime, be very careful not to despise or violate that authority of magistrates, full of venerable majesty, which God has established by the weightiest of decrees, even though it may reside with the most unworthy men, who defile it as much as they can with their own wickedness. For, if the correction of unbridled despotism is the Lord's to avenge, let us not at once think that it is entrusted to us, to whom no command has been given except to obey and suffer.

I am speaking all the while of private individuals. For if there are now any magistrates of the people, appointed to restrain the willfulness of kings, . . . I am so far from forbidding them to withstand, in accordance with their duty, the fierce licentiousness of kings, that, if they wink at kings who violently fall upon and assault the lowly common folk, I declare that their dissimulation involves nefarious perfidy, because they dishonestly betray the freedom of the people, of which they know that they have been appointed protectors of God's ordinance. . . .

The Lord, therefore, is the King of Kings, who, when he has opened his sacred mouth, must alone be heard, before all and above all men; next to him we are subject to those men who are in authority over us, but only in him. If they command anything against him, let it go unesteemed. And here let us not be concerned about all that dignity which the magistrates possess; for no harm is done to it when it is humbled before that singular and truly supreme power of God. . . . (1518–20)

9.11 Calvin: The Geneva Catechism (1545)
CStA 2: 71–5

185. Let us go to the second table [of the Ten Commandments]
      It begins: Honor your father and mother.
186. What do you understand here by "honor"?
      Children shall with humility and subordination be obedient to parents, relate to
      them with respect, help them where necessary, and work and do their utmost for
      them. In these three parts is the honor due parents.
187. Continue
      A promise is added to the commandment: That you may live long in the land
      that the Lord God has given you.
188. What does this mean?
      Whoever shows this required honor to parents will receive long life from God's
      benevolent will.
189. But this life is full of suffering. Why then does God promise us such long life as
      a benefit?
      Even though this life may have so much misery, it is nevertheless a blessing
      of God for the faithful, and it may also be on that account that it is a testi-
      mony to his fatherly affection, when he nurtures and preserves us here
      [on earth].
190. Conversely, does it follow from this that whoever is quickly snatched from this
      world without a long life is cursed by God?
      Not at all. Rather it sometimes happens that the more God loves someone, the
      quicker he takes him from this life.
191. But if God acts this way, how does he keep his promise?
      When God promises us earthly goods it is only under the condition that they
      serve the good and health of our soul. It would be truly a reverse of all order if
      regard for the soul were not foremost.
192. What happens to those who disobey their parents?
      They will be punished not only at the Last Judgment, but God will also take
      revenge on them in this earthly life, snatching them away in the prime of life,
      letting them suffer a wretched death, or through other means.
193. Is the land of Canaan spoken of in this promise, but not literally?
      Yes, in so far as it concerns the Israelites. But for us this promise has a com-
      prehensive meaning and must be expanded. Because the whole earth is God's,
      he secures us in whatever land we may dwell (Psalms 24:1; 89:11–12;
      115:16).
194. Is this commandment valid in any other way?
      Although it speaks only of father and mother, it is to be understood that all
      superiors are included under this heading.
195. What then?
      God has raised them to a higher position. There is no authority, no honorary
      office, be it parents, princes, or office holder apart from God's decree because it
      is his will the world be so ordered (Romans 13:1).

9.12 Ordinances Concerning Church Polity in Geneva (1546)
Hughes 1966: 53–9

Concerning Sermons

1. All the members of each household shall attend church on Sundays, unless it is necessary to leave someone behind to look after children or livestock, under penalty of 3 sous.
2. If on a weekday there is a service ordered by good authority, those who are able to attend and have no legitimate excuse are to attend; at least one member of each household shall be present, under penalty as above. . . .
5. During the sermon everyone shall listen attentively and there shall be no unseemly or scandalous behaviour.

Faults Which Contravene the Reformation apart from Those Mentioned Above

Superstitions
1. Those who are found in possession of paternosters or images for the purpose of worshipping them shall be sent before the Consistory, . . .
2. Those who have been on pilgrimages or similar journeys.
3. Those who observe the Romish festivals or fasts shall only be reprimanded, unless they remain obstinately rebellious.
4. Those who have attended the mass shall, besides being reprimanded, be summoned before Messieurs.
5. For this offence Messieurs shall decide whether to punish them by imprisonment or by special fines, according to their discretion. . . .

Drunkenness
1. People are not to invite one another to excessive drinking, under penalty of three sous.
2. Taverns are to be closed during public worship. . . .
3. If anyone is found drunk he shall pay three sous on the first occasion and shall be summoned before the Consistory; on the second occasion he shall pay the sum of five sous; and on the third he shall be fined ten sous and be put in prison. . . .

Songs and dances
Anyone who sings indecent, dissolute, or outrageous songs or dances the fling or some similar dance shall be imprisoned for three days and shall then be sent before the Consistory. . . .

Fornication
1. Any who are found practicing fornication, if they are an unmarried man and an unmarried woman, shall be imprisoned for six days on bread and water and shall pay sixty sous into public funds.

2. If it is a case of adultery, that is to say, that one or the other is married, they shall be imprisoned for nine days on bread and water and pay into public funds a sum at the discretion of Messieurs, according to the greater seriousness of the offence.
3. Those who are engaged to be married shall not live together as man and wife until the marriage has been solemnized in church, otherwise they shall be punished as fornicators. . . .

9.13 Calvin: *Short Treatise on the Holy Supper of our Lord Jesus Christ* (1542)
Calvin 1954: 163–6

As to the contention which has been so keenly debated in our time [the Lord's Supper], . . . I could wish that the memory of it be quite abolished, . . . Nevertheless, because I see many good consciences troubled, since they know not to which side to turn, I shall briefly state what seems to me to be necessary advice for showing them how they ought to decide. First, I pray all the faithful, in the name of God, not to be too offended at the great difference which has arisen between those who ought to be leaders in bringing back truth to the light of day. . . .

When Luther began to teach, he regarded the matter of the supper in such a way, that, with respect to the corporeal presence of Christ, he appeared ready to leave it as the world generally conceived it. For while condemning transubstantiation, he said the bread was the body of Christ, insofar as it was united with him. Further, he added some similes which were a little harsh and rude. But he did so as by constraint, because he could not otherwise explain his meaning. For it is difficult to give an explanation of so high a matter, without using some impropriety of speech.

On the other hand, there arose Zwingli and Oecolampadius, who, considering the abuse and deceit which the devil had employed to establish such a carnal presence of Christ as had been taught and held for more than six hundred years, thought it wrong to dissimulate; since this view implied an execrable idolatry in that Jesus Christ was adored as if enclosed under the bread. Now because it was very difficult to remove this opinion, rooted so long in the hearts of men, they applied all their mind to decry it, remonstrating that it was a quite gross error not to acknowledge what is so clearly testified in Scripture, concerning the ascension of Jesus Christ, that he was in his humanity received up into heaven, where he dwells until he descend to judge the world. While they were absorbed with this point, they forgot to define what is the presence of Christ in the Supper in which one ought to believe, and what communication of his body and his blood one there received. So Luther thought that they had intended to leave nothing else but bare signs without any corresponding spiritual substance. Hence he began to resist and oppose them, even to the extent of denouncing them as heretics. Once the contention had begun, it became more inflamed with time, and so has continued too bitterly for a period of fifteen years or thereabouts, without either party listening to the other. . . .

Both parties failed altogether to have patience to listen to each other, in order to follow truth without passion, wherever it might be found. None the less, we must not leave off thinking what is our duty. It is not to forget the gifts which our Lord bestowed on them, and the blessings which he distributes to us at their hands and by means of them. . . . In short, since we see that they were and still are distinguished by holy life and excellent knowledge and by conspicuous zeal to edify the Church, we ought always to judge and speak with modesty and reverence; just because it has pleased God at last, having humbled them thus, to bring to an end this unhappy disputation, or at least to calm it, in anticipation of it being quite resolved. I say this because there is not yet any published formula in which agreement has been framed, as would be expedient. But this will happen when God is pleased to bring into one place all those who are to draw it up. Meanwhile, it must content us that there is brotherliness and communion between the Churches, and that all agree in what is necessary for meeting together, according to the command of God. We all confess, then, with one mouth that, in receiving the sacrament in faith, according to the ordinance of the Lord, we are truly partakers of the real substance of the body and blood of Jesus Christ. How this is done, some may deduce better and explain more clearly than others. . . .

9.14 Calvin on Luther: Letter to Heinrich Bullinger (1544)
CStA 8: 98–100

I hear Luther is soon going to attack with frightful abuse not only you [in Zurich] but all of us. . . .

But it is my desire that you consider what a great man Luther is, by what extraordinary gifts of the Spirit he is distinguished, how brave and unshakeable, how skilled, how effective he has been in working continuously up to now for the destruction of the lordship of the Antichrist and for the spread of the doctrine of salvation. I have often said: If he should call me the devil, I would nevertheless honor him, regarding him as an outstanding servant of God. He certainly also suffers from great faults just as he is rich in splendid virtues. If he had only endeavored better to control his stormy character! If he had only always turned his innate vehemence against the enemies of the truth instead of letting it flash against the servants of the Lord! If he had only made more effort to see his own faults! . . . [N]evertheless it is our obligation so to reprove what is faulty in him that we give him credit for his brilliant gifts. I ask you this as your colleague, think above all that you have to do here with a first-born among the servants of Christ to whom we all owe so much. . . . And if Luther has angered us, it is better to refrain from a fight than to make the damage greater to the detriment of the whole church. . . .

9.15 The *Consensus Tigurinus* (1549)
Hughes 1966: 115–23

I have thought it worthwhile to summarize and arrange in order the main articles on which we conferred together, so that, if my plan receives your approval it will be possible for anyone to find tabulated as it were what was done and transacted between us [Geneva and Zurich]. . . . At the same time I would like them to know that nothing is included which all our own colleagues who serve Christ under the jurisdiction of the republic of Geneva or in the territory of Neuchâtel, have not approved by their subscription. . . .

The Purposes of the Sacraments:

The purposes of the sacraments are these: that they should be marks and badges of the Christian profession and fellowship or brotherhood, and that they should be incitements to thanksgiving and exercises of faith and godly living, indeed contracts binding us to this; but among the other purposes this is the principal one, that by means of the sacraments God may testify, represent, and seal His grace to us. . . .

The Sacraments Do Not Confer Grace:

By this teaching that fabrication of the sophists is overthrown which teaches that the sacraments of the new law confer grace on all who do not interpose the impediment of mortal sin [Council of Trent, Session VII, Canon 6]. For, apart from the fact that in the sacraments nothing is appropriated except by faith, it must also be maintained that the grace of God is least of all bound to them in such a way that whoever has the sign also possesses the reality. For the signs are administered to the reprobate equally with the elect, but the truth of which they are signs belongs only to the latter.

The Idea of a Local Presence Must Be Put Away:

It is especially important that any idea of a local presence of Christ should be put away. For while the signs are here in the world, seen by our eyes and touched by our hands, Christ in so far as He is man must be sought nowhere else than in heaven and in no other way than with the mind and the understanding of faith. . . .

Against Transubstantiation and Other Follies:

In this way not only is the fiction of the papists concerning transubstantiation refuted but also all the gross figments and futile theorizings which either detract from Christ's heavenly glory or are incompatible with the truth of His human nature. For we consider it no less absurd to locate Christ under the form of bread, or to conjoin Him with the bread, than for the bread to be transubstantiated into His body.

The Body of Christ Is Locally in Heaven:

And lest there should be any ambiguity when we say that Christ is to be sought in heaven this manner of speaking signifies and expresses the distance between places. For although philosophically speaking there is no place above the heavens, yet because the body of Christ, in that it bears the nature and mode of a human body is finite and is contained in heaven as in a place, it is necessarily as far distant from us in terms of separation between places as heaven is from earth. . . .

9.16 A Letter from the Geneva Company of Pastors to the Swiss Churches on Jerome Bolsec (1551)
Hughes 1966: 169–72

There is a certain Jerome here who, having abandoned the monk's cowl, became one of those wandering physicians who by deception and trickery accumulate so much impudence that they are ready and eager for any audacity. It is now eight months since this man endeavored, in the public assembly of our church, to overthrow the doctrine of the free election of God which we, together with you, teach as it is received from the Word of God.

[T]his worthless fellow stood up and protested that it was a false and wicked opinion . . . that the will of God is the cause of all things. It was in this way, he said, that sin and the blame for all evils were ascribed to God, so that He became saddled with a tyrannical will such as the ancient poets had invented for their god Jupiter.

Jerome then turned to the other article, affirming that men did not obtain salvation because they were elect, but that they were elect because they believe, and that no man was reprobated merely because God so willed it, but only those who turned away from the election which is common to all.

In raising this question he assailed us with many atrocious insults. On hearing of the matter the prefect of the city put him in prison, chiefly because he had incited the people in a tumultuous manner not to let themselves be deceived by us. Next, a report of the affair was made to the Council, where he proceeded to defend himself with no less obstinacy than temerity. Meanwhile, when he kept on claiming that there were many ministers in the other churches who agreed with him, we requested our Council not to pronounce a final judgment before the answer of your church had been received showing that this worthless fellow was dishonestly laying claim to your support. . . .

Now we desire that our church should be rid of this pestilential person, but in such a way that he does not become injurious to our neighbors. . . .

It is generally agreed that we are justified by faith; but the substance of God's mercy is seen when we understand that faith is the fruit of free adoption, and that adoption is the consequence of the eternal election of God. This impostor, however, not only pretends that election depends on faith but also that faith itself springs no less from man's own impulse than from heavenly inspiration.

9.17 Calvin: "The Consent Of The Pastors Of The Church Of Christ At Geneva, Concerning 'The Eternal Predestination Of God,' By Which He Has Chosen Some Men Unto Salvation, While He Has Left Others To Their Own Destruction . . ."
Dennison 2008: 693, 695, 712

The free election of God, by which He adopts unto Himself whom He will out of the lost generation of men, has been hitherto publicly declared by men, in this city, . . . But now, Satan, the father of all disturbances, has subtly introduced a wide spreading error, and has attempted to root out my doctrine, which is drawn from the pure Word of God, and to shake the faith of the whole people. But since this hungry hunter after vain glory [i.e., Bolsec] wishes to gain notoriety out of the very flames of the temple of God, . . . let his name remain buried in our silence, while I leave it purposely unmentioned. . . .

[W]hosoever shall hold faith to be the earnest and pledge of adoption, will assuredly confess that it flows from Divine election as its eternal source. And yet the knowledge of salvation is not to be sought from the secret counsel of God. Life is set before us in Christ, who not only makes Himself known, but presents Himself to our enjoyment in the Gospel. Into this mirror let the eye of faith ever fixedly look. Nor let it ever desire to penetrate where access to its sight is not given. . . .

I will now enter upon the more express subject and object of the present undertaking, which are to prove that nothing has been taught by me concerning this important doctrine but that which God Himself clearly teaches us all in the Sacred Oracles. The sum of which is this: that the salvation of believers depends on the eternal election of God, for which no cause or reason can be rendered but His own gratuitous good pleasure. . . .

9.18 Servetus: Letter to Abel Poupin, Minister in Geneva (1547?)
Bainton 1960: 145, 147

Your gospel is without God, without true faith, without good works. Instead of a God you have a three-headed Cerberus [i.e., the Trinity]. For faith you have a deterministic dream, and good works you say are inane pictures. With you the faith of Christ is mere deceit effecting nothing. Man is with you an inert trunk, and God is a chimera of the enslaved will. You do not know the celestial regeneration by water and you have as it were a fable. You close the Kingdom of Heaven before men. . . . Woe! Woe! Woe! This is the third letter that I have written to warn you that you may know better. I will not warn you again. Perhaps it will offend you that I meddle in this fight of Michael [the Archangel] and wish to involve you. Study that passage carefully and you will see that they are men who will fight there, giving their souls to death in blood and for a testimony to Jesus Christ. Before the fight there will be a seduction of the world. The fight then follows, and the time is at hand. . . . I know that I shall certainly die on this account, but I do not falter that I may be a disciple like the Master. This I regret, that I am not able to amend for you some passages in my works which are with Calvin. Goodbye, and do not expect to hear from me again.

9.19 The Trial of Michael Servetus (1553)
Hughes 1966: 223–4

On 13 August of this year Michael Servetus was recognized by certain brethren and it was decided that he should be imprisoned lest he should further infect the world with his blasphemies and heresies, seeing that he was known to be altogether beyond hope of correction. Thereupon, a certain person [Nicolas de la Fontaine, Calvin's secretary] had filed a criminal action against him, setting down . . . the most notorious errors of Servetus. Several days later the Council ordered that we should be present when he was examined. When this was done the impudence and obstinacy of Servetus became all the more obvious; for, to begin with, he maintained that the name of the Trinity had been in use only since the Council of Nicea [325] and that all the theologians and martyrs prior to that had not known what it was. And when the plainest evidences were produced from Justin Martyr, Irenaeus, Tertullian, Origen, and others, so far was he from showing any shame that he poured out all sorts of absurdities in a most insulting and offensive manner.

9.20 Servetus: Plea for Religious Liberty
Bainton 1960: 62

The greatest of the apostles were sometimes in error. Even though you see Luther erring egregiously at some points you do not condemn him. . . . Such is human frailty that we condemn the spirits of others as impostors and impious and except our own, for no one recognizes his own errors. . . . I beg you, for God's sake, spare my name and fame. . . . You say that I want all to be robbers and that I will not suffer any to be punished and killed. I call Almighty God to witness that this is not my opinion and I detest it, but if ever I said anything it is that I consider it a serious matter to kill men because they are in error on some question of scriptural interpretation, when we know that the very elect may be led astray.

9.21 Servetus: Petition from Prison to the Geneva Council
Bainton 1960: 197

I humbly beg that you cut short these long delays and deliver me from prosecution. You see that Calvin is at the end of his rope, not knowing what to say and for his pleasure wishes to make me rot here in prison. The lice eat me alive. My clothes are torn and I have nothing for a change, neither jacket nor shirt, but a bad one. . . . I have been caged here for five weeks and he [Calvin] has not urged against me a single passage. . . .

I petition you that my case be referred to the Council of Two Hundred with my requests, and if I may appeal there I do so ready to assume all the cost, loss and interest of the law of an eye for an eye, both against the first accuser and against Calvin, who has taken up the case himself.

9.22 The Sentence of the Geneva Council (1553)
Bainton 1960: 207–9

The sentence pronounced against Michael Servet de Villeneuve of the Kingdom of Aragon in Spain who some twenty-three or twenty-four years ago printed a book at Hagenau in Germany against the Holy Trinity containing many great blasphemies. . . .

In consequence he became a fugitive from Germany. Nevertheless he continued in his errors and, in order the more to spread the venom of his heresy, he printed secretly a book . . . full of the said heresies and horrible, execrable blasphemies against the Holy Trinity, against the Son of God, against the baptism of infants and the foundations of the Christian religion. He confesses that in this book he called believers in the Trinity Trinitarians and atheists. He calls this Trinity a diabolical monster with three heads. He blasphemes detestably against the Son of God, saying that Jesus Christ is not the Son of God from eternity. He calls infant baptism an invention of the devil and sorcery. His execrable blasphemies are scandalous against the majesty of God, the Son of God and the Holy Spirit. This entails the murder and ruin of many souls. Moreover he wrote a letter to one of our ministers in which, along with other numerous blasphemies, he declared our holy evangelical religion to be without faith and without God and that in place of God we have a three-headed Cerberus. . . .

Wherefore we Syndics, judges of criminal cases in this city, having witnessed the trial conducted before us . . . and having seen your voluntary and repeated confessions and your books, judge that you, Servetus, have for a long time promulgated false and thoroughly heretical doctrine, despising all remonstrances and corrections . . . and that you have tried to make a schism and trouble the Church of God by which many souls may have been ruined and lost, a thing horrible, shocking, scandalous and infectious. And you have had neither shame nor horror of setting yourself against the divine Majesty and the Holy Trinity, and so you have obstinately tried to infect the world with your stinking heretical poison. . . . For these and other reasons, desiring to purge the Church of God of such infection and cut off the rotten member, having taken counsel with our citizens and having invoked the name of God to give just judgment . . . speaking in the name of the Father, Son and Holy Spirit, we now in writing give final sentence and condemn you, Michael Servetus, to be bound and taken to Champel and there attached to a stake and burned with your book to ashes. And so you shall finish your days and give an example to others who would commit the like.

9.23 Castellio: *Concerning Heretics*
Bainton 1951: 111–12

The true fear of God and charity are fallen and grown cold. Our life is spent in contention and in every manner of sin. We dispute, not as to the way by which we may come to Christ, which is to correct our lives, but rather as to the state and office of Christ, where he now is and what he is doing, how he is seated at the right hand of the Father, and how he is one with the Father; likewise with regard to the Trinity, predestination, free will; so, also, of God, the angels, the state of souls after this life, and other like things, which do not need to be known for salvation by faith. . . . Nor if these are known do they make a man better, as Paul says, "Though I understand all mysteries, and have not love, it profiteth me nothing." This perverse curiosity engenders worse evils. Men are puffed up with knowledge or with a false opinion of knowledge and look down upon others. Pride is followed by cruelty and persecution so that now scarcely anyone is able to endure another who differs at all from him. Although opinions are almost as numerous as men, nevertheless there is hardly any sect that does not condemn all others and desire to reign alone. Hence arise banishments, chains, imprisonments, stakes, and gallows and this miserable rage to visit daily penalties upon those who differ from the mighty about matters hitherto unknown, for so many centuries disputed, and not yet cleared up.

If, however, there is someone who strives . . . to live justly and innocently, then all others with one accord cry out against him if he differ from them in anything, and they confidently pronounce him a heretic on the ground that he seeks to be justified by works. Horrible crimes of which he never dreamed are attributed to him, and the common people are prejudiced by slander until they consider it a crime merely to hear him speak. Hence arises such cruel rage that some are so incensed by calumny as to be infuriated when the victim is first strangled instead of being burned alive at a slow fire. This is cruel enough, but a more capital offense is added when this conduct is justified under the robe of Christ and is defended as being in accord with his will, when Satan could not devise anything more repugnant to the nature and will of Christ!

10

The Reformation in France

In spite of early French Humanist contributions to Reformation theology and reform programs, the evangelical movement in France remained a "church under the cross." The biblical Humanist Lefèvre's emphasis on what would become the "solas" of the Reformation – grace, faith, Scripture (10.1–3) – marked him and the Humanist center in Meaux as the source of French evangelicalism (10.4), in spite of the fact that he remained in the Roman Catholic Church. In his *Histoire de l'Hérésie en France* (1605), Florimond de Raemond noted that after heresy was welcomed into France by Marguerite, the sister of Francis I, and Bishop Briçonnet, it rooted itself in the town of Meaux (10.5). Marguerite's continuing interest in reform led her to request an account of the events in Geneva from Marie Dentière, a former French nun active in Genevan reform with her husband. Dentière's *Epistle* is the first French account of reformed theology by a woman (10.6). During the night of October 17–18, 1534, placards (10.7) condemning the mass were posted in various places, including the door to the king's bedchamber. The infuriated king then decided to move against the "Lutherans," including students (10.8) and those caught worshiping at Calvinist services (10.9). Swiss missionary pastors to France appealed to Geneva for advice (10.10) and were exhorted to remain faithful to God's will (10.11). In spite of persecution, the French Reformed church grew to an estimated 400,000 by 1555. Calvin, in consultation with Beza and Viret, drafted a confession of faith that was reworked by twenty delegates representing seventy-two French churches. The following year the French Confession (10.12) was presented to King Francis II with a plea for justice in the face of persecution. In 1571, at La Rochelle, the Confession was confirmed by all the French churches; hence it is also known as the Confession of La Rochelle. Religious conflict caused both the Venetian ambassador and the French chancellor to voice concern about civil war (10.13–14). The Crown's attempt to promote peace foundered at the Colloquy of Poissy (10.15). The aftermath included the St. Bartholomew's Day massacre (10.16–17), assassinations (10.18–19), and renewed efforts for peace (10.20–22) leading to the Edict of Nantes (10.23).

The European Reformations Sourcebook, Second Edition. Edited by Carter Lindberg.
© 2014 John Wiley & Sons, Ltd. Published 2014 by John Wiley & Sons, Ltd.

10.1 Jacques Lefèvre: *Commentary on the Epistles of St. Paul* (1512)
Hughes 1984: 85

Christ truly forgives our sins, setting us free from them in this life's pilgrimage. . . . But he who trusts in works trusts in himself and leans on a cane which breaks of itself. . . . By grace alone [*per solam gratiam*] can we be saved. . . . For we are saved by his grace through faith – saved not because of ourselves, but by God's grace. For grace is a gift, not a work. And lest we should think that the faith by means of which we are justified is ours, even this is God's gift. Therefore we should attribute everything to God and nothing to ourselves, and so we should glory neither in ourselves nor in works, but in God's grace and mercy alone.

10.2 Lefèvre: Preface to Latin Commentary on the Gospels (1522)
Hughes 1984: 155

The word of God is sufficient; this alone is enough for the discovery of the life which knows no end; this rule alone is the guide to eternal life; all else on which the word of God does not shine is as unnecessary as it is superfluous.

10.3 Lefèvre: Letters to Farel (1524)
Mousseaux 1967: 51–2

20 April 1524. I received right away from the Bishop of Meaux the books which you sent to me. . . . I have also received your second letter and the two books of Zwingli. All the works you have sent me from Germany please me greatly. Greet Oecolampadius, Ugwald, Zwingli, Roussel, Antoine, Matthieu, the elect and his father, Pierre du Fosse, the men and women who love Christ, greet you.
6 July 1524. The New Testament translation into French has been received with an extraordinary eagerness by the common people to whom it is read in our diocese on Sundays and Feast Days. The king has set aside the obstacles which some want to put in the way of the spread of the Word. The letters of Oecolampadius made a vivid impression on our bishop who has charged Gerard Roussel to instruct the people daily in Paul's epistles, and has commissioned me to care for our more evangelical preachers in other areas of the diocese.

You will not believe with what power, in some places, God inclines the spirit of the people toward his Word since the publication of our books in French. But still you are right to lament about those which are not widely accepted. Several, backed by the authority of the Parlement, endeavor to stop the movement; but we have in Christ a faithful patron who, notwithstanding every obstacle, desires that his Word be freely declared and his reign proclaimed in a language that each can understand. Now the gospel and epistles are read to the people in their language on Feast Days and every Sunday, and in addition the priest gives some exhortations.

10.4 The Sorbonne Condemnation of Lefèvre's "Fifty-Two Sundays" (1525)
Screech 1964: 41–51 (the "propositions" are extracts from Lefèvre)

Proposition 1. Everything is given and pardoned to us in Jesus Christ alone if we have faith in him.

Censure. This proposition that faith alone is necessary and sufficient for the remission of sins and justification perniciously removes the pious works of the faithful from procuring salvation and is a heresy of Luther.

Proposition 12. My brothers, do not consider at all that the gifts of grace which are in you have come by your merit, but only by the grace, generosity, and infinite benevolence of Jesus Christ.

Censure. This indication that the gifts of grace are not given to man by good works and merit, is condemned according to the previous censure [i.e., a Manichaean and Lutheran heresy].

Proposition 27. Faith and the works of faith are done in God, in the Spirit of Jesus Christ, and not at all in man nor in the flesh.

Censure. This proposition that states that nothing of man is effectual in good works, but only that of God, is consistent with the errors of the Manichaeans and Lutherans, and is heretical.

Proposition 43. St. Paul says, Jesus Christ has died for our sins, therefore we do not have to do anything for our sins because Jesus Christ has atoned for us.

Censure. This proposition that alleges nothing else is required for the satisfaction of sins besides Christ's death, gives rash and foolish hope, and deceives those who have sinned; and is heretical.

Proposition 46. If you have this faith that Jesus Christ has died for you and for the remission of your sins, it is so; and your sins are blotted out and his death is yours, and the merit of his death is yours; and if you believe thus that he was raised for your justification, it is so; and his resurrection is yours and your justification, and you are truly justified by faith . . . by the Word of God.

Censure. This proposition which assigns all merit to faith or to believing the passion, resurrection, and all other mysteries of Christ, and rejects all penances, is a condemned Lutheran heresy.

10.5 Florimond de Raemond: Heresy at Meaux
Mousseaux 1967: 79–80

It was the town of Meaux that harbored heresy first and which sheltered it. . . . Therefore as the everlasting mark of its infamy, there is the proverb: "Lutherans of Meaux." . . .

Four Lutheran-Zwinglians: Guillaume Farel from Dauphiné, Jacques Lefèvre, Arnaud and Gérard Roussel from Picardy, eloquent men well versed in letters and languages, were all school companions taught in Paris. Their hands fed the leaven of heresy in France which they poured out in various regions due to the very great pliancy of that bishop [Briçonnet].

Thus they arrived at Meaux cloaked in appearance by a Catholic habit, but quasi-Lutherans, disguised idols, insinuating themselves into the homes of the town and among the people. . . .

But to what [purpose] are the apostles, priests, and doctors of the church, who according to the Scriptures are ordained of God, if the distribution and interpretation of holy writings or the treatment of sacred books are connected to artisans and women regarded as good as them? God has given to his church its heralds and ambassadors. They are the only voice it is necessary for us to hear, and not the voices of these bastards, strangers or unknowns, trumpets of sedition, and furies which hell has vomited forth to drown this miserable century in murders, impieties, filth, and sacrilege. . . .

10.6 Marie Dentière: *Epistle to Marguerite de Navarre* (1539)
Dentière 2004: 52–6, 59, 61, 81–2

[M]y most honored Lady, I wanted to write to you, not to teach you, but so that you might take pains with the King, your brother, to obviate all these divisions which reign in the places and among the people over whom God commissioned him to rule and govern. And also over your people whom God gave you to provide for and to keep in order. For what God has given you and revealed to us women, no more than men should we hide it and bury it in the earth. . . .

Not only will certain slanderers and adversaries of truth try to accuse us of excessive audacity and temerity, but so will certain of the faithful, saying that it is too bold for women to write to one another about matters of scripture. We may answer them by saying that all those women who have written and have been named in holy scripture should not be considered too bold. . . .

Even though in all women there has been imperfection, men have not been exempt from it. Why is it necessary to criticize women so much, seeing that no woman ever sold or betrayed Jesus, but a man named Judas? Who are they, I pray you, who have invented and contrived so many ceremonies, heresies, and false doctrines on earth if not men? . . . Never was a woman found to be a false prophet, but women have been misled by them. . . .

The Lord God desires that all without exception come to the pure and true knowledge of truth through one mediator, Jesus Christ alone, by asking for that understanding only through a true and living faith, . . .

It was not enough for the wickedness of men to attribute and bestow the honor that belongs to Jesus Christ on those visible things that were ordained by God, but also on things ordained and invented by men, without the authority of scripture, such as pilgrimages and money given for indulgences, and pardons, and a full lot of other evil idolatries that men have discovered, created, and invented through their good intentions, or rather to pillage and rob the poor people, going against the holy word of God. . . .

What do you fear from the cardinals and bishops who are in your courts? If God is on your side, who will be against you? Why don't you make them support their case publicly before everybody? . . . What good are they to you, I ask you, if they will not show that their cause is good, ordained by God? Will you put up with them and let them dominate you? . . .

O adherents and supporters of the pope ["kings, princes, and lords"] don't you see that you are manifestly waging a battle against God? . . . [Y]ou will destroy one another rather than the church. And the more you persecute, the more you light that great consuming fire. . . . It is clear that you are too cowardly, too full of Roman venom. . . . The sword of God is yours, and the pope takes it away from you. You are ordered by God to defend and protect the good and punish the wicked, but for the love of the pope, you do just the opposite. For the love of God, leave that cruel master and accept good Jesus and his word. . . . Wake up, kings, princes, and lords; you have slept too long.

10.7 The Message of the Placards
Kidd 1911: 528–32

I invoke heaven and earth in witness of the truth against the pompous and vain Papal Mass by which the whole world (unless God intervene) is and will be totally destroyed, ruined, lost and sunk. In it our Lord is outrageously blasphemed and the people seduced and blinded. It must no longer be tolerated or endured. . . .

It is and ought to be very certain to all Christian faithful that our Lord and only Savior Jesus Christ, as the great Bishop and Pastor eternally appointed by God, gave his body, soul, life, and blood for our sanctification in perfect sacrifice. That sacrifice cannot and ought not ever be repeated by any visible sacrifice as though the original sacrifice were of no value or power, insufficient and incomplete; or that Jesus Christ had not fully satisfied God, His Father's justice for us, and that He is not the true Christ, Saviour, Pastor, Bishop and Mediator. . . .

[T]he Pope, and all his vermin of cardinals, bishops and priests, monks and other sanctimonious Mass-sayers and all those who agree with them are false-prophets, damned cheats, apostates, wolves, false-pastors, idolaters, seducers, liars and wretched blasphemers, killers of souls, renouncers of Christ, of His death and passion, perjurers, traitors, thieves, rapers of God's honor and more detestable than devils. . . .

The fruit and use of the Mass are wholly contrary to the fruit and use of the holy Supper of Jesus Christ. . . . By it [the Mass] all knowledge of Christ is erased, the preaching of the Gospel is rejected and impeded, the time is occupied in bells, howls, chants, vain rituals, lights, incense, disguises and all kinds of sorceries. In this way the poor world (like lambs and sheep) is miserably deceived, diverted, and misled, and consumed, preyed upon, and devoured by these ravaging wolves.

10.8 Letter to Geneva from Five Evangelical Students Imprisoned in Lyon (1552)
Hughes 1966: 191–2

Very dear brothers in our Lord Jesus Christ, since you have been informed of our captivity and of the fury which drives our enemies to persecute and afflict us, we felt it would be good to let you know of the liberty of our spirit and of the wonderful assistance and consolation which our good Father and Savior gives us in these dark prison cells, so that you may participate not only in our affliction of which you have heard but also in our consolation, as members of the same body who all participate in common both in the good and in the evil which comes to pass. . . . So far, indeed, are we from wishing to regard our affliction as a curse of God, as the world and the flesh wish to regard it, that we regard it rather as the greatest blessing that has ever come upon us, for in it we are made the children of God, brothers and companions of Jesus Christ, the Son of God, and are conformed to His image; and by it the possession of our eternal inheritance is confirmed to us. . . .

We pray you most affectionately to thank our good God with us for granting us so great a blessing, so that many may return thanks to Him, beseeching Him that, as He has commenced this work in us, so He will complete it, to the end that all glory may be given to Him, and that, whether we live or die, all may be to His honor and glory, to the edification of His poor Church, and to the advancement of our salvation, Amen!

10.9 Nicolas des Gallars, Pastor in Paris, to His Genevan Colleagues (1557)
Hughes 1966: 329–30

I imagine that you have already heard, if only by way of rumors, of the great misfortune that our congregation suffered three days ago. Almost two hundred persons are held captive by the enemy who threaten them with all kinds of dire consequences. Among them are many distinguished individuals, both men and women; but not the least respect is shown either for their family or for their station. . . . Tell me, what action can I take in the face of this great disaster? . . . The dangers of this war are now so great that I cannot remain here any longer. . . . My comrades in battle are unaware of the condition on which I was sent, since they have not received your letter. They consider me to be entirely committed and bound to them, and although I have from the beginning declared that it could not be so, yet they are unwilling to believe me. I rejoice and give thanks to Almighty God that I have been present in these troubles; for, if I have achieved nothing else, at least I have blocked many misconceived and pernicious plans, which would not only have caused the greatest offence but would also have brought upon us worse disaster and the utmost calamity. It is for this reason that I pray and beseech you to send a letter to them without delay so that, instead of making some rash move, they may submit to sound counsel. Should you delay to write, I fear it will be of little use; for it is difficult to restrain the impulse of many persons. The rest I will tell you when I am able to communicate freely with you.

10.10 Calvin's Response to Des Gallars (1557)
Hughes 1966: 331–2

Now with respect to the advice for which you ask, the united judgment of your colleagues is as follows: if you leave your post during these first disturbances we fear, not without reason, that your departure will cast down the spirits of all, indeed almost drive them to the extremes of despair. . . . Therefore so long as turbulent movements may in some measure be checked it is desirable that you should be close at hand, so that they may be assured by indisputable evidence that you are a partner in their perils. This proof will be a source of no little encouragement not only to them but also to all who are in sympathy with them. . . . If you see that your presence is necessary, for holding things together, we beseech you most earnestly to remain for some time longer, until, with the slackening of the enemy's fury, a measure of tranquillity affords justification for your departure, or until some greater exigency forces you out. If, however, the fear of others restricts your effectiveness, or you see the way to be closed before you, it is not our wish that you should sit by in idleness; for, so long as you are there, you should especially be prompt to stir up the whole flock of Christ to follow their Master. Doubtless, also, you are aware that there are many who are waiting to seize on any word of yours which may provide an excuse for timidity. This makes the importance of your presence all the more plain. . . . We would advise you also, to do nothing without the approval of your colleagues, lest, by withdrawing in defiance of their judgment, you should be setting a harmful precedent. May the Lord guide you and them in this crisis by the spirit of wisdom, understanding, and uprightness; may He be present with you and with the cover of His wings protect, strengthen, and sustain both you and the whole church.

10.11 Letter from the Company of Pastors to the Church in Paris (1557)
Hughes 1966: 333–5

Most dear sirs and brethren, there is no need for us to tell you at greater length how saddened and distressed we are at the news of your affliction, . . . But, apart from assuring you of our prayers, there is little that we are able to do; though whatever action we feel may be helpful has not been overlooked. Be that as it may, however, never doubt that our God will watch over you and will hear your tears and groanings. If, indeed, we do not trust in His providence, even the slightest disturbance will be an abyss to engulf us, any puff of wind will unsettle us, and we shall be thoroughly per-plexed and confused; in short, our whole life will be a puzzle – especially when Satan and his servants are given their head to torment and trouble the poor Church of God. We must always hold fast to this truth, that if God cares for all His creatures He will not abandon those who call on Him. If not a single sparrow falls to the ground without His will, His fatherly care for those who are His own children will never fail. It is true that when we see a calamity like this which could bring in its train a state of extreme desolation, we are strongly tempted to suppose that God is tardy to intervene and put things right. But it is not said without reason that God wishes to test our faith like gold in a furnace [I Pet. 1:6f.]. Although, then, He does not stretch out His hand to help us as soon as we would like, let us never waver in the assurance that every hair on our head is counted by Him. And if at times He permits the blood of those who are His to be spilt, even so He does not cease to hold their tears precious, keeping them as it were in His bottle, as David says in Psalm 56 [Ps. 56:8]. It is certain that He has only permitted what has happened as a preparation for some great thing which surpasses all our thoughts. . . . May we not believe that God has already prepared an outcome of this which will cause us doubly to rejoice and glorify Him? Be that as it may, if we are truly wise we shall subject ourselves to Him and, even if all should be thrown into confusion, calmly await the deliverance which He has promised us. . . .

We are giving you the same advice as that by which we ourselves would wish to be governed and restrained in similar circumstances. The fact is that it would be much better for us all to be overwhelmed, rather than that the Gospel of God should be exposed to the accusation that it caused people to take up arms for the purpose of sedition and rioting. For God will always cause the ashes of His servants to bear fruit, but excessive and violent behavior can lead only to sterility. Therefore, most dear sirs and brethren, show that you have profited in the school of Him who demands that we should sacrifice ourselves for Him, sparing no effort to maintain His cause by suffering until such time as He smashes the weapons of His enemies or wills them to His side. . . .

10.12 The French Confession of Faith (1559)
Cochrane 1966: 141, 150–2, 154

To the King: Sire, we thank God that hitherto having had no access to your Majesty to make known the rigor of the persecutions that we have suffered, and suffer daily, for wishing to live in the purity of the Gospel and in peace with our own consciences, he now permits us to see that you wish to know the worthiness of our cause. . . . This emboldens us to speak, which we have been prevented from doing hitherto through the injustice and violence of some of your officers, incited rather by hatred of us than by love of your service. . . . [W]e humbly beseech that you will see and hear our Confession of Faith, which we present to you, hoping that it will prove a sufficient answer to the blame and opprobrium unjustly laid upon us by those who have always made a point of condemning us without having any knowledge of our cause. In the which, Sire, we can affirm that there is nothing contrary to the Word of God, or to the homage which we owe to you. . . .

18. We believe that all our justification rests upon the remission of our sins, in which also is our only blessedness, . . . We therefore reject all other means of justification before God, and without claiming any virtue or merit, we rest simply in the obedience of Jesus Christ, which is imputed to us as much to blot out all our sins as to make us find grace and favor in the sight of God. . . .
20. We believe that we are made partakers of this justification by faith alone, . . . And this is done inasmuch as we appropriate to our use the promises of life which are given to us through him, and feel their effect when we accept them, being assured that we are established by the Word of God and shall not be deceived. Thus our justification through faith depends upon the free promises by which God declares and testifies his love to us.
21. We believe that we are enlightened in faith by the secret power of the Holy Spirit, that it is a gratuitous and special gift which God grants to whom he will, so that the elect have no cause to glory, but are bound to be doubly thankful that they

have been preferred to others. We believe also that faith is not given to the elect only to introduce them into the right way, but also to make them continue in it to the end. For as it is God who hath begun the work, he will also perfect it.

24. We believe, as Jesus Christ is our only advocate, and as he commands us to ask of the Father in his name, and as it is not lawful for us to pray except in accordance with the model God hath taught us by his Word, that all imaginations of men concerning the intercession of dead saints are an abuse and a device of Satan to lead men from the right way of worship. We reject, also, all other means by which men hope to redeem themselves before God, as derogating from the sacrifice and passion of Jesus Christ.

Finally, we consider purgatory as an illusion proceeding from the same shop, from which have also sprung monastic vows, pilgrimages, the prohibition of marriage, and of eating meat, the ceremonial observance of days, auricular confession, indulgences, and all such things by which they hope to merit forgiveness and salvation. These things we reject, not only for the false idea of merit which is attracted to them, but also because they are human inventions imposing a yoke upon the conscience.

28. In this belief we declare that, properly speaking, there can be no Church where the Word of God is not received, nor profession made of subjection to it, nor use of the sacraments. Therefore we condemn the papal assemblies, as the pure Word of God is banished from them, their sacraments are corrupted, or falsified, or destroyed, and all superstitions and idolatries are in them. We hold, then, that all who take part in these acts, and commune in that Church, separate and cut themselves off from the body of Christ. Nevertheless, as some trace of the Church is left in the papacy, and the virtue and substance of baptism remain, and as the efficacy of baptism does not depend upon the person who administers it, we confess that those baptized in it do not need a second baptism. But on account of its corruptions, we can not present children to be baptized in it without incurring pollution.

29. As to the true Church, we believe that it should be governed according to the order established by our Lord Jesus Christ. That there should be pastors, overseers, and deacons, so that true doctrine may have its course, that errors may be corrected and suppressed, and the poor and all who are in affliction may be helped in their necessities; and that assemblies may be held in the name of God, so that great and small may be edified.

10.13 The Report of the Venetian Ambassador in France (1561)
Kidd 1911: 679–81

Unless it otherwise pleases the Almighty, religious affairs will soon be in an evil case in France, because there is not one single province uncontaminated. Indeed in some provinces, such as Normandy, almost the whole of Brittany, Touraine, Poitou, Gascony, and a great part of Languedoc, of Dauphiny, and of Provence, comprising three-fourths of the kingdom, congregations and meetings, which they call assemblies, are held; and in these assemblies they read and preach, according to the rites and usages of Geneva, without any respect either for the ministers of the king or the commandments of the king himself. This contagion has penetrated so deeply that it affects every class of persons, and, what appears more strange, even the ecclesiastical body itself. . . . If these disaffected individuals continue to attend Mass and the Divine Offices, and externally to practise Catholic rites, they do so for show and from fear; because when they either are, or believe themselves to be, unobserved, they avoid and even fly from the Mass above all things, and also from the churches as far as they are able. . . . Your Serenity will hardly believe the influence and the great power which the principal minister of Geneva, by name Calvin, a Frenchman, and a native of Picardy, possesses in this kingdom; he is a man of extraordinary authority, who by his mode of life, his doctrines, and his writings, rises superior to all the rest; and it is almost impossible to believe the enormous sums of money which are secretly sent to him from France to maintain his power. It is sufficient to add that if God does not interfere, there is great and imminent danger that one of two things will happen in this kingdom: either that the truce, which is desired and sought publicly, will end by the heretics having churches wherein they can preach, read, and perform their rites, according to their doctrine, without hindrance . . . or, else, that we shall see an obedience to the Pope and to the Catholic rites enforced, and shall have to resort to violence and imbrue [stain] our hands in noble blood. For these reasons I foresee a manifest and certain division in the kingdom, and a civil war as a consequence. . . .

10.14 Michel de L'Hôpital: Speech to the Estates-General of Orleans (1560)
Knecht 1996: 101

It is true that if men were good and perfect they would never take up arms for the sake of religion; yet it cannot be denied that religion, good or bad, can arouse men's passions more than anything else. It is madness to hope for peace, repose and friendship among persons of different religion. No belief penetrates more deeply into the hearts of men than religion or divides them more widely from each other. . . . We experience this to-day and see that a Frenchman and an Englishman sharing the same faith are closer in love and friendship than are two Frenchmen of the same city, subject to the same lord, who have different faiths. Whereas religious unity transcends national unity, religious division separates more than any other. It divides father from son, brother from brother, husband from wife. . . . It deters the subject from obeying his king and produces rebellion. . . .

For this reason we must remove the cause of the evil and provide a remedy by means of a council, as was recently suggested at Fontainebleau and of which the pope has given us hope in response to the urgent request of the late King Francis. Meanwhile, gentlemen, let us obey our young king. Let us not take up new opinions too hastily, each in his own way. Let us think carefully first and educate ourselves; for what is at stake is no trifling matter: it is the salvation of our souls. For if it is allowable for each of us to adopt a new faith at will, then be prepared to see as many kinds of faith as there are families and leaders of men. Your religion, you say, is better than mine; I defend mine. Which is the more reasonable way: that I should follow your opinion or you mine? Who will judge if it is not a sacred council?

Let us not be careless; let us not bring war into the kingdom through sedition or disturb and confuse everything. I promise you that the king and queen will do everything to bring about a council, and, if this remedy fails, they will resort to other means used by their predecessors. . . . If the decline of our church has given birth to heresies, then its reformation may serve to extinguish them. We have behaved so far like bad captains who attack the enemy's fort with all their might but leave their own homes undefended. We must henceforth . . . assail our enemies with charity, prayer, persuasion and the word of God, which are the proper weapons for such a conflict . . . Sweetness will achieve more than severity. And let us banish those devilish names – "Lutheran," "Huguenot," "Papist" – which breed only faction and sedition; let us retain only one name: "Christian."

10.15 Beza's Account of the Colloquy of Poissy (1561)
Knecht 1996: 102–3

[T]he king spoke as follows:

"Messieurs, I have summoned you from various parts of my kingdom so that you may advise me on what my chancellor will propose to you. I beg you to set aside all prejudice so that we may achieve something which will bring peace to my subjects, honor to God, the salving of consciences and public tranquillity. I desire this so much that I have decided to keep you here until you have reached a settlement that will enable my subjects to live in unity and peace with each other, as I trust you will do. By acting thus you will make it possible for me to protect you as my royal predecessors have done."

The twelve ministers and twenty-two representatives of the provincial churches who assisted them were then called and presented by the duke of Guise, as was his duty, and by the *sieur* de la Ferté, captain of the guard. They were led to the bar against which they leant, bareheaded. Théodore de Bèze, who had been elected as their mouthpiece, spoke as follows:

"Sire, since the success of any enterprise great or small depends on God's help and favour, especially when the issue at stake concerns His service and transcends our understanding, we hope that Your Majesty will not be offended or surprised if we start with the following prayer: 'Lord God, eternal and all-powerful Father, we confess and acknowledge before Your sacred Majesty that we are poor, wretched sinners, conceived and born in sin and corruption, inclined to evil, incapable of good, and that our sinfulness causes us to break your sacred commandments continually and endlessly: thus we fairly deserve by your judgment ruin and damnation'."

[Beza then gave an account of Calvin's doctrine.]

This speech satisfied the whole assembly, as some of its most difficult and awkward members have since admitted. It was listened to with close attention until de Bèze had nearly finished speaking of the Real Presence of Jesus Christ in the Last Supper. Although, he explained, the body of Christ is truly offered and communicated to us therein, it is as far removed from the bread as are the heavens from the earth. This caused the prelates to stir and murmur, although he had said much else that was contrary and repugnant to the doctrine of the Roman church. While some of them exclaimed: "*blasphemavit*," others got up to leave, but they could do nothing more because of the king's presence . . . .

The Cardinal of Tournon then rose and spoke so quietly that he was barely audible. In brief, he begged the king not to believe what he had heard and to remain loyal to the faith of his forebears since King Clovis, in which he had been and would continue to be nurtured by the queen his mother, and he prayed to the glorious Virgin Mary and all the saints to assist him in this. He also asked for a chance to reply to the speech, adding that he would give a good answer. The king, he said, after hearing it, would be won back, but he suddenly corrected. himself "not won back," he said, "but continue to follow the right path." He spoke these words very angrily and as though much distraught.

10.16 St. Bartholomew's Eve (From Amsterdam, August 30, 1572)
Matthews 1959: 43–4

[T]he Admiral of France was on his way on horseback to court on the 22nd day of this month. As he was reading a letter in the street, a musket was fired at him from a window. He was but hit in the arm, yet stood in danger of his life. Whereupon it is said that the King evinced great zeal to probe into this matter. With this the Admiral did not rest content, but is reported to have said, he well knew who was behind this, and would take revenge, were he to shed royal blood. So when the King's brother, the Duke of Anjou, and the Guises and others heard of this, they decided to make the first move and speedily to dispose of the whole matter. On, the night of the 23rd day of this month they broke into the Admiral's house, murdered him in his bed, and then threw him out of the window. The same day they did likewise unto all his kin, upon whom they could lay their hands. It is said that thirty people were thus murdered, among them the most noble of his following, and also Monsieur de La Rochefoucauld, the Marquis de Retz, the King's bastard brother, and others. This has been likened unto Sicilian Vespers, by which the Huguenots and the Gueux of this country had their wings well trimmed. The Admiral has reaped just payment. We hear that the Prince and his retinue are being watchful that no such fate befall them. Truly, potentates do not permit themselves to be trifled with, and whosoever is so blind that he cannot see this learns it later to his sorrow. Since the Admiral, as has been reported, has now been put out of the way, it is to be supposed that all his scheming plots and secrets will be brought to the light of day. This may in time cause great uproar, as it is more than probable that many a one at present regarded as harmless was party to this game.

10.17 The Duke of Sully's Account of the St. Bartholomew's Day Massacre
Sully 1877: 85–7

Intending on that day to wait upon the king my master [King Henry of Navarre, later Henry IV of France], I went to bed early on the preceding evening; about three in the morning I was awakened by the cries of people, and the alarm-bells, which were everywhere ringing. M. de Saint Julian, my tutor, and my valet, who had also been roused by the noise, ran out of my apartments to learn the cause of it, but never returned, nor did I ever after hear what became of them. Being thus left alone in my room, my landlord, who was a Protestant, urged me to accompany him to mass in order to save his life, and his house from being pillaged; but I determined to endeavor to escape to the Collège de Bourgogne, and to effect this I put on my Scholar's gown, and taking a book under my arm, I set out. In the streets I met three parties of the Life-guards; the first of these, after handling me very roughly, seized my book, and, most fortunately for me, seeing it was a Roman Catholic prayer-book, suffered me to proceed, and this served me as a passport with the two other parties. As I went along I saw the houses broken open and plundered, and men, women, and children butchered, while a constant cry was kept up of, "Kill! Kill! O you Huguenots! O you Huguenots!" This made me very impatient to gain the college, where, through God's assistance, I at length arrived, without suffering any other injury than a most dreadful fright. The porter twice refused me entrance, but at last, by means of a few pieces of money, I prevailed on him to inform M. La Faye, the principal of the college and my particular friend, that I was at the gate, who, moved with pity, brought me in, though he was at a loss where to put me, on account of two priests who were in his room, and who said it was determined to put all the Huguenots to death, even the infants at the breast, as was done in the Sicilian vespers. However, my friend conveyed me to a secret apartment, where no one entered except his valet, who brought me food during three successive days, at the end of which the king's proclamation prohibiting any further plunder or slaughter, was issued. . . .

10.18 The Murder of Henry, Third Duke of Guise, at Blois (1588)
Knecht 1996: 117–18

Although this enterprise [King Henry III's plot to kill Henry of Guise] was planned as secretly as possible, some knowledge of it leaked out. As Monsieur de Guise left his room to attend the council, he met on the terrace of the chateau a nobleman from Auvergne, called La Sale, who warned him against proceeding any further because of a trap that had been laid for him. Thanking him, Guise said: "my good friend, I have long been cured of that fear." Four or five steps further on, he received a similar warning from a Picard, called Aubencour (unless I am mistaken), who had once been his servant. The duke called him a fool. But on entering the council chamber, he seemed to draw back, for he noticed at the door several guards belonging to the seigneur, de Larchant, and then Marshal d'Aumont, who did not usually attend the council. He asked for an explanation and Larchant said that he had come to ask for the wages due to his soldiers whose quarter had just ended; but he could not say why d'Aumont was there.

Standing in front of the hearth, Guise dropped a handkerchief by chance or design and stepped on it. It was picked up by the seigneur de Fontenay, treasurer of the *Epargne*, and the duke asked him to take it to his secretary, Péricart, and to bring him another at once. Many people believe (but this is only an opinion) that the duke's action was to warn his friends of the danger in which he saw himself. As Péricart tried to enter the chamber his way was barred by the archers of the guard.

Meanwhile, the Cardinal of Guise and the archbishop of Lyons arrived . . . Monsieur de Guise complained of feeling unwell, whereupon St Prix, the king's *valet de chambre*, brought him the king's box of plums. Soon afterwards, the secretary of state, Nervol [i.e., Revel], entered, saying that the king wished to see the duke. Guise rose to his feet and, twirling his cloak this way and that, as if in jest, entered the king's chamber, its door being closed immediately behind him. He found himself surrounded by a dozen noblemen who had been waiting for him in silence. They greeted him with many blows of such violence that he merely groaned.

This could not be done quietly. The cardinal and the archbishop, suspecting the truth, tried to rush in, but were stopped by Marshal d'Aumont, who, putting his hand upon his sword as an officer of the Crown, forbade anyone to move on pain of death. . . . At the same time the Cardinal of Guise, the archbishop of Lyons and, soon afterwards, the Cardinal of Bourbon, messieurs de Nemours, d'Elboeuf and the Prince of Joinville were taken prisoner. . . .

There was much alarm in town: all the shops were shut, and it rained heavily all day, as if to warn us of the calamities in store. . . . That same day the Cardinal of Guise was stabbed to death in his cell by four soldiers of Captain Gast, and the bodies of the two brothers were burnt on the following night, for the king was afraid that if they were buried their hones would be taken as relics by the Parisians (which seems likely). As for the archbishop of Lyons, his life was spared by the intercession of his nephew. . . .

We are now waiting like a bird on a branch for news. Four days have passed since this tragedy took place and not a word has come from Paris, which makes me fear the worst for our interests. Farewell. From Blois, 27 December 1588. E. Pasquier

10.19 Report of the Assassination of Henry III (1589)
Matthews 1959: 170–1

On the first day of the month of August, a young Dominican friar betook himself to St. Cloud where the late King sojourned, . . . On his arrival he informed the guard that he had something which he wished to communicate to the King. The King ordered that he might be permitted to deliver his message on the following day. . . . The following day the Provost-Marshal led the monk to the King's chamber. But, as there were several persons present, the monk demanded that the King might receive him alone. He led him into his cabinet and read various scripts which the monk handed to him. When the King had perused the last, he asked the monk whether he had any more. The latter thereupon replied "Yes," and, in place of the script, drew forth from his sleeve a short knife, the width of two fingers, which lie thrust into the King's abdomen below the navel. He left it sticking in the wound. The King pulled it out himself and thus enlarged the wound. He then himself inflicted a stab upon the monk. At his calls for help several people came into the room, among them La Bastida, who helped to murder the late Guise, and he with his dagger slashed at the monk. Also one of the halberdiers thrust his halberd into the monk so that he was mortally wounded. He said that he hadn't hoped to come off so easily. After his death his corpse was dragged along the streets, rent asunder by four horses, and publicly burnt. The King did not expect to die of his wound. He walked up and down his room, and showed himself to his servants and to the soldiery at the window. But at four o'clock in the evening he felt great pains and when the doctors visited him they found the injury to be most grievous. They gave him an enema, and discovered that the intestine had been injured. The wound turned black and the King was informed of his perilous condition. He did not at first believe this, because he was feeling fairly well. But by and by he became weaker and a Capuchin was sent for to comfort him. But when he arrived the King no longer spoke. He died upon the 2nd day of this month at midnight.

10.20 Henry IV Ascends the Throne (1589)
Matthews 1959: 171

From France confirmation is received of the fact that the King of Navarre has adopted the large coat of arms of France. He causes himself to be publicly acclaimed and styled King of France. The body of the young murdered King Henry he had buried in Senlis.

In all parish churches of Paris obsequies have been celebrated for Jacques Clément, who murdered the King. It is thought that the Paris people wish to erect a statue in eternal memory of him as the liberator of his country.

10.21 Henry IV Becomes a Catholic (1593)
Matthews 1959: 209

We have received tidings in what manner the King of Navarre on his birthday, the 28th day of July, was pronounced at St. Denis to be a member of the Church of Rome. Thereupon, it was urged on the Princes of the League by the common people in Paris as well as by Parliament that peace should be made. Although the Spanish Ambassador and the Legate of the Pope had declaimed against this, nevertheless a general peace for three months was declared. It is supposed that peace will become effective thereafter. Preachers shout and rave against this from the chancel and make an outcry that the King will not keep faith with the Catholics. In Vivarais, Languedoc and other places round here this peace has already been hailed with great rejoicing. The King had arrived at his country seat of La Roquette near Paris, which belongs to the former Chancellor, and the Princes were agreed to come to meet him from Paris. But the Spanish Ambassador and the Papal Legate like it not and were ready to depart. . . .

10.22 The Pope's Pardon for Henry IV (1595)
Matthews 1959: 215–16

Last Sunday morning at 8 o'clock the Pope caused himself to be carried in pontifical vestments to the square in front of the church of St. Peter. Nearly all the Cardinals present and a great number of prelates and gentlemen followed him thither. When he had taken his place with the Cardinals, there soon appeared the proxies of the King of Navarre, Messieurs Duperron and d'Ossat. They prostrated themselves before the Pope, kissed his feet and tendered to him their letters of introduction, in which the absolution which had oft been craved before, was submissively craved once again. The Pope showed himself favorably inclined to this petition, but he first commanded that a document be read out to the said proxies, in which it was declared that he was right willing to absolve the King, but that after receiving absolution the King was to say his rosary daily, attend Mass and conform to other spiritual exercises. Thereupon the aforesaid proxies first foreswore all heresies in the name of His Majesty, and publicly professed themselves to be of the Roman Faith. They likewise promised to carry through the conventions which had been agreed upon, and accepted the penance imposed on them.

10.23 The Edict of Nantes (1598)
Knecht 1996: 121–4

General Articles:

1. That the memory of . . . preceding troubles, and the occasion of the same, shall remain extinguished and suppressed, as things that had never been. . . .
2. We prohibit all our subjects of whatever state and condition they be, to renew the memory thereof, to attack, resent, injure, or provoke one another by reproaches for what is past, under any pretext or cause whatsoever, by disputing, contesting, quarrelling, reviling, or offending by factious words; but to contain themselves, and live peaceably together as brethren, friends, and fellow-citizens, upon penalty for acting to the contrary, to be punished for breakers of peace, and disturbers of the public quiet.
3. We ordain that the Catholic religion shall be restored and reestablished in all places and quarters of this kingdom and country under our obedience, . . .
6. And not to leave any occasion of trouble and difference among our subjects, we . . . permit those of the Reformed Religion to live and dwell in all the cities and places of this our kingdom and country under our obedience, without being inquired after, vexed, molested, or compelled to do any thing in religion contrary to their conscience, nor by reason of the same be searched after in houses or places where they live, they comporting themselves in other things as is contained in this our present edict or statute.
14. [They will not] exercise the said religion in our Court, nor in our territories and countries beyond the mountains, nor in our City of Paris, nor within five leagues of the said city: nevertheless those of the said religion dwelling in the said lands and countries beyond the mountains, and in our said city, and within five leagues about the same, shall not be searched after in their houses, nor constrained to do any thing in religion against their consciences, comporting themselves in all other things according as is contained in our present edict or law.
16. [W]e grant to those of the said religion power to build places for its exercise in cities and places where it is granted them, and that those shall be rendered to them which they have heretofore built. . . .

20. They shall also be obliged to keep and observe the festivals of the Catholic church, and shall not on the same days work, sell, or keep open shop, and likewise the artisans shall not work out of their shops, in their chambers or houses privately on the said festivals, and other forbidden days, of any trade, the noise whereof may be heard without by those that pass by, or by the neighbours.

21. Books concerning the said reformed religion shall not be printed or sold publicly, save in the cities and places where its public exercise is permitted. . . .

22. We ordain, that there shall not be made any difference or distinction on account of the said religion in receiving scholars to be instructed in the universities, colleges, or schools, or of the sick and poor into hospitals, sick houses or public almshouses.

25. We will and ordain that all those of the reformed religion shall be obliged . . . to pay tithes to the curates and other ecclesiastics and to all others to whom they shall appertain. . . .

27. [W]e declare all those . . . of the said reformed religion to be capable of holding and exercising all estates, dignities, offices and public charges whatsoever. . . .

58. We declare all sentences, judgments, procedures, seizures, sales and decrees made and given against those of the reformed religion, as well living as dead, from the death of the deceased King Henry II . . . upon the occasion of the said Religion, tumults and troubles since happening, as also the execution of the same judgments and decrees, henceforth cancelled, revoked and annulled.

Royal Warrant (30 April 1598)

His Majesty in addition to what is contained in the edict he has recently drawn up . . . has granted and promised them that all the fortified places, towns, chateaux which they held up to the end of last August, in which there will be garrisons, shall . . . remain in their hands under the authority and allegiance of His Majesty for the space of eight years, counting from the day the said edict is published. . . . For the upkeep of the garrisons to be stationed in these towns, His Majesty has apportioned a sum not to exceed 180,000 crowns not including those in the province of Dauphine, which will be paid for in addition to the said sum. . . .

11

The Reformation in the Netherlands

The emperor's direct control of the Netherlands meant strict enforcement of the Edict of Worms. Hence the early introduction of Luther's writings was vigorously combated by the authorities. Augustinian monks in Antwerp who followed Luther's teachings were imprisoned and their monastery leveled. Persecution of evangelicals became even more intense upon Charles V's resignation of the Crown of the Netherlands on October 26, 1555 to his son Philip II of Spain. Philip inherited his father's debts and policy of persecution of heresy, but not his popularity, for Philip was a foreigner (11.1). Upon his accession to the throne, Philip reenacted earlier prohibitions of Protestantism (11.2). Calvinism received confessional shape with the Belgic Confession (11.3), whose major author, Guy de Brès, was executed on May 31, 1567. The Belgic Confession, closely paralleling the French Confession (10.12), was presented to Philip II in 1562 with the vain hope of convincing him that Calvinists were not seditious. It was formally adopted by the synods of Antwerp (1566), Dort (1574), Middelburg (1581), Veere (1610), and Dort (1619). Reformed congregations increased in the 1560s through an influx of Huguenots fleeing the religious wars in France. The spread of Calvinism both encouraged its adherents in public preaching and iconoclasm and confirmed Philip II's commitment to eliminate heresy (11.4–9). Calvinists sought to distance themselves from mob rule and to enlist assistance from the nobles against Spanish occupation and oppression (11.10–11), but the wars continued. The Calvinist Peter Beutterich's pessimism about the possibilities for toleration (11.12) in light of the effort to depose Philip II (11.13) appears realistic in light of Philip II's conviction that there could be no concession to heresy (11.14).

The European Reformations Sourcebook, Second Edition. Edited by Carter Lindberg.
© 2014 John Wiley & Sons, Ltd. Published 2014 by John Wiley & Sons, Ltd.

11.1 The Venetian Ambassador on Philip II (1559)
Kidd 1911: 682–4

The Catholic king was born in Spain in the month of May 1527. He passed his early days and the greater part of his youth in that kingdom where either from the custom of the country or by the will of his mother, who was a Portuguese, he was educated with all the care and respect which could become the son of the greatest Emperor in Christendom and the heir of possessions of such vast magnitude.

Having been brought up after this manner, his Majesty, when he first quitted Spain, passed through Italy and Germany to Flanders, and conveyed a universal impression that he was of a severe and intractable disposition, and therefore he was not much liked by the Italians, thoroughly disliked by the Flemings, and hated by the Germans. Consequently he was first warned by the Cardinal of Trent, then by Queen Mary, and even more effectually by his father, that a character for severity did not become the ruler of various nations and people of various habits and customs. . . .

The Emperor governed entirely according to his own views, but the king governs according to the views of others, and he has no esteem for any nation except the Spanish; he consorts only with Spaniards, and with these only he takes counsel and governs. . . .

11.2 Philip II: The Edict of 1555
Motley 1856: 1.228–30

No one shall print, write, copy, keep, conceal, sell, buy or give in churches, streets, or other places, any book or writing made by Martin Luther, John Ecolampadius, Ulrich Zwinglius, Martin Bucer, John Calvin, or other heretics reprobated by the Holy Church . . . nor break, nor otherwise injure the images of the holy virgin, or canonized saints . . . nor in his house hold conventicles, or illegal gatherings, or be present at any such in which the adherents of the above-mentioned heretics teach, baptize, and form conspiracies against the Holy Church and the general welfare. . . . Moreover, we forbid all lay persons to converse or dispute concerning the Holy Scriptures, openly or secretly, especially on any doubtful or difficult matter, or to read, teach, or expound the Scriptures unless they have duly studied theology and been approved by some renowned university . . . or to preach secretly, or openly, or to entertain any of the opinions of the above-mentioned heretics on pain, should any one be found to have contravened any of the points above mentioned, as perturbators of our state and of the general quiet, to be punished in the following manner. . . .

That such perturbators of the general quiet are to be executed, to wit: the men with the sword and the women to be buried alive, if they do not persist in their errors; if they do persist in them, then they are to be executed with fire; all their property in both cases being confiscated to the crown. . . .

We forbid all persons to lodge, entertain, furnish with food, fire, or clothing, or otherwise to favor with any one holden or notoriously suspected of being a heretic . . . and any one failing to denounce any such we ordain shall be liable to the above-mentioned punishments. . . .

All who know of any person tainted with heresy are required to denounce and give them up to all judges, officers of the bishops, or others having authority on the premises, on pain of being punished according to the pleasure of the judge. Likewise, all shall be obliged, who know of any place where such heretics keep themselves, to declare them to the authorities, on pain of being held as accomplices, and punished as such heretics themselves would be if apprehended. . . .

[T]he informer, in case of conviction [of the alleged heretic], should be entitled to one-half the property of the accused, if not more than one hundred pounds Flemish; if more, then ten per cent of all such excess. . . .

[I]f any man being present at any secret conventicle, shall afterwards come forward and betray his fellow members of the congregation, he shall receive full pardon.

11.3 The Belgic Confession of Faith (1561)
Cochrane 1966: 190–2, 197, 204, 210–11

Art. 3: Of the Written Word of God

We confess that this Word of God was not sent nor delivered by the will of man, but that holy men of God spake as they were moved by the Holy Ghost. . . . And that afterwards God . . . commanded his servants, the Prophets and Apostles, to commit his revealed Word to writing; and he himself wrote with his own finger the two tables of the law. Therefore we call such writings holy and divine Scriptures.

Art. 5: Whence Do the Holy Scriptures Derive Their Dignity and Authority

We receive all these books, and these only, as holy and canonical, for the regulation, foundation, and confirmation of our faith; believing without any doubt, all things contained in them, not so much because the Church receives and approves them as such, but more especially because the Holy Ghost witnesseth in our hearts that they are from God, whereof they carry the evidence in themselves. . . .

Art. 7: The Sufficiency of the Holy Scriptures to Be the Only Rule of Faith

We believe that these Holy Scriptures fully contain the will of God. Therefore we reject with all our hearts whatsoever doth not agree with this infallible rule. . . .

Art. 13: Of Divine Providence

We believe that the same God, after he had created all things, did not forsake them, or give them up to fortune or chance, but that he rules and governs them, according to his holy will, so that nothing happens in this world without his appointment; nevertheless, God neither is the author of, nor can be charged with, the sins which are committed. . . .

This doctrine affords us unspeakable consolation, since we are taught thereby that nothing can befall us by chance, but by the direction of our most gracious and heavenly Father, who watches over us with a paternal care, keeping all creatures so under his power that not a hair of our head (for they are all numbered), nor a sparrow, can fall to the ground, without the will of our Father, in whom we do entirely trust; being persuaded that he so restrains the devil and all our enemies that, without his will and permission, they can not hurt us. . . .

Art. 23: Our Justification Consists in the Forgiveness of Sin and the Imputation of Christ's Righteousness

We believe that our salvation, consists in the remission of our sins for Jesus Christ's sake, and that therein our righteousness before God is implied; as David and Paul teach us, declaring this to be the happiness of man, that God imputes righteousness to him without works. . . .

Art. 29: Of the Marks of the True Church, and Wherein She Differs from the False Church

The marks by which the true Church is known are these: If the pure doctrine of the gospel is preached therein; if she maintains the pure administration of the sacraments as instituted by Christ; if church discipline is exercised in punishing of sin; in short, if all things are managed according to the pure Word of God, all things contrary thereto rejected, and Jesus Christ acknowledged as the only Head of the Church. . . .

As for the false Church, she ascribes more power and authority to herself and her ordinances than to the Word of God, and will not submit herself to the yoke of Christ. Neither does she administer the Sacraments, as appointed by Christ in his Word, but adds to and takes from them as she thinks proper; she relieth more upon men than upon Christ; and persecutes those who live holily according to the Word of God, and rebuke her for her errors, covetousness, and idolatry. These two Churches are easily known and distinguished from each other.

11.4 Pieter Titelmans, Inquisitor to Regent Margaret of Parma Kortrijk (1562)
Naphy 1996: 81

I heard gossip about some scandalous behavior in the village of Boescepe, near Steenvoorde. So I went there on Tuesday to find out the truth of the matter. I looked into the situation and found out that on the previous Sunday, during High Mass a man . . . had climbed up on a spot from where one can preach in the churchyard. He then gave a sermon attacking our Holy Mother, the Church, the Pope's (our Holy Father's) authority, the Mass' holy sacrifice, the altar's sacrament, and other parts and rites of our Holy Catholic faith. He caused a lot of concern and shock among the good people and insulted our Lord Jesus Christ and the Church. Some of the people there estimated that there was a crowd of about 150 to 200 people from the local area. To protect the preacher some of the crowd carried rusty swords and stout staffs, some pistols. Also, it is said that there were other supporters in the nearby hills ready to help if needed but I could not be sure of that because I had to get back to Ieper that same day. . . .

I thought I should pass along this news to advise that Your Highness act, although I have also reported the matter to the Council of Flanders. It is about time that everyone did as much as possible, or so I think, though I am not able to do as much as I would like.

The normal methods for maintaining law and order are inadequate as Your Highness will find out. This is especially true in the countryside and villages where the poor simple people have been misled by these people who can go back and forth to England and other places. The same is true of the Anabaptists. . . .

11.5 Description of "Hedge-Preaching" Given to Regent Margaret (1566)
Naphy 1996: 81–3

I am forced to tell Your Highness that last night there were two more preaching. The largest had 4,000 people . . . on the road to Tournai and was led by a preacher named (or so I believe) Cornille de La Zenne, a blacksmith's son from Roubai. His beliefs have made him a fugitive from justice for quite a while now. . . . We fear that as soon as the harvest is in and the barns full (in two or three weeks' time) they will take over the countryside and starve the cities. Thus they will use poverty to force people to follow them. I think, therefore, that orders should be given soon to find some way to stop these meetings. I have been told by some that certain French gentlemen are ready to aid the treasonous rebellion when it comes. . . . I am hopeful that we can rely on the nobles of the Low Countries. . . .

On Sunday 7 July 1566 – despite the rules – there were more sermons, this time at noon in Stallendriesche. Thousands of people from the city and the country came along including many of the common people who had little training in the Bible and the Church Fathers. The [preachers] said that the truth was being presented and the Gospel preached correctly for the first time. To prove this the preachers quoted the Bible loudly and forcefully. They encouraged the audience to check what they said against what was in their Bibles to see that they were preaching truthfully.

11.6 Philip Marnix on Mob Violence in the Netherlands (1567)
Naphy 1996: 85

I admit that among the image-breakers there were people who claimed to be of the [Protestant] religion. However, I also assert that there were just as many who made, and never would make, such a claim. In some places only women and children were involved in the destruction. In other places the bishops and priests began to hide all their valuables – many citizens did the same – because they thought that an order had been issued to hide what could be saved until the children and street urchins had finished destroying everything else. Elsewhere, the magistrates sent along their officers, accompanied by commoners, to do the work. Even now no one knows who started it. However, there are good reasons for thinking that this was started by the priests themselves in an attempt to get the civil officials to turn on the followers of the [Protestant] religion. They had obviously done this a number of times before to provoke new persecutions. It was also intended to wreck the churches' plan to send a letter to Her Highness [the Regent]. The priests and their supporters realised that this letter would ruin their petty schemes and that time was of the essence. In fact, no sooner had the violence in Antwerp died down than some men forced their way into the Church of Our Lady and started another riot. Six of them were arrested and hanged the next day. Of these, four were known papists of whom one was a well-known nobleman who had been urging on the rest. Thus, we must conclude that they tried to ruin the churches' plan by this plan. Later events prove this correct. The plan was abandoned and from then on those of the [Protestant] religion faced nothing but disapproval and hatred.

11.7 "Request" of the Nobles, Presented to Regent Margaret by Henry Brederode (1566)
Limm 1989: 120

We are not in doubt . . . that whatever His Majesty formerly ordained and now again ordains regarding the inquisition and the strict observance of the edicts concerning religion, has some foundation and just title and is intended to continue all that the late emperor, Charles – blessed be his memory – decreed with the best of intentions. Considering however that different times call for different policies, and that for several years past those edicts . . . have caused most serious difficulties, His Majesty's recent refusal to mitigate the edicts in any way, . . . and his strict orders to maintain the inquisition, and to execute the edicts in all their rigor, makes us fear that the present difficulties will undoubtedly increase. But in fact the situation is even worse. There are clear indications everywhere that the people are so exasperated that the final result, we fear, will be an open revolt and a universal rebellion bringing ruin to all the provinces and plunging them into utter misery. . . . [The edicts] are the source and origin of all difficulties; thus His Majesty should be asked kindly to repeal them . . . we implore His Majesty very humbly that it may please him to seek the advice and consent of the assembled States-General for new ordinances and other more suitable and appropriate ways to put matters right without causing such apparent dangers.

We also most humbly entreat Your Majesty that while His Majesty is listening to our just petition and making his decisions at his good and just pleasure, Your Majesty may meanwhile obviate the dangers which we have described by suspending the inquisition as well as the execution of the edicts until His Majesty has made his decision. And finally we declare with all possible emphasis before God and men that in giving this present warning we have done all we can do according to our duty, and state that if there should occur disasters, disorder, sedition, revolt or bloodshed later on, because no appropriate measures were taken in time, we cannot be criticised for having concealed such an apparent abuse.

11.8 "The Request of Those of the New Religion to the Confederate Nobles" (1567)
Naphy 1996: 85–6

Now, contrary to what we have expected (based on your promises), the edicts have been strenuously carried out. Some who would not promise to remain faithful to the Roman Church have been jailed or banished. The ministers of God's Word have been persecuted, some even hanged, others have had their beards torn off, they have been shot at, and some who were close by have been fatally wounded. The crowds which had gathered were attacked, some cruelly killed for attending the services, some for singing the psalms on their way home, some for baptising their children in the Reformed Church. Children of others who had been baptised were taken away and rebaptised in public. This looked more like an Anabaptist spectacle than the behavior of those adhering to the old rules. Letters were circulated ordering death for those practising the [Protestant] religion. As a result preaching stopped in many places and many of the king's faithful servants fled the country and their families to escape persecution. Because of hatred towards our faith the people of Valenciennes and the vicinity have been attacked more cruelly than they were by their enemies in the last war [against France]. Clearly, if defeated, the same fate will befall all churches immediately. In Gelderland, Friesland and elsewhere there have been similar attacks every day. Not only are secret schemes used by the magistrates and the provincial States to destroy our religion in many other places but also the attacks are often open and force is used. Armed men swarm over the land. Supporters of the [Protestant] religion in several towns and villages are mistreated worse by [these armed men] than they would be by a Foreign enemy. They are attacked, pillaged, assaulted, their wives and daughters are raped – many other horrible things take place which need not be mentioned.

11.9 Philip II: Letter to Pope Pius V on the Religious Question in the Netherlands (1566)
Limm 1989: 119

If possible I will settle the religious problem in those states [i.e., the Netherlands] without taking up arms, for I know that to do so would result in their total destruction; but if things cannot be remedied as I desire without recourse to arms, I am determined to take them up and go myself to carry out everything; and neither danger [to myself] nor the ruin of these states, nor of all the others which are left to me, will prevent me from doing what a Christian prince fearing God ought to do in his service, [and for] the preservation of the Catholic faith and the honor of the apostolic see.

11.10 The Goals of William of Orange (1572)
Limm: 1989: 121–2

I have only the following objectives in this war: That with full respect for the king's sovereign power, all decrees contrary to conscience and to the laws, shall be annulled and that every one who so wishes, shall be free to adopt the teaching of the prophets, of Christ and the apostles which the Churches have taught until now and that those who reject these doctrines may do so without any injury to their goods as long as they are willing to behave peacefully and can show that they did so in the past.

That the name of the inquisition shall be erased for ever. . . .

That those who have no right at all to be in this country and, of course, are not allowed to oppress the souls of our humble people by force of arms, shall be banished.

That people be given back their houses, possessions, hereditary estates, their good name, their freedoms, privileges and laws, by which liberty is maintained.

That state affairs shall be discussed in the States of the provinces in accordance with the custom of our ancestors.

That political matters will be dealt with by the king himself and by the States which are chosen in every province and not be dispatched secretly by hired foreigners through whose faithlessness and greed the present troubles have come about. . . .

I pray you once again, because of the loyalty which you and I owe to our dearest fatherland, that with my help you rescue, take back and protect what you don't want to lose for ever. If you do not do so, then I assert most solemnly that it will not be my fault if severer measures are taken. But if you take my admonition to heart (and I sincerely hope you will do this for your own sake) then swear allegiance firstly to Christ the only God our Savior, next to the king who takes delight in the sworn laws, finally to me as patron of the fatherland and champion of freedom.

11.11 Calvinists Appeal to the King for a Truce (1578)
Naphy 1996: 87–8

The Protestants promise to accept all reasonable conditions and to maintain and conform to all conditions which Your Majesty might be pleased to suggest. They beg you to recall that they have suffered much for their country – indeed they are ready to give themselves, their lives and possessions for their homeland – and their loyalty and obedience has been great since the [Pacification of Ghent]. Appropriate action has been taken whenever one of them has behaved in a manner which did not command common consent. These errors are not like those done by the people who say they are for the common good and then openly side with the enemy. The Protestants, should any wrong befall them (one hopes it will not), are determined to continue to fulfil their duty to their homeland.

11.12 Beutterich on the Possible Consequences of a Truce (1578)
Naphy 1996: 88–9

[P]reserving the Roman Catholic Church and preserving tyranny amount to the same thing here. I will say it again, preserving the Roman Catholic Church here is the same thing as preserving a tyranny which is worse than the one inflicted by the barbarians and Turks. At least the Turks, who are dictators over the body leave the conscience alone. The supporters of the Roman Catholic Church want to be tyrants over the body and the mind.

Keeping the Roman Catholic Church means bringing back banishments and confiscations, burning people at the stake again, re-building the gallows throughout the provinces, bringing back the Inquisition, and, finally, dredging up from Hell those vile, accursed laws. Remembering those laws fills every true patriot with dread and disgust. They recall the pouring of so much South Netherlandish [Belgian] blood from so many martyrs and that for one sole reason: the one and only Roman Catholic religion. . . .

Maintaining real freedom and the Roman Catholic Church are mutually exclusive. Keeping the Roman Catholic religion means nothing less than restoring the Spanish tyranny. The goals of the Spanish and the Roman Catholics are identical. The Spanish want the Roman religion established, so do the Catholics. The Catholics want the king to be accepted and given his due, so do the Spanish. We accept, rather than deny, that the king should receive his due as sovereign lord. However, there is a vast difference between what is lawfully due to the king and what the supporters of the Roman Catholic religion have in mind. They do not mean that one should obey the King in law, justice and fairness by keeping to the old customs and traditions. Rather, they mean that one should do everything the tyrant commands without a word of complaint, without a challenge, without resistance. In sum, it means being a serf and a slave.

This then is the goal these tin-pot dictators, the supporters of the Roman Catholic religion, have in mind; this has always been the goal of the Spanish.

11.13 Act of Abjuration (1581)
Limm 1989: 127

Let all men know that, in consideration of the matters considered above and under pressure of utmost necessity . . . we have declared and declare hereby by a common accord, decision and consent the king of Spain, *ipso jure* forfeit of his lordship, principality, jurisdiction and inheritance of these countries, and that we have determined not to recognize him hereafter in any matter concerning the principality, supremacy, jurisdiction or domain of these Low Countries, nor to use or permit others to use his name as Sovereign Lord over them after this time.

11.14 Philip II Refuses to Concede Toleration (1585)
Limm 1989: 122–3

In spite of everything I would regret very much to see this toleration conceded without limits. The first step [for Holland and Zealand] must be to admit and maintain the exercise of the Catholic religion alone, and to subject themselves to the Roman Church, without allowing or permitting in any agreement the exercise of any other faith whatever in any town, farm or special place set aside in the fields or inside a village. . . . And in this there is to be no exception, no change, no concession by any treaty of freedom of conscience. . . . They are all to embrace the Roman Catholic faith and the exercise of that alone is to be permitted.

12

The Reformations in England and Scotland

Reformation beginnings in England were steeped in concern for clerical standards (12.1) and anticlericalism (12.2), against the background of the earlier reform movement of Lollardy (12.3). Luther's writings reached England by the 1520s, influencing people such as Barnes, prior of the Cambridge Augustinians (12.4). Efforts by church authorities to prevent the spread of evangelical literature and Bible translations were frustrated by English merchants in Antwerp who facilitated the infiltration of Protestant publications into England (12.5). Henry VIII (12.6), in the Act of Supremacy (12.7), declared that the monarch was head of the Church of England, thus effectively replacing the authority of the pope with that of the king in all ecclesiastical affairs. Henry proceeded to enforce uniformity in religion by the Act of the Six Articles (12.8), that reflected his conservative determination to protect traditional practices. It was for denying the first of the Six Articles, transubstantiation, that Anne Askew was tortured and executed. Askew, one of the few women martyrs of the gentry, ably responded to her inquisitors by citing Scripture and refusing to implicate members of Queen Katherine Parr's household. Her *Examinations*, written in prison, articulated her right to read and interpret the Bible (12.9).

Although an Oxford Synod decree of 1408 forbade translation of or even reading the Bible in English without special permission, English translations (12.10–12) soon began to appear, led by the masterful work of William Tyndale, himself much influenced by Luther's German translation of the Bible. After the final break with Rome, the Convocation of Canterbury petitioned Henry VIII to order that an English translation of the Bible be made available to the people. The king's advisors gave Miles Coverdale authority to revise existing versions, and the work came to be called the Great Bible. Henry ordered this Bible to be placed in every parish church. During the reign of Elizabeth it was replaced by the Geneva Bible (1560). English Catholic exiles at Rheims produced their own translation based on the Vulgate to

The European Reformations Sourcebook, Second Edition. Edited by Carter Lindberg.
© 2014 John Wiley & Sons, Ltd. Published 2014 by John Wiley & Sons, Ltd.

counter "heretical" Protestant Bibles (12.13). The translation had numerous defects and never equaled the Geneva Bible in popularity. At the Hampton Court Conference (1604), King James I accepted the proposal to prepare a new translation of the Bible for general use (12.14).

Upon Edward VI's succession to the throne, the Reformers compiled a fresh set of sermons for use by the parish clergy. Cranmer's sermon on salvation (12.15) is from the "First Book of Homilies." The Act of Uniformity (12.16) established the First Prayer Book of Edward VI, composed by Cranmer, as the only legal form of worship. In England, as elsewhere, clerical marriage was a central issue. Under Edward VI, clerical marriage was legalized (12.17). Queen Mary's view of the matter is evident in her Injunctions (12.18), sent to the bishops with a letter ordering their enforcement. Elizabeth sought a "middle way" between Rome and Geneva that essentially restored the Church of England to pre-Marian Protestantism (12.19). Elizabeth's Injunctions (12.20) repeat most of those of Edward VI. Her policy was defended by John Jewel, a Marian exile, who on the accession of Elizabeth returned and became Bishop of Salisbury (12.21). Thomas Cranmer's Forty-Two Articles, drawn up during Edward's reign, became the basis for the Thirty-Nine Articles (12.22) which remain standard for Episcopal churches. The Vestiarian Controversy (1563–66) began during the reign of Edward VI with the protest of John Hooper (12.23), who had studied at Zurich. Hooper declined the bishopric of Gloucester because it would require wearing "Catholic" vestments which he did not understand to be adiaphora, i.e., "indifferent." Issues at stake included the regulative principle of Scripture that would be affirmed far more vigorously by the Puritans, and the concern that use of traditional vestments could easily imply continuation of Roman Catholic theology to the congregation. John à Lasco, born into the Polish nobility, was active in reform throughout Europe including the Rhineland, Belgium, and England. His understanding of reform according to Scripture and free from the jurisdiction of the English Church led to tension with Nicholas Ridley. After the death of Edward, Lasco returned to Poland. The Abolition of Vestments (12.24), first printed by the English Puritans in 1566, supports the position of Hooper. In 1570 Elizabeth was excommunicated (12.25) and in 1587 Mary Queen of Scots was executed (12.26).

12.1 William Melton, Chancellor of York Minster: Sermon to Ordinands (c.1510)
Gee & Hardy 1896; cf. Dickens & Carr 1967: 15

For it is from this stupidity and from this darkness of ignorance that there arises that great and deplorable evil throughout the whole Church of God, that everywhere throughout town and countryside there exists a crop of oafish and boorish priests, some of whom are engaged on ignoble and servile tasks, while others abandon themselves to tavern-haunting, swilling and drunkenness. Some cannot get along without their wenches; others pursue their amusement in dice and gambling. . . .

We must avoid and keep far from ourselves that grasping, deadly plague of avarice for which practically every priest is accused and held in disrepute. . . .

12.2 Simon Fish: *A Supplication for the Beggars* (1529)
Gee & Hardy 1896; cf. Dickens & Carr 1967: 16–19

These are not the [shep]herds but the ravenous wolves going in [shep]herds' clothing, devouring the flock: the bishops, abbots, priors, deacons, archdeacons, suffragans, priests, monks, canons, friars, pardoners and summoners. . . .

And what do all this greedy sort of sturdy, idle, holy thieves, with these yearly exactions that they take of the people? Truly nothing, but exempt themselves from the obedience of your Grace! Nothing, but translate all rule, power, lordship, authority, obedience and dignity from your Grace unto them! Nothing, but that all your subjects should fall into disobedience and rebellion against your Grace, and be under them. . . .

Yea, and what do they more? Truly, nothing but apply themselves, by all the sleights they may, to have to do with every man's wife, every man's daughter, and every man's maid, that cuckoldry and bawdry should reign over all among your subjects, that no man should know his own child; that their bastards might inherit the possessions of every man, to put the right-begotten children clear beside their inheritance, in subversion of all estates and godly order. . . . These be they that have made a hundred thousand idle, [dissolute women] in your realm, who would have gotten their living honestly, in the sweat of their faces, had not their [the clergy's] superfluous riches [allured] them to unclean lust and idleness. . . .

Oh, how all the substance of your realm (your sword, power, crown, dignity and obedience of your people) runneth headlong into the insatiable whirlpool of these greedy gulfs, to be swallowed and devoured! . . .

Tie these holy idle thieves to the carts, to be whipped naked about every market town till they will fall to labor, that they by their importunate begging take not away the alms that the good Christian people would give unto us, sore, impotent, miserable people, your beadsmen. Then shall as well the number of our aforesaid monstrous sort, as of the [profligate men and women], thieves and idle people, decrease; then shall these great yearly exactions cease; then shall not your sword, power, crown, dignity, and obedience of your people be translated from you; then shall you have full obedience of your people; then shall the idle people be set to work; then shall matrimony be much better kept; then shall the generation of your people be increased; then shall your commons increase in riches; then shall the gospel be preached. . . .

12.3 John Foxe's *Acts and Monuments*: Lollardy on the Eve of the Reformation
Catley & Townsend 1837–41; cf. Dickens & Carr 1967: 26–7

In turning over the registers and records of Lincoln likewise, and coming to the year of our Lord 1520, and to 1521, I find that as the light of the Gospel began more to appear, and the number of [its] professors to grow, so the vehemency of persecution and stir of the bishops began also to increase; whereupon ensued great perturbation and grievous affliction in divers and sundry quarters of this realm. . . . And this was before the name of Luther was heard of in these countries among the people. Wherefore they are much beguiled and misinformed, who condemn this kind of doctrine now received, of novelty; asking, "Where was this church and religion forty years ago, before Luther's time?" To whom it may be answered, that this religion and form of doctrine was planted by the Apostles, and taught by true bishops; afterward decayed, and now reformed again. . . .

[The Lollards were] against the Church of Rome: in pilgrimage, in adoration of saints, in reading Scripture-books in English, and in the carnal presence of Christ's body in the sacrament. After the great abjuration aforesaid, which was under William Smith, Bishop of Lincoln, they were noted and termed among themselves by the name of "known-men," or "just-fast-men": as now they are called by the name of Protestants.

12.4 John Foxe on Robert Barnes
Catley & Townsend 1837–41; cf. Dickens & Carr 1967: 30

This Barnes, after he came from the university of Louvain, went to Cambridge, where he was made prior and master of the house of the Augustines. . . . [H]e caused the house shortly to flourish with good letters. . . . After these foundations laid, then did he read openly in the house Paul's Epistles, and put by Duns and Dorbel [renounced the scholastic authors] . . . and only because he would have Christ there taught, and his holy word, he turned their unsavory problems and fruitless disputations to other better matter of the holy Scripture; and thereby in short space he made divers good divines. . . . Thus Barnes, what with his reading, disputation and preaching, became famous and mighty in the Scriptures, preaching ever against bishops and hypocrites. . . .

The first sermon that ever he preached of this truth was the Sunday before Christmas day [1525] at St. Edward's church . . . following the Scripture and Luther's Postil; and for that sermon he was immediately accused of heresy by two fellows of the King's Hall. Then the godly learned in Christ both of Pembroke Hall, St. John's, Peterhouse, Queen's College, the King's College, Gonville Hall and Benet College showed themselves and flocked together in open sight, both in the schools and at open sermons at St. Mary's and at the Augustines and at other disputations; and then they conferred continually together.

The house that they resorted most commonly unto was the White Horse, which for despite of them, to bring God's word into contempt, was called Germany. This house especially was chosen because many of them of St. John's, the King's College and the Queen's College, came in on the back side. At this time much trouble began to ensue.

12.5 Edward Hall: A Protestant Merchant Outwits a Bishop (1529)
Gee & Hardy 1896; cf. Dickens & Carr 1967: 36–7

William Tyndale had newly translated and imprinted the New Testament in English, and the Bishop of London [Cuthbert Tunstall], not pleased with the translation thereof, debated with himself how he might . . . destroy that false and erroneous translation (as he said). And so it happened that one Augustine Packington, a mercer and merchant of London, and of great honesty, the same time was in Antwerp, where the Bishop then was, and this Packington was a man that highly favored William Tyndale, but to the Bishop utterly showed himself to the contrary.

The Bishop, desirous to have his purpose brought to pass, communed of the New Testaments, and how gladly he would buy them. Packington . . . said unto the Bishop, "My lord, if it be your pleasure, I can in this matter do more, I dare say than most of the merchants of England that are here, for I know the Dutchmen and strangers that have bought them of Tyndale, and have them here to sell, so that if it be your lordship's pleasure to pay for them . . . I will then assure you to have every book of them, that is imprinted and is here unsold." The Bishop, thinking that he had God by the toe, when indeed he had (as after he thought) the Devil by the fist, said, "Gentle Master Packington, do your diligence and get them, and with all my heart I will pay for them, whatsoever they cost you, for the books are erroneous and naughty, and I intend surely to destroy them all, and to burn them at Paul's Cross."

Augustine Packington came to William Tyndale and said, "William, I know thou art a poor man, and hast a heap of New Testaments and books by thee, for the which thou hast both endangered thy friends and beggared thyself, and I have now gotten thee a merchant, which with ready money shall dispatch thee of all that thou hast, if you think it so profitable for yourself." "Who is the merchant?" said Tyndale. "The Bishop of London," said Packington. "O, that is because he will burn them," said Tyndale. "Yea, Mary," quod Packington. "I am the gladder," said Tyndale, "for these two benefits shall come thereof; I shall get money of him for these books, to bring myself out of debt, and the whole world shall cry out upon the burning of God's word. And the overplus of the money that shall remain to me shall make me more studious to correct the said New Testament, and so newly to imprint the same once again, and I trust the second will much better like you than ever did the first."

And so forward went the bargain; the Bishop had the books, Packington the thanks, and Tyndale had the money. Afterwards, when more New Testaments were imprinted, they came thick and threefold into England. The Bishop of London, hearing that still there were so many New Testaments abroad, sent for Augustine Packington and said unto him, "Sir, how cometh this that there are so many New Testaments abroad, and you promised and assured me that you had bought all?" Then said Packington, "I promise you I bought all that then was to be had; but I perceive they have made more since, and it will never be better as long as they have the letters and stamps [the type]; therefore it were best for your lordship to buy the stamps too, and then are you sure." The Bishop smiled at him and said, "Well, Packington, well." And so ended this matter.

12.6 A Report of Henry VIII by the Venetian Ambassador (1519)
Brown 1864: vol. 2, 559–61

King Henry was 29 years old, and much handsomer than any other Sovereign in Christendom – a great deal handsomer than the King of France. He was very fair, and his whole frame admirably proportioned. Hearing that King Francis wore a beard, he allowed his own to grow, and as it was reddish, he had then got a beard which looked like gold. He was very accomplished and a good musician; composed well; was a capital horseman, and a fine jouster; spoke good French, Latin, and Spanish; was very religious; heard three masses daily when he hunted, and sometimes five on other days, besides hearing the office daily in the Queen's chamber. . . . He was extremely fond of hunting. . . . He was also fond of tennis, at which game it was the prettiest thing in the world to see him play. . . .

He was very rich. His father left him ten millions of ready money in gold, of which he was supposed to have spent one half in the war against France, . . .

He was the best dressed sovereign in the world. His robes were very rich and superb, and he put on new clothes every holiday.

12.7 The Act of Supremacy (1534)
Englander 1997: 442–3

Be it enacted by authority of this present Parliament that the King our sovereign lord, his heirs and successors kings of this realm, shall be taken, accepted and reputed the only supreme head in earth of the Church of England called *Anglicana Ecclesia*, and shall have and enjoy annexed and united to the imperial crown of this realm as well the title and style thereof, as all honors, dignities, preeminences, jurisdictions, privileges, authorities, immunities, profits and commodities, to the said dignity of supreme head of the same Church belonging and appertaining. And that our said sovereign lord, his heirs and successors kings of this realm, shall have full power and authority from time to time to visit, repress, redress, reform, order, correct, restrain and amend all such errors, heresies, abuses, offences, contempts and enormities, whatsoever they be, which by any manner spiritual authority or jurisdiction ought or may lawfully be reformed, repressed, ordered, redressed, corrected, restrained or amended, most to the pleasure of Almighty God, the increase of virtue in Christ's religion, and for the conservation of the peace, unity and tranquillity of this realm: any usage, custom, foreign laws, foreign authority, prescription or any other thing or things to the contrary hereof notwithstanding.

12.8 The Act of the Six Articles (1539)
Bray 1994: 224

First, that in the most blessed sacrament of the altar, by the strength and efficacy of Christ's mighty word (it being spoken by the priest), is present really, under the form of bread and wine, the natural body and blood of our Savior Jesus Christ, conceived of the Virgin Mary; and that after the consecration there remaineth no substance of bread and wine, nor any other substance, but the substance of Christ, God and man.

Secondly, that communion in both kinds is not necessary *ad salutem*, by the law of God, to all persons; and that it is to be believed, and not doubted of, but that in the flesh, under the form of bread, is the very blood; and with the blood, under the form of wine, is the very flesh; as well apart, as though they were both together.

Thirdly, that priests after the order of priesthood received, as afore, may not marry, by the law of God.

Fourthly, that vows of chastity or widowhood, by man or woman made to God advisedly, ought to be observed by the law of God; and that it exempts them from other liberties of Christian people, which without that they might enjoy.

Fifthly, that it is meet and necessary that private masses be continued and admitted in this the King's English Church and Congregation, as whereby good Christian people, ordering themselves accordingly, do receive both godly and goodly consolations and benefits; and it is agreeable also to God's law.

Sixthly, that auricular confession is expedient and necessary to be retained and continued, used and frequented in the Church of God. . . .

12.9 Anne Askew: *The Examinations* (1545, 1546)
Beilin 1996: 117, 127, 130, 132 (the text is modernized)

I Anne Askew of good memory although God has given me the bread of adversity and the water of trouble, yet not so much as my sins have deserved, desire this to be known to your grace [Henry VIII]. That for as much as I am condemned by the law as an evil doer, I here take heaven and earth to record that I shall die in my innocence. . . .

Then they did put me on the rack because I confessed no ladies nor gentlemen to be of my opinion. And they kept me on it a long time. And because I did not cry, my Lord Chancellor and Master Rich took pains to rack me with their own hands till I was nigh dead. . . .

Then the lieutenant caused me to be loosed from the rack. Incontinently I fainted, and then they recovered me again. After that I sat two long hours upon the bare floor reasoning with my Lord Chancellor, where he with many flattering words [tried to persuade] me to leave my opinion. But my Lord God (I thank his everlasting goodness) gave me grace to persevere, and will do (I hope) to the very end. . . .

Then I was brought to a house and laid in a bed with as weary and painful bones as ever had patient Job. . . . Then my Lord Chancellor sent me word [that] if I would forsake my opinion, I should lack nothing. If I would not, I should be sent to Newgate [prison], and so be burned. I again sent him word that I would rather die than to break my faith. Thus [may] the Lord open the eyes of their blind hearts that the truth may take place. Farewell dear friend, and pray, pray, pray.

12.10 Tyndale's Preface to the New Testament (1526)
Bray 1994: 20–1, 24

Also ye see that two things are required to begin a Christian man. The first is a steadfast faith and trust in Almighty God, to obtain all the mercy that he hath promised us, through the deserving and merits of Christ's blood only, without all respect to our own works. And the other is that we forsake evil and turn to God, to keep his laws and to fight against ourselves and our corrupt nature perpetually, that we may do the will of God every day better and better. . . .

My deeds, if I keep the law, are rewarded with the temporal promises of this life. But if I believe in Christ, Christ's deeds have purchased for me the eternal promise of the everlasting life. . . .

12.11 Thomas Cranmer's Preface to the Great
Bible (1540)
Bray 1994: 239, 241

Therefore . . . I will here conclude and take it as a conclusion sufficiently determined and approved, that it is convenient and good the Scripture to be read of all sorts and kinds of people, and in the vulgar tongue, . . .

Therefore now to come to the second and latter part of my purpose. There is nothing so good in this world, but it may be abused, and turned from fruitful and wholesome to hurtful and noisome. . . .

I say not this to dissuade men from the knowledge of God, and reading or studying of the Scripture. For I say that it is as necessary for the life of man's soul, as for the body to breathe. . . . I forbid not to read, but I forbid to reason. Neither forbid I to reason so far as is good and godly. . . . Let us not sing the song of our Lord in a strange land; that is to say, let us not dispute the Word of God at all adventures, as well where it is not to be reasoned as where it is, and as well in the ears of them that be not fit therefore as of them that be. . . . This contention and debate about Scriptures and doubts thereof. . . dost most hurt to ourselves, and to the furthering of the cause and quarrels that we would have furthered above all things. . . .

12.12 The Preface to the Geneva Bible (1560)
Bray 1994: 356–7, 359

To the most virtuous and noble Queen Elizabeth, Queen of England, France and Ireland, etc., Your humble subjects of the English Church at Geneva, with grace and peace from God the Father through Christ Jesus our Lord. . . .

[W]e persuaded ourselves that there was no way so expedient and necessary . . . as to present unto your Majesty the Holy Scriptures faithfully and plainly translated according to the languages wherein they were first written by the Holy Ghost. For the Word of God is an evident token of God's love and our assurance of his defence, wheresoever it is obediently received; it is the trial of the spirits, and as the prophet saith, it is a fire and hammer to break the stony hearts of them that resist God's mercies offered by the preaching of the same (Jer. 23:29). . . .

Last of all (most gracious Queen) . . . two things are necessary; first, that we have a lively and steadfast faith in Christ Jesus, who must dwell in our hearts as the only means and assurance of our salvation; for he is the ladder that reacheth from the earth to heaven; . . . The next is that our faith bring forth good fruits, so that our godly conversation may serve us as a witness to confirm our election, and be an example to all others to walk as appertaineth to the vocation whereunto they are called. . . .

12.13 The Preface to the Rheims New Testament (1582)
Bray 1994: 365, 367, 375–6

[W]e do not . . . publish, upon [the] erroneous opinion . . . that the Holy Scriptures should always be in our mother tongue, or that they ought, or were ordained by God, to be read indifferently of all, or could be easily understood of everyone that readeth or heareth them in a known language, or that they were not often through man's malice or infirmity, pernicious and much hurtful to many; or that we generally and absolutely deemed it more convenient in itself, and more agreeable to God's Word and honor, or edification of the faithful, to have them turned into vulgar tongues, than to be kept and studied only in the ecclesiastical learned languages; not for these nor any such like causes do we translate this sacred book, but upon special consideration of the present time, state and condition of our country, unto which divers things are either necessary, or profitable and medicinable now, that otherwise in the peace of the Church were neither much requisite, nor perchance wholly tolerable. . . .

Now since Luther's revolt also, divers learned Catholics, for the more speedy abolishing of a number of false and impious translations put forth by sundry sects, and for the better preservation or reclaim of many good souls endangered thereby, have published the Bible in the several languages of almost all the principal provinces of the Latin Church, no other books in the world being so pernicious as heretical translations of the Scriptures, poisoning the people under colour of divine authority, and not many other remedies being more sovereign against the same (if it be used in order, discretion and humility) than the true, faithful and sincere interpretation opposed thereunto. . . .

Finally, all sect-masters and ravening wolves, yea the devils themselves pretend Scriptures, allege Scriptures, and wholly shroud themselves in Scriptures, as in the wool and fleece of simple sheep, whereby the vulgar, in these days of general disputes, cannot but be in extreme danger of error. . . .

[T]he Protestants . . . have so abused the people . . . that by their false translations they have, instead of God's Law and Testament, and for Christ's written will and word, given them their own wicked writing and fantasies . . . corrupting both the letter and sense by false translation, adding, detracting, altering, transposing, pointing, and all other guileful means; specially where it serveth for the advantage of their private opinions. . . .

12.14 The Preface to the Authorized (King James) Version of the Bible (1611)
Bray 1994: 419, 421

But now what piety without truth? What truth (what saving truth) without the Word of God? What Word of God (whereof we may be sure) without the Scripture? . . .

But how shall men meditate in that, which they cannot understand? How shall they understand that which is kept close in an unknown tongue? . . . Translation it is that openeth the window, to let in the light; that breaketh the shell, that we may eat the kernel; that putteth aside the curtain, that we may look into the most holy place. . . . Indeed without translation into the vulgar tongue, the unlearned are but like children. . . .

12.15 Thomas Cranmer: Certain Sermons, or Homilies (1547)
Parker 1966: 262, 270

Because all men be sinners and offenders against God, and breakers of his law and commandments, therefore can no man by his own acts, works, and deeds, seem they never so good, be justified and made righteous before God; but every man of necessity is constrained to seek for another righteousness or justification, to be received at God's own hands, that is to say, the remission, pardon, and forgiveness of his sins and trespasses in such things as he hath offended. And this justification or righteousness, which we so receive by God's mercy and Christ's merits, embraced by Faith, is taken, accepted, and allowed of God for our perfect and full justification. . . .

For the right and true Christian faith is, not only to believe that Holy Scripture and all the foresaid articles of our faith are true, but also to have a sure trust and confidence in God's merciful Promises to be saved from everlasting damnation by Christ; whereof doth follow a loving heart to obey his commandments. . . .

12.16 The Act of Uniformity (1549)
Bray 1994: 267

Wherefore the Lords spiritual and temporal and the Commons in this present Parliament assembled, . . . do give to his Highness most hearty and lowly thanks for the same [Book]; and humbly pray that it may be ordained and acted by his Majesty, with the assent of the Lords and Commons in this present Parliament assembled, and by authority of the same, that all and singular person and persons that have offended concerning the premises, other than such person and persons as now be and remain in ward in the Tower of London, or in the Fleet, may be pardoned thereof, and that all and singular ministers in any cathedral or parish church or other place within this realm of England, Wales, Calais and the marches of the same, or other the King's dominions, shall from and after the feast of Pentecost next coming (9 June 1549), be bound to say and use the Matins, Evensong, celebration of the Lord's Supper, commonly called the Mass, and administration of each of the sacraments, and all their common and open prayer, in such order and form as is mentioned in the said book, and none other or otherwise.

12.17 Act to Take Away All Positive Laws Against Marriage of Priests (1549)
Gee & Hardy 1896; cf. Dickens & Carr 1967

Although it were not only better for the estimation of priests and other ministers in the Church of God, to live chaste, sole, and separate from the company of women and the bond of marriage, but also thereby they might the better intend to the administration of the gospel, and be less intricated and troubled with the charge of household, being free and unburdened from the care and cost of finding wife and children, and that it were most to be wished that they would willingly and of their selves endeavor themselves to a perpetual chastity and abstinence from the use of women.

Yet forasmuch as the contrary hath rather been seen, and such uncleanness of living, and other great inconveniences, not meet to be rehearsed, have followed of compelled chastity, and of such laws as have prohibited those (such persons) the godly use of marriage; it were better and rather to be suffered in the commonwealth that those which could not contain, should, after the counsel of Scripture, live in holy marriage, than feignedly abuse with worse enormity outward chastity or single life.

Be it therefore enacted . . . that all and every law and laws positive, canons, constitutions, and ordinances heretofore made by the authority of man only, which doth prohibit or forbid marriage to any ecclesiastical or spiritual person or persons . . . shall be utterly void and of none effect. . . .

12.18 The Marian Injunctions (1554)
Gee & Hardy 1896; cf. Dickens & Carr 1967: 380–3

I. That every bishop and his officers, with all other having ecclesiastical jurisdiction, shall with all speed and diligence, and all manner of ways to them possible, put in execution all such canons and ecclesiastical laws heretofore in the time of King Henry VIII used within this realm of England, and the dominions of the same. . . .

VII. Item, that every bishop, and all the other persons aforesaid, proceeding summarily, and with all celerity and speed, may and shall deprive, or declare deprived . . . all such persons from their benefices and ecclesiastical promotions, who . . . have married and used women as their wives. . . .

IX. Item, that every bishop, and all persons aforesaid, do foresee that they suffer not any religious man, having solemnly professed chastity, to continue with his woman or wife; but that all such persons, after deprivation of their benefice or ecclesiastical promotion, be also divorced every one from his said woman, and due punishment otherwise taken for the offence therein. . . .

XI. Item, that all and all manner of processions of the Church be used, frequented, and continued after the old order of the Church, in the Latin tongue. . . .

12.19 The Act of Supremacy (1559)
Bray 1994: 322–3

And for the better observation and maintenance of this Act [of Supremacy], may it please your Highness that it may be further enacted by the authority aforesaid, that all and every archbishop, bishop, and all and every other ecclesiastical person, and other ecelesiastical officer and minister, of what estate, dignity, pre-eminence or degree soever he or they be or shall be, and all and every temporal judge, justice, mayor and other lay and temporal officer and minister, and every other person having your Highness's fee or wages, within this realm, or any your Highness's dominions, shall make, take and receive a corporal oath . . . :

"I, A. B., do utterly testify and declare in my conscience, that the Queen's Highness is the only Supreme Governor of this realm, and of all other her Highness's dominions and countries, as well in all spiritual or ecclesiastical things or causes, as temporal, and that no foreign prince, person, prelate, state or potentate has, or ought to have, any jurisdiction, power, superiority, preeminence or authority ecclesiastical or spiritual, within this realm; and therefore I do utterly renounce and forsake all foreign jurisdictions, powers, superiorities and authorities, and do promise that from henceforth I shall bear faith and true allegiance to the Queen's Highness, her heirs and lawful successors, and to my power shall assist and defend all jurisdictions, pre-eminences, privileges and authorities granted or belonging to the Queen's Highness, her heirs and successors, or united and annexed to the imperial crown of this realm. So help me God, and by the contents of this book."

12.20 The Elizabethan Injunctions (1559)
Bray 1994: 335–8, 341

[A]ll deans, archdeacons, parsons, vicars and other ecclesiastical persons shall faithfully keep and observe . . . all and singular laws and statutes made for the restoring to the Crown the ancient jurisdiction over the state ecclesiastical, and abolishing of all foreign power repugnant to the same. . . .

Besides this, to the intent that all superstition and hypocrisy crept into men's hearts may vanish away, they shall not set forth or extol any images, relics or miracles, for any superstition or lucre, nor allure the people by any enticements, to the pilgrimage of any saint or image, but reproving the same, they shall teach that all goodness, health and grace ought to be both asked and looked for only of God, as of the very author and giver of the same, and of none other.

Item, that they, the persons above rehearsed, shall preach in their churches and every other cure they have, one sermon, every quarter of the year at the least, wherein they shall purely and sincerely declare the Word of God, and in the same, exhort their hearers to the works of faith, mercy and charity specially prescribed and commanded in Scripture, and that works devised by men's fantasies, besides Scripture, as wandering to pilgrimages, offering of money, candles or tapers to relics, or images, or kissing and licking of the same, praying upon beads, or such like superstition, have not only no promise of reward in Scripture, for doing of them, but contrariwise, great threats and maledictions of God, for that they be things tending to idolatry and superstition. . . .

Also that they shall provide within three months next after this visitation, one book of the whole Bible, of the largest volume, in English. And within one twelve-months next after the said visitation, the Paraphrasis of Erasmus also in English upon the Gospels, and the same set up in some convenient place, within the said church that they have cure of, whereas their parishioners may most commodiously resort unto the same and read the same, out of the time of common service. . . . And they shall discourage no man (authorized and licensed thereto) from the reading of any part of the Bible, either in Latin or in English, but shall rather conform and exhort every person to read the same. . . .

Also, that the parson, vicar or curate and parishioners of every parish within this realm shall in their churches and chapels keep one book or register, wherein they shall write the day and year of every wedding, christening and burial made within their parish for their time, and so every man succeeding them likewise. . . .

Furthermore, because the goods of the Church are called the goods of the poor, . . . all parsons, vicars, pensionaries, prebendaries and other beneficed men within this deanery . . . shall distribute hereafter among their poor parishioners, or other inhabitants there, in the presence of the churchwardens or some other honest men of the parish, the fortieth part of the fruits and revenues of this said benefice. . . .

Also, they shall provide and have within three months after this visitation, a strong chest with a hole in the upper part thereof, to be provided at the cost and charge of the parish, having three keys, whereof one shall remain in the custody of the parson, vicar or curate, and the other two in the custody of the churchwardens, or any other two honest men to be appointed by the parish from year to year. Which chest you shall set and fashion in a most convenient place, to the intent the parishioners should put into it their oblation and alms, for their poor neighbours. And the parson, vicar and curate shall diligently from time to time, and specially when men make their testaments, call upon, exhort and move their neighbours to confer and give (as they may well spare) to the said chest, declaring unto them, whereas heretofore they have been diligent to bestow much substance otherwise than God commanded upon pardons, pilgrimages, trentals, decking of images, offering of candles, giving to friars and upon other like blind devotions, they ought at this time to be much more ready to help the poor and needy, knowing that to relieve the poor is a true worshipping of God. . . .

12.21 John Jewel: *An Apologie of the Church of England* (1560/61)
Parker 1966: 17–19, 38, 45, 47, 55

For where they [Papacy and Council of Trent] call us heretics, it is a crime so heinous, that . . . it ought not lightly to be judged or believed. . . . For heresy is a forsaking of salvation, a renouncing of God's grace, a departing from the body and spirit of Christ. . . .

Wherefore, if we be heretics, and they (as they would fain be called) be Catholics. . . . Why do they not convince and master us by the divine Scriptures? . . . It is God's cause: why are they doubtful to commit it to the trial of God's Word? . . .

For where these men bid the Holy Scriptures away, as dumb and fruitless, and procure us to come to God himself rather, who speaketh in the Church and in Councils, which is to say, to believe their fancies and opinions; this way of finding out the truth is very uncertain, and exceeding dangerous. . . .

We truly have renounced that Church, wherein we could neither have the Word of God sincerely taught, nor the sacraments rightly administered, nor the name of God duly called upon. . . .

But, not to tarry about rehearsing all points wherein we and they differ (for they have well nigh no end), we turn the Scriptures into all tongues: they scant suffer them to be had abroad in any tongue. We allure the people to read and to hear God's Word: they drive the people from it. We desire to have our cause known to all the world: they flee to come to any trial. We lean unto knowledge: they unto ignorance. We trust unto light: they unto darkness. We reverence, as it becometh us, the writings of the apostles and prophets: and they burn them. Finally, we in God's cause desire to stand to God's only judgment: they will stand only to their own. Wherefore, if they will weigh all these things with a quiet mind, and fully bent to hear and to learn, they will not only allow this determination of ours, who have forsaken errors, and followed Christ and his apostles, but themselves also will forsake their own selves, and join of their own accord to our side. . . .

For whereas some use to make so great a vaunt, that the Pope is only [alone] Peter's successor, as though thereby he carried the Holy Ghost in his bosom, and cannot err, this is but a matter of nothing, and a very trifling tale. God's grace is promised to a good mind, and to one that feareth God, not unto sees and successions. . . .

12.22 The Thirty-Nine Articles of the Church of England (1571)
Hardwick 1851

6. Holy Scripture contains all things necessary to salvation, so that whatsoever is not read therein nor may be proved thereby is not to be required of any man, that it should be believed as an article of the faith or be thought requisite as necessary to salvation.

10. The condition of man after the fall of Adam is such that he cannot turn and prepare himself by his own natural strength and good works to faith and calling upon God. Wherefore we have no power to do good works pleasant and acceptable to God without the grace of God by Christ. . . .

11. We are accounted righteous before God, only for the merit of our Lord and Savior Jesus Christ, by faith, and not for our own works or deservings. . . .

12. Albeit that good works, which are the fruits of faith and follow after justification, cannot put away our sins and endure the severity of God's judgment, yet are they pleasing and acceptable to God in Christ and do spring necessarily out of a true and lively faith, in so much that by them a lively faith may be as evidently known as a tree discerned by the fruit.

17. Predestination to life is the everlasting purpose of God whereby (before the foundations of the world were laid) he has constantly decreed by his council secret to us, to deliver from curse and damnation those whom he has chosen in Christ out of mankind, and to bring them by Christ to everlasting salvation, as vessels made to honor. . . .

19. The visible church of Christ is a congregation of faithful men in which the pure Word of God is preached and the sacraments are duly ministered according to Christ's ordinance in all those things that of necessity are requisite to the same. . . .

21. General councils may not be gathered together without the commandment and will of princes. And when they are gathered together (forasmuch as they are an assembly of men, whereof all are not governed with the Spirit and Word of God) they may err, and sometimes have erred, even in things pertaining unto God. Wherefore, things ordained by them as necessary to salvation have neither strength nor authority, unless it may be declared that they be taken out of holy Scripture.

25. Sacraments ordained of Christ are not only badges or tokens of Christian men's profession, but rather they are certain sure witnesses and effectual signs of grace and God's good will toward us, by the which he does work invisible in us and does not only quicken, but also strengthen and confirm our faith in him.

    There are two sacraments ordained of Christ our Lord in the gospel, that is to say, baptism and the supper of the Lord.

Those five, commonly called sacraments, that is to say, confirmation, penance, orders, matrimony, and extreme unction, are not to be counted for sacraments of the gospel, being such as have grown partly of the corrupt following of the apostles, partly are states of life allowed in the Scriptures, but yet have not like nature of sacraments with baptism and the Lord's supper, for that they have not any visible sign or ceremony ordained of God.

The sacraments were not ordained of Christ to be gazed upon, or to be carried about, but that we should duly use them. And in such only, as worthily receive the same, they have a wholesome effect or operation. But they that receive them unworthily purchase to themselves damnation, as Saint Paul says.

28. The supper of the Lord is not only a sign of the love that Christians ought to have among themselves one to another, but rather it is a sacrament of our redemption by Christ's death. . . .

Transubstantiation . . . cannot be proved by holy Writ, but is repugnant to the plain words of Scripture, overthrows the nature of a sacrament, and has given occasion to many superstitions.

The body of Christ is given, taken, and eaten in the supper only after a heavenly and spiritual manner. And the mean whereby the body of Christ is received and eaten in the supper is faith.

The sacrament of the Lord's supper was not by Christ's ordinance reserved, carried about, lifted up, or worshiped.

32. Bishops, priests, and deacons are not commanded by God's Law either to vow the estate of single life or to abstain from marriage. Therefore it is lawful also for them, as for all other Christian men, to marry at their own discretion, . . .

37. . . . Where we attribute to the Queen's Majesty the chief government . . . we give not to our princes the ministering either of God's Word or of sacraments, the which thing the injunctions also lately set forth by Elizabeth our Queen, do most plainly testify, but that only prerogative which we see to have been given always to all godly princes in holy Scriptures by God himself, that is, that they should rule all estates and degrees committed to their charge by God, whether they be ecclesiastical or temporal, and restrain with the civil sword the stubborn and evildoers.

The bishop of Rome has no jurisdiction in this Realm of England. . . .

12.23 John Hooper: *The Regulative Principle and Things Indifferent* (1550)
Murray 1965: 55–8

Nothing should be used in the Church which has not either the express Word of God to support it, or otherwise is a thing indifferent in itself which brings no profit when done or used, but no harm when not done or omitted.

The peculiar and special vestments in the ministry are not enjoined by the Word of God nor are they things indifferent in themselves. Therefore they should not be used. . . .

Although a thing may have its origin in Scripture, if it is to be indifferent, it is nevertheless required that there be no positive precept by which it is ordered, nor any negative one by which it is prohibited, but that it be left to us as something free, to use or not to use, as shall seem useful or otherwise to the conscience of the person using it. . . . For those things which are ordained by God must always of necessity be kept. But those things which are prohibited, those must always and of necessity be avoided and shunned. But not only what is ordained or prohibited by the express Word of God, but also every judgment of the Divine will, which follows by necessary inference and can be gathered from a collation and comparison of the Scriptures. . . .

If that first token of indifferent things is sought concerning vestments, whether they have their origin and source in the Word of God, so that a minister might use them in the Church. . . . But the statutes, canons and decrees of the apostles and evangelists make no mention of this matter. Therefore . . . we do exclude vestments from the number of indifferent things. . . .

What is prohibited by God can in no way be indifferent, as we have given warning above. . . . [Paul] clearly teaches that the priesthood of Aaron has been abolished by the priesthood of Christ (Heb. 7, 8, 10) with all its rites, vestments, shavings, anointings, consecrations, and other similar things. If then those semblances of Aaron's priesthood cannot stand with Christ's priesthood, far less can that Popish priesthood. . . .

12.24 John à Lasco: *The Abolition of Vestments* (1552?)
Murray 1965: 63–9

It is my belief that among all things in the Church of Christ, some ought to be preserved perpetually, some are indifferent, but others are not on any account to be tolerated. Those that ought to be permanent in the Church are the pure teaching of the prophets and apostles, which ought to be set forth diligently through God's ministers to the flock of Christ, as the food of the soul. Additional to this are the sacraments of Baptism and the Lord's Supper administered according to the apostolic rite described in three apostolic gospels; to these ecclesiastical discipline is most fittingly joined. But whatever things are done for the useful and convenient administration of the Word and sacraments are indifferent; so long as they have their source in the Scriptures let there be no prohibition, let their usefulness to the Church be clear, and let there be no tyranny which strangles men's consciences. Of this kind are questions of gathering at this or that hour of day in church, using this or that sort of speech in administration of the sacraments, and celebrating the Lord's Supper once or more often in the year.

The things which ought definitely to be kept out of the Church are twofold: certain things are so obviously impious that they can never deceive even those who are but little instructed in the Word of God, such as the worship of images, adoration of the bread and wine, profanation of the Lord's Supper by the mass, invocation of the sacraments, prayer for the dead, and innumerable similar monstrosities which Antichrist has brought into Christ's Church. There are other things, introduced by the same Antichrist, which contend strongly with Christian liberty, obscure Christ, increase hypocrisy, and bring pride into the Church. At the same time, however, they bear upon them the appearance of utility and splendour. Of this sort are appointed fast days, limitation of foods, much singing which is not understood in the Church, the playing of organs, and the use of vestments in the administration of the sacraments. There is not now the space to record how much harm has crept into the Church from these individual things, and how much more could creep in if they are not abolished; I can here only treat of the use of vestments, because they must by no means be tolerated any longer in the reformed Church of Christ by a pious teacher. . . .

We know that the Roman Pope is the very Antichrist; wherefore his priesthood also is Antichristian, by which the whole priesthood of Christ is utterly trampled upon. But forasmuch as the principal part of the papistical priesthood consists in ceremonies, annointing, shaving of hair, mitres and vestments, (for without these things they do not regard anyone as a bishop, and by the quality of these ornaments they judge the quality of the bishop) it follows that if we condemn the Pope's priesthood because it is of Antichrist, we ought also to avoid all its parts and manifestations.

12.25 The Excommunication and Deposition of Elizabeth: Pope Pius V's Bull "Regnans in Excelsis" (1570)
Barry 1965: 70–2

He who reigns on high, to whom is given all power in heaven and on earth, has entrusted his holy Catholic and Apostolic Church, outside which there is no salvation, to one person alone on earth, namely to Peter the prince of the apostles, and to Peter's successor, the Roman pontiff, to be governed by him with plenitude of power. Him alone he appointed prince over all nations and kingdoms, to root up, pull down, waste, destroy, plant and build, so that he might preserve his faithful people . . .

In fulfillment of this office, we . . . spare no labor. . . . But the number of the ungodly has grown so strong in power, that no place is left in the world which they have not tried to corrupt with their abominable doctrines; among others assisting in this work is the servant of vice, Elizabeth, pretended Queen of England, with whom, as in a place of sanctuary, the most nefarious wretches have found refuge. . . .

For having by force prohibited the practice of the true religion (which had formerly been overthrown by Henry VIII, an apostate from it, and restored by Mary, the legitimate queen of famous memory, with the help of this See) and following and embracing the errors of heretics . . . she has suppressed the followers of the Catholic faith. . . .

We have seen that the impieties and crimes have been multiplied, one upon the other, and that also the persecution of the faithful and the affliction of religion through the pressure and action of the said Elizabeth grows greater every day, and since we understand her spirit to be hardened and obstinate . . . we are necessarily compelled to take up against her the weapons of justice. . . . [W]e declare the aforesaid Elizabeth to be heretic and an abetter of heretics, and we declare her, together with her supporters in the above-said matters, to have incurred the sentence of excommunication and to be cut off from the unity of the Body of Christ.

Furthermore we declare her to be deprived of her pretended claim to the aforesaid kingdom and of all lordship, dignity and privilege whatsoever.

Also we declare that the lords, subjects and peoples of the said kingdom, and all others who have sworn allegiance to her in any way, are perpetually absolved from any oath of this kind and from any type of duty in relation to lordship, fidelity and obedience; consequently we absolve them by the authority of our present statements, and we deprive the same Elizabeth of her pretended claim to the kingdom. . . . And we command and forbid all and sundry among the lords, subjects, peoples and others aforesaid that they have not to obey her or her admonitions, orders or laws. We shall bind those who do the contrary with a similar sentence of excommunication. . . .

12.26 Eyewitness Account of the Execution of Mary Stuart on the 18th Day of February of the New Calendar, in the Castle of Fotheringhay in England (1587)
Matthews 1959: 127–34

Thereupon Parliament decided thus: the life of the Scottish Queen would mean the death of the English Queen and the ruin and destruction of England and of her religion. Therefore . . . the Scottish Queen, has to be put to death. Shortly thereafter, a conspiracy was discovered against the person of Her Majesty. . . . Thereupon, latterly, the Queen of England has resolved to abolish the cause of such evil and of the above-mentioned danger, although she agreed to the execution with but a heavy heart. . . .

There, in the large hall [of the castle], in front of the fireplace, in which burnt a great fire, a dais had been set up, which was twelve feet wide and eight feet high. It was completely covered with black cloth, and thereon stood a chair with a cushion. As now all was ready . . . a message was sent to the imprisoned Queen . . . to know whether she were ready. . . .

She was led between two men of her retinue into the antechamber. There she found all her people assembled. She exhorted them all to fear God and to live in humility of spirit. She took leave of them all. . . . She begged them not to grieve on her account but to be of good cheer and to pray for her. Then she was led to the stairway. . . .

Near her stood a doctor of theology . . . who, at the command of the gentlemen spoke words of Christian comfort to her, exhorting her to die as a Christian with a repentant heart. She at once interrupted him and begged him to keep his peace, for she was fully prepared for death. The Dean answered that he had been commanded to speak the truth to her. But she said for the second time: "I will not listen to you, Mr. Dean. You have naught to do with me. You disturb me." Thereupon he was bidden to be silent by the gentlemen. . . .

Then the aforesaid Doctor fell on his knees on the steps of the dais and read in an over loud voice a fervent and godly prayer for her . . . [and] for the Queen of England and the welfare of the Kingdom. All those standing round repeated the prayer. But as long as it lasted the Queen was praying in Latin and fairly audibly, holding the crucifix in her hand.

When this prayer was now ended on both sides, the executioner knelt in front of the Queen. Him she forgave his deed, as also all those who lusted after her blood, or desired her death.. She further forgave all and sundry and craved from God that He might also forgive her own trespasses. . . .

Afterwards she fell on her knees with great courage, did not change color, and likewise gave no sign of fear. One of her tirewomen bound a kerchief before her eyes. As she knelt down she repeated the 70th Psalm: "*In te, Domine, speravi. . . .*" When she had said this to the end, she, full of courage, bent down with her body and laid her head on the block, exclaiming: "*In manuas tuas, Domine, commendo spiritum meum.*" Then one of the executioners held down her hands, and the other cut off her head with two strokes of the chopper. Thus ended her life.

The executioner took the head and showed it to the people, who cried: "God spare our Queen of England!" When the executioner held up the head, it fell in disarray so that it could be seen that her hair was quite grey and had been closely cropped.

13

Catholic Renewal and Counter-Reformation

The numerous calls for renewal of the church on the eve of the Reformations were deeply rooted in an ascetic and theological tradition concerned with spiritual and ecclesiastical renewal through moral reform. Savonarola, the fervent Dominican preacher of Florence, proclaimed God's judgment on the corruption of the church and society. His sermon "On the Renovation of the Church" (13.1) was delivered in Florence at the height of his influence before conflict with Pope Alexander VI led to his execution in 1498. John Colet, dean of St. Paul's in London, and friend of Erasmus, preached on reform (13.2) at the invitation of the Archbishop of Canterbury. Egidio da Viterbo, General of the Augustinian Order, renowned scholar and preacher in Italy and later Bishop of Viterbo, called upon the Fifth Lateran Council (13.3) to take up his ideal of reform of the church by reform of its members and restoration of its discipline. The Fifth Lateran Council (1512–17), called by Pope Julius II to oppose the French-sponsored Council at Pisa, ended under Pope Leo X only months before Luther posted the Ninety-Five Theses. Cardinal Contarini's aspiration for religious renewal and church reform found expression in his roles on the papal reform commission and his efforts for ecumenical compromise at the Regensburg Colloquy (1541). His conversion experience (13.4) and his understanding of justification (13.5) paralleled Luther's. The very brief pontificate of Pope Adrian VI (January 1522–September 1523) disappointed those who hoped he would reform the church and hence the world. His instruction to the Diet of Nuremberg (13.6) exemplifies the injunction that had been addressed to Adrian himself: *Purga Romam, purgatur mundus* ("Cleanse Rome and the world will be cleansed"). In preparation for a general council, Pope Paul III requested nine prelates to recommend responses to the major issues facing the church (13.7). The committee included some of the most outspoken advocates of reform: Cardinals Contarini, Carafa (later Pope Paul IV), Sadoleto, and Pole. A German translation of their recommendations appeared in 1538 and was republished by Luther with sarcastic marginal comments (see LW 34: 233–67). The report failed to gain acceptance at the papal court, but it does illustrate the concerns of Italian reform thought. One of the

The European Reformations Sourcebook, Second Edition. Edited by Carter Lindberg.
© 2014 John Wiley & Sons, Ltd. Published 2014 by John Wiley & Sons, Ltd.

most famous tracts associated with the Italian movement for reform was the anonymous *Beneficio di Christo* (13.8), with citations from Calvin's *Institutes*. Similarly, the *Diálogo de doctrina Christiana* (1529) by the Spanish theologian and founder of a reformist circle in Naples, Juan de Valdés, contains material from Luther. Although the *Beneficio* was prohibited by the Inquisition in 1549, its wide distribution, as well as its approval by at least three of the cardinals who signed the Counsel for Reform of the Church, attest to its enthusiastic reception. The ideas of the Reformers were available in Italy not only through their own tracts but also through evangelical circles. One of these was that around Renée of France (1510–75), a daughter of Louis XII of France (d. 1515), raised at the court of Francis I and influenced by his sister Marguerite d'Angoulême. Married to Hercule d'Este, duke of Ferrara, Renée provided hospitality to various dissidents, including John Calvin in 1536. The intellectual star of this court was Olympia Morata. An exceptionally brilliant scholar, she embraced Calvinism, and, after marrying a German physician, moved to Germany. Dubbed the "Calvinist Amazon," she strove during her brief life to provide Reformation materials to her countrymen (13.9–11). Agrippa of Nettesheim, who studied at Cologne and Paris as well as with Colet, roused the ire of the scholastics by his biblical orientation, and exposed corruption among inquisitors with *The Vanity and Uncertainty of the Arts and Sciences* (13.12). Ignatius de Loyola, founder of the Jesuits, was one of the most influential figures of Catholic renewal and Counter-Reformation (13.13). Pope Paul III formally approved the Society of Jesus in 1540 (13.14). Loyola's *Spiritual Exercises* posited renewal of the church through personal reform. The first part of the *Exercises* details a 30-day retreat for prayer, meditation, and self-examination. The second part is the so-called "Rules for Thinking with the Church" (13.15). Loyola himself proposed combating Protestantism by education (13.16). The Council of Trent (1545–63) responded to specific Protestant theological challenges (13.17–23), even while echoing Pope Adrian's earlier confession and call for extirpation of Lutheran heresy.

Expressions of the Catholic mission to counter the Reformations were wide-ranging and included the theological rationalization of tyrannicide and disparate approaches to colonialism. The Jesuit Juan de Mariana, in *The King and the Education of the King* (13.24), dedicated to the Spanish king Philip III, expanded political theory from the right of resistance to approval of tyrannicide. The Jesuits required him to remove his description of the assassination of the French king Henry III (cf. 10.18) from later editions. After the assassination of Henry IV of France in 1610, copies of Mariana's books were publicly burned in Paris. The Spanish theologian Juan Ginés de Sepúlveda championed paternalism in the Spanish colonies (13.25) whereas Bartolomé de las Casas, a Spanish Dominican, advocated for the voiceless in the face of Christian imperialism (13.26).

13.1 Girolamo Savonarola: "On the Renovation of the Church" (1495)
Olin 1992: 5–6, 14

[A]ll of Italy must be turned upside down, Rome as well, and then the Church must be renewed. But you do not believe! You should believe, however, for God has said it to you rather than I.

Now, let us begin with the reasons that I have cited to you in the several years that have passed until now, which demonstrate and prove the renovation of the Church. Some of the reasons are probable and can be contradicted; some are demonstrable and cannot be contradicted, for they are based on Holy Scripture. . . .

When you see a good head, you know that the body is well; when the head is wicked, woe to that body. However, when God permits that there be at the head of government ambition, lust and other vices, believe that God's flagellation is near. . . . Therefore, when you see that God permits the heads of the Church to be weighed down by evils and simonies, say that the flagellation of the people is near. I am not saying that this condition is found in the heads of the Church, but I am saying "when you will see it." . . .

Look, today it seems as though no one believes and has faith, . . .

Go, See what is done for the churches of God and what devotion is there, for the worship of God seems and is today lost. You will say: "Oh, there are so many religious and so many prelates, more than there have ever been!" Would that there were fewer of them! O tonsured ones, tonsured ones! . . . You are the cause of all this evil! And nowadays everyone thinks he is holy, if he has a priest in his house; and I say to you that the time will come when it will be said: "Blessed is that house that does not have a shaved head!" . . .

Believe me that the knife of God will come and soon. . . . Believing does not harm you at all, as a matter of fact it benefits you, for it makes you turn to penance and makes you walk in God's way; and do not believe that it can harm you rather than benefit you. Therefore believe that it is soon, although the precise time cannot be given, for God does not wish it, so that his elect remain always in fear, in faith and in charity, and continually in the love of God. And so I have not told you the appointed time, in order that you may always do penance and always please God. For example, if I were to say to men: The tribulation is to come here in ten years, everyone would say: I can delay longer before I mend my ways; and it would be almost giving you the license to commit evil in the meantime; it would be harmful. And therefore God does not want the appointed time preached. But I tell you wholeheartedly that now is the time for penance. . . .

O Italy, O princes of Italy, O prelates of the Church, the wrath of God is over you, and you will not have any cure unless you mend your ways! . . .

13.2 John Colet: Convocation Sermon (1512)
Olin 1992: 32–6, 38

I am about to exhort you, reverend fathers, to endeavor to reform the condition of the Church; because nothing has so disfigured the face of the Church as the secular and worldly way of living on the part of the clergy. . . .

In the first place, to speak of pride of life – what eagerness and hunger after honor and dignity are found in these days amongst ecclesiastical persons! What a breathless race from benefice to benefice, from a less to a greater one, from a lower to a higher! Who is there who does not see this? . . .

As to the second worldly evil, which is the lust for the flesh – has not this vice, I ask, inundated the Church as with the flood of its lust, so that nothing is more carefully sought after, in these most troublous times, by the most part of priests, than that which ministers to sensual pleasure? . . .

Covetousness also, which is the third worldly evil, which the Apostle John calls the lust of the eye, and Paul idolatry – this most horrible plague – has so taken possession of the hearts of nearly all priests, and has so darkened the eyes of their minds, that nowadays we are blind to everything but that alone which seems to be able to bring us gain. . . .

The fourth worldly evil which mars and spots the face of the Church is the incessant worldly occupations in which many priests and bishops in these days entangle themselves – servants of men rather than of God, soldiers of this world rather than of Christ. . . .

Now let us come to the second part – concerning Reformation. . . .

[T]his reformation and restoration in ecclesiastical affairs must needs begin with you, our fathers, and then afterwards descend upon us your priests and the whole clergy. For you are our chiefs – you are our examples of life. To you we look as way-marks for our direction. In you and in your lives we desire to read, as in living books, how we ourselves should live. . . .

The way, moreover, by which the Church is to be reformed and restored to a better condition is not to enact any new laws (for there are laws enough and to spare) . . . but for the observance of those already enacted. . . .

Lastly, let those laws and constitutions be renewed concerning the holding of Councils, which command that Provincial Councils should be held more frequently for the Reformation of the Church. For nothing ever happens more detrimental to the Church of Christ than the omission of Councils, both general and provincial.

13.3 Egidio da Viterbo: "Address to the Fifth Lateran Council" (1512)
Olin 1992: 44–5, 47

Thus I shall say of a Council both how useful it is for the Church at all times and how necessary it is for our times, with the preface that I would not dare alter the prophetic writings, but would make use of the words and speeches in their entirety, as they are accustomed to be read, not only because men must be changed by religion, not religion by men, but because the language of truth is straightforward. . . .

As often as the holding of Councils was delayed, we saw the divine Bride forsaken by her Spouse. . . . We saw, I say, violence, pillage, adultery, incest, in short, the scourge of every crime so confound all that is sacred and profane, and so attack the holy bark, that this bark has been almost swamped by the waves of sin and nearly engulfed and destroyed. . . .

Since time does not permit, I pass over what should be hardly passed over, namely the question of those in charge of the churches and the shepherds of the people on whom certainly rest the entire Christian faith and salvation. For just as this lower world is ruled by the movement and light of heaven, so the Christian peoples are governed by rulers as though by heavenly shepherds, who, if they are to be good, must teach others while shining themselves with the light of learning, and must lead the way by their own actions, practicing the pious deeds they preach. . . .

13.4 Gasparo Contarini's Conversion Experience (1511)
Oberman 1981: 211–12

On Holy Saturday I went to confession at the church of San Sebastiano. There I spoke a while with a very pious and holy father. As he recognized my inner turmoil, he began in various ways to make clear to me that the path to salvation is broader than many think. And although he did not otherwise know me at all, he spoke at length and persuasively with me. As I left, I began to think about blessedness and our situation here on earth. And I conceived truly that even if I did all the penitential services and even much more, it would hardly be sufficient to merit that blessedness, but would merely make amends for past sins.

. . . I had recognized that infinite good, that love, which without end always burns and loves us poor worms so much that our understanding cannot comprehend it. . . .

God, constrained simply by this glowing love, decided to send his only-begotten Son who should by his passion atone for all those who desire to have him as their head, and who become members of the body whose head is Christ. And although not all can have the grace to be members near the head, nevertheless all who are united with this body through the power of satisfaction [for sins] that our head has achieved, can easily hope for the atonement of their sins. We only have to strive to unite ourselves with this head through faith, through hope, and by the few things in love of which we are capable. With regard to the satisfaction for past sins and for those into which the person falls by weakness, Christ's passion is completely sufficient and more than enough.

These thoughts changed my great fear and sadness into joy. . . . Shall I not thus be able to sleep securely . . . because I have such a one who pays for my guilt? . . .

And so I shall certainly live without any anxiety in the face of my evils, for his mercy is greater than all his other works.

13.5 Contarini on Justification (1523)
Gleason 1981: 32–3

I have truly arrived at the following firm conclusion; although I had formerly read it and knew how to repeat it, nevertheless only now, as a result of experience, do I fully grasp its meaning. It is this: nobody can justify himself or purge his soul of worldly affections through works. We must have recourse to divine grace which we obtain through faith in Jesus Christ, as Saint Paul writes, and we must say with him: "Blessed is the man to whom the Lord will not impute sins, without works."

Consequently, I understand the ancient philosophers clearly: although they saw the truth in the idea that purification of the soul from desires is necessary for happiness, and said so, nevertheless they were capital fools in thinking that this purification could be brought about through habit, by acquiring the habitual practice of virtues that suppress worldly affections. Now I seem to see through my own example as well as that of others that man falls down more easily precisely at the point when he thinks he has acquired these virtues. From this I conclude that any man that lives is but nothingness [Ps. 38:6] and that we must justify ourselves through the justice of another, namely Christ. Joining ourselves to him, his justice becomes ours. We must not trust ourselves at all but say: "For ourselves we could find no outcome but death" [II Cor. 1:9].

13.6 Pope Adrian VI: Instruction to the Diet of Nuremberg (1522)
Olin 1992: 122–5

You will especially make clear to them the very great sorrow which afflicts us because of the progress of the Lutheran sect, above all because we see countless souls who have been redeemed by the blood of Christ and entrusted to our pastoral care being turned away from the true faith and religion and going to perdition. . . . Therefore, you will declare that we most strongly desire that this pestilence be more quickly countered before it infects Germany, as it once infected Bohemia. You will declare that we are most prepared to do everything that can be expected of us to this effect. . . . Moreover, the following should spur them to this task:

First, and above all, the honor of God, which is seriously offended by these heresies. . . .

Second, the dishonor of their own nation should move them. . . .

Third, let regard for their own honor move them – an honor greatly damaged, if these men who hold authority and power in Germany do not strive with all their energy to expel those heresies. . . .

Fourth, let the injury inflicted by Luther upon them and their parents and ancestors move them. . . .

Fifth, let them look to the end toward which the Lutherans go: namely, that under the guise of evangelical liberty which they proclaim to men every source of authority is destroyed. . . . [W]hile the secular princes believe that this stratagem is not directed against themselves, but only against the clergy (to whom the laity generally are hostile). . . . [I]t is certain that the people will attempt the same thing against those very secular princes.

Sixth, let the enormous scandals, disturbances, plundering of goods, homicides, quarrels, and dissensions, which this most mischievous sect has stirred up and daily stirs up throughout all Germany, move them. . . .

Seventh, let them consider the fact that Luther employs almost the same method in seducing the Christian people as that most detestable Mohammed used in deceiving so many thousands of souls, namely, by permitting those things toward which carnal men are inclined. . . . Luther, in order to win for himself the favor of monks and virgins consecrated to God and of priests lusting for the delights of the flesh, proclaims that vows of perpetual chastity are illicit, to say nothing of not being binding, and therefore that those persons may marry because of evangelical liberty. . . .

Since therefore Luther and his followers condemn the Councils of the holy fathers, burn the sacred canons, throw everything into confusion as they will, and disturb the whole world, it is clear that they must be outlawed as enemies and disturbers of the public peace by all who love that peace.

You will also say that we frankly confess that God permits this persecution to afflict His Church because of the sins of men, especially of the priests and prelates of the Church. . . . All of us . . . have strayed from our paths; nor for a long time has anyone done good; no not even one. Therefore, we must all give glory to God and humble our souls before Him, and each one of us must consider how he has fallen and judge himself, rather than await the judgment of God with the rod of His anger. As far as we are concerned, therefore, you will promise that we will expend every effort to reform first this Curia, whence perhaps all this evil has come, so that, as corruption spread from that place to every lower place, the good health and reformation of all may also issue forth. We consider ourselves all the more bound to attend to this, the more we perceive the entire world longing for such a reformation.

13.7 *Proposal of a Select Committee of Cardinals and other Prelates Concerning the Reform of the Church, Written and Presented by Order of His Holiness Pope Paul III (1537)*
Gleason 1981: 85, 87–90, 95, 98–100

Most holy Father! . . . You ordered that without any regard either to your own interest or that of anyone else we should point out to you the abuses, indeed the most serious ills with which the church of God and especially the court of Rome have long been afflicted. . . .

Obeying your command, we have therefore listed as briefly as possible the diseases and such remedies as we could suggest in spite of our limited abilities. . . .

The first abuse is the ordination of clerics, especially priests, in which neither care nor diligence is employed. Everywhere those that are the least educated, of lowest birth, conspicuous for their bad habits, or too young are admitted to holy orders and especially to the priesthood. . . . From this cause stem countless scandals and contempt of the clergy; for this reason respect for divine worship is not only diminished, but well-nigh extinct. . . .

Another extremely grave abuse consists in bestowing ecclesiastical benefices, especially parishes, and above all bishoprics. Here the custom has come to prevail of providing for persons on whom the benefices are conferred, not for the flock of Christ and the church. . . .

Still another abuse consists in the exchange of benefices, done by agreements which are all simoniacal, and where no regard is shown for anything but profit. . . .

Another abuse distresses the Christian people through the nuns who are under the care of conventual friars. In a great many monasteries public sacrilege is committed to the greatest scandal of all men. . . .

Indulgences should not be granted more than once a year in each large city. . . .

Having laid before you as clearly as we could all those matters which concern the pontiff of the universal church, we should say some things pertaining to the bishop of Rome. The city and church of Rome is the mother and teacher of other churches; thus divine worship and virtuous customs should be especially conspicuous here. For this reason, most holy Father, all strangers are scandalized who enter St. Peter's basilica, where slovenly and ignorant priests celebrate mass, dressed in vestments and attire with which they could not really appear even in a squalid house. . . .

In this city courtesans go about or ride on mules like honest women. In broad daylight they are followed by men of noble families who are members of households of cardinals, and by clerics. In no other city do we see such corruption save in this, which should be an example to all others. Moreover, these women live in fine houses. This shameful abuse must be corrected. . . .

These, then, Holy Father, are the points which we have drawn up. . . . Our hope is that you are truly chosen to restore our hearts and actions by the name of Christ, which is forgotten by the nations and by us, the clergy, to heal our diseases, to lead the sheep of Christ to one fold, and to turn away from us the wrath of God and the vengeance we deserve, which is hanging over our heads and ready to fall on us.

13.8 Anonymous: The *Beneficio di Christo* (1543)
Gleason 1981: 108–10, 112, 123, 128, 133–4

Therefore, the first office performed by the Law is to make sin known. . . . The second office performed by the Law is to make sin grow. . . . The third office of the Law is to reveal the wrath and judgment of God, who threatens death and eternal punishment to those who do not fully observe his Law. . . . When the Law has uncovered and increased sin, and has demonstrated the wrath and anger of God, who threatens death, it performs its fourth office by terrifying man. . . . The fifth office of the Law, which is its proper end, and the most excellent and necessary one, is that it compels man to go to Christ. . . .

Then our God sent that great prophet he had promised us, namely, his only-begotten Son, so that he might free us from the curse of the Law, reconcile us with our God, make our will capable of doing good works, heal our free will, and restore to us that divine image which we lost through the fault of our first parents. . . .

For our works cannot be good, unless we ourselves are made good and just through faith before we do them. . . .

Comparing the justice of the Law to the justice of the Gospel, he [St. Paul] says to the Romans that the former consists in acts and the latter in belief. . . . Here then you see how clearly St. Paul demonstrates that faith makes man just without any aid from works. . . .

And what can man do in order to merit such a great gift and treasure as Christ? This treasure is given only through the grace, favor, and mercy of God, and it is faith alone that receives such a gift, and allows us to enjoy the remission of sins. Therefore, when St. Paul and the doctors say that faith alone justifies without works, they mean that it alone enables us to enjoy the general pardon and to receive Christ, who lives in the heart through faith as St. Paul says. . . .

From this discussion, one can clearly see the difference between us and those who defend justification by faith and works. We agree in that we also uphold works, affirming that justifying faith cannot be without good works, and they say that those who are justified by faith do works which can truly be called good. We differ in that we say faith justifies without the aid of works, and the reason is ready, that through faith we clothe ourselves in Christ and make his justice and sanctity our own. Since it is true that we are given Christ's justice through faith, we cannot be so ungrateful, blind, and impious, as to believe that this is not sufficient to make us pleasing and just before God without our works.

13.9 Morata: Letter to Lavinia della Rovere
Orsini (1551/52)
Parker 2003: 117

I sent you a rather long letter this summer, . . . I don't know whether you got it. Letters are very rarely delivered in these turbulent times, in which everything seems to rage with war. . . . Indeed, if Germany did not give me the comfort of being allowed to have books of theology that we could not have there [Italy], I would not be able to bear my longing for my friends, especially you. . . . I'm also sending you some writings by Dr. Martin Luther, which I enjoyed reading. They may be able to move and restore you, too. Work hard at these studies, for God's sake, ask that He enlighten you with true religion. You will not lose. You don't think that God lies, do you? Why would He have made so many promises, unless He wished to keep them? He invites and summons all the wretched to him. He turns away no one.

13.10 Morata: Letter to Matthias Flacius Illyricus (1553)
Parker 2003: 133

My dear sir: After I had thought long and hard about how I might enrich my own family and other Italians with the good things with which Germany overflows, but found no place of counsel or ability to help in myself, I realized that I might be able to obtain this easily through other learned men. And since your writings have made you well-known to me, you were the first to come into my mind as one who seemed able to help my fellow Italians, who are lost in so many errors and are in need of the good things of heaven. If you were to translate into Italian any of Luther's German books in which he argues against the general errors (for I do not yet understand German, although I have worked hard at it) or if you would write something in Italian on the same subject (you could do it far better than I, since you have unrolled the books of sacred Scripture, which I have barely touched with my lips), I am sure that you would save many pious men from the errors by which they are misled. . . . I think it would be even more useful for them if you were to write in Italian, since many of them are ignorant of letters. I beg and beseech you again and again to do this through Christ, Who will account this a kindness done to Himself. . . .

13.11 Morata to Pietro Paolo Vergerio (1555)
Parker 2003: 167–8

I would have answered your letter a long time ago if I had not been prevented by a severe illness, from which I am only now recovering. But now I can put it off no longer. A great desire to write to you has held me ever since I read your books and saw that your soul was ready and eager to help the church. . . . And so first, I give you great thanks for your book which you gave me. Next, I demand that which before I did not dare to ask. It is this: since you strive with all your heart to advance the cause of the church, for that very reason please translate into Italian the Latin version by Vincent Opsopaeus of Martin Luther's book titled the *Greater Catechism*. If you read the book diligently, you know how much benefit it will give to us Italians, especially the young. Therefore, over and over I beg you and beseech you through Christ that you please undertake this work for the sake of your brothers, for whom we ought even to seek death. Furthermore, I am not ignorant that there is a great controversy among Christians about the sacrament, which would have already been easily resolved if men in council had consulted not their own glory but that of Christ and the health of the church, which is preserved by concord. And so to return to my previous point, I think that book would be of the greatest assistance to our fellows if you were willing to render assistance to them in this matter. I cannot urge you enough to do it.

13.12 Henry Cornelius Agrippa: "The Art of the Inquisitors" (1530)
Englander 1997: 209–11

To this company [of thieves and robbers] also belong the Inquisitors of heretics of the order of preaching friars [Dominicans]. Though their authority ought to be based on theological traditions and the Holy Scriptures, they most cruelly exercise this whole art rather in accordance with the Canon Law and the decrees of the Popes, as if the Pope were infallible. They neglect the Holy Scriptures as if it were a dead letter and a shadow of the truth. Indeed they cast it aside, saying it is the shield and bulwark of heretics. . . . They accept only the Church of Rome, whose head is the Pope – who, according to what they say, is infallible and whose office they make the object of their faith. . . .

[T]hese bloodthirsty vultures nonetheless exceed the powers of the office of the Inquisition granted to there. . . .

In this way they show their stern and extreme cruelty towards poor countrywomen who are accused of witchcraft or sorcery and condemned without first being examined by a lawful judge. They put these women to atrocious and frightful suffering, till they are forced to confess what it had never crossed their minds to believe. . . . They really suppose they are fulfilling the role of Inquisitors when they do not cease from their duty until the defenceless woman is burned or had put gold into the Inquisitor's hand, on account of which he takes pity on her and releases her as sufficiently purged by tortures. For often the Inquisitor can change the pain of the body into the punishment of the purse and apply it to his Inquisitorial office. Because of this they accumulate no small profit and not a few of these unfortunate women are obliged to pay them an annual fee. . . .

13.13 Loyola's Conversion
Englander 1997: 233–5

Until the age of twenty-six he was a man given over to vanities of the world; with a great and vain desire to win fame he delighted especially in the exercise of arms. Once when he was in a fortress that the French were attacking, . . . he persuaded him [the commander] at last to defend it; this was contrary to the views of all the knights, but they were encouraged by his valour and energy. . . . After the bombardment had lasted a good while, a shot hit him in the leg, breaking it completely; since the ball passed through both legs, the other one was also badly damaged.

[A grisly account of setting the broken bones, re-breaking and resetting the bones, and finally sawing off a protruding bone!] [H]e suffered martyrdom for many days. But Our Lord was restoring his health, and he was getting well. In everything else he was healthy except that he could not stand easily on his leg and had to stay in bed. As he was much given to reading worldly and fictitious books, usually called books of chivalry, when he felt better he asked to be given some of them to pass the time. But in that house none of those he usually read could be found, so they gave him a Life of Christ [by Ludolf of Saxony; see 1.23] and a book of the lives of the saints in Spanish.

As he read over them many times, he became rather fond of what he found written there. Putting his reading aside, he sometimes stopped to think about the things he had read and at other times about the things of the world that he used to think about before. . . . Yet there was this difference. When he was thinking about the things of the world, he took much delight in them, but afterwards, when he was tired and put them aside, he found that he was dry and discontented. But when he thought of going to Jerusalem, barefoot and eating nothing but herbs and undergoing all the other rigours that he saw the saints had endured, not only was he consoled when he had these thoughts, but even after putting them aside, he remained content and happy. . . .

From this reading he obtained not a little insight, and he began to think more earnestly about his past life and about the great need he had to do penance for it. At this point the desire to imitate the saints came to him, though he gave no thought to the circumstances, but only promised with God's grace to do as they had done. All he wanted to do was to go to Jerusalem as soon as he recovered . . . performing all the disciplines and abstinences which a generous soul, inflamed by God, usually wants to do. . . .

13.14 Pope Paul III: *Regimini Militantis Ecclesiae* (1540)
Olin 1992: 203–5

[O]ur beloved sons, Ignatius of Loyola, Pierre Favre, and Diego Laynez, as also Claude Le Jay, Paschase Broet, and Francis Xavier, and further Alphonso Salmeron, and Simon Rodriguez, Jean Codure, and Nicholas Bobadilla, all priests, . . . all Masters of Arts, graduates of the University of Paris, and trained for a number of years in theological studies; . . . have come together from various regions of the globe, and entering into association have renounced the pleasures of this world and have dedicated their lives to the perpetual service of our Lord Jesus Christ, and of ourselves and the other Roman Pontiffs who shall succeed us. . . .

We append herewith this [their] plan of life . . . :

Whoever shall desire to bear the arms of God under the banner of the cross, and to serve the one God and the Roman Pontiff, His Vicar upon earth, in our Society, which we wish to be called by the name of Jesus, having made a solemn vow of perpetual chastity, must purpose to become a member of a society principally instituted to work for the advancement of souls in Christian life and doctrine, and for the propagation of the faith. . . .

Let all the members of the Company know and bear in mind, not only in the early days of their profession but through all the days of their life, that this entire Company and all who compose it are engaged in a conflict for God under the obedience of the most sacred Lord the Pope, and his successors in the pontificate. And although we have learned from the Gospel, and know by the orthodox faith, and firmly profess that all the faithful in Christ Jesus are subject to the Roman Pontiff, as the Head and the Vicar of Jesus Christ, nevertheless, for the greater humility of our Society, and the perfect mortification of each, and the abnegation of our wills, we have deemed it to be very helpful to take upon ourselves, beyond the bond common to all the faithful, a special vow. It is meant so to bind that whatsoever the present Roman Pontiff and his successors may command us concerning the advancement of souls and the spreading of the faith, we shall be obliged to obey instantly as far as lies in us, without evasion or excuse. . . .

13.15 Loyola: "Rules for Thinking with the Church"
Englander 1997: 241–3

1. We should put away completely our own opinion and keep our minds ready and eager to give our entire obedience to our holy Mother the hierarchical Church, Christ our Lord's undoubted Spouse.

4. We should speak with particular approval of religious orders, and the states of virginity and celibacy, not rating matrimony as high as any of these.

6. We should approve of relics of the saints, showing reverence for them and praying to the saints themselves; . . .

7. We should approve of the laws of fasting and abstinence. . . .

9. Finally, all the Church's commandments should be spoken of favourably, our minds being always eager to find arguments in her defence, never in criticism.

11. Theology . . . should be praised by us; . . .

13. To arrive at complete certainty, this is the attitude of mind we should maintain: I will believe that the white object I see is black if that should be the decision of the hierarchical Church, for I believe that linking Christ our Lord the Bridegroom and His Bride the Church, there is one and the same Spirit, ruling and guiding us for our souls' good. . . .

17. Nor should we talk so much about grace and with such insistence on it as to give rise to the poisonous view that destroys freedom. . . . [O]ur language and way of speaking should not be such that the value of our activities and reality of human freedom might be in any way impaired or disregarded, especially in times like these which are full of dangers. . . .

13.16 Loyola: Letter to Father Peter Canisius on Opposing Heresy (1554)
Tylenda 1985: 97–9

The heretics have made their false theology popular and presented it in a way that is within the capacity of the common people. They preach it to the people and teach it in the schools, and scatter pamphlets that can be bought and understood by many; they influence people by their writings when they cannot reach them by preaching. Their success is largely due to the negligence of those who should have shown some interest; and the bad example and the ignorance of Catholics, especially the clergy, have made such ravages in the vineyard of the Lord. Hence it would seem that our Society should use the following means to end and cure the evils which the Church has suffered through these heretics.

In the first place, sound theology . . . requires a long time to acquire, . . . [therefore] it would be good to prepare a summary of theology dealing briefly with topics that are essential but not controversial. In matters controversial there could be more detail, but it should be accommodated to the present needs of the people. . . .

The principal conclusions of this theology could be taught to children from a short catechism, . . . and also to the common people who are not yet too corrupted by heresy and are incapable of subtleties. . . .

Another excellent means for helping the Church in this trial would be to increase the colleges and schools of the Society in many lands. . . .

The heretics write a good many pamphlets and booklets, by which they aim to remove all authority from the Catholics, and especially from the Society, and set up their false dogmas. It would seem imperative, therefore, that Ours also write answers in pamphlet form, short and well written, so that they can be produced without delay and purchased by many. . . . These works should be modest, but stimulating; they should point out the evil that is abroad and uncover the deceits and evil purposes of the adversaries. . . .

13.17 The Council of Trent on the Canonical Scriptures (1546)
Schroeder 1955: 17–19

[T]hese truths and rules [of the gospel] are contained in the written books and in the unwritten traditions, which received by the Apostles from the mouth of Christ Himself, or from the Apostles themselves, the Holy Ghost dictating, have come down to us, transmitted as it were from hand to hand. Following, then, the examples of the orthodox Fathers, it receives and venerates with a feeling of piety and reverence all the books both of the Old and New Testaments, since one God is the author of both; also the traditions, whether they relate to faith or to morals, as having been dictated either orally by Christ or by the Holy Ghost, and preserved in the Catholic Church in unbroken succession. It has thought it proper, moreover, to insert in this decree a list of the sacred books, lest a doubt arise in the mind of someone as to which are the books received by this council. [Here follows the list, including the Apocrypha.] . . . If anyone does not accept as sacred and canonical the aforesaid books in their entirety and with all their parts, as they have been accustomed to be read in the Catholic Church and as they are contained in the old Latin Vulgate Edition, and knowingly and deliberately rejects the aforesaid traditions, let him be anathema. . . .

Furthermore, . . . it decrees that no one relying on his own judgment shall presume to interpret them [the Scriptures] contrary to that sense which holy mother Church . . . has held and holds. . . .

13.18 Decree and Canons Concerning Justification (1547)
Schroeder 1955: 31–3, 42–4, 46

It is furthermore declared that in adults the beginning of that justification must proceed from the predisposing grace of God through Jesus Christ . . . without any merits on their part . . . ; that they who by sin had been cut off from God, may be disposed through His quickening and helping grace to convert themselves to their own justification by freely assenting to and cooperating with that grace; . . . Hence, when it is said in the sacred writings: *Turn ye to me, and I will turn to you* (Zach. 1:3), we are reminded of our liberty; and when we reply: *Convert us, O Lord, to thee, and we shall be converted* (Lam. 5:21), we confess that we need the grace of God.

[Justification] is not only a remission of sins but also the sanctification and renewal of the inward man through the voluntary reception of the grace and gifts whereby an unjust man becomes just. . . . The causes of this justification are: the final cause is the glory of God and of Christ and life everlasting; the efficient cause is the merciful God . . . ; the meritorious cause is His most beloved only begotten, our Lord Jesus Christ . . . ; the instrumental cause is the sacrament of baptism . . . ; finally, the single formal cause is the justice of God, not that by which He Himself is just, but that by which He makes us just. . . .

Canon 1. If anyone says that man can be justified before God by his own works, whether done by his own natural powers or through the teaching of the law, without divine grace through Jesus Christ, let him be anathema.

Can. 4. If anyone says that man's free will moved and aroused by God, by assenting to God's call and action, in no way cooperates toward disposing and preparing itself to obtain the grace of justification, that it cannot refuse its assent if it wishes, but that, as something inanimate, it does nothing whatever and is merely passive, let him be anathema.

Can. 5. If anyone says that after the sin of Adam man's free will was lost and destroyed, or that it is a thing only in name, indeed a name without a reality, a fiction introduced into the Church by Satan, let him be anathema.

Can. 9. If anyone says that the sinner is justified by faith alone, meaning that nothing else is required to cooperate in order to obtain the grace of justification, and that it is not in any way necessary that he be prepared and disposed by the action of his own will, let him be anathema.

Can. 12. If anyone says that justifying faith is nothing else than confidence in divine mercy, which remits sins for Christ's sake, or that it is this confidence alone that justifies us, let him be anathema.

Can. 13. If anyone says that in order to obtain the remission of sins it is necessary for every man to believe with certainty and without any hesitation arising from his own weakness and indisposition that his sins are forgiven him, let him be anathema.

Can. 33. If anyone says that the Catholic doctrine of justification as set forth by the holy council in the present decree, derogates in some respect from the glory of God or the merits of our Lord Jesus Christ, and does not rather illustrate the truth of our faith and no less the glory of God and of Christ Jesus, let him be anathema.

13.19 Canons on the Sacraments in General, Seventh Session (1547)
Schroeder 1955: 51–4

Canon 1. If anyone says that the sacraments of the New Law were not all instituted by our Lord Jesus Christ, or that there are more or less than seven, namely, baptism, confirmation, Eucharist, penance, extreme unction, order and matrimony, or that any one of these seven is not truly and intrinsically a sacrament, let him be anathema.

Can. 4. If anyone says that the sacraments of the New Law are not necessary for salvation but are superfluous, and that without them or without the desire of them men obtain from God through faith alone the grace of justification, though all are not necessary for each one, let him be anathema.

Can. 6. If anyone says that the sacraments of the New Law do not contain the grace which they signify, or that they do not confer that grace on those who place no obstacles in its way, as though they are only outward signs of grace or justice received through faith and certain marks of Christian profession, whereby among men believers are distinguished from unbelievers, let him be anathema.

Can. 8. If anyone says that by the sacraments of the New Law grace is not conferred. *ex opere operato*, but that faith alone in the divine promise is sufficient to obtain grace, let him be anathema.

13.20 Decree Concerning the Eucharist (1551)
Schroeder 1955: 73, 75, 79–80

Chapter I. The Real Presence of Our Lord Jesus Christ in the Most Holy Sacrament of the Eucharist

First of all, the holy council teaches and openly and plainly professes that after the consecration of bread and wine, our Lord Jesus Christ, true God and true man, is truly, really and substantially contained in the august sacrament of the Holy Eucharist under the appearance of those sensible things. . . . [I]t is a most contemptible action on the part of some contentious and wicked men to twist them [the words of institution] into fictitious and imaginary tropes by which the truth of the flesh and blood of Christ is denied, contrary to the universal sense of the Church, which . . . has detested as satanical these untruths devised by impious men.

Chapter IV. Transubstantiation

But since Christ our Redeemer declared that to be truly His own body which He offered under the form of bread, it has, therefore, always been a firm belief in the Church of God, and this holy council now declares it anew, that by the consecration of the bread and wine a change is brought about of the whole substance of the bread into the substance of the body of Christ our Lord, and of the whole substance of the wine into the substance of His blood. This change the holy Catholic Church properly and appropriately calls transubstantiation.

Canons on the Most Holy Sacrament of the Eucharist
Can. 3. If anyone denies that in the venerable sacrament of the Eucharist the whole Christ is contained under each form and under every part of each form when separated, let him be anathema.
Can. 6. If anyone says that in the holy sacrament of the Eucharist, Christ, the only begotten Son of God, is not to be adored with the worship of *latria*, also outwardly manifested, and is consequently neither to be venerated with a special festive solemnity, nor to be solemnly borne about in procession according to the laudable and universal rite and custom of holy Church, or is not to be set publicly before the people to be adored and that the adorers thereof are idolaters, let him be anathema.
Can. 8. If anyone says that Christ received in the Eucharist is received spiritually only and not also sacramentally and really, let him be anathema.

13.21 Antonius Caucus: Sermon for the Opening of Session Eighteen (1562)
Oberman 1981: 227–8

We shall hold a free ecumenical council in this distinguished and thriving city in order to root out heresy, re-establish peace in the Catholic Church, and improve the ruined morals of the Christian people. Unfortunately we live in a grievous time . . . boundless injustice and sacrilege have resulted for the Church of God due to the recently arisen abominable heresy of Luther, for the uprooting of which we are gathered: church property has been robbed, church buildings destroyed, cloisters not only pillaged and their members robbed but completely destroyed; and the most holy representative of Christ and true disciple of Peter, the Pope, as well as bishops and other priests of God are no longer respected, no longer properly honored but slandered and extremely vilified. In addition virgins dedicated to God are dishonored and their goods stolen, venerable images of the saints despised and relics disdained, the sacraments of the Church ridiculed and trodden under foot, and finally the holy laws and ordinances of the Church thrown in the fire and all the divinely instituted traditions completely overthrown. Indeed, these unholy men desire to revive the ancient and long suppressed heresies of Mani, Jovinian, Vigilantius, Pelagius, Eutyches, Felix, the Albigensians, the Waldensians, of Berengar, Marsilius of Padua, John Wyclif, Jan Huss and Jerome of Prague as well as the errors of others which our holy fathers have so often refuted and repudiated in Councils. And they [the heretics] dare to overthrow the divine and Christian teachings founded by our savior Christ which have been transmitted to us by these same holy fathers, defined in Councils with God's help, and confirmed by the popes. Indeed, what is more, they babble that these doctrines are nothing and worthless; and they set forth a broad way that does not lead to heaven. . . . The conflagration has already spread so far that there is nearly no untouched corner left in the Church of God in which this vile heresy has not invaded with all its power.

Esteemed fathers! If we would carefully search out the origin of these contemporary evils and without prejudice carefully consider everything, and if each of us will be an incorruptible judge, then we will easily see that we ourselves are, so to speak before all eyes, the cause. We, who have been appointed by God as shepherds of the Church, have done this. That is to say, we have so much offended the immortal God and the Christian people that we – put briefly – have not in the least done our duty.

13.22 The Sacrifice of the Mass, Twenty-Second Session (1562)
Schroeder 1955: 145–6, 148

And inasmuch as in this divine sacrifice which is celebrated in the mass is contained and immolated in an unbloody manner the same Christ who once offered Himself in a bloody manner on the altar of the cross, the holy council teaches that this is truly propitiatory. . . . Wherefore, according to the tradition of the Apostles, it is rightly offered not only for the sins, punishments, satisfactions and other necessities of the faithful who are living, but also for those departed in Christ but not yet fully purified. . . .

Though the mass contains much instruction for the faithful, it has nevertheless not been deemed advisable by the Fathers that it should be celebrated everywhere in the vernacular tongue. . . .

13.23 Ten Rules Concerning Prohibited Books Drawn Up By The Fathers Chosen By the Council of Trent and Approved by Pope Pius IV
Schroeder 1955: 273–8

II. The books of those heresiarchs, who after the aforesaid year [the first rule reaffirmed the prior condemnations of books up to 1515] originated or revived heresies, as well as of those who are or have been the heads or leaders of heretics, as Luther, Zwingli, Calvin, Balthasar Friedberg, Schwenkfeld, and others like these, whatever may be their name, title or nature of their heresy, are absolutely forbidden. . . .

III. . . . Translations of the books of the Old Testament may in the judgment of the bishop be permitted to learned and pious men only, provided such translations are used only as elucidations of the Vulgate . . . and not as the sound text. Translations of the New Testament made by [suspect] authors shall be permitted to no one. . . .

IV. Since it is clear from experience that if the Sacred Books are permitted everywhere and without discrimination in the vernacular, there will by reason of the boldness of men arise therefrom more harm than good, the matter is in this respect left to the judgment of the bishop or inquisitor, who may . . . permit the reading of the Sacred Books translated into the vernacular by Catholic authors to those who they know will derive . . . an increase of faith and piety.

VII. Books which professedly deal with, narrate or teach things lascivious or obscene are absolutely prohibited. . . .

X. . . . The bishops and general inquisitors, however, in view of the authority which they have, are free to prohibit even those books which appear to be permitted by these rules, if they should deem this advisable in their kingdoms, provinces or dioceses. . . . And if anyone should read or possess books by heretics or writings by any author condemned and prohibited by reason of heresy or suspicion of false teaching, he incurs immediately the sentence of excommunication.

13.24 Juan de Mariana, SJ: "Whether It Is Right to Destroy a Tyrant?" (1599)
Zuck 1975: 192–5

Tyranny, which is the most evil and disadvantageous type of government. exercises an oppressive power over its subjects, and is built up generally by force. . . . Although the duties of a real king are to protect innocence, punish wickedness, provide safety, to enlarge the commonwealth with every blessing and success, on the contrary the tyrant establishes his maximum power on himself – abandonment to boundless licentiousness and the advantages therefrom, thinks no crime to be a disgrace to him, no villany so great that he may not attempt it; through force he brings blemish to the chaste, he ruins the resources of the powerful, violently snatches life away from the good, and there is no kind of infamous deed that he does not undertake during the course of his life. . . .

Henry III, King of France, lies dead, stabbed by a monk in the intestines with a poisoned knife, a detestable spectacle and one especially to be remembered; but also by this princes are taught that impious attempts by no means go unpunished, and that the power of princes is weak once reverence has departed from the minds of the subjects. . . .

In this I see that both the philosophers and theologians agree, that the Prince who seizes the State with force and arms, and with no legal right, no public, civic approval, may be killed by anyone and deprived of his life and position. Since he is a public enemy and afflicts his fatherland with every evil, since truly and in a proper sense he is clothed with the title and character of tyrant, he may be removed by any means. . . .

13.25 Juan Ginés de Sepúlveda: "On the Indians" (c.1547)
Englander 1997: 321–2

You should remember that authority and power are not only of one kind but of several varieties, since in one way and with one kind of law the father commands his children, in another the husband commands his wife, in another the master commands his servants, in another the judge commands the citizens, in another the king commands the peoples and human beings confined to his authority. . . . Although each jurisdiction may appear different, they all go back to a single principle, as the wise men teach. That is, the perfect should command and rule over the imperfect, the excellent over its opposite. . . .

The man rules over the woman, the adult over the child, the father over his children. That is to say, the most powerful and most perfect rule over the weakest and most imperfect. This same relationship exists among men, there being some who by nature are masters and others who by nature are slaves. Those who surpass the rest in prudence and intelligence, although not in physical strength, are by nature the masters. On the other hand those who are dim-witted and mentally lazy . . . are by nature slaves. It is just and useful that it is this way. We even see it sanctioned in divine law itself, for it is written in the Book of Proverbs: "He who is stupid will serve the wise man." And so it is with the barbarous and inhumane people [the Indians]. . . . It will always be just and in conformity with natural law that such people submit to the rule of more cultured and human princes and nations. . . . Such being the case, you can well understand . . . if you know the customs and natures of the two peoples, that with perfect right the Spaniards rule over these barbarians of the New World and the adjacent islands, who in wisdom, intelligence, virtue, and humanitas are as inferior to the Spaniards as infants to adults and women to men.

13.26 Bartolomé de las Casas: "On the Indians" (1552)
Englander 1997: 324–9

1. The Roman Pontiff . . . has the authority and the power of Christ himself, the Son of God, over all men in the world, believers or infidels, insofar as it necessary to guide and direct men to the end of eternal life and to remove any impediments to this goal. . . .

10. Among the infidels who have distant kingdoms that have never heard the tidings of Christ or received the faith, there are true kings and princes. Their sovereignty, dignity, and royal pre-eminence derive from natural law and the law of nations. . . . Therefore with the coming of Jesus Christ to such domains, their honors, royal pre-eminence, and so on, do not disappear in fact or in right.

11. The opinion contrary to [the above] is erroneous and most pernicious. He who persistently defends it will fall into formal heresy. It is likewise most impious and iniquitous and has been the cause of innumerable thefts, violent disturbances, tyrannies, massacres, larcenies, irreparable damages, the gravest sins, infamy, stench, and hatred against the name of Christ and the Christian religion. . . .

20. The kings of Castille are obligated by the Apostolic See and also by divine law to procure, to provide, and to send with all diligence qualified ministers to preach the faith everywhere, calling and inviting the people in the Indies to come to the wedding and banquet of Christ. . . .

22. The gospel should be preached peacefully, with love, charity, sweetness, and affection, with meekness and good example. The infidels, especially the Indians (who by nature are very gentle, humble, and peaceful) should be persuaded by gifts and presents, and nothing should be taken away from them. . . .

23. To conquer them first by war is contrary to the law, gentle yoke, light load, and sweetness of Jesus Christ. It is the same approach that Mohammed and the Romans followed when they disturbed and plundered the world. It is the same manner that the Turks and Moors have adopted today. . . . Therefore it is iniquitous, tyrannical, and infamous to the sweet name of Christ, causing infinite new blasphemies against the true God and against the Christian religion. And we have abundant evidence of the damage that this warlike approach has done and is still doing in the Indies. Since the Indians regard our God as the most cruel, unjust, and pitiless god of all, the conversion of the Indians has been hindered, and it has become impossible to convert infinite numbers of infidels. . . .

28. The Devil could invent no worse pestilence to destroy all that world and to kill all the people there . . . than the . . . institution used to distribute and entrust Indians to the Spaniards. This was like entrusting the Indians to a gang of devils or delivering herds of cattle to hungry wolves. [It] . . . was the most cruel sort of tyranny that can be imagined, and it is most worthy of infernal damnation.

Bibliography

Appold 2012: Kenneth G. Appold, "Women's Ministry and Ordination in Early Lutheranism," *Lutheran Forum* 46/2 (Summer), 34–43.

Bainton 1951: Roland Bainton, *The Travail of Religious Liberty: Nine Biographical Studies.* Philadelphia, PA: Westminster Press.

Bainton 1960: Roland Bainton, *Hunted Heretic: The Life and Death of Michael Servetus, 1511–1553.* Boston: Beacon Press.

Barry 1965: Colman J. Barry, ed., *Readings in Church History, 2: The Reformation and the Absolute States 1517–1789.* Westminster, MD: Newman Press.

Baylor 1991: Michael G. Baylor, ed. and trans., *The Radical Reformation* (Cambridge Texts in the History of Political Thought). Cambridge: Cambridge University Press.

Beaty 1991: Mary Beaty and Benjamin W. Farley, trans., *Calvin's Ecclesiastical Advice.* Louisville, KY: Westminster Press/John Knox.

Beilin 1996: Elaine V. Beilin, ed., *The Examinations of Anne Askew.* New York: Oxford University Press.

Benrath 1967: Gustav Benrath, ed., *Wegbereiter der Reformation.* Bremen: Carl Schünemann Verlag.

Bentzinger 1983: Rudolf Bentzinger, ed., *Die Wahrheit muss ans Licht! Dialoge aus der Zeit der Reformation,* Leipzig: Verlag Philipp Reclam.

Birdsall & Newhall 1953: Jean Birdsall (trans.) and Richard Newhall (notes), *The Chronicles of Jean de Vennette.* New York: Columbia University Press.

Bray 1994: Gerald Bray, ed., *Documents of the English Reformation.* Minneapolis, MN: Fortress Press.

Bromiley 1953: G. W. Bromiley, ed. and trans., *Zwingli and Bullinger* (Library of Christian Classics, 24). Philadelphia, PA: Westminster Press.

Brown 1864: Rawdon Brown ed., *The Calendar of State Papers Relating to English Affairs in the Archives of Venice,* vol. 2: *1509–1519.* London: Longmans, Green, Reader, & Dyer.

Burnett 2011a: Amy Nelson Burnett, ed. and trans., *The Eucharistic Pamphlets of Andreas Bodenstein von Karlstadt.* Kirksville: Truman State University Press.

Burnett 2011b: Amy Nelson Burnett, *Karlstadt and the Origins of the Eucharistic Controversy: A Study in the Circulation of Ideas.* New York: Oxford University Press.

The European Reformations Sourcebook, Second Edition. Edited by Carter Lindberg.
© 2014 John Wiley & Sons, Ltd. Published 2014 by John Wiley & Sons, Ltd.

Calvin 1954: John Calvin, *Theological Treatises*, trans. J. K. S. Reid (Library of Christian Classics, 22), Philadelphia: Westminster Press.

Calvin 1958: John Calvin, *Tracts and Treatises on the Reformation of the Church*, trans. Henry Beveridge, introd. Thomas F. Torrance. Grand Rapids, MI: Eerdmans. Includes Theodore Beza, "Life of John Calvin."

Calvin 1960: John Calvin, *Institutes of the Christian Religion*, 2 vols. (continuously paginated), ed. John T. McNeill, trans. Ford Lewis Battles. Philadelphia, PA: Westminster Press.

Calvin 1981: John Calvin, *Commentary on the Book of Psalms* [French edn., 1563] (Calvin's Commentaries). Grand Rapids, MI: Baker Book House.

Caponetto 1999: Salvatore Caponetto, *The Protestant Reformation in Sixteenth-Century Italy*, trans. Anne C. Tedeschi and John Tedeschi. Kirksville, MO: Thomas Jefferson University Press.

Catley & Townsend 1837–41: S. R. Catley and George Townsend, eds., *John Foxe, Acts and Monuments*, 8 vols. London: R. B. Seeley and W. Burnside.

Clarkson 1955: John F. Clarkson, SJ, et al., eds., *The Church Teaches: Documents of the Church in English Translation*. St. Louis, MO: B. Herder.

Cochrane 1966: Arthur C. Cochrane, ed., *Reformed Confessions of the 16th Century*. Philadelphia, PA: Westminster Press.

Dennison 2008: James T. Dennison, Jr., *Reformed Confessions of the 16th and 17th Centuries in English Translation*, vol. 1: *1523–1552*. Grand Rapids, MI: Reformation Heritage Books.

Dentière 2004: Marie Dentière, *Epistle to Marguerite de Navarre and Preface to a Sermon by John Calvin*, ed. and trans. Mary B. McKinley. Chicago: University of Chicago Press.

Dickens & Carr 1967: A. G. Dickens and Dorothy Carr, eds., *The Reformation in England to the Accession of Elizabeth I*. London: Edward Arnold.

Douglass 1985: Jane Dempsey Douglass, *Women, Freedom & Calvin*. Philadelphia, PA: Westminster Press.

Edwards 1994: Mark U. Edwards, Jr., *Printing, Propaganda, and Martin Luther*. Berkeley: University of California Press.

Eire 1979: Carlos M. N. Eire, "Calvinism and Nicodemism: A Reappraisal," *Sixteenth Century Journal* 10/1, 45–69.

Engen 1988: John Van Engen, trans., *Devotio Moderna: Basic Writings*. New York: Paulist Press.

Englander 1997: David Englander, Diana Norman, Rosemary O'Day, and W. R. Owens, eds., *Culture and Belief in Europe 1450–1600*. Oxford: Blackwell.

Furcha 1984: E. J. Furcha, ed., *Huldrych Zwingli Writings*. Allison Park, PA: Pickwick Publications.

Furcha 1995: E. J. Furcha, ed. and trans., *The Essential Carlstadt: Fifteen Tracts*. Waterloo, Ont.: Herald Press.

Gee & Hardy 1896: H. Gee and W. J. Hardy, *Documents Illustrative of English Church History*. London: Macmillan.

Gleason 1981: Elisabeth G. Gleason, ed. and trans., *Reform Thought in Sixteenth-Century Italy*. Chico, CA: Scholars Press.

Greef 1994: Wulfert de Greef, *The Writings of John Calvin: An Introductory Guide*, trans. Lyle D. Bierma. Grand Rapids, MI: Baker Books. Expanded edn.: Louisville: Westminster John Knox, 2008.

Harder 1985: Leland Harder, ed., *The Sources of Swiss Anabaptism: The Grebel Letters and Related Documents*. Scottdale, PA: Herald Press.

Hardwick 1851: Charles Hardwick, *A History of the Articles of Religion*. Cambridge: John Deighton.

Higman 1970: Francis M. Higman, ed., *Jean Calvin. Three French Treatises*. London: Athlone Press.

Hillerbrand 1964: Hans J. Hillerbrand, *The Reformation: A Narrative History Related by Contemporary Observers and Participants*. New York: Harper & Row.

Hoffman 1980: Bengt Hoffman, trans., *The Theologia Germanica of Martin Luther*. New York: Paulist Press.

Holtrop 1993: Philip C. Holtrop, *The Bolsec Controversy on Predestination, from 1551 to 1555*, 2 vols. Lewiston: Edwin Mellen Press.

Hughes 1966: Philip Edgcumbe Hughes, ed. and trans., *The Register of the Company of Pastors of Geneva in the Time of Calvin*. Grand Rapids, MI: Eerdmans.

Hughes 1984: Philip Edgcumbe Hughes, *Lefèvre: Pioneer of Ecclesiastical Renewal in France*. Grand Rapids, MI: Eerdmans.

Jackson 1972: Samuel Macauley Jackson, ed., *Ulrich Zwingli (1484–1531)*. Philadelphia, PA: University of Pennsylvania Press. Reprint of 1901 edn.

Jackson 1987: Samuel Macauley Jackson, ed., *Ulrich Zwingli: Early Writings*. Durham, NC: Labyrinth Press. Reprint of 1912 edn.

Janz 1982: Denis Janz, ed., *Three Reformation Catechisms: Catholic, Anabaptist, Lutheran*. New York: Edwin Mellen Press.

Jensen 1973: De Lamar Jensen, ed. and trans., *Confrontation at Worms: Martin Luther and the Diet of Worms*. Provo, UT: Brigham University Press.

Joestel 1992: Volkmar Joestel, *Legenden um Martin Luther und andere Geschichten aus Wittenberg*. Berlin: Schelzky & Jeep.

Junghans 1967: Helmar Junghans, ed., *Die Reformation in Augenzeugenberichten*. Düsseldorf: Karl Rauch Verlag.

Jussie 2006: Jeanne de Jussie, *The Short Chronicle: A Poor Clare's Account of the Reformation of Geneva*, ed. and trans. Carrie F. Klaus. Chicago: University of Chicago Press.

Kähler 1952: Ernst Kähler, *Karlstadt und Augustin: Der Kommentar des Andreas Bodenstein von Karlstadt zu Augustin Schrift De Spiritu et Litera*. Halle (Scale): Niemeyer Verlag.

Karant-Nunn & Wiesner-Hanks, 2003: Susan Karant-Nunn and Merry E. Wiesner-Hanks, ed. and trans., *Luther on Women: A Sourcebook*. Cambridge: Cambridge University Press.

Kenney 1998: Theresa M. Kenney, ed. and trans., *"Women Are Not Human": An Anonymous Treatise and Responses*. New York: Crossroad.

Kidd 1911: B. J. Kidd, ed., *Documents Illustrative of the Continental Reformation*. Oxford: Clarendon Press.

Kidd 1941: B. J. Kidd, ed., *Documents Illustrative of the History of the Church*, vol. 3. London: SPCK.

Kingdon 1974: Robert M. Kingdon, ed., *Transition and Revolution*. Minneapolis, MN: Burgess.

Klug 1996: Ronald Klug, ed., *Prayers from the "Imitation of Christ"*. Minneapolis, MN: Augsburg.

Knecht 1996: R. J. Knecht, *The French Wars of Religion 1559–1598*, 2nd edn. New York: Longman.

Leppin 2005: Volker Leppin, ed., *Reformation* (Kirchen- und Theologiegeschichte in Quellen. Ein Arbeitsbuch, III). Kempton: Neukirchener Verlag.

Lietzmann 1911: Hans Lietzmann, ed., *Von Abtuhung der Bylder und das keyn Bedtler unther den Christen seyn sollen*. Bonn: de Gruyter.

Lietzmann 1935: Hans Lietzmann, ed., *Die Wittenberger und Leisniger Kastenordnung*. Berlin: de Gruyter.

Limm 1989: Peter Limm, *The Dutch Revolt 1559–1648*. London: Longman.

Lindberg 1979: Carter Lindberg, "Karlstadt's Dialogue on the Lord's Supper," *Mennonite Quarterly Review* 53/1, 35–77.

Lindberg 1993: Carter Lindberg, *Beyond Charity: Reformation Initiatives for the Poor*. Minneapolis, MN: Fortress Press.

Löscher 1723: Ernst Löscher, *Vollständige Reformations-Acta und Dokumenta*. Leipzig.

MacKenzie 2006: Paul A. MacKenzie, trans., *Caritas Pirckheimer: A Journal of the Reformation Years 1524–1528*. Cambridge: D. S. Brown.

Manschreck 1965: Clyde Manschreck, ed., *A History of Christianity: Readings in the History of the Church from the Reformation to the Present*. Englewood Cliffs, NJ: Prentice-Hall.

Matheson 1988: Peter Matheson, ed. and trans., *The Collected Works of Thomas Müntzer*. Edinburgh: T. & T. Clark.

Matheson 1995: Peter Matheson, ed., *Argula von Grumbach: A Woman's Voice in the Reformation*. Edinburgh: T. & T. Clark.

Matthews 1959: George T. Matthews, ed., *The Fugger Newsletters*. New York: Capricorn Books.

McKee 2006: Elsie McKee, ed. and trans., *Katharina Schütz Zell: Church Mother. The Writings of a Protestant Reformer in Sixteenth-Century Germany*. Chicago: University of Chicago Press.

Motley 1856: John Lathrop Motley, *The Rise of the Dutch Republic*, 3 vols. London: Everyman Library.

Mousseaux 1967: Maurice Mousseaux, *Aux sources françaises de la Réforme (Textes et Faits)*. Paris: Librairie protestante.

Murray 1965: Iain Murray, ed., *The Reformation of the Church: A Collection of Reformed and Puritan Documents on Church Issues*. London: The Banner of Truth Trust.

Naphy 1995: William G. Naphy, "Baptisms, Church Riots and Social Unrest in Calvin's Geneva," *Sixteenth Century Journal* 26/1, 87–97.

Naphy 1996: William G. Naphy, ed. and trans., *Documents on the Continental Reformation*. London: Macmillan.

Noble 2009: Bonnie Noble, *Lucas Cranach the Elder: Art and Devotion of the German Reformation*. Lanham, MD: University Press of America, 2009.

Noll 1991: Mark A. Noll, ed., *Confessions and Catechisms of the Reformation*. Grand Rapids, MI: Baker Book House.

Oberman 1981: Heiko A. Oberman, ed., *Die Kirche im Zeitalter der Reformation* (Kirchen- und Theologiegeschichte in Quellen, III, ed. H. A. Oberman, A. M. Ritter., and H.-W. Krumweide). Neukirchen-Vluyn: Neukirchener Verlag.

Olin 1966: John C. Olin, ed., *John Calvin & Jacopo Sadoleto: A Reformation Debate. Sadoleto's Letter to the Genevans and Calvin's Reply*. New York: Harper & Row.

Olin 1975: John C. Olin, ed., *Christan Humanism and the Reformation: Selected Writings of Erasmus with the Life of Erasmus by Beatus Rhenanus*, revised edn. New York: Fordham University Press.

Olin 1992: John C. Olin, ed., *The Catholic Reformation: Savonarola to Ignatius Loyola*. New York: Fordham University Press.

Ozment 1974: Steven Ozment, "Luther and the Late Middle Ages: The Formation of Reformation Thought," in Robert M. Kingdon, ed., *Transition and Revolution*. Minneapolis, MN: Burgess, pp. 109–52.

Parker 1966: T. H. L. Parker, ed., *English Reformers* (Library of Christian Classics, 26). Philadelphia, PA: Westminster Press.

Parker 2003: Holt N. Parker, ed. and trans., *Olympia Morata: The Complete Writings of an Italian Heretic*. Chicago: University of Chicago Press.

Petry 1962: Ray C. Petry. ed., *A History of Christianity: Readings in the History of the Early and Medieval Church*. Englewood Cliffs, NJ: Prentice-Hall.

Pfeilschifter 1983: Frank Pfeilschifter, *Das Calvinbild bei Bolsec und sein Fortwirken im französischen Katholizismus bis ins 20. Jahrhundert*. Augsburg: FDL Verlag.

Pipkin 1984: H. Wayne Pipkin, ed. and trans., *Huldrych Zwingli: Writings*, vol. 2. Allison Park, PA: Pickwick Publications.

Plöse & Vogler 1989: Detlof Plöse and Günter Vogler, eds., *Buch der Reformation. Eine Auswahl zeitgenossischer Zeugnisse (1476–1555)*. Berlin: Union Verlag.

Potter 1978: G. R. Potter, ed., *Huldrych Zwingli*. London: Edward Arnold.

Quellenbuch 1966: Hermann Schuster et al., eds., *Quellenbuch zur Kirchengeschichte*, I/II. Frankfurt am Main: Verlag Moritz Diesterweg.

Radice 1971: Betty Radice, trans., *Praise of Folly*. Harmondsworth: Penguin Books.

Reinis 2006: Austra Reinis, *Reforming the Art of Dying: The* ars moriendi *in the German Reformation (1519–1528)*. Aldershot: Ashgate.

Reu 1930: J. M. Reu, *The Augsburg Confession. A Collection of Sources with an Historical Introduction*. Chicago: Wartburg Publishing.

Robinson 1906: J. H. Robinson, trans., *Readings in European History*, vol. 2. Boston: Ginn & Co.

Russell 2006: Camilla Russell, *Giulia Gonzaga and the Religious Controversies of Sixteenth-Century Italy*. Turnhout: Brepols.

Sachsse & Tennstedt 1980: Christoph Sachsse and Florian Tennstedt, eds., *Geschichte der Armenfürsorge in Deutschland: Vom Spätmittelalter bis zum 1. Weltkrieg*. Stuttgart: Kohlhammer.

Schade 1966: Oskar Schade, ed., *Satiren and Pasquille aus der Reformationszeit*, vols. 1–3. Hildesheim: Georg Olms. Reprint of 2nd edn. of 1863.

Schaff 1917: David S. Schaff, trans., *De ecclesia. The Church, by John Huss*. New York: Charles Scribner's Sons

Schramm & Stjerna 2012: Brooks Schramm and Kirsi Stjerna, eds., *Martin Luther, the Bible, and the Jewish People: A Reader*. Minneapolis: Fortress Press.

Schroeder 1955: H. J. Schroeder, OP, *Canons and Decrees of the Council of Trent*, 3rd printing. St. Louis, KY: B. Herder.

Scott & Scribner 1994: Tom Scott and Bob Scribner, ed. and trans., *The German Peasants' War: A History in Documents*. Atlantic Highlands, NJ: Humanities Press International.

Screech 1964: M. A. Screech, ed., *Jacques Lefèvre d'Etaples et ses disciples: épistles & évangiles pour les cinquante & deux sepmaines de l'an*. Geneva: Librairie Droz.

Shrady 1985: Maria Shrady, trans., *Johannes Tauler: Sermons*. New York: Paulist Press.

Sider 1978: Ronald J. Sider, ed. and trans., *Karlstadt's Battle with Luther: Documents in a Liberal–Radical Debate*. Philadelphia, PA: Fortress Press.

Skocir & Wiesner-Hanks, 1996: Joan Skocir and Merry Wiesner-Hanks, ed. and trans., *Convents Confront the Reformation: Catholic & Protestant Nuns in Germany*. Milwaukee: Marquette University Press.

Spalatin 1851: Georg Spalatin, *Friedrichs des Weisen. Leben und Zeitgeschichte*, ed. C. G. Neudecker and L. Preller. Jena: Friedrich Mauke.

Spijker 2001: Willem van't Spijker, *Calvin: Biographie und Theologie* (Die Kirche in ihrer Geschichte, 3/J2). Göttingen: Vandenhoeck & Ruprecht.

Spitz 1974: Lewis W. Spitz, "Humanism and the Reformation," in Robert M. Kingdon, ed., *Transition and Revolution*. Minneapolis: Burgess International Group.

Stjerna 2009: Kirsi Stjerna, *Women and the Reformation*. Oxford: Blackwell.

Strauss 1971: Gerald Strauss, ed. and trans., *Manifestations of Discontent in Germany on the Eve of the Reformation*. Bloomington: Indiana University Press.

Sully 1877: *Memoirs of the Duke of Sully*, vol. 1. London: G. Bell.

Summers 1928: Montague Summers, trans., *Malleus Maleficiarum*. John Rodker.

Tappert 1959: Theodore G. Tappert, ed. and trans., *The Book of Concord: The Confessions of the Evangelical Lutheran Church*. Philadelphia, PA: Muhlenberg Press.

Thatcher & McNeal 1905: O. J. Thatcher and E. H. McNeal, *A Sourcebook for Medieval History*. New York: Charles Scribner's Sons.

Thulin 1966: Oscar Thulin, *A Life of Luther*. Philadelphia, PA: Fortress Press.

Tylenda 1985: Joseph N. Tylenda, SJ, ed., *Counsels for Jesuits: Selected Letters and Instructions of Saint Ignatius Loyola*. Chicago: Loyola University Press.

Vaughan 1845: Robert Vaughan, ed., *Tracts and Treatises of John de Wycliffe*. London: Wycliffe Society.

Wallmann 1987: Johannes Wallmann, "The Reception of Luther's Writing on the Jews from the Reformation to the End of the 19th Century," *Lutheran Quarterly* 1/1, 72–97.

Wendebourg 2012: Dorothea Wendebourg, "Jews Commemorating Luther in the Nineteenth Century," *Lutheran Quarterly* 26/3, 249–70.

Wiesner 1993: Merry E. Wiesner, *Women and Gender in Early Modern Europe*. Cambridge: Cambridge University Press.

Wiesner-Hanks 1996: Merry Wiesner-Hanks, ed., *Convents Confront the Reformation: Catholic and Protestant Nuns in Germany*. Milwaukee, WI: Marquette University Press.

Williams 1957: George H. Williams, ed., *Spiritual and Anabaptist Writers: Documents Illustrative of the Radical Reformation* (Library of Christian Classics, 25). Philadelphia, PA: Westminster Press.

Wilson 1987: Katharina M. Wilson, ed., *Women Writers of the Renaissance and Reformation*. Athens: University of Georgia Press.

Wulfert 2009: Heiko Wulfert, *Die Kritik an Papsttum und Kurie bei Ulrich von Hutten (1488–1523)*. Berlin: Lit Verlag.

Zeydel 1962: Edwin H. Zeydel, trans., *The Ship of Fools*. New York: Dover Publications.

Ziegler 1969: Donald J. Ziegler, ed., *Great Debates of the Reformation*. New York: Random House.

Zuck 1975: Lowell Zuck, ed., *Christianity and Revolution: Radical Christian Testimonies 1520–1650*. Philadelphia, PA: Temple University Press.

Acknowledgments to Sources

The editor and publisher gratefully acknowledge permission to reproduce copyright material.

"A Contemporary Description of Indulgence Selling," from B. J. Kidd (ed.), *Documents Illustrative of the Continental Reformation* (Clarendon Press, Oxford, 1911).

"A Conversation Concerning the Common Chest of Schwabach, Namely by Brother Heinrich, Knecht Ruprecht, Spuler and Their Master of the Wool Trade" (1524), in Oskar Schade (ed.), *Satiren and Pasquille aus der Reformationszeit*, vols. 1–3 (Georg Olms, Hildesheim, 1966; reprint of 2nd edition of 1863). Translated by the editor.

"Act of Abjuration" (July 25, 1581), from Peter Limm, *The Dutch Revolt 1559–1648* (Longman, London, 1989). Reproduced by permission of Pearson Education.

"Act to Take Away All Positive Laws Against Marriage of Priests" (1549), from H. Gee and W. J. Hardy, *Documents Illustrative of English Church History* (Macmillan, London, 1896).

"Aftermath of the Peasants' War: Report of the Bernese Chronicler, Valerius Anshelm," from Tom Scott and Bob Scribner (ed. and trans.), *The German Peasants' War: A History in Documents* (Humanities Press

International, Atlantic Highlands, NJ, 1994). Copyright ©1994. Reproduced by permission of Prometheus Books.

Agrippa, Henry Cornelius, "The Art of the Inquisitors" (1530), from David Englander, Diana Norman, Rosemary O'Day, and W. R. Owens (eds.), *Culture and Belief in Europe 1450–1600* (Blackwell, Oxford, 1997). Reproduced by permission of John Wiley & Sons Ltd.

à Lasco, John, "The Abolition of Vestments" (1552?), from Ian Murray (ed.), *The Reformation of the Church: A Collection of Reformed and Puritan Documents on Church Issues* (The Banner of Truth Trust, London, 1965). Reproduced by permission of The Banner of Truth www.banneroftruth.co.uk.

"A Letter from the Geneva Company of Pastors to the Swiss Churches on Jerome Bolsec" (November 14, 1551), from Philip Edgcumbe Hughes (ed. and trans.), *The Register of the Company of Pastors of Geneva in the Time of Calvin*, © 1966 Wm. B. Eerdmans Publishing Company, Grand Rapids, Michigan. Reproduced by permission of Wm. B. Eerdmans Publishing.

"Anabaptism Begins" (February 7, 1525), from B. J. Kidd (ed.), *Documents Illustrative of the Continental Reformation* (Clarendon Press, Oxford, 1911).

Anonymous, "The *Beneficio di Christo*" (1543), from Elisabeth G. Gleason (ed. and trans.), *Reform Thought in Sixteenth-Century Italy* (Scholars Press, Chicago, 1981).

Anonymous, "What is Loan-Interest Other than Usury?" (1522), in Detlof Plöse and Günter Vogler (eds.), *Buch der Reformation. Eine Auswahl zeitgenossischer Zeugnisse (1476–1555)* (Union Verlag, Berlin, 1989). Translated by the editor.

"Appeal to Outsiders to Join the 'New Jerusalem' in Munster," from Hans J. Hillerbrand, *The Reformation: A Narrative History Related by Contemporary Observers and Participants* (Harper & Row, New York, 1964). Reproduced by kind permission of the author.

Archbishop Albert of Mainz, "The Commission of Indulgences," from Hans J. Hillerbrand, *The Reformation: A Narrative History Related by Contemporary Observers and Participants* (Harper & Row, New York, 1964). Reproduced by kind permission of the author.

"A Report of Henry VIII by the Venetian Ambassador" (1519), from Rawdon Brown (ed.), *The Calendar of State Papers Relating to English Affairs in the Archives of Venice*, vol. 2: *1509–1519* (Longmans, Green, Reader, and Dyer, London, 1864).

"Argula von Grumbach (c.1492–1554)," from Peter Matheson (ed.), *Argula von Grumbach: A Woman's Voice in the Reformation* (T. & T. Clark, Edinburgh, 1995). Reproduced by permission of Bloomsbury.

Askew, Anne, "The Examinations" (1545, 1546), from Elaine V. Beilin (ed.), *The Examinations of Anne Askew* (Oxford University Press, New York, 1996). Reproduced by permission of Oxford University Press.

"Aspects of Müntzer's Military Campaign," from Tom Scott and Bob Scribner (ed. and trans.), *The German Peasants' War: A History in Documents* (Humanities Press International, Atlantic Highlands, NJ). Copyright © 1994. Reproduced by permission of Prometheus Books.

"Beutterich on the Possible Consequences of a Truce" (1578), from William G. Naphy (ed. and trans.), *Documents on the Continental Reformation* (Macmillan, London, 1996). Reproduced by permission of Palgrave Macmillan.

"Beza's Account of the Colloquy of Poissy" (September 9–October 18, 1561), from R. J. Knecht, *The French Wars of Religion 1559–1598*, 2nd edn. (Longman, New York, 1996). Reprinted by permission of Pearson Education.

Biel, Gabriel, "Doing What is in One," from Steven Ozment, "Luther and the Late Middle Ages: The Formation of Reformation Thought," in Robert N. Kingdon (ed.), *Transition and Revolution* (Burgess, Minneapolis, 1974).

Brant, Sebastian, "The Ship of Fools," from Edwin H. Zeydel (ed.), *The Ship of Fools* (Dover Publications, New York, 1962). Reproduced by permission of Dover Publications Inc.

Bucer's Description of Luther at the Heidelberg Disputation (1518), from Helmar Junghans (ed.), *Die Reformation in Augenzeugenberichten* (Düsseldorf: Karl Rauch Verlag, 1967). Translated by the editor.

Bullinger, Heinrich, "Account of Zwingli's Preaching Against Mercenary Service in 1521," from B. J. Kidd (ed.), *Documents Illustrative of the Continental Reformation* (Clarendon Press, Oxford, 1911).

Calvin, John, "Apology of John Calvin to the Gentlemen, the Nicodemites," from Eberhard Busch et al. (eds.), *Calvin-Studienausgabe*, 8 vols., vol. 3 (Neukirchener Verlagsgesellschaft, Neukirchen-Vluyn, 1994–2011). Translated by the editor.

Calvin, John, "A Very Useful Account Concerning the Great Benefit that

Christianity will Receive if it takes an inventory . . . ," from Henry Beveridge (trans.), *John Calvin, Tracts and Treatises on the Reformation of the Church*, introd. Thomas F. Torrance (Eerdmans, Grand Rapids, MI, 1958). Reproduced by permission of Wm B. Eerdmans Publishing.

Calvin, John, "Calvin to Kaspar Olevianus regarding the church in Heidelberg," from Eberhard Busch et al. (eds.), *Calvin-Studienausgabe*, 8 vols., vol. 8 (Neukirchener Verlagsgesellschaft, Neukirchen-Vluyn, 1994–2011).Translated by the editor.

Calvin, John, "Conversion and Development," in John Calvin, *Commentary on the Book of Psalms* [French edn., 1563] (Baker Book House, Grand Rapids, MI, 1981). Translated by the editor.

Calvin, John, "Institutes of the Christian Religion," from John T. McNeill (ed.) and Ford Lewis Battles (trans.), John Calvin, *Institutes of the Christian Religion*, 2 vols. (The Westminster Press, Philadelphia, 1960). Reproduced by permission of Westminster John Knox Press.

Calvin, John, *Short Treatise on the Holy Supper of our Lord Jesus Christ* (1542), from John Calvin, *Theological Treatises*, trans. J. K. S. Reid (Library of Christian Classics, 22) (Westminster Press Philadelphia, 1954). Reproduced by permission of Westminster John Knox Press and Hymns Ancient and Modern Limited.

Calvin, John, "The Consent of the Pastors . . . Concerning 'The Eternal Predestination of God' . . . ," from James T. Dennison, Jr., *Reformed Confessions of the 16th and 17th Centuries in English Translation*, vol. 1: *1523–1552* (Reformation Heritage Books, Grand Rapids, MI, 2008). Reproduced by permission of Reformation Heritage Books.

Calvin, John, "The Geneva Catechism, 1545," from Eberhard Busch et al. (eds.), *Calvin-Studienausgabe*, 8 vols., vol. 2 (Neukirchener Verlagsgesellschaft, Neukirchen-Vluyn, 1994–2011). Translated by the editor.

"Calvin on Luther: Letter to Heinrich Bullinger" (November 25, 1544), from Eberhard Busch et al. (eds.), *Calvin-Studienausgabe*, 8 vols., vol. 3 (Neukirchener Verlagsgesellschaft, Neukirchen-Vluyn, 1994–2011). Translated by the editor.

"Calvinists Appeal to the King for a Truce" (June 22, 1578), from William G. Naphy (ed. and trans.), *Documents on the Continental Reformation* (Macmillan, London, 1996). Reproduced by permission of Palgrave Macmillan.

"Calvin's Response to Des Gallars" (September 16, 1557), from Philip Edgcumbe Hughes (ed. and trans.), *The Register of the Company of Pastors of Geneva in the Time of Calvin*. © 1966 Wm. B. Eerdmans Publishing Company, Grand Rapids, Michigan. Reproduced by permission of Wm. B. Eerdmans Publishing.

"Canon Law," from Carter Lindberg, *Beyond Charity: Reformation Initiatives for the Poor* (Fortress Press, Minneapolis, 1993). Copyright © 1993 Fortress, Minneapolis. Reproduced by permission of Augsburg Fortress.

"Canons on the Sacraments in General, Seventh Session, March 3, 1547," from H. J. Schroeder, *Canons and Decrees of the Council of Trent* (Herder, St. Louis, 1955).

Capito, "Letter of Support to Luther" (1519), from Helmar Junghans (ed.), *Die Reformation in Augenzeugenberichten* (Karl Rauch Verlag, Dusseldorf, 1967). Translated by the editor.

"Cardinal Campeggio's Instructions to the Emperor" (January 1530), from B. J. Kidd (ed.), *Documents Illustrative of the Continental Reformation* (Clarendon Press, Oxford, 1911).

"Cardinal Legate Campeggio's Response to the Augsburg Confession" (July 1530), from B. J. Kidd (ed.), *Documents Illustrative of the Continental Reformation* (Clarendon Press, Oxford, 1911).

Castellio, "Concerning Heretics," from Roland Bainton, *The Travail of Religious Liberty: Nine Biographical Studies* (Westminster Press, Philadelphia, PA, 1951). Reproduced by permission of Westminster John Knox Press.

Caucus, Antonius, "Sermon for the Opening of Session Eighteen, February 26, 1562," from Heiko A. Oberman (ed.), *Die Kirche im Zeitalter der Reformation* (Kirchen- und Theologiegeschichte in Quellen, III, ed. H. A. Oberman, A. M. Ritter, and H.-W. Krumweide) (Neukirchener Verlag, Neukirchen-Vluyn, 1981). Translated by the editor.

Charles V, "Abdication Speech, Brussels" (1556), from J. H. Robinson (trans.), *Readings in European History*, vol. 2 (Ginn & Co., Boston, 1906).

Charles V, "Message to his Council" (April 19, 1521), from Oscar Thulin, *A Life of Luther*. Copyright © 1966 Fortress Press, Philadelphia. Reproduced by permission of Augsburg Fortress.

"Christopher Froschauer's Defense" (April 1522), from B. J. Kidd (ed.), *Documents Illustrative of the Continental Reformation* (Clarendon Press, Oxford, 1911).

Colet, John, "Convocation Sermon" (1512), from John C. Olin (ed.), *The Catholic Reformation: Savonarola to Ignatius Loyola* (Fordham University Press, New York, 1992). Reproduced by permission of Fordham University Press.

"Communism in the City of Munster," from Hans J. Hillerbrand, *The Reformation: A Narrative History Related by Contemporary Observers and Participants* (Harper & Row, New York, 1964). Reproduced by kind permission of the author.

"Conciliarism: Opinion of the University of Paris" (1393), from O. J. Thatcher and E. H. McNeal, *A Sourcebook for Medieval History* (Charles Scribner's Sons, New York, 1905).

"Confutation of the Augsburg Confession" (August 3, 1530), from J. M. Reu, *The*

Augsburg Confession: A Collection of Sources with an Historical Introduction (Wartburg, Chicago, 1930). Reproduced by permission of Augsburg Fortress.

"Conrad Grebel and Companions to Müntzer" (September 5, 1524), from Peter Matheson (ed. and trans.), *The Collected Works of Thomas Müntzer* (T. & T. Clark, Edinburgh, 1988). Reproduced by permission of Bloomsbury.

"Contarini on Justification" (February 7, 1523), from Elisabeth G. Gleason (ed. and trans.), *Reform Thought in Sixteenth-Century Italy* (Scholars Press, Chicago, 1981).

Cop, Nicolas, "Rector's Address to the University of Paris" (November 1, 1533), from Eberhard Busch et al. (eds.), *Calvin-Studienausgabe*, 8 vols., vol. 1 (Neukirchener Verlagsgesellschaft, Neukirchen-Vluyn, 1994–2011). Translated by the editor.

Cranmer, Thomas, "Certain Sermons, or Homilies" (1547), from T. H. L. Parker (ed.), *English Reformers* (Library of Christian Classics, 26) (Westminster Press, Philadelphia, 1966). Reproduced by permission of Westminster John Knox Press.

D'Ailly, Pierre, "Conciliar Principles" (1409), from Ray C. Petry (ed.), *A History of Christianity: Readings in the History of the Early and Medieval Church* (Prentice-Hall, Englewood Cliffs, 1962).

da Viterbo, Egidio, "Address to the Fifth Lateran Council" (1512), from John C. Olin (ed.), *The Catholic Reformation: Savonarola to Ignatius Loyola* (Fordham University Press, New York, 1992). Reproduced by permission of Fordham University Press.

de Bonivard, François, "On the Ecclesiastical Polity of Geneva," from Robert M. Kingdon (ed.), *Transition and Revolution* (Burgess International Group, Minneapolis, 1974).

"Decree and Canons Concerning Justification" (January 13, 1547), from H. J. Schroeder, *Canons and Decrees of the Council of Trent* (Herder, St. Louis, 1955).

"Decree Concerning the Eucharist" (October 11, 1551), from H. J. Schroeder, *Canons and Decrees of the Council of Trent* (Herder, St. Louis, 1955).

de Jussie, Jeanne, *The Short Chronicle: A Poor Clare's Account of the Reformation of Geneva*, ed. and trans. Carrie F. Klaus (University of Chicago Press, Chicago, 2006). Reproduced by permission of University of Chicago Press.

de las Casas, Bartolomé, "On the Indians" (1552), from David Englander, Diana Norman, Rosemary O'Day, and W. R. Owens (eds.), *Culture and Belief in Europe 1450–1600* (Blackwell, Oxford, 1997). Reproduced by permission of John Wiley & Sons Ltd.

de L'Hôpital, Michel, "Speech to the Estates-General of Orleans" (December 13, 1560), from R. J. Knecht, *The French Wars of Religion 1559–1598*, 2nd edn. (Longman, New York, 1996). Reprinted by permission of Pearson Education.

de Mariana, Juan, SJ, "Whether It Is Right to Destroy a Tyrant?" (1599), from Lowell Zuck (ed.), *Christianity and Revolution: Radical Christian Testimonies 1520–1650* (Temple University Press, Philadelphia, 1975), © Lowell H. Zuck. Reproduced by kind permission of the author.

Dentière, Marie, *Epistle to Marguerite de Navarre and Preface to a Sermon by John Calvin*, ed. and trans. Mary B. McKinley (University of Chicago Press, Chicago, 2004). Reproduced by permission of University of Chicago Press.

de Raemond, Florimond, "Heresy at Meaux," from Maurice Mousseaux, *Aux sources françaises de la Réforme (Textes et Faits)* (Librairie protestante, Paris, 1967). Translated by the editor.

"Description of 'Hedge-Preaching' given to Regent Margaret," from William G. Naphy (ed. and trans.), *Documents on the Continental Reformation* (Macmillan, London, 1996). Reproduced by permission of Palgrave Macmillan.

de Sepúlveda, Juan Ginés, "On the Indians" (c.1547), from David Englander, Diana Norman, Rosemary O'Day, and W. R. Owens (eds.), *Culture and Belief in Europe 1450–1600* (Blackwell, Oxford, 1997). Reproduced by permission of John Wiley & Sons Ltd.

de Venette, Jean, "Chronicle," from Jean Birdsall (trans.) and Richard Newhall (notes) *The Chronicles of Jean de Vennette* (Columbia University Press, New York, 1953) pp. 48–52 (extracts). Reproduced by permission of Columbia University Press.

"Dukes William IV and Louis X of Bavaria to the Theological Faculty of Ingolstadt University" (February 13, 1530), from J. M. Reu, *The Augsburg Confession: A Collection of Sources with an Historical Introduction* (Wartburg, Chicago, 1930). Reproduced by permission of Augsburg Fortress.

Dürer, Albrecht, "Rumors of Luther's Capture" (1521), from Oscar Thulin, *A Life of Luther*. Copyright © 1966 Fortress Press, Philadelphia. Reproduced by permission of Augsburg Fortress.

Eck, Johannes, "'404 Articles' on the Errors of the Reformers" (March 1530), from M. Reu, *The Augsburg Confession: A Collection of Sources with an Historical Introduction* (Wartburg, Chicago, 1930). Reproduced by permission of Augsburg Fortress.

Eck, Johannes, "Letter to Duke George of Saxony on the Anabaptists (1527), from Helmar Junghans (ed.), *Die Reformation in Augenzeugenberichten* (Karl Rauch Verlag, Düsseldorf, 1967). Translated by the editor.

Erasmus, Desiderius, "Praise of Folly" (1509), from Betty Radice (trans.), *Praise of Folly* (Penguin Books, Harmondsworth, 1971). Reproduced by permission of Penguin Books UK.

Erasmus, "Letter to Martin Dorp" (1515), from John C. Olin (ed.), *Christian Humanism and the Reformation: Selected Writings of Erasmus with the Life of Erasmus by Beatus Rhenanus*, revised edn. (Fordham

University Press, New York, 1975). Reproduced by permission of Fordham University Press.

Erasmus, "Paraclesis" (1516), in Gustav Benrath (ed.), *Wegbereiter der Reformation* (Carl Schünemann Verlag, Bremen, 1967). Translated by the editor.

"Erasmus to Martin Bucer" (November 11, 1527), from William G. Naphy (ed. and trans.), *Documents on the Continental Reformation* (Macmillan, London, 1996). Reproduced by permission of Palgrave Macmillan.

"Eyewitness Account of the Execution of Mary Stuart on the 18th Day of February of the New Calendar, in the Castle of Fotheringhay in England" (1587), from George T. Matthews (ed.), *The Fugger Newsletters* (Capricorn Books, New York, 1959).

Fish, Simon, "A Supplication for the Beggars" (1529), from H. Gee and W. J. Hardy, *Documents Illustrative of English Church History* (Macmillan, London, 1896).

Gallus, Nicholas, et al., "A Confession of the Magedeburg Pastors Concerning Resistance to the Superior Magistrate" (April 13, 1550), from Lowell Zuck (ed.), *Christianity and Revolution: Radical Christian Testimonies 1520–1650* (Temple University Press, Philadelphia, 1975). © Lowell H. Zuck. Reproduced by kind permission of the author.

"Gasparo Contarini's Conversion Experience" (April 19, 1511), in Heiko A. Oberman (ed.), *Die Kirche im Zeitalter der Reformation* (Kirchen- und Theologiegeschichte in Quellen, III, ed. H. A. Oberman, A. M. Ritter, and H.-W. Krumweide) (Neukirchener Verlag, Neukirchen-Vluyn, 1981). Translated by the editor.

Geiler of Kaysersberg, Johann, "Concerning Begging," from Christoph Sachsse and Florian Tennstedt (eds.), *Geschichte der Armenfursorge in Deutschland: Vom*

Spätmittelalter bis zum 1. Weltkrieg (Kohlhammer, Stuttgart, 1980). Translated by the editor.

Hall, Edward, "A Protestant Merchant outwits a Bishop" (1529), from H. Gee and W. J. Hardy, *Documents Illustrative of English Church History* (Macmillan, London, 1896).

Hausmann, Nicholas, "A Report Concerning the Zwickau Prophets" (1521), from Lowell Zuck (ed.), *Christianity and Revolution: Radical Christian Testimonies 1520–1650* (Temple University Press, Philadelphia, 1975). © Lowell H. Zuck. Reproduced by kind permission of the author.

"Henry IV Ascends the Throne" (September 1589), from George T. Matthews (ed.), *The Fugger Newsletters* (Capricorn Books, New York, 1959).

"Henry IV Becomes a Catholic" (August 1593), from George T. Matthews (ed.), *The Fugger Newsletters* (Capricorn Books, New York, 1959).

Hooper, John, "The Regulative Principle and Things Indifferent" (1550), from Ian Murray (ed.), *The Reformation of the Church: A Collection of Reformed and Puritan Documents on Church Issues* (The Banner of Truth Trust, London, 1965). Reproduced by permission of The Banner of Truth www.banneroftruth.co.uk.

"Hubmaier to Oecolampadius on Baptism" (January 16, 1525), from B. J. Kidd (ed.), *Documents Illustrative of the Continental Reformation* (Clarendon Press, Oxford, 1911).

Hus, John, "The Treatise on the Church," from David S. Schaff(trans.), *De ecclesia. The Church by John Huss* (Charles Scribner's Sons, New York, 1917).

Institution of the Prophesy in Zurich, from Helmar Junghans (ed.), *Die Reformation in Augenzeugenberichten* (Karl Rauch Verlag, Düsseldorf, 1967). Translated by the editor.

Jewel, John, "An Apologie of the Church of England" (1560/61), from T. H. L. Parker (ed.), *English Reformers* (Library of Christian Classics, 26) (Westminster Press, Philadelphia, 1966). Reproduced by permission of Westminster John Knox Press.

"Johann Rühl, Mansfeld Councillor, to Martin Luther" (May 21 and 26, 1525), from Tom Scott and Bob Scribner (ed. and trans.), *The German Peasants' War: A History in Documents* (Humanities Press International, Atlantic Highlands, NJ, 1994). Copyright © 1994. Reproduced by permission of Prometheus Books.

"John Foxe on Robert Barnes," from S. R. Catley and George Townsend (eds.), *John Foxe, Acts and Monuments*, 8 vols. (R. B. Seeley and W. Burnside, London, 1837–41).

"John Foxe's Acts and Monuments: 'Lollardy on the Eve of the Reformation'," from S. R. Catley and George Townsend (eds.), *John Foxe, Acts and Monuments*, 8 vols. (R. B. Seeley and W. Burnside, London, 1837–41).

"Judgment of the Saxon Jurists" (October 1530), from Jaroslav Pelikan and Helmut T. Lehmann (eds.), *Luther's Works*, vol. 47. Copyright © 1955–86 Augsburg Fortress. Reproduced by permission of Augsburg Fortress.

Karlstadt, Andreas Bodenstein von, "'Dialogue' on the Lord's Supper" (1524), from Carter Lindberg, "Karlstadt's Dialogue on the Lord's Supper," *Mennonite Quarterly Review* 53/1 (January). Reproduced by permission of the Mennonite Quarterly Review.

Karlstadt, Andreas Bodenstein von, "Exposition of Numbers 30 Which Speaks of Vows" (1522), from E. J. Furcha (ed. and trans.), *The Essential Carlstadt* (Herald Press, Waterloo, 1995). © 1995 Herald Press. Reproduced by permission of Herald Press.

Karlstadt, Andreas Bodenstein von, "On the Abolition of Images and That There Should Be No Beggars Among Christians" (January 27, 1522), from Hans Lietzmann (ed.), *Von Abtuhung der Bylder und das keyn Bedtler*

unther den Christen seyn sollen (de Gruyter, Bonn, 1911). Translated by the editor.

Karlstadt, Andreas Bodenstein von, "Several Main Points of Christian Teaching Regarding Which Dr. Luther Brings Andreas Carlstadt Under Suspicion through False Accusation and Slander" (1525), from E. J. Furcha (ed. and trans.), *The Essential Carlstadt: Fifteen Tracts* (Herald Press, Waterloo, 1995). Copyright © 1995 by Herald Press, Harrisburg, VA. Reproduced by permission of Herald Press, Scottdale, PA 15683, USA.

Karlstadt, Andreas Bodenstein von, "The 151 Theses" (1517), from Ernst Kahler, *Karlstadt und Augustin: Der Kommentar des Andreas Bodenstein von Karlstadt zu Augustin Schrift De Spiritu et Litera* (Niemeyer Verlag, Halle (Scale), 1952). Translated by the editor.

Karlstadt, Andreas Bodenstein von, "The Meaning of the Term 'Gelassen' and Where in Holy Scripture It Is Found" (1523), from E. J. Furcha (ed. and trans.), *The Essential Carlstadt* (Herald Press, Waterloo, 1995). Reproduced by permission of Herald Press, Scottdale, PA 15683, USA.

Karlstadt, Andreas Bodenstein von, "Whether One Should Proceed Slowly" (November 1524), from Ronald J. Sider (ed. and trans.), *Karlstadt's Battle with Luther: Documents in a Liberal–Radical Debate*. Copyright © 1978 Fortress Press, Philadelphia. Reproduced by permission of Augsburg Fortress.

Kempis, Thomas à, "The Imitation of Christ," from Ronald Klug (ed.), *Prayers from the "Imitation of Christ"*. Copyright © 1996 Augsburg Fortress, Minneapolis. Reproduced by permission of Augsburg Fortress.

Kolde, Dietrich, *A Fruitful Mirror or Small Handbook for Christians*, from Denis Janz (ed.), *Three Reformation Catechisms: Catholic, Anabaptist, Lutheran* (New York: Edwin Mellen Press, 1982). Reproduced by permission of the Edwin Mellen Press.

Lefèvre, Jacques, "Commentary on the Epistles of St. Paul" (1512), from Philip Edgcumbe Hughes, *Lefèvre: Pioneer of Ecclesiastical Renewal in France* (Eerdmans, Grand Rapids, MI, 1984). Reprinted by permission of Wm. B. Eerdmans Publishing.

Lefèvre, Jacques, "Letters to Farel" (1524). in Maurice Mousseaux, *Aux sources françaises de la Réforme (Textes et Faits)* (Librairie protestante, Paris, 1967). Translated by the editor.

Lefèvre, Jacques, "Preface to Latin Commentary on the Gospels" (1522), from Philip Edgcumbe Hughes, *Lefèvre: Pioneer of Ecclesiastical Renewal in France* (Eerdmans, Grand Rapids, MI, 1984). Reprinted by permission of Wm. B. Eerdmans Publishing.

"Letter from the Company of Pastors to the Church in Paris" (September 16, 1557), from Philip Edgcumbe Hughes (ed. and trans.), *The Register of the Company of Pastors of Geneva in the Time of Calvin.* © 1966 Wm. B. Eerdmans Publishing Company, Grand Rapids, Michigan. Reproduced by permission of Wm. B. Eerdmans Publishing.

"Letter from Nicolas des Gallars, Pastor in Paris, to his Genevan Colleagues" (September 7, 1557), from Philip Edgcumbe Hughes (ed. and trans.), *The Register of the Company of Pastors of Geneva in the Time of Calvin.* © 1966 Wm. B. Eerdmans Publishing Company, Grand Rapids, Michigan. Reproduced by permission of Wm. B. Eerdmans Publishing.

"Letter to Geneva from Five Evangelical Students Imprisoned in Lyon" (July 1552), from Philip Edgcumbe Hughes (ed. and trans.), *The Register of the Company of Pastors of Geneva in the Time of Calvin.* © 1966 Wm. B. Eerdmans Publishing Company, Grand Rapids, Michigan. Reproduced by permission of Wm. B. Eerdmans Publishing.

Loyola, "Letter to Father Peter Canisius on Opposing Heresy" (August 13, 1554), from Joseph N. Tylenda (ed.), *Counsels for Jesuits: Selected Letters and Instructions of Saint Ignatius Loyola* (Loyola University Press, Chicago, 1985).

Loyola, "Rules for Thinking with the Church," from David Englander, Diana Norman, Rosemary O'Day and W. R. Owens (eds.), *Culture and Belief in Europe 1450–1600* (Blackwell, Oxford, 1997). Reproduced by permission of John Wiley & Sons Ltd.

"Loyola's Conversion," from David Englander, Diana Norman, Rosemary O'Day, and W. R. Owens (eds.), *Culture and Belief in Europe 1450–1600* (Blackwell, Oxford, 1997). Reproduced by permission of John Wiley & Sons Ltd.

Ludolf of Saxony, "Vita Jesu Christi," from Gustav Benrath (ed.), *Wegbereiter der Reformation* (Carl Schünemann Verlag, Bremen, 1967). Translated by the editor.

Luther, Martin, "A Brief Instruction on What to Look for and Expect in the Gospels" (1521), from Jaroslav Pelikan and Helmut T. Lehmann (eds.), *Luther's Works,* vol. 38. Copyright © 1955–86 Augsburg Fortress. Reproduced by permission of Augsburg Fortress.

Luther, Martin, "Admonition to Peace. A Reply to the Twelve Articles of the Peasants in Swabia" (1525), from Jaroslav Pelikan and Helmut T. Lehmann (eds.), *Luther's Works,* vol. 46. Copyright © 1955–86 Augsburg Fortress. Reproduced by permission of Augsburg Fortress.

Luther, Martin, "Against the Heavenly Prophets" (1525), from Jaroslav Pelikan and Helmut T. Lehmann (eds.), *Luther's Works,* vol. 40. Copyright © 1955–86 Augsburg Fortress. Reproduced by permission of Augsburg Fortress.

Luther, Martin, "Against the Robbing and Murdering Hordes of Peasants" (1525), from Jaroslav Pelikan and Helmut T. Lehmann (eds.), *Luther's Works,* vol. 46. Copyright © 1955–86 Augsburg Fortress. Reproduced by permission of Augsburg Fortress.

Luther, Martin, "An Open Letter on the Harsh Book Against the Peasants" (1525), from Jaroslav Pelikan and Helmut T. Lehmann (eds.) *Luther's Works*, vol. 46. Copyright © 1955–86 Augsburg Fortress. Reproduced by permission of Augsburg Fortress.

Luther, Martin, "A Sermon on Keeping Children in School" (1530), from Jaroslav Pelikan and Helmut T. Lehmann (eds.), *Luther's Works*, vol. 46. Copyright © 1955–86 Augsburg Fortress. Reproduced by permission of Augsburg Fortress.

Luther, Martin, "Confession Concerning Christ's Supper" (1528), from Jaroslav Pelikan and Helmut T. Lehmann (eds.), *Luther's Works*, vol. 37. Copyright © 1955–86 Augsburg Fortress. Reproduced by permission of Augsburg Fortress.

Luther, Martin, "Disputation Against Scholastic Theology" (September 4, 1517), from Jaroslav Pelikan and Helmut T. Lehmann (eds.), *Luther's Works*, vol. 31. Copyright © 1955–86 Augsburg Fortress. Reproduced by permission of Augsburg Fortress.

Luther, Martin, "Disputation Concerning the Right to Resist the Emperor," from Lowell Zuck (ed.), *Christianity and Revolution: Radical Christian Testimonies 1520–1650* (Temple University Press, Philadelphia, 1975). © Lowell Zuck. Reproduced by kind permission of the author.

Luther, Martin, "Dr. Martin Luther's Warning to his Dear German People" (1531), from Jaroslav Pelikan and Helmut T. Lehmann (eds.), *Luther's Works*, vol. 47. Copyright © 1955–86 Augsburg Fortress. Reproduced by permission of Augsburg Fortress.

Luther, Martin, "Foreword" to Mathias Hutlin's *The Book of Vagabonds* (1510), from *D. Martin Luthers Werke: Kritische Gesamtausgabe*, 58 vols., vol. 26 (Böhlau, Weimar, 1883–51). Translated by the editor.

Luther, Martin, "Letter to Elector Frederick" (March 5, 1522), from Jaroslav Pelikan and Helmut T. Lehmann (eds.), *Luther's Works*, vol. 48. Copyright © 1955–86 Augsburg Fortress. Reproduced by permission of Augsburg Fortress.

Luther Martin, "Letter to Lazarus Spengler in Nuremberg" (March 18, 1531), from Lowell Zuck (ed.), *Christianity and Revolution: Radical Christian Testimonies 1520–1650* (Temple University Press, Philadelphia, 1975). © Lowell H. Zuck. Reproduced by kind permission of the author.

Luther, Martin, "Letter to the Christians at Strassburg in Opposition to the Fanatic Spirit" (1524), from Jaroslav Pelikan and Helmut T. Lehmann (eds.), *Luther's Works*, vol. 40. Copyright © 1955–86 Augsburg Fortress. Reproduced by permission of Augsburg Fortress.

Luther, Martin, "Letter to the Princes of Saxony Concerning the Rebellious Spirit" (July, 1524), from Jaroslav Pelikan and Helmut T. Lehmann (eds.), *Luther's Works*, vol. 40. Copyright © 1955–86 Augsburg Fortress. Reproduced by permission of Augsburg Fortress.

Luther, Martin, "On Translating: An Open Letter" (1530), from Jaroslav Pelikan and Helmut T. Lehmann (eds.), *Luther's Works*, vol. 35. Copyright © 1955–86 Augsburg Fortress. Reproduced by permission of Augsburg Fortress.

Luther, Martin, "Recollections of Becoming a Monk," from Jaroslav Pelikan and Helmut T. Lehmann (eds.), *Luther's Works*, vol. 54. Copyright © 1955–86 Augsburg Fortress. Reproduced by permission of Augsburg Fortress.

Luther, Martin, "Temporal Authority: To What Extent it Should be Obeyed" (1523), from *Luther's Works*, vol. 45, ed. Jaroslav Pelikan and Helmut T. Lehmann. Copyright © 1955–86 Augsburg Fortress. Reproduced by permission of Augsburg Fortress.

Luther, Martin, "That Clergy Should Preach Against Usury" (1540), from *D. Martin Luthers Werke: Kritische Gesamtausgabe*, 58 vols., vol. 51 (Böhlau, Weimar, 1883–51). Translated by the editor.

Luther, Martin, "The Babylonian Captivity of the Church" (October 6, 1520), from Jaroslav Pelikan and Helmut T. Lehmann (eds.), *Luther's Works*, vol. 36, Copyright © 1955–86 Augsburg Fortress. Reproduced by permission of Augsburg Fortress.

Luther, Martin, "The Blessed Sacrament of the Holy and True Body of Christ and the Brotherhoods" (1519), from Jaroslav Pelikan and Helmut T. Lehmann (eds.), *Luther's Works*, vol. 35. Copyright © 1955–86 Augsburg Fortress. Reproduced by permission of Augsburg Fortress.

Luther, Martin, "The Estate of Marriage" (1522), from Jaroslav Pelikan and Helmut T. Lehmann (eds.), *Luther's Works*, vol. 45. Copyright © 1955–86 Augsburg Fortress. Reproduced by permission of Augsburg Fortress.

Luther, Martin, "The Freedom of a Christian" (early November 1520), from Jaroslav Pelikan and Helmut T. Lehmann (eds.), *Luther's Works*, vol. 31. Copyright © 1955–86 Augsburg Fortress. Reproduced by permission of Augsburg Fortress.

Luther, Martin, "The Invocavit Sermons" (March 9, 1522), from Jaroslav Pelikan and Helmut T. Lehmann (eds.), *Luther's Works*, vol. 51. Copyright © 1955–86 Augsburg Fortress. Reproduced by permission of Augsburg Fortress.

Luther, Martin, "The Judgment of Martin Luther on Monastic Vows" (1521), from Jaroslav Pelikan and Helmut T. Lehmann (eds.), *Luther's Works*, vol. 44. Copyright © 1955–86 Augsburg Fortress. Reproduced by permission of Augsburg Fortress.

Luther, Martin, "The Large Catechism" (1529), from Robert Kolb and Timothy J. Wengert (eds.), *The Book of Concord: The Confessions of the Evangelical Lutheran Church* (Fortress Press, Minneapolis, 2000).

Luther, Martin, "The Ninety-five Theses" (October 31, 1517), from Jaroslav Pelikan and Helmut T. Lehmann (eds.), *Luther's Works*, vol. 31. Copyright © 1955–86 Augsburg Fortress. Reproduced by permission of Augsburg Fortress.

Luther, Martin, *The Small Catechism* (1529), from from Robert Kolb and Timothy J. Wengert (eds.), *The Book of Concord: The Confessions of the Evangelical Lutheran Church* (Fortress Press, Minneapolis, 2000).

Luther, Martin, "To the Christian Nobility of the German Nation Concerning the Reform of the Christian Estate" (August 18, 1520), from Jaroslav Pelikan and Helmut T. Lehmann (eds.), *Luther's Works*, vol. 44. Copyright © 1955–86 Augsburg Fortress. Reproduced by permission of Augsburg Fortress.

Luther, Martin, "To the Councilmen of All Cities in Germany that They Establish and Maintain Christian Schools" (1524), from Jaroslav Pelikan and Helmut T. Lehmann (eds.), *Luther's Works*, vol. 45. Copyright © 1955–86 Augsburg Fortress. Reproduced by permission of Augsburg Fortress.

Luther, Martin, "Trade and Usury" (1524), from Jaroslav Pelikan and Helmut T. Lehmann (eds.), *Luther's Works*, vol. 45. Copyright © 1955–86 Augsburg Fortress. Reproduced by permission of Augsburg Fortress.

Luther, Martin, "Treatise on Good Works" (1520), from Jaroslav Pelikan and Helmut T. Lehmann (eds.), *Luther's Works*, vol. 44. Copyright © 1955–86 Augsburg Fortress. Reproduced by permission of Augsburg Fortress.

"Luther before Emperor and Empire at the Diet of Worms," from Oscar Thulin, *A Life of Luther*. Copyright ©1966 Fortress Press, Philadelphia. Reproduced by permission of Augsburg Fortress.

"Luther's Conversion," from Jaroslav Pelikan and Helmut T. Lehmann (eds.), *Luther's*

Works, vol. 34. Copyright © 1955–86 Augsburg Fortress. Used by permission of Augsburg Fortress.

"Luther's Hearing before Cardinal Cajetan at Augsburg" (1518), from Oscar Thulin, *A Life of Luther*. Copyright © 1966 Fortress Press, Philadelphia. Reproduced by permission of Augsburg Fortress.

"Luther's Theological Emphases," from Jaroslav Pelikan and Helmut T. Lehmann (eds.), *Luther's Works*, vol. 12. Reproduced by permission of Concordia Publishing House.

"Mandate of the Zurich Mayor and Council for Scriptural Preaching" (December 1520), from B. J. Kidd (ed.), *Documents Illustrative of the Continental Reformation* (Clarendon Press, Oxford, 1911).

"Mantz's Petition of Defense" (December 1524), from Leland Harder (ed.), *The Sources of Swiss Anabaptism: The Grebel Letters and Related Documents* (Herald Press, Scottdale, 1985). Copyright © 1985 by Herald Press, Harrisonburg, Virginia. Reproduced by permission of Herald Press.

Marsilius of Padua, "Defensor Pacis" (1324), from Ray C. Petry (ed.), A *History of Christianity: Readings in the History of the Early and Medieval Church* (Prentice-Hall, Englewood Cliffs, 1962).

Melanchthon, Philipp, "On Improving the Studies of Youth" (1518), from Lewis W. Spitz, "Humanism and the Reformation," in Robert M. Kingdon (ed.), *Transition and Revolution* (Burgess International Group, Minneapolis, 1974).

Melanchthon, Philipp, "Report to Frederick on the Situation in Wittenberg" (1521), in Heiko A. Oberman (ed.), *Die Kirche im Zeitalter der Reformation* (Kirchen- und Theologiegeschichte in Quellen, III, ed. H. A. Oberman, A. M. Ritter, and H. W. Krumweide) (Neukirchener Verlag, Neukirchen-Vluyn, 1981). Translated by the editor.

Melanchthon, Philipp, "Theses Against Scholastic Theology" (1520), in Heiko A. Oberman (ed.), *Die Kirche im Zeitalter der Reformation* (Kirchen- und Theologiegeschichte in Quellen, III, ed. H. A. Oberman, A. M. Ritter, and H. W. Krumweide) (Neukirchener Verlag, Neukirchen-Vluyn, 1981). Translated by the editor.

Melton, William, Chancellor of York Minster, "Sermon to Ordinands" (c.1510), from H. Gee and W. J. Hardy, *Documents Illustrative of English Church History* (Macmillan, London, 1896).

Morata, Olympia, "Letter to Lavinia della Rovere Orsini" (1551/52), from Holt N. Parker (ed. and trans.), *Olympia Morata: The Complete Writings of an Italian Heretic* (Chicago: University of Chicago Press, 2003). Reproduced by permission of the University of Chicago Press.

Morata, Olympia, "Letter to Matthias Flacius Illyricus" (1553), from Holt N. Parker (ed. and trans.), *Olympia Morata: The Complete Writings of an Italian Heretic* (Chicago: University of Chicago Press, 2003). Reproduced by permission of the University of Chicago Press.

Morata, Olympia, "Letter to Pietro Paulo Vergerio" (1555), from Holt N. Parker (ed. and trans.), *Olympia Morata: The Complete Writings of an Italian Heretic* (Chicago: University of Chicago Press, 2003). Reproduced by permission of the University of Chicago Press.

Mosellanus, Peter, "Description of Luther, Karlstadt, and Eck at the Leipzig Debate," from Helmar Junghans (ed.), *Die Reformation in Augenzeugenberichten* (Düsseldorf: Karl Rauch Verlag, 1967). Translated by the editor.

Müntzer, Thomas, "Prague Manifesto" (1521), from Peter Matheson (ed. and trans.), *The Collected Works of Thomas Müntzer* (T. & T. Clark, Edinburgh, 1988). Reproduced by permission of Bloomsbury.

Müntzer, Thomas, "Sermon to the Princes" (July 13, 1524), from Peter Matheson (ed. and trans.), *The Collected Works of Thomas Müntzer* (T. & T. Clark, Edinburgh, 1988). Reproduced by permission of Bloomsbury.

Müntzer, Thomas, "Vindication and Refutation" (1524), from Peter Matheson (ed. and trans.), *The Collected Works of Thomas Müntzer* (T. & T. Clark, Edinburgh, 1988). Reproduced by permission of Bloomsbury.

"Müntzer to Frederick the Wise" (August 3, 1524), from Peter Matheson (ed. and trans.), *The Collected Works of Thomas Müntzer* (T. & T. Clark, Edinburgh, 1988). Reproduced by permission of Bloomsbury.

"Müntzer to Luther" (July 13, 1520), from Peter Matheson (ed. and trans.), *The Collected Works of Thomas Müntzer* (T. & T. Clark, Edinburgh, 1988). Reproduced by permission of Bloomsbury.

"Müntzer to Melanchthon" (March 29, 1522), from Peter Matheson (ed. and trans.), *The Collected Works of Thomas Müntzer* (T. & T. Clark, Edinburgh, 1988). Reproduced by permission of Bloomsbury.

"Müntzer to the People of Allstedt" (April 26 or 27, 1525), from Peter Matheson (ed. and trans.), *The Collected Works of Thomas Müntzer* (T. & T. Clark, Edinburgh, 1988). Reproduced by permission of Bloomsbury.

"Müntzer to the People of Erfurt" (1525), from Peter Matheson (ed. and trans.), *The Collected Works of Thomas Müntzer* (T. & T. Clark, Edinburgh, 1988). Reproduced by permission of Bloomsbury.

"Müntzer's Revolutionary 'Ring of Justice' in the Camp of the Frankenhausen Army," from Tom Scott and Bob Scribner, *The German Peasants' War* (Humanities Press International, Atlantic Highlands, NJ, 1994). Copyright © 1994. Reprinted by permission of Prometheus Books.

Nicholas of Lyra, "Interpretation of the Bible," from Gustav Benrath (ed.), *Wegbereiter der Reformation* (Carl Schunemann Verlag, Bremen, 1967). Translated by the editor.

"Official Catalogue of Relics in the Wittenberg Castle Church," from Hans J. Hillerbrand, *The Reformation: A Narrative History Related by Contemporary Observers and Participants* (Harper & Row, New York, 1964). Reproduced by the kind permission of the author.

"Ordinance for the Reform of the Great Minster" (September 29, 1523), from B. J. Kidd (ed.), *Documents Illustrative of the Continental Reformation* (Clarendon Press, Oxford, 1911).

"Ordinances Concerning Church Polity in Geneva" (December 17, 1546), from Philip Edgcumbe Hughes (ed. and trans.), *The Register of the Company of Pastors of Geneva in the Time of Calvin*, © 1966 Wm. B. Eerdmans Publishing Company, Grand Rapids, Michigan. Reproduced by permission of Wm. B. Eerdmans Publishing.

"Petition of Certain Preachers of Switzerland to the Most Reverend Lord Hugo, Bishop of Constance, That He Will Not Suffer Himself to be Persuaded to Make any Proclamation to the Injury of the Gospel, Nor Endure Longer the Scandal of Harlotry, But Allow Priests to Marry Wives or at Least Would Wink at Their Marriages" (July 2, 1522), from Samuel Macauley Jackson (ed.), *Ulrich Zwingli: Early Writings* (The Labyrinth Press, Durham, NC, 1987; reprint of 1912 edition).

"Philip Marnix on Mob Violence in the Netherlands" (1567), from William G. Naphy (ed. and trans.), *Documents on the Continental Reformation* (Macmillan, London, 1996). Reproduced by permission of Palgrave Macmillan.

Philip II, "Letter to Pope Pius V on the Religious Question in the Netherlands," from Peter Limm, *The Dutch Revolt 1559–1648* (Longman, London, 1989). Reproduced by permission of Pearson Education.

"Philip II Refuses to Concede Toleration" (August 17, 1585), from Peter Limm, *The Dutch Revolt 1559–1648* (Longman, London, 1989). Reproduced by permission of Pearson Education.

"Philip II: The Edict of 1555," from John Lathrop Motley, *The Rise of the Dutch Republic*, 3 vols. (Everyman Library, London, 1856).

"Pieter Titelmans, Inquisitor to Regent Margaret of Parma Kortrijk," from William G. Naphy (ed. and trans.), *Documents on the Continental Reformation* (Macmillan, London, 1996). Reproduced by permission of Palgrave Macmillan.

Pirckheimer, Caritas, "A Journal of the Reformation Years 1524–1528," from Paul A. MacKenzie (ed. and trans.), *Caritas Pirckheimer: A Journal of the Reformation Years 1524–1528* (D. S. Brewer, Cambridge, 2006). Reprinted by permission of Boydell & Brewer Limited.

Pirckheimer, Willibald, "Humanist Disappointment with the Reformation" (1530), from Detlof Plöse and Günter Vogler (eds.), *Buch der Reformation. Eine Auswahl zeitgenossischer Zeugnisse (1476–1555)* (Union Verlag, Berlin, 1989). Translated by the editor.

Pope Adrian VI, "Instruction to the Diet of Nuremberg" (1522), from John C. Olin (ed.), *The Catholic Reformation: Savonarola to Ignatius Loyola* (Fordham University Press, New York, 1992). Reproduced by permission of Fordham University Press.

Pope Boniface VIII, "Unam Sanctam" (1302), from Ray C. Petry (ed.), *A History of Christianity: Readings in the History of the Early and Medieval Church* (Prentice-Hall, Englewood Cliffs, 1962).

Pope Clement VI, "Unigenitus Dei Filius" (January 27, 1343), from John F. Clarkson et al. (eds.), *The Church Teaches: Documents of the Church in English Translation* (Herder, St. Louis, 1955).

Pope Leo X, "Exsurge Domine" (June 15, 1520), from Oscar Thulin, *A Life of Luther*. Copyright © 1966 Fortress Press, Philadelphia. Reproduced by permission of Augsburg Fortress.

Pope Leo X, "Pastor Aeternus" (March 16, 1516), from Oscar Thulin, *A Life of Luther*. Copyright © 1966 Fortress Press, Philadelphia. Reproduced by permission of Augsburg Fortress.

Pope Paul III, "Regimini Militantis Ecclesiae" (September 27, 1540), from John C. Olin (ed.), *The Catholic Reformation: Savonarola to Ignatius Loyola* (Fordham University Press, New York, 1992). Reproduced by permission of Fordham University Press.

Pope Pius II, "Execrabilis" (January 18, 1460), from B. J. Kidd (ed.), *Documents Illustrative of the History of the Church*, vol. III (SPCK, London, 1941). Reproduced by permission of SPCK and Sheldon Press.

Pope Sixtus IV, "Salvator Noster" (August 3, 1476), from B. J. Kidd (ed.), *Documents Illustrative of the History of the Church*, vol. III (SPCK, London, 1941). Reproduced by permission of SPCK and Sheldon Press.

Prierias, "Dialogue Against the Arrogant Theses of Martin Luther on the Power of the Pope" (1518), from Ernst Löscher, *Vollständige Reformations-Acta and Dokumenta* (Leipzig, 1723). Translated by the editor.

"Proposal of a Select Committee of Cardinals and other Prelates Concerning the Reform of the Church, Written and Presented by Order of His Holiness Pope Paul III" (1537), from Elisabeth G. Gleason (ed. and trans.), *Reform Thought in Sixteenth-Century Italy* (Scholars Press, Chicago, 1981).

Rabelais, François, "On Education," from David Englander, Diana Norman, Rosemary O'Day, and W. R. Owens (eds.), *Culture and Belief in Europe 1450–1600* (Blackwell, Oxford, 1997). Reproduced by permission of John Wiley & Sons Ltd.

"Reform Programme of the Bishop of Pomerania" (January 1, 1525), from B. J. Kidd (ed.), *Documents Illustrative of the Continental Reformation* (Clarendon Press, Oxford, 1911).

Rem, Katherine, "A Nun Rejects the Reformation" (1523), from Merry Wiesner-Hanks (ed.), *Convents Confront the Reformation: Catholic and Protestant Nuns in Germany* (Marquette University Press, Milwaukee, 1996). © 1996 Marquette University Press, Wisconsin, USA. Reproduced by permission of the publisher. All rights reserved. www.marquette.edu/mupress.

"Removal of Relics and Organs" (June 1524), from B. J. Kidd (ed.), *Documents Illustrative of the Continental Reformation* (Clarendon Press, Oxford, 1911).

"Report of the Assassination of Henry III" (August 1, 1589), from George T. Matthews (ed.), *The Fugger Newsletters* (Capricorn Books, New York, 1959).

"Request of the Nobles Presented to Regent Margaret by Henry Brederode" (April 5, 1566), from Peter Limm, *The Dutch Revolt 1559–1648* (Longman, London, 1989). Reproduced by permission of Pearson Education.

Roset, Michel, "Chronicles of Geneva" (1562), from Robert M. Kingdon (ed.), *Transition and Revolution* (Burgess International Group, Minneapolis, 1974).

Rothmann, Bernard, "A Confession of Faith and Life in the Church of Christ of Münster" (1534), from Lowell Zuck (ed.), *Christianity and Revolution: Radical Christian Testimonies 1520–1650* (Temple University Press, Philadelphia, 1975). © Lowell H. Zuck. Reproduced by kind permission of the author.

Rothmann, Bernhard, "A Restitution of Christian Teaching, Faith, and Life" (October 1534), from Lowell Zuck (ed.), *Christianity and Revolution: Radical Christian Testimonies 1520–1650* (Temple

University Press, Philadelphia, 1975). © Lowell H. Zuck. Reproduced by kind permission of the author.

Rothmann, Bernard, "Concerning Revenge" (December 1534), from Lowell Zuck (ed.), *Christianity and Revolution: Radical Christian Testimonies 1520–1650* (Temple University Press, Philadelphia, 1975). © Lowell H. Zuck. Reproduced by kind permission of the author.

"Sastrow's Account of Preaching in the Interim," in Helmar Junghans (ed.), *Die Reformation in Augenzeugenberichten* (Karl Rauch Verlag, Düsseldorf, 1967). Translated by the editor.

Savonarola, Girolamo, "On the Renovation of the Church" (1495), from John C. Olin (ed.), *The Catholic Reformation: Savonarola to Ignatius Loyola* (Fordham University Press, New York, 1992). Reproduced by permission of Fordham University Press.

Servetus, "Letter to Abel Poupin, Minister in Geneva" (1547?), from Roland Bainton, *Hunted Heretic: The Life and Death of Michael Servetus 1511–1553* (Beacon Press, Boston, 1960). Copyright © 1953 The Beacon Press. Reproduced by permission of Beacon Press, Boston.

Servetus, "Petition from Prison to the Geneva Council," from Roland Bainton, *Hunted Heretic: The Life and Death of Michael Servetus 1511–1553* (Beacon Press, Boston, 1960). Copyright © 1953 The Beacon Press. Reproduced by permission of Beacon Press, Boston.

Servetus, "Plea for Religious Liberty," from Roland Bainton, *Hunted Heretic: The Life and Death of Michael Servetus 1511–1553* (Beacon Press, Boston, 1960). Copyright © 1953 The Beacon Press. Reproduced by permission of Beacon Press, Boston.

"Social Tensions: The Reformation of the Emperor Sigismund" (c.1438), from Gerald Strauss (ed. and trans.), *Manifestations of Discontent in Germany on the Eve of the Reformation* (Indiana University Press,

Bloomington, 1971). Reproduced by kind permission of Daphne Patai.

"Social Welfare Legislation: Leisnig" (1523), from Jaroslav Pelikan and Helmut T. Lehmann (eds.), *Luther's Works*, vol. 45. Copyright © 1955–86 Augsburg Fortress. Reproduced by permission of Augsburg Fortress.

"Social Welfare Legislation: The City of Wittenberg" (1522) in Hans Lietzmann (ed.), *Die Wittenberger and Leisniger Kastenordnung* (de Gruyter, Berlin, 1935). Translated by the editor.

Spalatin, Georg, "Recollections of Frederick the Wise on Luther," from Georg Spalatin, *Friedrichs des Weisen. Leben and Zeitgeschichte*, ed. C. G. Neudecker and L. Preller (Friedrich Mauke, Jena, 1851). Translated by the editor.

"St. Bartholomew's Eve" (August 30, 1572), from George T. Matthews (ed.), *The Fugger Newsletters* (Capricorn Books, New York, 1959).

Tauler, Johannes, OP, "Sermons," from Maria Shrady (trans.), *Johannes Tauler: Sermons* (Paulist Press, New York, 1985). Reproduced by permission of Paulist Press.

"Ten Rules Concerning Prohibited Books Drawn Up By The Fathers Chosen By the Council of Trent and Approved by Pope Pius IV," from H. J. Schroeder, *Canons and Decrees of the Council of Trent* (Herder, St. Louis, 1955).

Tetzel, "A Sample Sermon," from Hans J. Hillerbrand, *The Reformation: A Narrative History Related by Contemporary Observers and Participants* (Harper & Row, New York, 1964). Reproduced by kind permission of the author.

"The Account of Hans Hut" (November 26, 1527), from Tom Scott and Bob Scribner (ed. and trans.), *The German Peasants' War* (Humanities Press International, Atlantic Highlands, NJ). Copyright © 1994. Reprinted by permission of Prometheus Books.

"The Act of Supremacy" (1534), from David Englander, Diana Norman, Rosemary O'Day, and W. R. Owens (eds.), *Culture and Belief in Europe 1450–1600* (Blackwell, Oxford, 1997). Reproduced by permission of John Wiley & Sons Ltd.

"The Act of Supremacy" (1559), from Gerald Bray (ed.), *Documents of the English Reformation*. Copyright © 1994 Fortress Press, Minneapolis. Reproduced by permission of Augsburg Fortress.

"The Act of the Six Articles" (1539), from Gerald Bray (ed.), *Documents of the English Reformation*. Copyright © 1994 Fortress Press, Minneapolis. Reproduced by permission of Augsburg Fortress.

"The Act of Uniformity" (1549), from Gerald Bray (ed.), *Documents of the English Reformation*. Copyright © 1994 Fortress Press, Minneapolis. Reproduced by permission of Augsburg Fortress.

"The Advice of Dr Brück, Chancellor of Electoral Saxony" (March 1530), from B. J. Kidd (ed.), *Documents Illustrative of the Continental Reformation* (Clarendon Press, Oxford, 1911).

"The Affair of the Sausages," from B. J. Kidd (ed.), *Documents Illustrative of the Continental Reformation* (Clarendon Press, Oxford, 1911).

"The Augsburg Confession" (June 25, 1530), from Theodore G. Tappert (ed. and trans.), *The Book of Concord: The Confessions of the Evangelical Lutheran Church* (Muhlenberg Press, Philadelphia, 1959). Reproduced by permission of Augsburg Fortress.

"The Banishment of Blaurock and Execution of Mantz," from Leland Harder (ed.), *The Sources of Swiss Anabaptism: The Grebel Letters and Related Documents* (Herald Press, Scottdale, 1985). Copyright © 1985 by Herald Press, Harrisonburg, Virginia. Reproduced by permission of Herald Press.

"The Belgic Confession of Faith" (1561), from Arthur C. Cochrane (ed.), *Reformed*

Confessions of the Sixteenth Century (Westminster Press, Philadelphia, 1966). Reproduced by permission of Westminster John Knox Press.

"The Capture, Torture, Confession and Execution of Jan van Leiden," from Hans J. Hillerbrand, *The Reformation: A Narrative History Related by Contemporary Observers and Participants* (Harper & Row, New York, 1964). Reproduced by kind permission of the author.

"The Consensus Tigurinus" (August 1, 1549), from Philip Edgcumbe Hughes (ed. and trans.), *The Register of the Company of Pastors of Geneva in the Time of Calvin* (Wm. B. Eerdmans Publishing Company, Grand Rapids, Michigan, 1966). Reproduced by permission of Wm. B. Eerdmans Publishing.

"The Consequences of Luther's Stance During the Peasants' War: Hermann Mühlpfort, Mayor of. Zwickau, to Stephan Roth at Wittenberg" (June 4, 1525), from Tom Scott and Bob Scribner, *The German Peasants' War* (Humanities Press International, Atlantic Highlands, NJ, 1994). Copyright © 1994. Reproduced by permission of Prometheus Books.

The Council of Constance, "Haec sancta" (May 6, 1415), from B. J. Kidd (ed.), *Documents Illustrative of the Continental Reformation* (Clarendon Press, Oxford, 1911).

The Council of Constance, "Frequens" (October 9, 1417), from Ray C. Petry (ed.), *A History of Christianity: Readings in the History of the Early and Medieval Church* (Prentice-Hall, Englewood Cliffs, NJ, 1962).

"The Council of Trent on the Canonical Scriptures" (April 8, 1546), from H. J. Schroeder, *Canons and Decrees of the Council of Trent* (Herder, St. Louis, 1955).

"The Council Orders Anabaptists to be Drowned" (March 7, 1526), from B. J. Kidd (ed.), *Documents Illustrative of the Continental Reformation* (Clarendon Press, Oxford, 1911).

"The Council's Mandate for Churchgoing" (August 10, 1531), from B. J. Kidd (ed.), *Documents Illustrative of the Continental Reformation* (Clarendon Press, Oxford, 1911).

"The Crisis of Values: Reynard the Fox" (1498), from Gerald Strauss (ed. and trans.), *Manifestations of Discontent in Germany on the Eve of the Reformation* (Indiana University Press, Bloomington, 1971). Reproduced by kind permission of Daphne Patai.

"The Death of the 'Prophet' Jan Matthijs," from Hans J. Hillerbrand, *The Reformation: A Narrative History Related by Contemporary Observers and Participants* (Harper & Row, New York, 1964). Reproduced by kind permission of the author.

"The Declaration of the Cities" (August 4, 1526), from B. J. Kidd (ed.), *Documents Illustrative of the Continental Reformation* (Clarendon Press, Oxford, 1911).

"The Duke of Sully's Account of the St. Bartholomew's Day Massacre," from *Memoirs of the Duke of Sully*, vol. 1 (G. Bell, London, 1877).

"The Ecclesiastical Ordinances of 1541," from Robert M. Kingdon (ed.), *Transition and Revolution* (Burgess International Group, Minneapolis, 1974).

"The Edict of Nantes" (April 13, 1598), from R. J. Knecht, *The French Wars of Religion 1559–1598*, 2nd edn. (Longman, New York, 1996). Reproduced by permission of Pearson Education.

"The Edict of Worms" (May 26, 1521), from De Lamar Jensen (ed. and trans.), *Confrontation at Worms: Martin Luther and the Diet of Worms* (Brigham University Press, Provo, 1973). Reproduced by permission of Brigham Young University Press.

"The Elizabethan Injunctions" (1559), from Gerald Bray (ed.), *Documents of the English Reformation*. Copyright © 1994 Fortress Press, Minneapolis. Reproduced by permission of Augsburg Fortress.

"The Excommunication and Deposition of Elizabeth: Pope Pius V's Bull 'Regnans in Excelsis'" (February 25, 1570), from Colman J. Barry (ed.), *Readings in Church History, 2: The Reformation and the Absolute States 1517–1789* (The Newman Press, Westminster, MA, 1965). Copyright © 1965 Paulist Press, Mahwah, NJ.

"The First Zurich Disputation" (January 23, 1523), from Samuel Macauley Jackson (ed.), *Ulrich Zwingli (1484–1531)* (University of Pennsylvania Press, Philadelphia, PA, 1972; reprint of 1901 edn.).

"The Fourth Lateran Council" (1215), from John F. Clarkson et al. (eds.), *The Church Teaches: Documents of the Church in English Translation* (Herder, St. Louis, 1955).

"The French Confession of Faith" (1559), from Arthur C. Cochrane (ed.), *Reformed Confessions of the Sixteenth Century* (Westminster Press, Philadelphia, 1966). Reproduced by permission of Westminster John Knox Press.

"The Goals of William of Orange" (June 16, 1572), from Peter Limm, *The Dutch Revolt 1559–1648* (Longman, London, 1989). Reproduced by permission of Pearson Education.

"The Hammer of Witches" (1486), from Montague Summers (trans.), *Malleus Maleficiarum* (John Rodker, 1928).

"The Introduction of Polygamy in the City of Munster," from Hans J. Hillerbrand, *The Reformation: A Narrative History Related by Contemporary Observers and Participants* (Harper & Row, New York, 1964). Reproduced by kind permission of the author.

"The Marburg Colloquy and Articles" (1529), from Donald J. Ziegler (ed.), *Great Debates of the Reformation*. Copyright © 1969 by Random House, Inc. Reproduced by permission of Modern Library, a division of Random House, Inc. Any third party use of this material is prohibited. Interested parties should apply to Random House, Inc. for permission.

"The Marian Injunctions" (1554), from H. Gee and W. J. Hardy, *Documents Illustrative of English Church History* (Macmillan, London, 1896).

"The Massacre of Weinsberg" (April 16, 1525) and "Report of the Parson Johann Herolt," from Tom Scott and Bob Scribner, *The German Peasants' War* (Humanities Press International, Atlantic Highlands, NJ, 1994). Copyright © 1994. Reproduced by permission of Prometheus Books.

"The Message of the Placards," from B. J. Kidd (ed.), *Documents Illustrative of the Continental Reformation* (Clarendon Press, Oxford, 1911).

"The Murder of Henry, Third Duke of Guise, at Blois" (December 23, 1588), from R. J. Knecht, *The French Wars of Religion 1559–1598*, 2nd edn. (Longman, New York, 1996). Reproduced by permission of Pearson Education.

"The Nuremberg Begging Order of 1478," from Christoph Sachsse and Florian Tennstedt (eds.), *Geschichte der Armenfursorge in Deutschland: Vom Spätmittelalter bis zum 1. Weltkrieg* (Kohlhammer, Stuttgart, 1980). Translated by the editor.

"Theologia Deutsch," from Bengt Hoffman (trans.), *The Theologia Germanica of Martin Luther* (Paulist Press, New York, 1980). Reproduced by permission of Paulist Press.

"The Papal Nuncio's Reports from the Diet of Worms," from Oscar Thulin, *A Life of Luther*. Copyright © 1966 Fortress Press, Philadelphia. Reproduced by permission of Augsburg Fortress.

"The Peace of Augsburg" (September 25, 1555), from B. J. Kidd (ed.), *Documents Illustrative of the Continental Reformation* (Clarendon Press, Oxford, 1911).

"'The Piper of Niklashausen': A Report of His Preaching" (1476), from Gustav Benrath (ed.), *Wegbereiter der Reformation* (Carl Schünemann Verlag, Bremen, 1967). Translated by the editor.

"The Pope's Pardon for Henry IV" (September 1595), from. George T. Matthews (ed.), *The Fugger Newsletters* (Capricorn Books, New York, 1959).

"The Preface to the Authorized (King James) Version of the Bible" (1611), from Gerald Bray (ed.), *Documents of the English Reformation.* Copyright © 1994 Fortress Press, Minneapolis. Reproduced by permission of Augsburg Fortress.

"The Preface to the Geneva Bible" (1560), from Gerald Bray (ed.), *Documents of the English Reformation.* Copyright © 1994 Fortress Press, Minneapolis. Reproduced by permission of Augsburg Fortress.

"The Preface to the Rheims New Testament" (1582), from Gerald Bray (ed.), *Documents of the English Reformation.* Copyright © 1994 Fortress Press, Minneapolis. Reproduced by permission of Augsburg Fortress.

"The Recess of the Diet" (August 27, 1526), from B. J. Kidd (ed.), *Documents Illustrative of the Continental Reformation* (Clarendon. Press, Oxford, 1911).

"The Recess of the Diet of Augsburg" (September 22, 1530), from M. Reu, *The Augsburg Confession: A Collection of Sources with an Historical Introduction* (Wartburg, Chicago, 1930). Reproduced by permission of Augsburg Fortress.

"The Report of the Venetian Ambassador in France" (1561), from B. J. Kidd (ed.), *Documents Illustrative of the Continental Reformation* (Clarendon Press, Oxford, 1911).

"The Request of Those of the New Religion to the Confederate Nobles" (February 8, 1567), from William G. Naphy (ed. and trans.), *Documents on the Continental Reformation* (Macmillan, London, 1996). Reproduced by permission of Palgrave Macmillan.

"The Resolution of the Majority" (April 7, 1529), from B. J. Kidd (ed.), *Documents Illustrative of the Continental Reformation* (Clarendon Press, Oxford, 1911).

"The Resolution of the Minority" (April 19–25, 1529), from B. J. Kidd (ed.), *Documents Illustrative of the Continental Reformation* (Clarendon Press, Oxford, 1911).

"The Robbing of Tetzel," from Volkmar Joestel, *Legenden um Martin Luther und andere Geschichten aus Wittenberg* (Schelzky & Jeep, Berlin, 1992). Translated by the editor.

"The Sacrifice of the Mass" (Twenty-Second Session, September 17, 1562), from H. J. Schroeder, *Canons and Decrees of the Council of Trent* (Herder, St. Louis, 1955).

"The Schleitheim Confession of Faith (Seven Articles)" (1527), from Lowell Zuck (ed.), *Christianity and Revolution: Radical Christian Testimonies 1520–1650* (Temple University Press, Philadelphia, 1975). © Lowell H. Zuck. Reproduced by kind permission of the author.

"The Second Council of Lyons" (1274), from John F. Clarkson et al. (eds.), *The Church Teaches: Documents of the Church in English Translation* (Herder, St. Louis, 1955).

"The Second Zurich Disputation" (October 26–28, 1523), from Leland Harder (ed.), *The Sources of Swiss Anabaptism: The Grebel Letters and Related Documents.* Copyright © 1985 by Herald Press, Harrisonburg, Virginia. Reproduced by permission of Herald Press, Scottdale, PA 15683, USA.

"The Sentence of the Geneva Council" (October 27, 1553), from Roland Bainton, *Hunted Heretic: The Life and Death of Michael Servetus 1511–1553* (Beacon Press, Boston, 1960). Copyright © 1953 The Beacon Press. Reproduced by permission of Beacon Press, Boston.

"The Sorbonne Condemnation of Lefèvre's 'Fifty-two Sundays'" (1525), from M. A. Screech (ed.), *Jacques Lefèvre d'Etaples et ses disciples: épistles & évangiles pour les cinquante & deux sepmaines de l'an* (Librairie Droz, Geneva, 1964). Translated by the editor.

"The Speech from the Throne" (June 25, 1526), from B. J. Kidd (ed.), *Documents Illustrative of the Continental Reformation* (Clarendon Press, Oxford, 1911).

"The Speech from the Throne" (March 15, 1529), from B. J. Kidd (ed.), *Documents Illustrative of the Continental Reformation* (Clarendon Press, Oxford, 1911).

"The Thirty-Nine Articles of the Church of England" (1571), from Charles Hardwick, *A History of the Articles of Religion* (John Deighton, Cambridge, 1851).

"The Trial and Martyrdom of Michael Sattler" (1527), from George H. Williams and Angel M. Mergal (eds.), *Spiritual and Anabaptist Writers* (Library of Christian Classics, 1957). Reproduced by permission of Westminster John Knox Press.

"The Trial of Michael Servetus" (August 1553), from Philip Edgcumbe Hughes (ed. and trans.), *The Register of the Company of Pastors of Geneva in the Time of Calvin*, (Wm. B. Eerdmans Publishing Company, Grand Rapids, Michigan, 1966). Reproduced by permission of Wm. B. Eerdmans Publishing.

"The Twelve Articles of the Upper Swabian Peasants" (1525), from Michael G. Baylor (ed.), *The Radical Reformation* (Cambridge Texts in the History of Political Thought) (Cambridge University Press, Cambridge, 1991). © Cambridge University Press 1991. Reproduced by permission of Cambridge University Press.

The Twelve Elders of Münster, "Thirteen Statements of the Order of Life" and "A Code for Public Behaviour" (mid-1534), from Lowell Zuck (ed.), *Christianity and Revolution: Radical Christian Testimonies 1520–1650* (Temple University Press, Philadelphia, 1975). © Lowell H. Zuck. Reproduced by kind permission of the author.

"The Venetian Ambassador on Philip II" (1559), from B. J. Kidd (ed.), *Documents Illustrative of the Continental Reformation* (Clarendon Press, Oxford, 1911).

"The Wittenberg Movement: The University Report to Elector Frederick" (1521), from Heiko A. Oberman (ed.), *Die Kirche im Zeitalter der Reformation* (Kirchen- und Theologiegeschichte in Quellen, III, ed. H. A. Oberman, A. M. Ritter., and H.-W. Krumweide) (Neukirchener Verlag, Neukirchen-Vluyn, 1981). Translated by the editor.

"The Wittenberg Movement by the End of 1522," from Helmar Junghans (ed.), *Die Reformation in Augenzeugenberichten* (Karl Rauch Verlag, Dusseldorf, 1967). Translated by the editor.

"The Zurich Council Orders Infant Baptism, and Silence" (January 18, 1525), from B. J. Kidd (ed.), *Documents Illustrative of the Continental Reformation* (Clarendon Press, Oxford, 1911).

"Thomas Cranmer's Preface to the Great Bible" (1540), from Gerald Bray (ed.), *Documents of the English Reformation*. Copyright © 1994 Fortress Press, Minneapolis. Reproduced by permission of Augsburg Fortress.

"Thomas More to Martin Dorp" (October 21, 1515), from William G. Naphy (ed. and trans.), *Documents on the Continental Reformation* (Macmillan, London, 1996). Reproduced by permission of Palgrave Macmillan.

"Tyndale's Preface to the New Testament" (1526), from Gerald Bray (ed.), *Documents of the English Reformation*. Copyright © 1994 Fortress Press, Minneapolis. Reproduced by permission of Augsburg Fortress.

Ursala of Münsterberg, "A Nun Explains Her Leaving the Convent" (1528), from Merry Wiesner-Hanks (ed.), *Convents Confront the Reformation: Catholic and Protestant Nuns in Germany* (Marquette University Press, Milwaukee, 1996). Reproduced by permission of the publisher. All rights reserved. www.marquette.edu/mupress.

Valla, Lorenzo, "The Falsely Believed and Forged Donation of Constantine," from Gustav Benrath (ed.), *Wegbereiter der Reformation* (Carl Schünemann Verlag, Bremen, 1967). Translated by the editor.

Vögeli, Jörg, "Letter to Konrad Zwick" (1523), in Heiko A. Oberman (ed.), *Die Kirche im Zeitalter der Reformation* (Kirchen- und Theologiegeschichte in Quellen, III, ed. H. A. Oberman, A. M. Ritter, and H. W. Krumweide) (Neukirchener Verlag, Neukirchen-Vluyn, 1981). Translated by the editor.

von Hutten, Ulrich, "Vadiscum oder die Römishe Dreifaltigkeit" (1519), from Rudolf Bentzinger (ed.), *Die Wahrheit muss ans Licht! Dialoge aus der Zeit der Reformation* (Verlag Philipp Reclam, Leipzig, 1983). Translated by the editor.

von Hutten, Ulrich, "Letters from Obscure Men" (1515), from Clyde Manschreck (ed.), *A History of Christianity: Readings in the History of the Church from the Reformation to the Present* (Prentice-Hall, Englewood Cliffs, 1965).

von Staupitz, Johannes, "Sermon Extracts" (1516) in Gustav Benrath (ed.), *Wegbereiter der Reformation* (Carl Schünemann Verlag, Bremen, 1967). Translated by the editor.

Wimpfeling, Jakob, "Grievances of the German Nation" (1513), from Gerald Strauss (ed. and trans.), *Manifestations of Discontent in Germany on the Eve of the Reformation* (Indiana University Press, Bloomington, 1971). Reproduced by kind permission of Daphne Patai.

Wimpfeling, Jakob, "The Origins of Printing," from *Epitome Rerum Germanicarum* (1505), in Detlof Plöse and Günter Vogler (eds.), *Buch der Reformation. Eine Auswahl zeitgenossicher Zeugnisse (1476–1555)* (Union Verlag, Berlin, 1989). Translated by the editor.

Wyclif, John, "On Indulgences," from Robert Vaughan (ed.), *Tracts and Treatises of John de Wycliffe* (The Wycliffe Society, London, 1845).

Zell, Katharina Schütz, Writings on Reformation and Marriage, from Elsie McKee (ed. and trans.), *Katharina Schütz Zell: Church Mother. The Writings of a Protestant Reformer in Sixteenth-Century Germany* (University of Chicago Press, Chicago, 2006). Reproduced by permission of the University of Chicago Press.

Zerbolt, Gerard, "The Spiritual Ascents," from John Van Engen (trans.), *Devotio Moderna: Basic Writings* (Paulist Press, New York, 1988). Reproduced by permission of Paulist Press.

Zwingli, "Concerning Choice and Liberty Respecting Food – Concerning Offense and Vexation – Whether Anyone Has Power to Forbid Foods at Certain Times – Opinion of Huldreich Zwingli" (April 16, 1522), from Samuel Macauley Jackson (ed.), *Ulrich Zwingli: Early Writings* (The Labyrinth Press, Durham, 1987; reprint of 1912 edition).

Zwingli, "Friendly Exegesis, that is, Exposition of the Matter of the Eucharist, addressed to Martin Luther by Huldrych Zwingli" (February 1527), from H. Wayne Pipkin (ed. and trans.), *Huldrych Zwingli: Writings*, vol. 2 (Pickwick Publications, Allison Park, PA, 1984). Reproduced by permission of Wipf & Stock Publishers Inc.

Zwingli, "Letter to Matthew Alber Concerning the Lord's Supper" (November 16, 1524), from H. Wayne Pipkin (ed. and trans.), *Huldrych Zwingli: Writings*, vol. 2 (Pickwick Publications, Allison Park, PA, 1984). Reproduced by permission of Wipf & Stock Publishers Inc.

Zwingli, "Of Baptism" (May 27, 1525), from G. W. Bromiley (ed. and trans.), *Zwingli and Bullinger* (Library of Christian Classics 1953). Reproduced by permission of Westminster John Knox Press and Hymns Ancient and Modern.

Zwingli, "Of the Clarity and Certainty of the Word of God" (September 6, 1522), from

G. W. Bromiley (trans.), *Zwingli and Bullinger* (Library of Christian Classics 1953). Reproduced by permission of Westminster John Knox Press and Hymns Ancient and Modern.

Zwingli, "Refutation of the Tricks of the Baptists" (July 31, 1527), from Samuel Macauley Jackson (ed.), *Ulrich Zwingli (1484–1531)* (University of Pennsylvania Press, Philadelphia, PA, 1972; reprint of 1901 edn.).

Zwingli, "Short Christian Instruction" (November 17, 1523), from H. Wayne Pipkin (ed. and trans.), *Huldrych Zwingli Writings*, vol. 2 (Pickwick Publications, Allison Park, PA, 1984). Reprinted by permission of Wipf & Stock Publishers Inc.

Zwingli, "The Sixty-Seven Articles" (1523), from Mark A. Noll (ed.), *Confessions and Catechisms of the Reformation* (Baker Books, Grand Rapids, 1991). © Mark Noll. Reproduced by kind permission of the author.

"Zwingli's Invitation to Zurich," from G. R. Potter (ed.), *Huldrych Zwingli* (Edward Arnold, London, 1978).

"Zwingli's View of Luther," from Hermann Schuster et al. (eds.), *Quellenbuch zur Kirchengeschichte*, I/II (Frankfurt am Main, Verlag Moritz Diesterweg, 1966). Translated by the editor.

Index